# CHILDREN

# *with*

# SPECIAL

# NEEDS

## *Family, Culture, and Society*

### SECOND EDITION

# CHILDREN

## *with*

# SPECIAL

# NEEDS

*Family, Culture, and Society*

SECOND EDITION

James L. Paul
*University of South Florida*

Rune J. Simeonsson
*University of North Carolina, Chapel Hill*

HARCOURT BRACE JOVANOVICH COLLEGE PUBLISHERS

Fort Worth   Philadelphia   San Diego   New York   Orlando   Austin   San Antonio
Toronto   Montreal   London   Sydney   Tokyo

| | |
|---:|:---|
| *Editor-in-Chief* | Ted Buchholz |
| *Acquisitions Editor* | Jo-Anne Weaver |
| *Project Editor* | Nicole Boyle |
| *Senior Production Manager* | Ken Dunaway |
| *Book Designer* | Melinda Huff |

*Address for Editorial Correspondence:* Harcourt Brace Jovanovich College Publishers, 301 Commerce Street, Suite 3700, Fort Worth, TX 76102.

*Address for Orders:* Harcourt Brace Jovanovich, Publishers, 6277 Sea Harbor Drive, Orlando, Florida 32887. 1-800-782-4479, or 1-800-433-0001 (in Florida).

ISBN: 0-03-055743-7

Library of Congress Catalog Card Number: 92-082769

Printed in the United States of America

2 3 4 5 6 7 8 9 0 1   039   9 8 7 6 5 4 3 2 1

*Dedicated to our families.*

James L. Paul
Rune J. Simeonsson

# ABOUT THE AUTHORS

**James L. Paul, Ed.D.,** is a professor and chair of the Department of Special Education at the University of South Florida. His policy-related writings include work in ethics, mainstreaming, advocacy, deinstitutionalization, and working with families who have children with disabilities. His clinical and education-related writings include work in the education of children with behavior disorders, learning disabilities, and developmental disabilities. Dr. Paul is currently involved in research on university-school collaboration in teacher education, the role of special education in restructured schools, integrating the humanities into the study of persons with disabilities, and ethics.

**Patricia B. Porter, Ph.D.,** is Chief of Developmental Disability Services for the North Carolina Department of Human Resources. She was instrumental in the construction of North Carolina's Plan for Delivery of Services that has a family centered service delivery focus. As a special educator and speech/language pathologist, Dr. Porter has served as a classroom teacher, resource teacher and mental retardation center program director. As a faculty member at the University of North Carolina, she taught special education and speech/language pathology courses and she served as Director of Clinical Programs at the Center for Development and Learning. She is committed to consumer and family participation in the policy-making process.

**Sondra Diamond,** now deceased, worked as a counselor with both disabled and able-bodied clients. She published several articles on issues concerning the disabled, including psychosocial needs, unmet medical needs, and the image of the disabled. She crusaded on behalf of people with disabilities through her "Bill of Rights for the Disabled," (1975), numerous media appearances, and two films— "I Am Not What You See" and "Sondra Diamond—Truly Alive." Ms. Diamond was disabled with cerebral palsy since birth. She recognized the need for change in regard to attitudes toward the disabled, and contributed to that end.

**George D. Falk** is presently completing his doctoral studies in the Department of Special Education at the University of South Florida. He received his B.A. and post B.A. document in Education at Simon Fraser University. He recently completed a research assistantship at Florida Mental Health Institute where he worked with children with severe emotional disorders. He has taught in the public school system in Canada both as a secondary school special education teacher for students with varying exceptionality and a regular education primary teacher. Mr. Falk currently works for Moose Jaw Public School Division in Moose Jaw, Saskatchewan, Canada.

**Rune J. Simeonsson, Ph.D., MSPH,** is professor of education and research professor of psychology at the University of North Carolina, Chapel Hill. He has graduate teaching responsibilities in the special education and school psychology programs focusing on the topics of exceptional child development, biomedical and psychological aspect of exceptionality, and assessment and intervention of children with special needs. He is also an investigator at the Frank Porter Graham Child Development Center where his research activities include low incidence assessment, childhood disability and its prevention, and issues pertaining to the evaluation of child and family outcomes in intervention.

**Nancy Simeonsson, BSN, MA, PNP,** is a pediatric nurse practitioner at the Frank Porter Graham Child Development Center, University of North Carolina, Chapel Hill. She has had extensive experience providing health care to children from infancy through adolescence in medical and educational settings. Her focus in nursing research includes the role of health factors in the early development of children and medical dimensions in the transition and integration of children with special needs. She is actively involved in inservice training of care providers as well as preservice nursing education at several levels of professional preparation on the issues of health care and the family.

**Paula J. Beckman, Ph.D.,** is an associate professor of special education at the University of Maryland. She has over 15 years experience working with families of infants and toddlers who have or are at risk of having disabilities. Dr. Beckman has conducted numerous studies of stress, coping, and adaptation in families. She currently directs Project Assist, a federally funded project designed to investigate the effectiveness of social support to families. She also provides training to students interested in working with infants and toddlers who have or are at risk of having disabilities and their families.

**Lee Smith, Ph.D.,** is an assistant professor at the University of South Florida at Sarasota. In the past, Dr. Smith has taught persons with severe emotional disabilities, persons with mental disabilities, and persons with autism, and has served as a curriculum specialist and assistant principal. His research interests include university and community collaboration, and persons with disabilities and their families.

**Brett Webb-Mitchell, Ph.D.,** has a broad interdisciplinary educational and professional background. Educationally, Dr. Brett Webb-Mitchell has a B.A. degree in music therapy from the University of Kansas; an M. Div. from Princeton Theological Seminary; a Th.M. from Harvard University; and a Ph.D. in Special Education from the University of North Carolina-Chapel Hill, with a focus in religious education and course work at Duke University. His interest in working with people with disabilities in the context of religious communities comes from his broad professional experiences. He has worked with people with disabilities and their families in various settings; he worked in a public school as a music therapist with children with developmental disabilities; he was a chaplain assistant with adolescents with behavioral disabilities. He also served as an assistant in a l'Arche community; and most recently he was the Director of Religious Life at Devereux Hospital and Children's Center of Florida.

**Cathleen Smith, B.A.,** is a specialist in early childhood education and a member of the faculty of Douglas College in British Columbia. She has had a long-standing committment to the integration of young children with disabilities and has been actively involved in addressing the special needs of children with HIV and AIDS. Currently she is heading up a project to examine friendship formation in young children and ways in which it can be facilitated in integrated settings. Drawing on her experiences in the multi-cultural context of Canada, she is a frequent contributor on the topic of cultural diversity at provincial, national, and international conferences.

**Daphne Thomas, M.S.W., Ph.D.,** is an assistant professor at the University of South Florida in Tampa. She teaches courses in working with families, consultation and collaboration, and preschool education for children with disabilities. Dr. Thomas directed an interdisciplinary statewide interagency program focusing on the needs of young children and their families. Her current research focuses on the longitudinal investigation of within group variability in a cohort of 150 African-American families with young disabled children.

**Agneta Hellstrom, B.S.,** works in the Department of Social Welfare Department in Stockholm, Sweden with responsibilities in the Child Care Division program for children with special needs. She has been involved in a number of projects to survey and document the nature of services for children with special needs in Sweden as well as the Nordic countries. Her interests include the integration of young children with disabilities, services for children with attention deficit disorders and family adaptation. In addition to contributions in the form of publications, she is engaged in extensive consultation and inservice training.

**Kofi Marfo, Ph.D.,** is a professor and director of the doctoral program in special education at the University of South Florida. Dr. Marfo's research interests include early intervention efficacy, parent-child interaction, and children's cognitive strategies in classroom learning contexts. He is the editor of two recent volumes: *Early intervention in transition: Current perspectives on programs for handicapped children,* and *Parent-child interaction and developmental disabilities: Theory, research, and intervention.* He currently serves as an associate editor of the *Journal of early intervention.*

**Tien Miau Wang, Ph.D.,** is an associate professor in the Department of Special Education at National Taiwan Normal University. Her major teaching and research interests are in the area of early childhood special education focusing on interventions with young children and their families. Dr. Wang contributes to the development of interdisciplinary efforts for children with special needs in Taiwan through publication and inservice training programs. She is active in conferences and professional development activities throughout South East Asia.

**Elaine Meyer, Ph.D.,** is a member of the pediatrics faculty at Brown University School of Medicine and works as a clinical psychologist at Women and Infants Hospital, Providence, Rhode Island. With professional credentials in nursing and psychology, Dr. Meyer's major interests include the psychosocial and ethical dimensions of childhood chronic illness and high risk infants in intensive care settings. These interests are reflected in publications and presentations on family-centered care to professionals as well as parents and caregivers.

**Donald B. Bailey, Jr, Ph.D.,** is the director of the Frank Porter Graham Child Development Center at the University of North Carolina, Chapel Hill. In addition to his administrative roles, he conducts research in the area of early intervention and has academic appointments in the Departments of Special Education and Medical Allied Health. He recently headed the Carolina Institute for Research on Infant Personnel Preparation, a multi-disciplinary effort, which has examined the nature and needs of personnel preparation. He enjoys national visibility based on his extensive contributions to the field of early childhood special education encompassing family focused intervention, team process and the design and implementation of developmental interventions for children.

**Pamela Winton, Ph.D.,** is an investigator at the Frank Porter Graham Child Development Center, University of North Carolina, Chapel Hill, whose major interests have focused on issues of working with families in the early intervention context. She is well known for her contributions to literature on the nature and form of interviewing and supporting families and is a frequent presenter at conferences and workshops on these topics. She has developed curricular materials for preservice and inservice training and is actively involved in the graduate education at the university through her course on families.

**Bonnie Strickland, Ph.D.,** is currently a staff member of the Maternal and Child Health Bureau, National Institute of Health, with major responsibilities to promote integration of federal efforts in the areas of child health and education. She has previously taught in the university setting, as well as working in the context of special education services in the public schools, including several years as an administrator in the Department of Defense Schools in Europe. She has a strong record of contributions to the field with particular reference to the relationship of parents and the schools in the development and implementation of the Individualized Education Plan.

**Craig Fiedler, Ph.D., JD.,** is an assistant professor of special education in the College of Education and Human Services at the University of Wisconsin, Oshkosh. Prior to 1987 he was an assistant professor of education at the University of New Hampshire. Dr. Fiedler has both a doctorate in special education and a law degree. In addition to his public school teaching experience in both regular and special education classrooms, he has worked as a legal services attorney in Kentucky and Wisconsin. Dr. Fiedler's interest and research areas include supporting families with exceptional children, special education law and policy issues, the integration of exceptional children into school and community settings, and the enhancement of positive attitudes toward people with disabilities. Dr. Fiedler is a parent of an exceptional child himself.

**Lee Kern-Dunlap** is presently completing her doctoral studies in the Department of Special Education at the University of South Florida. She has taught for several years in both regular and special education. Ms. Kern-Dunlap's current research focuses primarily on children with behavioral disorders/emotional disturbance.

**James J. Gallagher, Ph.D.,** is Kenan Professor of Education at the University of North Carolina at Chapel Hill. He is a leading figure in the field of special education, having served as a pioneer in the federal commitment to exceptional children in the establishment of the Bureau of Education for the Handicapped. He was the first director of the Frank Porter Graham Child Development Center, guiding its program of research, policy analysis, and technical assistance efforts over a period of two decades. His international visibility is reflected by extensive scholarly contributions on exceptional children and their families, gifted education and policy issues, and special education.

# PREFACE

The way we view families has changed remarkably during the last third of the 20th century. Variability in social arrangements for the rearing of children has increased so dramatically during this period that it has been necessary to reconsider the traditional image of the family. Our culturally diverse society brings together different traditions, each with its own image of family structure and functions. The different family forms that now exist are increasingly recognized as alternative social patterns, rather than deviant, compromised, or undesirable. Prior to this period, the metaphor of brokenness was applied to families that were not "in tact," that is, with a biological father and mother married and living together.

In the last decade of this century we are in transition from a uniform image of a "healthy" and "whole" family to a social pluralism that recognizes different and alternative family forms. Changes in the structures and memberships in families have been produced by the complex interaction of different social, economic, and political forces. Economic circumstances, creating the necessity for both parents to work, have helped launch a massive entry of women into the workforce. At the same time there has been an increased consciousness of individual rights and equality promoting an egalitarian perspective and challenging the predominantly patriarchal Eurogenic political structure of families in our society. There also has emerged a moral stance that questions the necessity of permanence in marriage commitments and a growing social philosophy that embraces individual mental health values. These values have displaced the ethic of duty embedded in traditional religious communities with the ethics of health and individual well-being. Public social-welfare policies have been, in many respects, insensitive to family needs. A major factor in the interaction to these social and moral forces has been an increasing sensitivity to the dominance of the Eurocentric family and child rearing ideology and public policy in our society. Extended families and different understandings of kinship patterns are part of the normative reality of some of the cultures that comprise our ethnically diverse society.

The assumptions and values embedded in our views of families with disabled children that form the basis for the vision of care and subsequent public policies have been seriously challenged. Changes in the philosophy of science have also challenged conventional approaches to research on families.

Class issues, specifically poverty, have historically confounded our study of and conclusions about families. It is difficult to understand different parenting patterns, for example, as reflecting ethnic differences, without having some understanding of the circumstances of the lives of those families and the history of their coping strategies across generations. This is well illustrated by racism, a present force in our society that has been a constant feature of the social context in which African-American children grow up and define themselves as individuals and, ultimately, as parents.

The impact of a disabled child on a family is another area of understanding that has changed dramatically. The predominant view has been that a disability is a negative condition and, therefore, the impact of a child with a disability on a family must be negative. The focus of much of the research in this area has been on the nature of the negative effects. Findings of positive effects were typically understood as symptomatic of the family's denial, having not yet come to accept the "reality" of the child's disability. This kind of tautological argument has been more difficult to defend in recent years with more research focusing on positive effects.

In the past, there were two general approaches to research on families who have children with disabilities. One approach treated family data as dependent variables, and the presence of a child with a disability as the independent variable. The effect of this approach, and the unidirectional causal assumption in which it was rooted, was to foster a view of the family as a victim of the child's disability. The other approach treated the family as the independent variable and the child with the disability as the dependent variable. This approach was common in research on children with autism, for example, until the late 1960s, when the flawed logic of unidirectional attribution became recognized.

While the bi-directionality of effects has been appreciated and accommodated in the research designs, data analyses, and interpretations of data since the late 1960s, most research continues to reflect assumptions about cause and effect, and a commitment to the empricist genre of inquiry. The correlational, regression, and multivariate models commonly used in research on families with disabled children provide the logical and statistical protocols for comparisons of family in terms of styles, efficacy, and other observable or reportable variables. While ecologically valid measures and contextualized interpretations of data are essential features of responsible inquiry, what may not obviously violate assumptions of the analysis of data may none-the-less reflect an insensitivity to the social meaning of findings and the political nature of the comparison itself.

Our research on child development and on families has changed during the past decade in response to increasing sensitivity to these issues. It is also changing as part of a larger change in the philosophy of inquiry in the social sciences. Postmodern science is changing the assumptions and approaches to inquiry. These changes include a growing understanding of the problematic assumption of objectivity in observation and a deeper appreciation for the storied nature of our lives. These views, which reflect different epistemological traditions, are represented in an increasing number of studies that seek to account for the experience of the observer's and those observed/heard—and examine the complexity of the subject/setting/event studied.

Interpretive research is beginning to help us understand more about the lives of individuals with disabilities and families. It is leading us into deeper understanding that complements and, in some instances, provides an alternative to inferential statistical models that guide comparisons. Both quantitative and interpretive research are subject to political construction that can ultimately serve or harm the interests of those studied. The current culture of inquiry, however, has created new opportunities for interdisciplinary work that is leading researchers to more interesting questions and more culturally sensitive approaches to research. This is producing different knowledge bases for clinical practice and for policy development and creating a context within which ethical reasoning in clinical and policy decisions is more informed. Further, interpretive research is expanding the discourse on both families and disabilities, including moral and spiritual topics that in the past were largely forbidden in academic parlance.

Many of these changes in our understanding of families with disabled children have occurred since the first edition of this text was published a decade ago. This is, therefore, a substantial revision of the earlier work, including several new chapters as well as a major updating and, in some instances, rethinking of chapters included from the first edition. The research reported here reflects the broad range of quantitative and interpretive contributions to our present knowledge. The addition of an entire section on families in different cultures accurately portrays the editors' value of a pluralistic framework for understanding families.

Four general principles guided the editors and the authors of individual chapters: 1) an appreciation for the developmental course of the life of a family with a child who has a disability; 2) a central interest in the experiences of the families; 3) respect for ethnicity as an organizing framework for understanding families; 4) a focus on the ethical implications of all aspects of professional decisions that affect families; 5) a particular emphasis on the social and cultural complexity of providing care for and with families who have children with disabilities, and 6) a commitment to sharing the current construction of a more diverse and morally sensitive vision of the spiritual and social lives of families.

JLP
RJS

# CONTENTS

# INTRODUCTION

The dynamic nature of the fields of special education and related services is evident in continuing changes in policies and priorities. Recent years are no exception with the introduction and adoption of a variety of concepts. Perhaps two of the most pervasive of these have been the increased press for integration of children and youth with disabilities into typical environments and a recognition of the centrality of the family in their life and development. While those concepts have found expression in specific terms such as mainstreaming, inclusion, regular education initiative, and family-centered intervention, they can be productively considered as exemplars of broader constructs. An ecological orientation and transactional view of development are constructs frequently advanced to account for child and family adaption. The significant role Bronfenbrenner (1977) assigned to the environment has provided a useful conceptualization of the embeddedness of the child in successive ecological levels at the micro (family), meso (culture), and exosystem (society). Of comparable influence has been Sameroff and Chandler's (1975) articulation of the transactional nature of development, reflecting the continuous interplay bewtween child and environment over time to account for varying outcomes. Given their inclusive scope and influence in the field, these two constructs serve as underlying frameworks for this volume. While these are widely endorsed central constructs, others relevant to specific content here are drawn upon in appropriate contexts.

Our overall purpose is thus to examine the development and adpatation of children with disabilities and their families. While it is recognized that individual adaptation and family reltaionships are life-span issues, this book focuses on disability in the developmental phase, encompassing the period from infancy through adolescence. Drawing on an ecological framework, such examination first considers the family, secondly, cultural factors, and thirdly, societyal factors as cumulative contexts to account for variations in child and family outcomes. Closely aligned with this ecological orientation is an interpretation of child and family adaptation within the transactional model of devleopment. To this end, the book is organized into five sections with the first consisting of two introductory chpaters designed to provide the conceptual base for the remaining sections. Successively, these sections consider the family context of the child with disability, the role of cultural factors, and thirdly, societal aspects. We conclude with a synthesis of issues and a view of future trends and directions involving children, families, and disability.

# 1

# FAMILIES OF CHILDREN WITH DISABLING CONDITIONS

*James L. Paul, Patricia B. Porter, George D. Falk*

## INTRODUCTION

It is in the family that we first learn about the world and about ourselves. The home is the social setting and the family provides the emotional context for our growth and development. When we are hurt it is usually a parent who comforts, bandages the cut, and reassures us that we will be all right. For most children it is a parent who brings calm and comfort to displace the terror of waking from a bad dream in the darkness of the night. The food we eat, the clothes we wear, and the shelter that keeps us safe, dry, and comfortable are provided by one or both parents or parent surrogate. Clean sheets and dishes, toothpaste and toys, ice cream and places to play—these, too, are usually provided in the context of a family.

Children first hear adults talk and see how people relate to each other from their families. It is here that they are forced to do some things they do not want to do and prohibited from doing other things that seem to them as necessary as life itself. They learn about resentment, anger, and feelings of power or lack of it. Parents provide children with the raw material from which they begin to fashion an answer to the questions "Who am I?" and "Who should I become?" They learn what little boys and little girls are like, what grown-ups are like, and what parents are like. They learn how to behave in socially acceptable ways, from the control of bodily functions to keeping their ears clean and wearing clothes that are appropriate to different situations and places. They learn things about themselves, and that the way they act can make people happy, sad, or angry. It is within the family that children become psychologically and socially a part of this world and learn of its trustworthiness or lack of it, that they distinguish themselves as individuals, separate and apart from those around them.

As children grow older, the family becomes a social point of departure. They leave the family to go to school, but they return. If they succeed or fail in school, it is the family who cares. As they grow older, they eventually leave the family residence, although they continue to be a member of that family even as they establish a separate family of their own in which they have the adult parent role.

The family in its many different forms plays a key role in our society and assumes primary responsibility for the transmission of culture. It is a primary unit of social control, especially for young children, and serves a protective function

3

for the young. The family serves the spiritual and psychological functions of nurturance and development of the human potential. Parents have the basic responsibility for seeing that the sociocultural goals of the family are met. While custom, social values, and law generally support and promote the functioning of the family, there are many barriers and challenges to effective and productive family life. The Gallup Poll News Service (1990) revealed that 81% of adults believe that raising children today is more difficult than when their parents raised them.

One major barrier to effective family life is economic. Resources are not distributed equally among families, and many are forced to survive in situations with insufficient resources, where basic human needs are unmet. This may cause parent absence from the home, affect nutrition and medical care, and limit cultural enrichment opportunities.

Another barrier is the lack of information about and skill in implementing primary roles within the family. While the socialization role of the parent is basic to our society, parents are generally provided little direct assistance in fulfilling their role effectively. In earlier periods of our history, the extended family structure provided a model of parents' roles. Opportunities for this apprenticeship are less available today because of the variety and diversity of family life and the interactions society makes available. The family has undergone dramatic changes within this century. Families vary depending on their culture, socioeconomic status, marital status, sexual orientation, education, and values.

While it would not be relevant in this context to attempt to enumerate all of the barriers to effective family functioning, it is important to note there are many social and economic forces that work against the interest of the integrity of the family. The family can become a reflection of conflict and unrest in society. There is an ongoing tension between family values and the constantly changing values in the society. Ultimately, it is in the family where the conflicting values are felt and acted out.

During the present century the complexity of the parent role has increased as the social boundary between the family and larger social and economic communities has become more permeable. There has been an increased sharing of authority and responsibility with community social institutions, such as education, the courts, police, welfare, health, and mental health. The blurring of boundaries has brought confusion as the family and community institutions wrestle with who is responsible for what, including who defines appropriate behavior.

In no area of family life are the issues of appropriate behavior and the boundary of responsibility between the family and community institutions more important than in those having to do with rearing children. The question of how to raise our children is made complex because it is essentially inseparable from the question of how to live our lives. The parent-child relationship is one of the most basic relationships in the human community. Most parents would give their life for that of their child or would gladly take the pain of any disease to prevent their child from suffering. It is in this relationship between parent and child that both learn much about themselves and about the other, where there is the opportunity for human experience, joy, and love not duplicated in the human community. Yet all that is wrong in our society—conflict, duplicity, and injustice—ultimately is dealt with in this context. The child's thousand questions of "Why?" are part of the child's exploration of the mind and values of the parent. The child wants to know how things work, and then he or she wants to know if it is all right that they work that way. And, in the end, the child's explanations of the way things are and his or her preferences about the way they ought to be will bear considerable resemblance to the understanding and preferences of the parent.

In a culturally pluralistic society with an ethical code that appears predominantly situation-dependent, the behavioral and intellectual content of what parents teach children is a matter of community concern. Their methods of teaching are also of concern to the community. Social and legal codes provide a context of expectations and standards for parental behavior relative to the disciplining of their children. While these standards are not always clear and certainly not consistently enforced, the community responds to *undisciplined* or inappropriately disciplined children in terms of the inadequacy of parenting. Traditionally, if the child behaves inappropriately in social settings, including the school, this has been viewed as symptomatic of inadequate or insufficient parenting. If the child fails in school, this failure has often been considered a result of problems of motivation, intellectual deficit, anxiety, or other psychological factors.

When children go to school they are understood to be the products of the genetic heritage and the behavioral models provided by their parents in the specific physical and social-psychological environment of the home. Parents take great pride in high achievement and high IQ scores of their children. They feel they have succeeded genetically and behaviorally. Conversely, when children do not do well, parents feel they have failed and have been less than adequate in their parenting. Children are viewed as extensions of the parents. After all, the parent is thought to be in complete control of things that happen to their children including their social, intellectual, perceptual, and affective development, as well as physical nutrition. It is in this context that parents of children with disabilities have been most vulnerable.

Parental responsibility for the action, behaviors, progress—the very life of their child—has the possibility, then, of being a tremendous source of emotional conflict for parents of children with disabilities. Fortunately, the perception of the nature of this parental impact has changed drastically over the past century. Parents, who were once viewed negatively as the cause of their child's disability, are now recognized as able to provide enormous positive change in the life of their child. Once censured by society, parents are now viewed as partners in their child's education and treatment. It is no longer assumed or expected that a child with a disability brings about a problem in the family. It is as important to review historically the roles and responsibilities held by parents of children with disabilities as it is to review changes in societal attitudes toward persons with disabilities and various forms of treatment. Retrospect allows identification of helpful, and hurtful, elements and should guide decisions that affect the future course.

History provides a base on which to build an understanding of the contemporary dynamics of parenting children with disabilities. Accordingly, we have included within this chapter and throughout the book a chronological review of the roles assigned to parents, parent participation in programming, and economic support for that participation. We have attempted to heighten the clarity of the perspective by mapping areas of parental participation against the changes over time of general attitudes toward exceptional persons in our society.

In the past three decades there has been a substantial uprooting of traditional views of human behavior. In the 1960s, there was considerable erosion of confidence in public institutions that had been largely unquestioned in the past. The ethic of responsibility for individual behavior began to change. Social institutional hypotheses regarding the nature and nurture of deviance replaced hypotheses regarding the psychopathology of individual deviance in the minds of many (Scheff, 1966). A more radical view that emerged during the same period was the valuing of diversity as a source of cultural renewal rather than an object for therapeutic intervention (Rhodes, 1975).

During this period of social change, there were very marked gains in the development of the sciences of behavior and understanding of the development of adaptive human functioning. Views of behavior as the product of single causes such as *bad genes*, poor home environment, *sick* parents, or a defective brain were largely replaced by views of behavior as a developmental product of the interaction between capacity, predisposition, and opportunity. These changing views are reflective of Sameroff and Chandler's (1975) distinction of main effect and transactional models respectively. Sophisticated technologies of behavior change and control have been developed and applied in many different settings.

The family has been affected by these changes. The balancing of the psychology of deviance with the sociology of deviance has provided a kind of existential renewal for the family: Society shares the burden of cause, effect, and treatment. Attitudes toward the family have changed, as evidenced by the family advocacy movement, to provide support, and where necessary, defense for the family. The prominence of the parental role in the education legislation as espoused in PL 101-476 is another example of the elevation of regard for parents as necessary allies in any programmatic intervention into the lives of their children.

Behavioral technologies previously viewed as the property of professional guilds are taught to parents in parent education programs. The parent education strategies developed by Gordon (1970) and others, which teach infant stimulation and other mothering behaviors, were a part of this fundamental shift in the attitude toward parents and the philosophy of service delivery. Now there are sophisticated parent education components in many service delivery systems (e.g., Dunst, Trivette, & Deal, 1988; Turnbull & Turnbull, 1990).

The 1990s will continue to clarify legal and societal issues in the treatment or lack of treatment of children with disabling conditions and their families. The Regular Education Initiative (REI) structured the debate about least restrictive education and placement in the 1980s (Reynolds, Wang, & Walberg, 1987; Sailor, 1991; Skrtic, 1991). This debate will continue as policies are developed to make human services more responsive to the complex needs and interests of individual children and their families. These policies will have to address the ethical issues involved in making treatment effectively available to people with severe medical involvement including those with AIDS and those affected by substance abuse.

# ROLES ASSIGNED TO PARENTS

The perceived role of parents of children with disabilities has changed over time. A major theme that has only begun to be modified in the last few years is that parents are in some sense responsible for their child's disability or behavioral deviation. This theme is easily identified in the historical literature on parents. In 1899, school dropouts, insubordination, and vagrancy were viewed as the result of a lack of cooperation between parents and teachers (Harpur, 1899). In 1912, Goddard published his famous study of the Kallekak family. Goddard traced the descendents of Martin Kallekak who, during the Revolutionary War, fathered several children by a woman considered mentally defective. After the war, Kallekak married a woman with normal intelligence and, from a study of the descendants of this marriage, Goddard made comparisons with Kallekak's other progeny. He found more *social degenerates* and *feebleminded individuals* among the descendants of the mentally deficient woman, and he presented his data as support for the view that feeblemindedness is genetically based. While the Kallekak study has been entirely discredited (Smith, 1985), its conclusions were long accepted as supporting the genetic hypothesis.

The intelligence movement in this country, substantially advanced by the work of Terman, Hall, and Thorndike, supported the view that intelligence was genetically based and unalterable by environmental influences. However, a different view of the nature and malleability of capacity gained popularity in the second quarter of the century. Behaviorism and basic principles of learning were experimentally validated. Also, out of political necessity, there was considerable attention given to the education and training of young children.

The progressive education movement in the late 19th century and up until World War II believed that the American family was unable to carry out several of its educative responsibilities (Cremin, 1988). Schlossman (1976), in a comprehensive review of parent education in America, writes that the 1920s saw our nation reeling under the results of military draft tests. Remarkably high rates of mental, emotional, and physical *unfitness* appeared to characterize American youth. The cause was identified as the incapacity of the family to be the principal educator and socializer of the young; the panacea was, therefore, a necessarily greater reliance on other public institutions to provide care and training outside the family unit (Cremin, 1988).

In addition to the genetic and training hypotheses, the emerging mental health field was advancing a developmental view that focused on the important role of mothers in the child's emotional health and functional capacity. In 1949, for example, Kanner described parents of autistic children as obsessive and humorless individuals. He described a syndrome of *refrigerator mothers*, which he viewed as a primary factor in producing autism in children.

There is an enormous volume of psychological and biomedical literature regarding the genetic basis of intelligence (Chamberlain, 1983; Hebb, 1949), the relationship between mothering and psychiatric disorders (Rutter, 1971), the psychological consequences of broken marriages (Wolff & Acron, 1963), the educational consequences of a culturally impoverished childhood (Hunt, 1961; Jencks et al., 1972), the behavioral consequences of poor nutrition (Bakan, 1970; Perkins, 1977), and the psychological consequences of stress, anxiety, and abuse in early life (Elmer & Gregg, 1967). At some points in history the genetic arguments and evidence were more pervasive; at other points the environmental arguments and data seemed more compelling.

As we noted earlier, for more than a decade most behavioral scientists have viewed behavior as a developmental product of the interaction between heredity and socialization. For many of the disabling conditions in children, the exact contribution of organic factors, on the one hand or environmental factors, on the other, is not well understood. With the child with learning disabilities there is a continuing debate regarding whether specific learning disabilities result from brain lesions or from other factors. The traditional literature on the problems of children who are now labeled learning disabled focused on defects in the central nervous system. Since the 1970s, however, the emphasis has shifted to a functional description of the manifest learning deficits, leaving the primary etiology open to question.

In the area of children with emotional disturbance, the traditional mental health literature focused more on environmental factors and the quality of the parent-child relationship, especially the relationship with the mother (Bowlby, 1958). Now we understand that aberrant behavior may have an organic base. With children with emotional and behavioral challenges, the behavioral deviation in the child may be viewed by some as a function of organic pathology; that is, something is wrong with the child's brain. This conclusion may rest upon *soft* signs. Others may view the problem as the result of faulty learning; that is, the child has learned to behave in ways that are inappropriate and defeating. Some may view the problem as a product of the child's social history; that is, the result of family psychopathology. Some may interpret the problem primarily as a consequence of the rules or norms of the settings in which the disruptive behavior occurs; that is, the system, especially the school, is unrealistic in its expectations. And still others view behavior problems as not being the exclusive problem of the child or the system, but an interaction between the child and the setting. This latter view is less likely to result in scapegoating the child, the teacher, or the parent.

During the last 20 years there has been a decreasing emphasis on primary etiology and an increasing emphasis on identifying the specific problem—whether of learning or behavior—and focusing on corrective, remedial, reeducative, or habilitative strategies to reduce the dysfunction. While there may be little prescriptive educational value in specific etiology, it is the development of knowledge of disabling conditions in children that will ultimately lead to preventive strategies.

Understanding of the etiology of mental retardation has gone through a similar historical metamorphosis, variously considering biological, genetic, organic, or biochemical defects, and/or cultural-familial factors. The majority of instances of mild mental retardation are now viewed as resulting from a combination of genetic and poor social and economic conditions (Kirk & Gallagher, 1979).

The point in this review of the history of our understanding of cognition and behavior is that parents are often perceptually connected to the cause of their child's disability. Depending on the clinical issues involved in a particular case, the scientific basis for the attribution of cause varies. Most professionals would agree that since behavior is a function of the interaction of the person and the environment, from the point of conception it is difficult to separate clearly the contributions of nature or nurture to the cause of behavior. The child has certain capacities and genetic ceilings, but he or she is a part of one or more social systems. The important question for treatment and education is, What can be done now to increase positive participation in society?

One role of parents historically has been that of scapegoat. Only during the last 30 years has this stigma begun to be removed. This past century has seen the emphasis of the parental role move from principal causative factor to principal agent of treatment and change. Parents won rights for their children and themselves in the 1960s, 1970s, and 1980s through litigation and the development of new laws, including PL 94-142 and its subsequent amendments, that guaranteed appropriate services and participation of parents in decisions about their children. During the 1980s, support grew for the positive role of parents as allies with professionals in providing services and for services to families. This support, buffered by a systems view of families (Turnbull & Turnbull, 1990), gained momentum as strategies were developed to empower families.

## FAMILY EXPERIENCE

When we think of serious disabling conditions, we are generally not talking about a circumscribed deficit that manifests itself in simple ways or in limited situations. We are talking about a child who may be a constant disruptive force at mealtime, with food that can never stay on the plate or be successfully negotiated into the child's mouth, or with drinks that are constantly spilled onto a clean tablecloth no matter who has come to dinner. We may be speaking of a child who has a high energy level and is constantly seeking the parent's help or attention in some way. Many of the children who have severe physical learning and/or behavior problems also have limited social skills. Consequently, these children have great difficulty in getting along with other children, whether siblings, children in the neighborhood, children of friends, or children at church or at school. Privacy for parents is virtually impossible, in many instances, and it is usually difficult for parents to find a sitter in whom they can have full confidence in order to enjoy a brief respite. We may be speaking of a child whose physical health is such that the parents live in a constant state of tension and fear. Many of these children are a source of great sadness to parents who hurt inside when their child must always be excluded from the games other children play. Some children with severe disabilities have behavior so bizarre and uncontrollable that the parents may live in a state of terror and feel forced to compromise their own sensibilities. In some instances these children are viewed by their parents and siblings as being in charge of family life and holding the reins on the pleasure and joy of the family. This, of course, is only one side of the picture. Many of these stories are sensitively told by parents in a superb publication, *Parents Speak Out* (Turnbull & Turnbull, 1985).

In addition to the physical, social, and psychological toll of having a child with disabilities in the family, there is also the opportunity for extraordinary reward and joy. The special needs and vulnerabilities of a child with disabilities can be a major rallying point. Family members see each other at weak moments when they are very tired, their resources gone, and their defenses virtually absent. It is possible that some families of children with disabilities learn more about themselves and about each other as a result of their intense common struggle.

Parents learn about their children's needs and their own abilities to perform and make adjustments in their expectations for their children. Having a successful meal, where a 6-year-old has succeeded in keeping food off the floor, not spilling his or her milk, and not having a temper outburst, can be an extraordinarily satisfying experience. Having this child assume even the smallest part in a school play and seeing him or her look forward to the event, prepare for it, and eventually succeed, can engender more pride and joy than that experienced by the parents and family of a more precocious child who has the leading role. Families with a child with disabilities may indeed learn to live with more emotional extremes and ultimately at greater human depths.

When parents of children with disabilities take their child to school, they come with many mixed feelings of hope and doubt, confidence and fear. They do not always know what to expect of their child as a student in the school. Sometimes their own feelings of inadequacy and self-doubt have become so intense that they believe the teacher, or anyone other than themselves, can probably work miracles with their child. Other parents, especially those with children with severe disabilities, have much lower expectations; in some instances lower than they should be. Some parents are understandably very protective of their child and are anxious to minimize the exploitation of their child's vulnerability. The teacher cannot overestimate the vital importance of some acknowledged success of this child in his or her early encounter with school. The child, the parent, and the teacher need a positive beginning and a large degree of understanding of the issues each experiences.

Many families experience a developmental progression toward acceptance of a child's disability. Upon diagnosis they may experience denial, then progress to strong feelings of both guilt and anger, followed by a period of despair. Emotional stability within the family is achieved when the parents can view their child's disability realistically (Bennett & Algozzine, 1983). However, many parents, especially those of children with physical disabilities, behavior disorders, and serious learning disabilities, who have not realistically come to accept their child's disability, live day by day with the idea that they are simply inadequate parents and have not been successful in finding ways to control their child and to help him or her learn. Many parents of young children with disabilities also believe what is happening with their child is phase-specific, and while the developmental phase may be somewhat extended for their child, he or she will outgrow it. There is considerable social reinforcement and cultural lore to reinforce self-defeating denial.

The advent of Part H of PL 101-476 has meant that parents are now legally required to deal with public institutions about their child with disabilities at an earlier age (between birth and age 3, depending on the state and its implementation policy). From this point forward the relationship between the parents, the child, and public institutions will become increasingly important and complex.

## THE CHILD, THE DISABILITY, AND THE SCHOOL

Children with disabilities are, by definition, unable to perform at appropriate age-grade levels with a regular educational curriculum in the same manner as other children. That is, they start at a disadvantage. They do not fit the normative achievement and/or behavior standards of the regular classroom. A modification of the expectations (goals) and/or the curriculum (content/methods) is required for these children. Some children, with orthopedic or sensory disabilities, for example, can adapt to most of the regular curriculum with the assistance of prosthetic devices, and modifications may only be necessary in areas such as physical education. Some children are not disabled until they are faced with the expectation of school. Some children are not identified as having special needs until they are faced with the increasing math and reading demands in the third or fourth grade. At that point the question of etiology is especially difficult. While our knowledge is increasing about the nature of disabilities in children, it continues to be limited. Professionals are realizing that children with disabilities will not always fit into a particular category of disability and that, in many instances, there is an overlapping among categories. This is further complicated by the use of several different labels, essentially meaning the same thing, as is the case with children with learning disabilities.

Our focus on a careful understanding of the present circumstances of learning and behavioral deficits, rather than on whom to hold responsible for things as they are, has made us less likely to scapegoat and alienate important members of the planning effort whose positive participation is essential. Collaboration between parents and professionals will enable a consistent and mutually agreed upon plan of action in the two most influential areas of a child's life—home and school. The inclusion of parents in the decision-making, planning, and implementation processes enhances the opportunity for success by empowering the parents as vital participants in their child's educational program (Dunst, Trivette, & Deal, 1988).

## PARENT ADVOCACY: HISTORICAL PERSPECTIVE

Parents have had to assume the role of advocates for their children. The compulsory school law was passed in 1919, but it did not apply to children with disabilities. If children did not *fit in* to the regular education curriculum, they could be excluded from the school. Parents of children with disabilities have led the way in demanding equal educational opportunity for their children. They have organized and, when unavailable, the parents have provided services themselves (President's Commission on Mental Retardation, 1977).

Educators simply did not know how to teach children with severe disabling conditions. Educational curricula had to be developed and professional special educators trained. After all, the children with disabling conditions were not a homogeneous group with common learning needs. There were more differences among the children who could not fit into a regular education curriculum than between these children and normal learners. A relevant classification system for learning and behavior problems had to be developed and appropriate services designed.

Before all this could occur, however, it had to be determined that the educational systems had a responsibility for educating these children. The law was on the side of the educational system, allowing it to make discretionary judgments about the inclusion of children with disabilities. It was not until 1975 that the Education for All Handicapped Children Act, PL 94-142 (now Individuals with Disabilities Act of 1990—IDEA, PL 101-476) was passed, which assured all children the right to a free, appropriate public education. The passage of PL 99-457 in 1985 (Part H of PL 101-476) extended those services to families and to children from birth (Office of Special Education and Rehabilitative Services, 1991).

Educational policies formulated by boards of education were necessarily developed in the context of prevailing philosophies and economic realities. Services for children with disabilities generally had been strongly influenced by the philosophy of social Darwinism—that is, the survival of the fittest. Places were made available in the public sector for *those who could make it*. Children with disabilities were set apart from society, and were generally kept out of sight and out of mind. The children with severe disabilities were feared and, in some instances, thought to be possessed by demons. Children with more moderate disabilities were generally kept at home and cared for in an extended family arrangement. Those who could do so were allowed to work around the house or the farm.

Society had a different experience with disability as a result of World War I. Young men, who had been known in communities and had been normal in every respect, returned from war to their communities blind, deaf, epileptic, and suffering a wide range of psychological and physical disabilities. This was a profound experience, and an education for families and communities about the nature of disabling conditions.

About the same time there was a strong push for reform of institutions for the insane. Clifford Beers, who had been a patient in a psychiatric hospital shortly before the turn of the century, was determined to call public attention to the inhumane conditions and circumstances in institutions. In 1908, he wrote *A Mind That Found Itself*, a description of his personal experience in an institution. Many consider this to be the beginning of the mental health movement.

This push for a more humane understanding and treatment of institution-alized persons forced a reconsideration, over time, of the nature of human devi-ance, the philosophy of human services, and community obligation as reflected in economic commitment to services. It was in this context that parents went to school boards and to legislators to make a case for the education of their children.

Commitments did not come quickly, and they were not evenly distributed across the country. Even to the present day, local economic support and varying sophistication of educational services are responsible for many different types of arrangements for children with disabilities.

The early success in developing services for children with disabilities came as a result of effective advocacy by parents and in many instances occurred in situations where members of the community power structure had some personal experience with disabilities in their own families. Parents learned quickly that they could be most effective when they worked together. As early as 1933, moth-ers in Cuyahoga County, Ohio, indignant that their children were excluded from school, were effective in working together to see that a special class was formed for their children. The class was sponsored by the parents themselves, and, in retrospect, must be seen as a very courageous step. It was not easy at this point in history, when intelligence was seen as the most valuable of all human attrib-utes, to bring into the open the fact that the family had a *defective* member (President's Commission on Mental Retardation, 1977).

In 1936, parents of institutionalized children formed the Children's Benev-olent League in Washington state. The league was composed of a few parents gathered around the common interest of having a child placed in a state insti-tution. Their combined goal was to make the institution a happy and constructive place (President's Commission on Mental Retardation, 1977).

It was not until 1950 that the National Association of Parents and Friends of Mentally Retarded Children, now the National Association of Retarded Cit-izens (NARC), was formed. This organization, which now has over 200,000 members, has been effective in lobbying for the interests of persons with mental retardation. The parents assumed a leadership role in accumulating technical information on exceptional children. In 1954, NARC launched a major cam-paign against the view of people with mental retardation as menaces to society.

In 1955, legislators and policymakers were beginning to turn to parents for information and to advise them about how to proceed in developing appropriate public policy and law to serve the interests of children with disabilities. In the early 1950s, *educable* children were being allowed to attend school in large cities.

During the 1950s, parents focused their work primarily on the legislative branch of government; in 1958, PL 85-926 was passed, which provided support for universities to prepare teachers to work with children with mental retardation. In the 1960s, parents focused their attention more on the executive branch of government and realized significant gains resulting from their work with legislators a decade before (Boggs, 1971). In 1960, a golden anniversary White House Conference on Children and Youth recommended that separation of a child from his or her family should be the last resort (President's Commission on Mental Retardation, 1977).

The social movement on behalf of the children with disabilities gained considerable momentum in the early 1960s as a result of the support provided by the Kennedy administration. The coupling of parent advocates with key members of the power structure who had personal experience with disabilities in the family—a strategy that had been so effective at the local level—worked well at the national level also.

During the 1960s the grass-roots structure for building an effective support system for the persons with disabilities in our society took hold and grew rapidly. The total society was undergoing a complete reexamination of its values. All vestiges of human indignity and inhumanity were being challenged. War, bigotry, racism, and human exploitation in all forms were torn from the dark underside of institutional policies and practices, from the courts to the corridors of institutions for persons with disabilities. These injustices were dragged out into the light for fresh analysis under old lamps—justice, civil liberty, fairness, decency, right to life, right to work, freedom, and the right to dignity.

It was a painful time for our society. University campuses became caldrons of action insisting on change. People were hurt and buildings were burned. Many streets were unsafe by day and closed by night. National political conventions were disrupted. Every sector of our society was involved and each had to attend to this period of change and growth in our society.

It was in this context that many human rights movements were born. Movements to support the rights of blacks, women, consumers, children, and persons with disabilities gained footing during the 1960s. It was during this period that the Comprehensive Mental Retardation Facilities Construction Act (PL 88-164) was passed. This act combined three pieces of legislation that provided support for a commitment to community services and embraced several provisions for persons with disabilities. It included the major source of support for mental retardation research centers and training grants to institutions of higher learning to develop doctoral level programs emphasizing provision of services to people with mental retardation.

During the late 1950s and 1960s, several important parent and professional organizations were formed, including the following: (1) the International Parents Organization, established in 1957, as the parents' arm of the Alexander G. Bell

Association (1979); (2) the Association for Children With Learning Disabilities, established in 1964 by a group of concerned parents (Association for Children With Learning Disabilities, 1985); (3) the National Society for Autistic Children, formed in 1965 by parents (National Society for Autistic Children, 1984); and (4) the Epilepsy Foundation of America, incorporated in 1967 (Epilepsy Foundation of America, 1974).

During this period there was more cooperative work between parents and professional organizations. The International Council for Exceptional Children, which was first established by faculty and students at Columbia University in 1922, developed into the major organization for special educators. This organization recognized small parent organizations as early as the late 1940s, but in the 1960s more active cooperative alliances were established. Similarly, the American Association for Mental Retardation (originally called the Medical Officers of American Institutions for Idiots and Feebleminded Persons, and later, the American Association for Mental Deficiency), formed in Media, Pennsylvania, by institution superintendents in 1876, and has been the major professional organization concerned with comprehensive services for persons with mental retardation. This organization also started recognizing small parent organizations in the late 1940s, and in the late 1960s developed more formal affiliations with them.

In the 1960s, parents developed a strong commitment to the policy whereby services for their children should be provided by the public sector. In 1965, for example, the National Association for Retarded Citizens developed the policy that they would obtain, not provide, services (President's Commission on Mental Retardation, 1977).

The 1960s, then, was a time when parents worked effectively with the executive branch of government. It also was a time when the nation developed a social agenda for the 1970s. Many of the human and civil rights claimed in principle during the 1960s now had to be institutionalized. Old laws had to be changed and new laws had to be passed. Institution policies and practices also needed change. In many ways the 1970s was a period for institutionalizing the changes of the 1960s. Both attitudes and bureaucracy had to change. Public education and awareness were a critical part of this transformation.

The Developmental Disabilities Construction Act of 1971 was an important advocacy development during the 1970s. It resulted in the implementation of a formula grant program to assist states in providing a broad range of services for the lifelong needs of the developmentally disabled. In addition, the 1971 Act extended construction authority for University Affiliated Facilities and provided operations support.

The Developmental Disabilities Assistance and Bill of Rights Act of 1975 extended and revised some provisions of the 1971 Act. The Bill of Rights specified basic rights of the person with developmental disabilities and called for appropriate treatment services. Conditions were identified that protected the rights of the person with disabilities. Among these conditions was included the concept of advocacy and state developmental disabilities councils.

Parent and child advocacy activities were organized and developed in the late 1960s and early 1970s (Paul, Neufeld, & Pelosi, 1977). A new role was created in the early 1970s to help move the government and public institutions beyond a verbal commitment to services for persons with disabilities to legal mandates and the designation of legal advocates, who, in some instances, were the catalytic agents for parents or parent organizations in their work with state and local agencies. In other instances, when parents had reached an impasse with public agencies that felt they should not or could not provide services for their children, the legal advocate took the case to court. Thus, in the 1970s, parents, who in the past had worked primarily with the legislative and executive branches of government, were now more involved with the judicial branch of government (Boggs, 1971).

During the early 1970s, parents were successful in their litigation. Public Law 94–142 established the right of all children to a free appropriate public education. It brought together into one instrument of law the major principles that had been established in many different court decisions ruling in favor of children with disabilities.

While there were tremendous advances in the commitment to providing services to children with disabilities in the 1960s and early 1970s, much of this commitment was articulated in terms of those with mild or moderate disabilities. It was not until the mid-1970s that a more concentrated effort to assure the provision of services for persons with severe and profound disabilities was made. In the 1950s and 1960s there was a major debate whether or not the public schools, being in the business of education, should have any responsibility for children who were not educable. Some argued that children with trainable mental retardation, who were limited in their capacity to learn, should not be included in the broad definition of educational responsibility.

In the past 20 years this debate has been closed. Public Law 94–142 provided that *all* children would receive an education appropriate to their level of functioning. There now are special schools and special classes within public schools for children with trainable mental retardation. Children with profound mental retardation are no longer served only in institutions or in small residential facilities. The public school system must also provide them with developmental opportunities for growth.

The priority placed on the children with severe and profound disabilities was established in parent organizations in the early 1970s (President's Commission on Mental Retardation, 1977). In 1975, the National Institute of Neurological and Communication Disorders and Stroke assumed major governmental responsibility for research on autism through the efforts of the National Society for Autistic Children, and in the late 1970s, the Bureau of Education for the Handicapped in the U.S. Office of Education developed as a major priority the training of professionals to work with children with severe disabilities. The implementation of PL 94-142 generated a tremendous amount of change with federal dollars (Blaschke, 1979).

The research spawned by PL 94-142 continued into the 1980s and contributed to the development of a subsequent amendment in 1986, PL 99-457, which authorized services for preschool children with special needs (Horne, 1991). This legislation reflects the research on child development and the following assumptions that were articulated about children: (1) the infant functions within the ecological context of the family (Bronfenbrenner, 1977), consequently early intervention should be specific to, and reflect the needs of, the family involved (Bricker & Casuso, 1979); (2) early intervention is most effective when parents and professionals work collaboratively (Blackard & Barsh, 1982); (3) the comprehensiveness and diversity of toddlers' disabilities and their families' needs necessitate an interdisciplinary approach to intervention (Bailey & Simeonsson, 1988; Gallagher, 1989); and (4) early intervention is effective and preferable to later intervention (Gallagher & Ramey, 1987).

In 1984, PL 98-524, the Vocational Education Act, was passed. This law guarantees that youth with disabilities will have access to vocational education opportunities. Its subsequent amendment, PL 101-392—the Carl Perkins Vocational and Applied Technology Act of 1990—functions as a companion piece of legislation with PL 101-476. However, its mandate is expanded to include individuals who are educationally and economically disadvantaged (Horne, 1991).

The parents' movement is credited with increasing public concern, local, state, and federal government involvement (Cruikshank & Johnson, 1958; Kirk, 1962), legislation for persons with disabilities, favorable public policy changes, developmental research, and direct services (President's Commission on Mental Retardation, 1977). From the period immediately following World War II until the present, there has been tremendous activity involving appropriate identification and treatment of persons with disabilities. This activity originated in the frustration of parents of children with disabilities caused by the institutional neglect of their children and the poor quality of existing services. Through concerted parental effort, progress has been made in the legislative, executive, and judicial branches of government and in the public citizenry at all levels.

The parents' movement contributed to antidiscrimination legislation for persons with disabilities in the work force and community with the passage of PL 93-112, the Rehabilitation Act of 1973. The Americans With Disabilities Act of 1990, PL 101-336, continues to remove the barriers faced by persons with disabilities that have restricted their access to community and employment opportunities (Simpkins & Kaplan, 1991). The American Disabilities Act (ADA) makes it illegal to discriminate against individuals with disabilities in employment, public accommodations, public services, and telecommunications. Architectural or communication barriers that restrict access to any employment or community activities must be removed (Horne, 1991; Simpkins & Kaplan, 1991).

## PARENT-PROFESSIONAL ALLIANCE

In addition to their active role as advocates in developing or affecting services for their children, parents have become increasingly involved with professionals in making decisions about appropriate programming. From the early 1950s to the early 1970s parents were busy getting their children into school. Simultaneously, public schools were gaining some experience in providing educational services for children with disabilities. As a rule, however, parents were involved relatively little in educational decisions. But several issues did evolve out of those experiences. First, the special class became a predominant strategy for serving children with disabilities. Research in the 1960s and early 1970s indicated that many children were inappropriately placed in special classes and that the educational experience there, especially in the area of academics, may have been inferior to that in the regular class (Goldstein, Moss, & Jordan, 1965; Johnson, 1962). Also, many children were inappropriately labeled as a result of culturally biased and inappropriate assessment (*Diana v. State Board of Education*, 1971; *Larry P. v. Wilson Riles*, 1971).

Accomplishing an appropriate match between the needs of children with disabilities and an appropriate educational program in the public school remains a very complex, technical, professional, and human task. A major hallmark of PL 94-142 is that it provides for an instrument of accountability in the form of a written individual educational program (IEP). It requires an unbiased assessment of the child and guarantees parents an important role in making educational decisions affecting their child. Parents and teachers must share responsibility to satisfy the spirit and letter of the law that requires a child to be provided with an appropriate education. Part H of PL 101-476 continues to recognize the importance of the family, and has a written individualized family service plan (IFSP) as its instrument of accountability.

## SERVICES FOR PARENTS

While parents have been successful in their advocacy for the interests of their children, services to parents have been developed more slowly. Parents have needs for technical information, for skill training, for counseling and support services, and for respite care for their child so that they and the child can, like other parents and children, be apart from each other for renewal. Services to parents have varied from educative counseling to training parents to be the primary service providers for their children (Gordon, 1970; Ora, 1973; Schopler & Reichler, 1971, 1976). In 1975, PL 94-142 established the standards for parent involvement in the educational process. In 1976, the Bureau of Education for the Handicapped established a funding priority to support the implementation of parent training programs.

Recent surveys have found that services for parents remains a high priority. Parents want more information about how to teach their child with disabilities, services effectively available now and in the future, more reading material from other parents in similar situations (Bailey & Simeonsson, 1988), and information regarding advocacy issues in areas such as due process, costs, obtaining appropriate services, and school personnel expectations (National Council on Disability, 1989).

No real understanding of the deficits, assets, and needs of the exceptional person can be achieved without comprehensive, in-depth attention to the values, expectations, resources, and circumstances of that person's social and physical environment. The family and community have a clear impact on the life of the exceptional child. The interaction overlaps among the child, his or her family, and resources in the community. These factors vary in intensity, duration, and importance, but they must be included in a thorough understanding of the child's abilities, needs, and available resources for meeting those needs.

## SUMMARY

It is through the family that each of us first learns about ourselves. Parents have assumed various roles within the family; the actual and perceived roles of parents and of families have changed. During the present century, the complexity of the parent role has increased as the social boundary between the family and larger social, economic, and educational communities has become more permeable. Changes have caused confusion regarding social values, economic stability, and child-rearing responsibilities. This is especially true for parents of children with disabilities. An historical perspective provides an interesting and important view of the magnitude of these changes and their effect on the child with disabilities, his or her family, and resources in the community.

Our understanding of parents of children with disabilities and the services we provided them based on that understanding has changed remarkably over the past 20 years. Part of the change has occurred as the result of research and the accumulation of clinical experience. We have learned a great deal about the impact of disabling conditions of children on their social and emotional development. We have a deeper appreciation of the subtle as well as profound effects of the quality of the nurturing environment on the child's development. In this text, we examine the research on the effects of illness and genetic disorders as well as the effects of nurturance on the development of children. We discuss the impact of that knowledge on services and the policies that govern the delivery of those services.

There is considerably more than the development of knowledge about child development and the education of children with disabilities that has influenced current views of education and treatment policies. The entire social context and structure of child rearing have changed, and those changes provide a theater within which the story of child development is being rethought and reformulated. The traditional two-parent family, with the mother at home taking care of the children, provided the backdrop for the study of child rearing. In 1940, 85% of the children in America were raised in this traditional family structure (Baca, Zinn & Eitzen, 1990). This family was buffered and extended by other resources including grandparents, aunts, and uncles. Families that did not have two parents with a mother at home to take care of the children were thought to be inadequate and characterized by demeaning metaphors, such as *broken*. The difficulties of children—behavior problems, delayed social and cognitive development—were often attributed to these atypical family circumstances. Now there are many family arrangements. Only 6% of the households are traditional families where the father works and the mother stays home to care for school-aged children (Hodgkinson, 1990). One out of every five families is headed by a single parent, however; one out of every two black families is headed by a single parent (Bureau of the Census, 1990). Approximately 90% of single-parent families are headed by the mother (Bureau of the Census, 1990). In addition, 1.9 million children do not live with either parent and are living predominantly in foster homes or with distant relatives (Hodgkinson, 1990). In two out of three two-parent households, both parents work at paying jobs to support the family (Baca, Zinn & Eitzen, 1990). Eleanor Macklin (1980) defines several nontraditional families, including children raised by gay couples, multiadult households (communal living and expanded families), and single parent—never married by choice.

The diversity of family structures is enriched by the multiethnic and multicultural nature of our society. The different ethnic and cultural families that are growing and constituting an increasing presence in our society have deep and well-established traditions about the rearing of children. The values and visions of child rearing in these different traditions differ from one another. Questions of which cultural traditions are *right* or, to put it more in the context of the American vocabulary, *more healthy*, are ethical, not medical, questions. The idea that there must be a single understanding of the social and emotional development of children in a pluralistic society is as problematic as the idea of a single educational curriculum that will meet the needs of all children.

Our understanding of families and the patterns of rearing children, then, has been enriched by the growing presence of African, Asian, European, and other cultural groups in our society. It has also been enriched by our beginning to understand the developmental consequences for children of the many different family forms that have emerged to adapt to socioeconomic circumstances in this country or to lifestyle preferences.

Teachers and parents are expected to be the primary agents in the education and socialization of children in our society. As the society has grown more complex, the task of educating children for life has become increasingly difficult. Pluralistic standards of behavior, increasing reliance on subtle social cues and language in communication, complex rules governing the social process, and the lack of clarity of the goals of education are among the factors contributing to the problems of knowing how best to teach and how best to parent children.

The changes in family patterns and child rearing are complex and raise questions about our traditional views of child development. The quality of the nurturing environment has important clinical consequences for children, including children with disabilities. Understanding those consequences for children broadly is a research challenge, which has only in recent years begun to be addressed with more sensitivity to and appreciation of the cultural complexity of our views of child rearing. Understanding the implications for a particular child and family is a clinical question. Understanding the nature of the different cultural perspectives and their implications for providing care for families with children with disabilities forms a major focus of this text.

The rapid accumulation of new knowledge and technology has not been effectively or efficiently absorbed by social institutions. While institutional policies and practices, as well as the roles of institutional members and consumers, have indeed changed, these changes have been guided more by political and economic forces than by a science of behavior, human development, and education.

The public education system's assumption of responsibility for children with disabilities is an example of institutional change caused by social forces. A need for new knowledge and better utilization of existing knowledge has been created. The change is extensive, evidenced by new philosophies and practices, policies and laws. A significant aspect of this change in which new concepts and knowledge are needed involves the relationship between teachers and parents of children with disabilities.

The division of responsibility in rearing children is not clear. The school has taken on responsibility for social and affective goals and for meeting an increasingly wider range of student needs. The relationship between the parent and teacher has changed as the perceived division of responsibility has changed.

The teacher-parent relationship may be challenging under the best of circumstances. It is especially important and can be particularly difficult when a child with disabilities is involved. In the socialization experience, someone usually is *perceived* to have failed. The child has failed to learn and/or behave, the teacher has failed to teach and/or control behavior, or the parent has failed to prepare the child for his or her role as a student. Blame is often in the picture when teachers and parents of children with disabilities work together: Who is at fault? Who is responsible? Parents often blame themselves. Their guilt and grief may go unrelieved and may even be compounded by professionals in helping systems—schools, mental health centers, health departments, welfare agencies, churches, or juvenile justice systems.

The teacher-parent relationship may be troubled by negativity and counterproductive behavior which, when understood, may be the result of parent behavior unconsciously designed to protect against further hurt to the already injured parental ego. The relationship may suffer from teacher behavior motivated by a need to be protected from the embarrassment of exposed ignorance of what to do. Trust and mutual respect are basic in a helpful teacher-parent relationship. It is also essential that the teacher have professional and technical competencies in programming for the child with disabilities. This is no longer sufficient, however; the law now stipulates that the parents have a right to be involved in educational decisions about their children.

In recent years the changes in our society have required us to examine the gender, lifestyle, ethnic, religious, and other cultural biases in our laws, policies, and practices working with families. This has been coupled by a blurring of the boundaries of traditional disciplines that have studied and/or provided services to the family, especially psychology, social work, sociology, anthropology, and several medical specialities. This is creating more integrated and, in some instances, more wholistic perspectives for understanding families and child rearing. The legal, policy, and ethical implications of emerging views and their implications for families with a child with disabilities form another major focus of the text.

In addition to the cultural-contextual and socioethical perspectives, it is important to consider the individual's own personal view. Each person's story, told in a language and with images of a particular culture, has its own texture and meaning. The personal story, always in some tension with the prevailing story of culture, provides a voice that cannot be heard with test data, theoretical perspectives, and general analysis.

## REFERENCES

Alexander G. Bell Association. (1979). *International parents' organization*. Washington, DC: Author.

Association for Children With Learning Disabilities. (1985). *Taking the first step to solving problems*. Pittsburgh: Author.

Baca Zinn, M., & Eitzen, D. (1990). *Diversity in families*. (2nd ed.). New York: HarperCollins.

Bailey, D., Jr., & Simeonsson, R. (1988). Assessing needs of families with handicapped infants. *Journal of Special Education, 22*, 117–127.

Bakan, R. (1970). Malnutrition and learning. *Phi Delta Kappan, 47*, 527–530.

Bennett, T., & Algozzine, B. (1983). *Effects of family-oriented intervention with young handicapped children on indicators of parental stress*. Washington, DC: ED/OSERS.

Blackard, M., & Barsh, E. (1982). Parents' and professionals' perceptions of the handicapped child's impact on the family. *Journal of the Association for the Severely Handicapped, 7*, No. 2 (pp. 62–70).

Blaschke, C. (1979). *Case study of the implementation of PL 94-142*. Washington, DC: Bureau of Education for the Handicapped.

Boggs, E. (1971). Federal legislation. In J. Wortis, (Ed.), *Mental Retardation* (Vol. III) (pp. 103–127). New York: Grune & Stratton.

Bowlby, J. (1958). Separation of mother and child. *Lancet, 1*, 480.

Bowlby, J. (1968). Effects on behavior of disruption of an affectional bond. In J. M. Thoday and H. Parker (Eds.), *Genetic and environmental influences on behavior* (pp. 94–108) Edinburgh: Oliver Boyd.

Bricker, D., & Casuso, V. (1979). Family involvement: A critical component of early intervention. *Exceptional Children, 12*, 108–116.

Bronfenbrenner, U. (1977). Toward an experimental ecology of human development. *American Psychologist, 32*, 513–531.

Bureau of the Census. (1990). Demographic state of the nation. In *How we're changing*, Series P-23, No. 164, Washington, DC.

Chamberlain, H. (1983). Mental retardation. In T. W. Farmer, (Ed.), *Pediatric Neurology* (2nd ed.), (pp. 153–190). New York: Harper & Row.

Cremin, L. A. (1988). *American education: The metropolitan experience*. New York: Harper & Row.

Cruikshank, W., & Johnson, G. (1958). *Education of exceptional children and youth*. Englewood Cliffs, NJ: Prentice-Hall.

Dunst, C., Trivette, C., & Deal, A. (1988). *Enabling and empowering families: Principles and guidelines for practice*. Cambridge, MA: Brookline.

Elmer, E., & Gregg G. (1967). Developmental characteristics of abused children. *Pediatrics, 4,* (40), 596–609.

Epilepsy Foundation of America. (1974). *The history of the epilepsy movement in the United States*. Washington, DC: Author.

Gallagher, J. (in press). The role of value and facts in policy development for handicapped infants and toddlers and their families. In *Handbook for the Development of Implementation Policies for P.L. 99–457 (Part H)*.

Gallagher, J., & Ramey, C. (Eds.). (1987). *The malleability of children*. Baltimore: Brookes.

Goldstein, H., Moss, J., & Jordan, L. (1965). The efficacy of special class training on the development of mentally retarded children. *Cooperative Research Project No. 619*. Washington, DC: U.S. Office of Education.

Gordon, I. (1970). *Parent involvement in compensatory education*. Urbana: University of Illinois Press.

Harpur, U. (1899). *The report of the educational commission of the City of Chicago*. Chicago: Lakeside Press.

Hebb, S. (1949). *The organization of behavior*. London: Chapman & Hall.

Hodgkinson, H. (1990). Perspectives on Southwest Florida: The region and educational system. West Central Regional Management Development Network, *Monograph Series 1: Report on the Regional Educational Executive Issues Forum*.

Horne, R. L. (1991). The education of children and youth with special needs: What do the laws say? *NICHCY News Digest,* 1, (1), 1–15.

Hunt, J. (1961). *Intelligence and experience*. New York: Ronald.

Jencks, C., Smith, M., Acland, H., Bane, M., Cohen, D., Gentis, H., Heyns, B., & Michelson, S. (1972). *Inequality: A reassessment of the effect of family and schooling in America*. New York: Basic.

Johnson, G. (1962). Special education for the mentally handicapped: A paradox. *Exceptional Children, 29,* 62–69.

Kirk, S. (1962). *Educating exceptional children*. Boston: Houghton Mifflin.

Kirk, S., & Gallagher, J. (1979). *Educating exceptional children*. (3rd ed.). Boston: Houghton Mifflin.

Macklin, E. (1980). Nontraditional family forms: A decade of research. *Journal of Marriage and the Family, 42,* 905–922.

National Council on Disability. (1989). *The education of children with disabilities: Where do we stand? A report to the president and Congress of the United States*. Washington, DC: Author.

National Society for Autistic Children. (1984). A brief history of N.S.A.C. *Advocate,* 16, 5.

Office of Special Education and Rehabilitative Services. (1991). Meeting the needs of infants, toddlers, and preschool children with disabilities. In *To assure the free appropriate public education of all children with disabilities* (pp. 51–86). Washington, DC: U.S. Department of Education.

Ora, J. (1973). Involvement and training of parents- and citizen-workers in early education for the handicapped. In M. Karnes (Ed.), *Not all little wagons are red* (pp. 66–75). Washington, DC: Council for Exceptional Children.

Paul, J. L., Neufeld, G. R., & Pelosi, J. W. (Eds.). (1977). *Child advocacy within the system*. Syracuse, NY: Syracuse University Press.

Perkins, S. (1977). Malnutrition and mental development. *Exceptional Children, 43*, 214–219.

President's Commission on Mental Retardation. (1977). *MR 76 mental retardation past and present*. Washington, DC: U.S. Government Printing Office.

Reynolds, M., Wang, M., & Walberg, H. (1987). The necessary restructuring of special and regular education. *Exceptional Children, 53*, 391–398.

Rhodes, W. C. (1975). *A study of child variance: Vol. 5. The Future*. Ann Arbor: University of Michigan Press.

Rhodes, W. C., & Head, S. (1974). *A study of child variance: Vol. 4. The future*. Ann Arbor: University of Michigan Press.

Rutter, M. (1971). Parent-child separation: Psychological effects on children. *Journal of Child Psychology and Psychiatry, 12*, 233–260.

Sailor, W. (1991). Special education in the restructured school. *Remedial and Special Education, 12*(6), 8–22.

Scheff, T. (1966). *Being mentally ill*. Chicago: Aldine.

Schlossman, S. (1976). Before home state: Notes toward a history of parent education in America 1897–1929. *Harvard Educational Review, 46*,(3), 436–466.

Schopler, E., & Reichler, R. (1971). Parents as cotherapists in the treatment of psychotic children. *Journal of Autism & Childhood Schizophrenia, 1*, 87–102.

Schopler, E., & Reichler, R. (Eds.). (1976). *Psychopathology and child development: Research and treatment*. New York: Plenum.

Simpkins, K. L., & Kaplan, R. K. (1991). Fair play for disabled persons: Our responsibilities under the new ADA. *Journal of Career Planning and Employment, 51*,(2), 40–46.

Skrtic, T. M. (1991). The special education paradox: Equity as the way to excellence. *Harvard Educational Review, 61*, 148–195.

Smith, J. (1985). *Minds made feeble: The myth and legacy of the Kallekaks*. Rockville, MD: Aspen.

The Gallup Poll News Service (June 4, 1990), Vol. 55, No. 5.

Turnbull, A., & Turnbull, H. R. (1985). *Parents speak out: Then and now* (2nd ed.). Columbus, OH: Merrill.

Turnbull, A., & Turnbull, H. R. (1990). *Families, professionals, and exceptionality: A special partnership* (2nd ed.). Columbus, OH: Merrill.

Wolff, S., & Acron, W. (1963). Characteristics of parents of disturbed children. *British Journal of Psychiatry, 104*, 593–601.

# 2

# CHILDREN, FAMILIES, AND DISABILITY: PSYCHOLOGICAL DIMENSIONS

*Rune J. Simeonsson, Nancy E. Simeonsson*

## INTRODUCTION

Perhaps the most pervasive and fundamental shift in the orientation of the help-ing professions in recent years has been a recognition of the centrality of the family system in the provision of services. Using one term or another, represen-tative fields such as medicine (Worthington, 1992), rehabilitation, (Zolko, 1991), and psychiatry (Jaffe-Ruiz, 1984) have each espoused the importance of approaching the family as the unit of analysis for assessment and intervention. Increasingly there is a recognition of the need for integrated and systemic views of the family (Sluzki, 1983). This shift in orientation is no less true in services for exceptional children, with the field of early intervention leading the way with models such as family-centered care (Shelton, Jeppson, & Johnson, 1987), family-focused intervention (Simeonsson & Bailey, 1991), as well as family enablement and empowerment (Dunst, Trivette, & Deal, 1988). While each of these models differs in their details, they share an implicit belief that strengthening the family is an important part of intervention. Given ongoing changes in roles of families in our society, a thorough consideration of conceptions about families and var-iations in their structure, functions, needs, and resources would constitute a useful base for the provision of services. Such consideration is of particular importance relative to families raising children with disabilities, since their concerns, needs, and resources may differ in form, frequency, and intensity from those of other families. This chapter reviews selected conceptualizations of the family, to iden-tify elements relevant to working with the family in which there is a disabled child, and to suggest implications for family-oriented services.

Like all families, those with disabled children are characterized by a range of needs, resources, and support. Such variability is important to understand in that it is likely to account for the adaptation of the family in terms of its trans-actions with the physical and psychological environment (Sameroff & Fiese, 1990). Approaching family work objectively may be difficult not only because of family diversity but also because each of us brings a personal, subjective frame to such work. In order to enhance our efforts with disabled children and their families, it is important to consider frameworks for serving families that build on available concepts and findings. There is an increasing availability of information on the family describing clinical approaches to therapy involving parents and siblings (Minuchin, 1974). Paralleling clinical interventions is a growing body of knowledge about families based on research and theory (Rossi, 1977; Tseng & McDermott, 1979). This information base can contribute to the identification of means to support and strengthen the family, a goal of particular significance for families who have children with disabilities. To this end this chapter considers: (1) conceptual approaches to the family; (2) characteristics of families with a disabled member; (3) change and continuity in family development and adaptation; and (4) approaches to promote family development.

## CONCEPTUAL APPROACHES TO THE FAMILY

The manner in which professionals conceptualize the family can be a significant factor, determining the form and manner of service provision by helping professions to families in need. Freeman (1976) has emphasized, "The framework that we bring to understanding how families behave can facilitate or retard our work. If we have too narrow a view of family functioning, the types of questions, goals, and strategies we can use become more of a disservice than help to families" (p. 746).

Conceptualizations of the family were historically oriented toward, and derived from, considerations of family pathology. Drawing on a diagnostic approach, primarily from the fields of psychiatry and psychology, interest focused on examining atypical conditions while typical features were only of passing interest as a reference point. With the growing multidisciplinary interest in the family, alternate conceptualizations are emerging that go well beyond a focus on pathology. Illustrative of this change is a comparison of approaches toward investigating family response to a child's disability or chronic illness (Kanfl & Deatrick, 1987). One approach was defined as objective, passive, and outcome focused, whereas the second was subjective, active, and process oriented. Not only were the assumptions for the two approaches different, but the implications for findings clearly differed as well.

Given Freeman's (1976) admonition about the importance of frameworks in serving families, a consideration of selected approaches would seem useful. Israelstam (1988) has contrasted four major family therapy models: the affective experiential, strategic, structural, and Milan school and identified the implications of each for therapy training. Steinhauer (1985) has proposed a systematic and integrated approach as a means to move beyond some of these established models. Two major ways in which the family has been conceptualized are of particular relevance to the focus of this chapter: the structural approach and the developmental approach.

# Structural Approach

The structural conceptualization of the family has as its primary focus the structure of relationships among family members. It is an approach commonly used in clinical settings (Tseng & McDermott, 1979) and is typically characterized by a focus on pathological dimensions and an emphasis on family dynamics.

Within a structural perspective an individual in the family is identified as the patient, and family pathology becomes conceptualized in terms of dysfunctional relationships and transactions of family subsystems. The pathological orientation of this approach is typified by the designation used in representative contributions. By virtue of its clinical origin and utility, a structural conceptualization emphasizes viewing the family in terms of pathology. Along with this pathological orientation is an interpretation of dynamic factors as causal of family dysfunction. The dynamic emphasis focuses on the nature of family relationships in terms of governing family behavior or roles assigned to family members. Rules, although typically unwritten and implicit, do govern the family and can be inferred from its repetitive and redundant behavior. For example, based on data collected on families in clinical settings, Ford and Herrick (1974) identified five rules that, because of their dominance, constituted maladaptive family lifestyles. These rules were (1) children come first; (2) two against the world; (3) share and share alike; (4) everyone for him or herself; and (5) until death do us part. Although these and other rules are also expressed in nondysfunctional families, it is the excessive dominance of a given rule on family life that contributes to family dysfunction.

The dynamic emphasis of the structural approach can also be seen in the roles assigned to family members. Rollins, Lord, Walsh, and Weil (1973) have identified four roles of the identified child as reflective of family psychopathology: scapegoat, baby, pet, and peacemaker. The assignment of roles is based on dynamics of conflict resolution and fixations. The scapegoat and baby roles are negative in nature and harmful to family adaptation in that the child is the object of excessive blame, or excessive investment, respectively. The pet and peacemaker roles, on the other hand, are positive in nature but still harmful to family functioning. The pet is showered with indiscriminate family attention and the peacemaker may be assigned or required to assume adultlike roles in mediating the aggression of feuding parents. In healthy family systems, roles result from group interaction and serve to promote the growth of the child and the family. Roles typically shift adaptively with development, but pathological factors influencing the family may result in family roles becoming fixed, resulting in maladaptive family functioning.

# Developmental Approach

Whereas the structural approach to families emphasizes dysfunction of roles and relationships within the family, the developmental approach centers on the needs and problems of families at different stages, or phases, of development. Major theories of human development (Erikson, 1963; Piaget, 1970) have served as models to define typical and atypical family development. A number of constructs from developmental psychology have been advanced as relevant for family therapy (Stratton, 1988), including attachment, identity, and competence. Two features of the developmental approach may have particular relevance for viewing families with a disabled child: the concept of developmental tasks and the concept of developmental stages. Both applications address changes in family structure and functioning due to development but do so from somewhat different perspectives with different emphases.

**Developmental Tasks.**    A developmental task is one that is encountered and has to be mastered at a certain stage of development as a prerequisite for the mastery of subsequent tasks. Throughout the individual's life span, from infancy through senescence, different tasks must be mastered at each phase of development. According to Havighurst (1972), some of the major tasks facing the adult members of the family are selecting a mate, learning to live with a partner in marriage, starting a family, rearing children, managing a home, and assisting children to become adults. For a more detailed treatment of these tasks and additional developmental tasks, a review of Havighurst's book would be in order. The concept of developmental tasks is valuable in that it identifies major tasks that both parents and children have to face. Most families, including those with disabled children, face these tasks, although as we later discuss, families with disabled children often have to face additional tasks.

**Developmental Stages.**    The concept of stages of development has been central to several theories. Piaget's major stages of cognitive development and Freud's stages of psychosexual development have served as frameworks for diagnoses and treatment in psychiatry. The theories of Piaget and Freud have had a rather specific focus—cognitive and psychosexual development—and have been limited to the period from infancy through adolescence. A more comprehensive theory of personal-social development across the life span has been developed by Erikson (1963), which he calls the "eight stages of man." In each of these stages, the individual strives to resolve a major crisis of development and achieve a satisfactory sense of achievement and competency. The last four stages have direct relevance for working with families. While the fifth stage focuses on adolescence, the crisis addressed in this stage is compounded when adolescents become parents. Teenage and single parenting are issues of special concern when working with minority families, and recommendations for interventions with these families are discussed in detail in Chapter 7. In the sixth stage, young adults seek companionship to acquire a sense of intimacy and solidarity and avoid a sense of isolation. In the seventh stage, with the establishment of a home and family, the person acquires a sense of generativity and relinquishes the sense of self-absorption. In the eighth and last stage, each parent seeks to acquire a sense of integrity and avoid a sense of despair as increasing age brings on constriction of roles. Maier (1965) has proposed that these stages reflect a universal and collective human life cycle which transcends that of individual development.

A developmental stage model similar to Erikson's, but focusing on the development of the family as a unit rather than on the individual, has been proposed by Solomon (1973). This approach is conceptualized around major life events and tasks that are faced by the family in its life cycle. Solomon contends that the tasks of one stage must be resolved for satisfactory mastery of subsequent stages. The degree to which the family is able to resolve stress and disorganization at each stage is indicative of the family's functioning.

Solomon's first developmental stage is the formation of the family in which two major tasks are for each partner to (1) give up the primary gratification derived from their family of origin; and (2) make an investment in the marital partnership. The second stage is associated with childbirth and child rearing, where the tasks are to strengthen and solidify marital roles, while at the same time developing and assuming new parental roles. The third stage of the family encompasses the period from the time the first child begins school through the adolescence of the last child. The major task of this stage is the successful modification of roles for each member of the family from the dependent interaction of children on parents in infancy and childhood to the progressive independence of adolescence. The departure of children from the home constitutes the fourth stage of the family, in which the task is similar to that of the first stage: namely, the ability to relinquish primary relationships between parent and child in favor of secondary relationships between parent and adult offspring with new expectations and demands. Solomon sees this final stage of the family as the integration of loss, characterized by the adjustment of husband and wife to the physical, social, and economic demands of being dependent, alone, and growing older. Satisfactory resolution of such problems requires an acceptance of changes and a reinvestment in spousal roles.

This brief review of two developmental approaches to the family has revealed several common themes. One assumption central to the developmental approach is that there are life tasks faced by most families which, if mastered satisfactorily, contribute to family stability and growth. On the other hand, failure to master or resolve significant tasks may prevent or distort family adjustment. The value of developmental approaches thus lies not only in the manner in which family development is viewed as parallel to individual development, but also in the frameworks they provide for identifying the family's stage of functioning and associated need for intervention.

# CONCEPTUAL APPROACHES TO FAMILIES WITH A DISABLED CHILD

In the search for frameworks to enhance interpretation of family functioning and plan appropriate services, there is a growing need to attend to the developmental characteristics of child and family. There are several contributions available for review that may have particular relevance in a consideration of families with disabled children.

One contribution has addressed the lack of a comprehensive classification system of the family for the helping professions. In response to this problem, Tseng and McDermott (1979) have proposed a multidimensional framework of the family designed to reflect the complexity of both family structure and function. The classification model builds on previous conceptualizations of the family by considering pathological and dysfunctional aspects, and, more importantly, it recognizes the structure and function of the normal nondysfunctional family as well. This multidimensional model of the family specifies family dimensions along three axes. The first axis represents developmental stages, and considers the family longitudinally from the first stage of marriage to the last stage of a family with adult children. The second axis views the family from a cross-sectional perspective by focusing on individual family members and the extent to which relationships are functional or dysfunctional. The third axis is also cross-sectional, but views the family as a group or system. Families can be classified as functional or dysfunctional in terms of internal processes (such as organization, interpretation, and role division) or external processes (such as nonconformity and social isolation). A summary of the three axes of the model is shown in Figure 2–1.

This triaxial model may have value for conceptualizations of families with disabled children because its classification system permits the simultaneous consideration of family development, family structure, and family function. Family adjustment can thus be determined more precisely, since we can see the family as experiencing difficulties along one dimension but not another. Such situations may often characterize families of disabled children in that specific reactions to stress may result in disorders of family functioning at a certain time but not another. Some of the classifications defined by Tseng and McDermott (1979) may be reflective of coping styles in families with disabled children. These classifications include child-related dysfunctions, parent-child triangular dysfunction, the socially isolated family, and the special theme family. A comparable application, for example, has been described by Kodadek and Haylor (1990), who identified family response to their child's blindness in terms of four family paradigms: the perfect blind child's family, the devoted parent family, the overwhelmed family, and the realistically accepting family. Goodyer (1986) has noted that family therapy is not a panacea for all families with disabled children but can be effective in appropriate cases. A second related value of the triaxial model is that it takes into account the major phases of family development and potential complications of each phase. Thus it should be possible to distinguish whether a family's reaction is indicative of an adjustment in a particular phase or stage, or reflective of more enduring adjustments. These characteristics of the triaxial model illustrate its potential utility as a framework in which to view the family with a disabled child. The recognition that the family is an internally dynamic system and subject to external change requires that conceptualizations about the family be flexible and open to reevaluation (Tseng & McDermott, 1979).

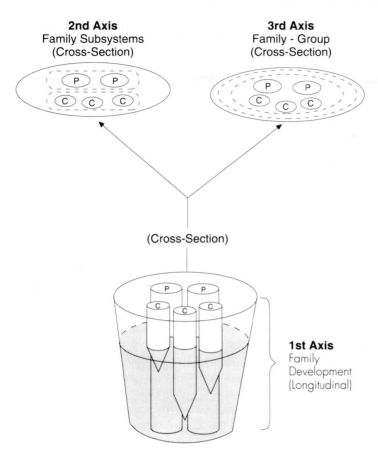

**2nd Axis**
Family Subsystems
(Cross-Section)

**3rd Axis**
Family - Group
(Cross-Section)

(Cross-Section)

**1st Axis**
Family
Development
(Longitudinal)

FIGURE 2–1

*Triaxis of family
dimensions*

# Other Developmental Approaches

Other developmental applications, narrower in scope than the triaxial classification model, may also have utility for considering families with disabled children. Several approaches represent extensions of Piaget's constructivist theory to clinical concerns with children and families. Melito (1985) has drawn on the Piagetian constructs of regulation and operations to describe adaptive processes in families. Two other applications have focused on the manner in which parents actively construct and reconstruct their conceptions of the child and are described more fully later.

Greenspan (1978) has proposed that effective parenting is a function of the parent's ability to discriminate among ambiguous and/or conflicting elements of a child's behavior and make appropriate coordinations. He suggests that operational parenting involves the process of "decentering" in responding to the child's behavior, or the simultaneous consideration of two or more dimensions of a child's acts or feelings. Such simultaneous consideration is of particular importance in child discipline, which involves a balance between the facilitation of autonomy (allowance of affect) and responsibility (assertion of limits). Parenting of disabled children may require a special form of decentering, that is, recognizing and making appropriate coordinations given limitations associated with the child's disabling condition. Inadequate decentration may be expressed by parents either making unrealistic demands on the child on the one hand or inappropriately indulging the child on the other.

Also operating from Piaget's theory, but in a somewhat different manner, Sameroff (1975, July) proposed that parental conceptions of child behavior can be seen to fit stages of development. These stages parallel those that the child traverses in cognitive growth from sensorimotor schemas to formal operations logic. A sensorimotor interpretation of child behavior focuses on the simple, physical, here-and-now interactions directly related to parental activity. A preoperational conception is one in which the parent views the child on the basis of generalized characteristics (e.g., pretty child, difficult child, etc.). In concrete operational terms the major feature of interpretation is that the parent is able to consider the child's behavior apart from the label. At this level a broader context is used to coordinate several aspects of a child's behavior, for example, age specificity of behavior is recognized. Only at the formal operations level, however, does a parent view a child's behavior as situation-specific. "At this level the parents are able to understand that a child's behavior is a function of its individual experience with its specific environments and that if the experience had been different that child's characteristics would be different" (Sameroff, 1975, July, p. 7).

The utility of Sameroff's proposal regarding the developmental nature of parental conceptions is that it builds on the transactional model, which asserts that child characteristics contribute to changes in the caretaking environments. Within this perspective, Sameroff suggests that parents whose interpretation of behavior is at a basic level may have difficulty with child behavior that deviates or differs from that conception. A parent whose view of the child is restricted to the preoperational level, for example, may persist in treating a child according to an earlier label (e.g., hyperactive), even though the child's behavior has changed. Variations in the construction of a child's development may apply to the family as a unit as well as to the individual parent. This is illustrated in Pollner and McDonald-Wikler's (1985) study that described a family's unrealistic attribution of competence to a family member with severe mental retardation. A parent whose interpretations are of a formal operations nature, however, will be able to place the child's behavior in perspective. "Deviances in the child are now perceived as being deviances in the relation of a particular child to a particular environment, rather than as concrete expressions of the essential nature of the child. Remediation can be proposed by altering the experience of the child through environmental changes" (Sameroff, 1975, July, p. 7). Given that this approach recognizes the complexity of parent-child relationships, an implication for families of disabled children is that intervention should not simply facilitate parental adaptation to specific behaviors but adaptation that is responsive to broader characteristics of the child as well.

# THE FAMILY WITH A DISABLED CHILD ████████████████

There is little doubt that the presence of a disabled child in a family can have profound effects on the structure, function, and developmental stage of the family. Not only may there be changes in family roles and relationships, but there may also be variations in developmental tasks and stages encountered by the family. To provide effective support, professionals need to understand the family as a system and consider the developmental course of the child, the parents, and the siblings.

## Developmental Course of the Child

The developmental course of a child with a disability is typically delayed in one or more areas compared to nondisabled peers. The nature and extent of the delay is likely to be a function of the disability and its severity. For children with disabilities of vision or hearing, delays may be most marked in the early formative years with subsequent compensation of skills by adolescence. For children with significant neuromuscular and/or mental impairment, there is often delayed development as well as an ultimate ceiling on motor and/or mental functioning. Although each child's development is a function of complex interactions involving experience, some common factors can be identified that influence the child's ultimate outcome. Bijou (1963), for example, has proposed that organismic as well as experiential variables contribute to developmental retardation. Organismic variables influence development in that the child's (1) physical or physiological deficits prohibit certain actions; (2) impairment of function or mobility may restrict physical and social experiences; and (3) physical characteristics may be aversive to others, thereby reducing social interactions and learning. In addition to these organismic factors, Bijou also suggests that a child's experience may functionally retard development through a life history of (1) inadequate reinforcement; (2) inconsistent or atypical reinforcement; or (3) punishment. Variability of developmental outcome can thus be seen to reflect the joint contribution of biological and experiential factors. Furthermore, although development may be differentially influenced by the nature as well as the severity of the disability, a particular condition may also have greater or lesser significance at different points in development (Fostel, 1978). With these considerations in mind, we draw some generalizations to provide a perspective on the development of disabled children.

In the first few years of life the emergence of independence can be significantly delayed by problems in motor coordination and difficulties in feeding and elimination. The normal course of emotional and social exchange in parent-child relationships may be delayed or distorted in children with sensory impairments (e.g., in blind, autistic, or motor-impaired children). The preschool development of disabled children is often characterized by a delay in the acquisition of spoken language or in a substitute communication system for deaf, autistic, and some severely motorically disabled children. Limited ability and restricted opportunities for exploration and social play with peers, combined with communication difficulties, contribute to functional deficits in skills essential for future academic performance. The early school years involving special education may serve as the occasion for many children with mild disabilities to become aware of the dimensions along which they differ from other children. It has been found that children with physical disabilities go through a well-defined crisis between the ages of 5 and 9, following a realization that the disability is permanent. First comes a period of depression followed by an equal period of emotional adjustment and acceptance of the condition (Minde, Hackett, Killou, & Silver, 1972). The disabled child's level of awareness and the supportiveness of the social environment are probably critical influences on the development of the disabled child's self-concept and identity.

The preadolescent and adolescent years may mark a period of particular difficulty for many disabled children in that growing societal expectations for independence are combined with complications of physical and sexual maturation. The identity problems of disabled adolescents have been delineated within Erikson's stages of development in terms of psychosexual role differences and enforced dependency roles due to cognitive and/or physical limitations (Travis, 1976).

In summary, the developmental course of disabled children from infancy to physical maturity is often characterized by delays or distortions of cognitive, social, affective, and communicative processes. In spite of multiple stressors, many children with disabilities achieve the physical and psychological maturity to function independently in society. Others reach physical maturity but fail to achieve levels of functioning in which they can cease to be dependent on others.

## Developmental Course of Parents

The adjustment of parents often seems to follow a developmental pattern, and substantial research has focused on describing the reaction of parents when they first learn their child's development may not be "normal." Traditionally two theories have been advanced to explain the shock, denial, and disbelief of parents faced with the crisis of having a disabled child (Fostel, 1978). One is Solnit and Stark's (1961) theory of a mourning reaction to the loss of the expected healthy child, and the other is Olshansky's (1962) premise of chronic sorrow, a reaction to the knowledge that the child will not become independent. While aspects of these reactions continue to be considered (Copley & Bodenstein, 1987), their pervasiveness and universality have been challenged.

As MacKeith (1973) has suggested, the feelings and behaviors of parents may be influenced by several factors including (1) the severity of the disability; (2) the degree to which the disability is obvious to others; (3) the attitude of others toward the disability; and perhaps most important (4) the time at which the disability became evident. Each of these factors, singly or in combination, will contribute to a family's feelings and reactions and define the extent of the family response from acceptance to rejection. It should be emphasized, however, that reactions and behaviors vary greatly across parents of disabled children, with most characterized by adaptive coping.

MacKeith's (1973) identification of varied feelings and behaviors does, however, accentuate the complexity of reactions that may be evoked in parents of disabled children. An appreciation of this complexity has prompted the development of models to approach the family as a unit for intervention and support.

Conclusions regarding long-range consequences of a disabled child's presence on a family are not uniform. It is apparent from the studies cited that simplistic conclusions about the impact of a physically disabled child on the family are inappropriate, since a variety of factors may interact to threaten or strengthen the family. A substantial body of research on family adaptation in the context of child disability supports a general interpretation that the adequacy of family functioning reflects the interplay of family resilience and vulnerability. This interactive interpretation is similar to the conception of adaptation as a reflection of the goodness of fit between capabilities and demands. The utility of the goodness of fit concept has been applied to the study of families with delayed infants and toddlers (Simeonsson, Bailey, Huntington, & Comfort, 1986) and families with chronically ill children (Wallander, Hubert, & Varni, 1988).

We must emphasize that the mixed interpretation of family reactions to the presence of a disabled child is not derived solely from the opinions of professionals. In Chapter 4, a number of poignant perspectives are described in personal terms by parents of disabled children. Evidence of such perspectives should turn attention away from a preoccupation by professionals with the negative aspects of parenting disabled children. Instead, more focus should be directed toward a delineation and enhancement of factors associated with positive adaptation of families (Gallagher, Haskins, & Farran, 1979).

## Developmental Course of Siblings

In many families with disabled children, there are often older as well as younger nondisabled siblings (Schulman, 1988). They occupy unique roles in that they, along with the disabled child, are the objects of their parents' socialization, but they may in many instances also serve as socializing agents for their disabled sibling. From studies of sibling influence in selected families, McMillan and Henao (1977) have concluded that, under some conditions, older siblings are as effective as parents in helping younger siblings.

The manner in which siblings function in families with a disabled child may vary widely, since they are frequently subjected to considerable direct as well as indirect stress (Davis, 1975). Siblings do not seem to be studied as often or as comprehensively as disabled children and their parents, and available research presents contradictory findings. Conflicting results of studies associating emotional disturbance of siblings of disabled children led Wing (1969) to suggest that the problem of dealing with disabled children represents universal experiences of disappointment and trauma. Variability of responses across families may thus be a function of inherent differences in families; while some seem to adapt, others are overwhelmed (Simeonsson & Bailey, 1986).

One factor that may contribute to the problems of siblings of disabled children is that more attention is given by parents to the disabled child than to the siblings. The excess need for attention or demand for time by the disabled children may in fact result in siblings having more severe emotional problems than the disabled child (Poznanski, 1973). Tew and Laurence (1973) found that maladjustment was four times higher in siblings of children with spina bifida than in siblings of controls. In another study comparing 174 siblings of Down syndrome children with a control group matched for social class, significantly more of the former were rated as deviant in behavior than control children (Gath, 1973).

The presence of a disabled child may also have unequal effects for brothers and sisters. Gath (1973), for example, reported that the presence of a Down syndrome child was uniquely associated with deviant behavior and educational problems of sisters. These findings are important to consider given the current emphasis on deinstitutionalization and advocacy for home care for the disabled. This emphasis could, as Poznanski (1973) has suggested, exaggerate the difference in needs and demands between the disabled children and their siblings and requires further investigation.

## CHANGE AND CONTINUITY IN FAMILIES WITH DISABLED CHILDREN

There can be no doubt that the introduction and continuing presence of a disabled child results in irrevocable and pervasive changes, whether beneficial or detrimental, in a family. Yet for many families in the face of such changes, there is remarkable adaptation and efforts to maintain the continuity of family functioning. If helping professionals are to be effective in providing support, they need to understand change and continuity as they are expressed in the lives of families with disabled children. To enhance such understanding it is useful to consider the family of the disabled in a framework that builds on available conceptualizations of the family and recognizes their common as well as unique problems. A developmental perspective seems the most appropriate approach for considering families and their children, given that problems in development constitute the major characteristic of disabled children and that parenting can be seen to follow a sequence of stages. Such a perspective builds on the assumption that changes within and outside the family are transactional in nature; that is, one change contributes to another, which in turn results in yet other changes over time. Transactions in family development may thus result in a wide range of developmental outcomes, as Sameroff and Chandler (1975) have noted in their concept of the "continuum of caretaking casualty." Factors that impact family transactions and thereby influence developmental outcome of disabled children and their families are (1) additional developmental tasks; (2) developmental crises they face; and (3) the extent to which alternate developmental goals are met. These factors serve as a basis for conceptualizing the disabled child and the family and form a framework for supporting and enhancing their development.

## Additional Developmental Tasks

Havighurst's (1972) concept of developmental tasks has previously been referred to as a series of tasks that an individual encounters and needs to master at different points in the life span. These tasks include the broad expectations that society holds for every individual, including those with disabilities and their families, even though mastery may not be achieved. A consideration of disabled children and their families further suggests that they may not be able to master some tasks but may also encounter additional developmental tasks not faced by anyone else. Some of these additional developmental tasks are encountered only by the disabled child, whereas others are faced by the child's family.

**Children With Disabilities.**   In an article addressing disruptions in the socialization process, Battle (1974) identified several additional developmental tasks that young disabled children face in adjusting to their condition, to their environment, and to themselves. These additional tasks include (1) adjustment to many medical examinations and hospitalizations; (2) acceptance or tolerance of associated treatments and procedures of exposure to large numbers of professionals for evaluation when quite young; (3) adjustments to the special concern of parents and other adults; (4) adjustment to ridicule or curiosity; and (5) acceptance of personal limitations such as being dependent and frustrated in performance and communication. Although nondisabled children may encounter some of these developmental tasks in a limited manner, disabled children experience them in severe and chronic forms. In a study on children with oral-facial clefts, for example, repeated medical operations were seen as particularly traumatic events for some children (Tisza, Irwin, & Scheide, 1973).

Another developmental event common to most children, but which assumes additional demands for the disabled child, is that of school experience. School experiences for the disabled child can be different from those of other children in that the disabled child may be assigned to homogeneous peer groups, which can mean geographical and/or social isolation from nondisabled peers (Travis, 1976). As Travis has pointed out, it may also mean being labeled, stereotyped, or treated in a certain way and experiencing unpredictable events or crises in their lives. Developmental tasks of adolescence may present serious challenges for adjustment and self-concept development among adolescents with disabilities. Physically disabled adolescents often must face the additional problem of using specific prostheses, aids, or wheelchairs for functioning. Dorner's (1973) findings of social isolation and reaction to using urinary appliances in spina bifida adolescents, particularly among boys, illustrate the reality of these additional developmental burdens.

**The Family.** Just as each disabled child faces additional tasks to individual development, so, too, does the family. One general task faced by the family, regardless of the type of disabling condition, is to assist the disabled child in mastering his or her developmental tasks. Another general task faced by families of disabled children is to deal with more stress than most families experience (Tew & Laurence, 1973). In regard to caretaking activities involving children with specific disabilities, families may face the additional task of decoding responses from the child other than contact or cuddling. Families of blind children will need to accept verbal and tactile responses (Fraiberg, 1976), whereas families of autistic children (Marcus, 1977) and of those with birth defects (Travis, 1976) may have to accept atypical or no overt responses.

Additional tasks for families of children with disabilities or chronic conditions often involve family routines. Travis (1976) has identified several of these burdens, such as (1) sleep interruption for families of disabled children beyond the infancy period; (2) provision of complicated diets or treatments; (3) extra cleaning and housework; (4) physical or structural adaptation of home; and (5) additional financial demands. For a number of disabled children, families face the prolonged, and in many cases more physically demanding, tasks of lifting, bathing, dressing, and diapering older children (Richards & McIntosh, 1973).

While families with disabled children face developmental tasks common to most families, they are also called on to varying degrees and in varying ways to deal with additional tasks or tasks with exaggerated or prolonged demands. The extent to which these tasks of the family and child are mastered is likely to be influenced not only by the nature and severity of the child's disability, but more substantively by the physical and social environment.

## Developmental Crises Periods

If a developmental framework is adopted to view disabled children and their families, their adjustment may take the form of response to sequential crisis periods. It is important for helping professionals to be aware of these in order to be prepared to assist families at times of particular difficulty. Furthermore, as Lowit (1973) has concluded, if the first crisis is dealt with in a positive manner, helping families in subsequent periods of need can be enhanced.

Although crisis periods do not correspond exactly with specific developmental stages of children and families as discussed earlier in this chapter, they do appear to reflect similar transitions. MacKeith (1973) has proposed four major crisis periods associated with the development of the disabled child. The first occurs when the parents initially become aware that their child is disabled. Although this usually occurs at the time the child is born, in families with a visually impaired child (Hancock, Wilgosh, & McDonald, 1990), for example, it may be delayed if the impairment is less readily evident. A number of studies have identified parental reactions to this crisis and emphasized the importance of guidance and support during this period. Five stages of reaction have been found in a study of the response of 20 parents to the development and care of their disabled child (Drotar, Baskiewicz, Irwin, Kennell, & Klaus, 1975). The first of these stages reflected shock, the second denial, the third consisted of sadness and anger, the fourth adaptation, and the fifth reorganization. The authors developed a hypothetical model to indicate that the stages emerged sequentially and varied in their impact.

A second major crisis period identified by MacKeith centers on the time when the child becomes eligible for educational services. It is at this point that many parents may have to face realistically the level and permanence of their child's disability and expectations for academic achievement and independence. Associated with the crisis faced by the family is a potential crisis experienced by some children as they come to realize the permanence of the condition. These crises faced by child and family may be eased and adjustment facilitated by anticipatory guidance and ongoing support by schools.

Associated with this crisis period for the family is the specific crisis faced by orthopedically disabled children as they come to realize the permanence of the condition. Periods involving depression and acceptance, mentioned previously, are typically experienced by these children between the ages of 5 and 9. These crises may be compounded or eased depending on adjustment to the broader demands of the school experience.

MacKeith identifies the third crisis period as the time when the disabled child or youth leaves school. From a more general perspective, this time of crisis involves problems associated with physical and physiological maturation in the context of social, psychological, and/or functional limitations. For the adolescent who is mentally retarded, it may be a period of personal confusion and frustration. For adolescents with an impairment such as spina bifida, it is often a period of severe restriction of social experiences (Dorner, 1973). The critical task faced by parents of adolescents is to deal with their concern about their future dependency status and whether or not they should continue to remain at home or be placed in a setting away from home as disabled adults. Although factors contributing to the resolution of these difficult periods are complex, the severity and visibility of the disability are probably significant influences. A study by McAllister, Butler, and Lei (1973) of families with children with mental retardation provides some evidence for the influence of a disabled child on the family's social life. Findings indicated that the presence of a child with mental retardation restricted social interaction within the nuclear family itself and also negatively influenced extrafamilial interactions, particularly those involving immediate neighborhood activity.

According to MacKeith, the final crisis period comes for parents when they are aging and can no longer assume responsibility or care for their disabled offspring. Viewed in the context of Solomon's (1973) developmental stages of the family, the critical stage for parents in this period focuses on resolving the difficult demands associated with the fourth and fifth stages. Specifically, at the fourth stage there may be difficulty in relinquishing the primary dependent relationship between parent and child for that of a more independent, secondary relationship of parent and adult offspring. At the fifth stage the continued presence and/or dependence of a disabled offspring may restrict, delay, or prevent the necessary adjustment that aging parents need to make at a time when their own abilities and resources decline.

The identification of periods of particular crises or stress by MacKeith and others is valuable because it provides an organized framework in which to consider present and potential needs of disabled families. This is particularly important since the reaction of parents to a disabled child may be extreme and they may get "stuck" in one phase (Martin, 1975). Reference to a framework can provide direction for helping professionals in assisting the parents of disabled children to progress toward more healthy and adaptive functioning.

## Developmental Goals

Thus disabled children and their families experience crisis periods and face additional developmental tasks beyond those of most families. Furthermore, broad developmental goals of growth and behavior may have to be modified by families with a disabled child because of that child's characteristics. Let's consider (1) some general developmental goals the helping professions hold for families of disabled children; and (2) some specific goals these families hold for themselves.

### Goals of Intervention.
A major goal in parent support is for parents to arrive at a realistic balance of probable and possible developmental outcomes for their disabled child (Gordon, 1972). This goal may not be achieved easily, and may in fact only be achieved sequentially as each crisis period is encountered.

Another goal held by helping professionals is to help parents determine priorities for the family. There is a danger that the additional parenting demands and energy investment required by the child with a disability may result in the abdication of other family responsibilities of being a spouse or being a parent to the nondisabled siblings. Solomon (1973) feels that the parents of a disabled child may be particularly vulnerable to the danger of substituting a parental role for the marital role. The role of helping professionals is to give objective assistance to parents in helping them gauge their involvement such that they are able to realize overall family priorities.

### Goals of Parents.
A consideration of goals that families hold for themselves suggest that they encompass at least two areas of concern as evidenced by research. The first of these areas reflects the expressed needs of parents for knowledge about their disabled child and the second pertains to the nature of services that parents feel are needed in meeting the child's needs. Research on the perceived family needs of infants and young children with disabilities indicated

general congruence between mothers and fathers with informational needs representing a primary priority (Bailey & Simeonsson, 1988). Mothers endorsed a higher proportion of needs than fathers, indicative of the primary nature of the maternal caregiving role with young children. Of interest, however, was the identification of needs specific to each parent supporting the importance of assessing more than one family member's perspective.

**Information Needs.**   The need for information is usually expressed as soon as the parents become aware of the child's disabling condition. A study by Gayton and Walker (1974) on the time and manner in which parents of Down syndrome infants were informed about their child's condition indicated that parents had very specific preferences in this regard. Parents wanted to be informed as promptly as possible. Cunningham and Sloper (1973) state that parents will not automatically resent the person informing them of their child's condition, but privacy and access to support are seen as important. Critical information may need to be presented several times and parents may need to repeat the information back to the professional to clear up any misunderstandings. After being informed that their child is disabled, parents will want more detailed information about the handicapping condition and management advice. In a study of supportive services for families of children with chronic disorders, Pless, Satterwhite, and Van Vechten (1978) found that care was fragmented. A particular gap was evident in the lack of sufficient advice and counseling for parents. The concerns of families thus include not only questions about the etiology and correlates of a particular disability but also advice and counseling regarding family life and future educational programs (Knott, 1979).

**Service Needs.**   Availability of needed services is the second set of goals expressed by parents (Bailey & Simeonsson, 1988). In general, as indicated by a survey of families (Dunlap, 1976), parents want social services that will enable their disabled children to become more independent and more self-sufficient. Necessary help and guidance is seen as a major problem in caring for the disabled child at home (Lloyd-Bostock, 1976). Lack of services such as babysitting and the need for supportive counseling for siblings of the disabled are specific needs of families (McAndrew, 1976). We cannot understate the importance of professional sensitivity to parental goals for services, since parents have judged problems associated with obtaining needed services to be more difficult than problems attributable to the child's disability (Lloyd-Bostock, 1976).

## ENHANCING FAMILY DEVELOPMENT

Since the major objective of helping professionals is to support and enhance the development of families with disabled children, it is essential that assumptions held about them are realistic as well as consistent with current knowledge. Some assumptions are relevant to families in general; others are specific to families of disabled children. Implementation of the assumptions requires that services for families take into account changing societal contexts and services be provided in a comprehensive manner addressing primary, secondary, and tertiary needs (Doherty & Burge, 1987). Central to this and other considerations of the family is the assumption that the individual is a member of the family and the family is embedded in a social network.

A primary challenge facing the multiple disciplines seeking to support families with disabled children is to derive a frame of reference of the psychologically healthy family. In examining this issue, Textor (1989) has indicated that the definition of psychological health of families can take a number of approaches, including statistical, sociocultural, and clinical. Within the clinical approach, there are options of defining health in terms of the absence of pathology (indirect), the achievement of tasks (functional), and the use of values and consensus (ideal). Within the context of the idealistic approach, Textor has described dimensions of psychological health that could serve as frames of reference in family-based services. From a dimensional standpoint, a healthy family personality is characterized by an appropriate expression of affect. Cognitive and behavioral characteristics of a healthy family include realism, creativity, and flexibility. The dimension of family communication is healthy to the extent that it is clear and complete and free of contradictions. In regard to roles and relationships, a healthy family is one in which roles are distinct and clearly defined and the relationship is characterized by mutuality of an I and you dialogue. Finally, health exists when the family's definition of itself as a system is distinct, and it possesses the ability to adapt to internal and external demands. The search for conceptual models of family health is consistent with the growing interest in defining and documenting strengths of families with a disabled member (Schwab, 1989).

In regard to assumptions specific to families of disabled children, it is important to recognize that priorities for services and resources identified by professionals are not necessarily those that parents of disabled children would select (Lonsdale, 1978). The primacy of parents in decision making is basic to current ideology and legislation about family-centered interventions. A final assumption needing consideration is that more is not always better in providing services to families. This has been demonstrated in a study by Sandow and Clarke (1978), in which disabled children who had less frequent home visitations from helping professionals ultimately made better progress than those visited more frequently. The authors concluded that infrequent visits made the parents less dependent on the therapist and gave them a greater sense of responsibility for the progress of their child. In the provision of services it is therefore important to personalize interventions for families on the basis of their desired level of involvement. As Simeonsson and Bailey (1991) have proposed, levels of involvement may vary not only across families but may also vary within families at different points of time.

# RESOURCES AND SUPPORT

Theoretical models of families and findings on family functioning can provide background for a better understanding of the nature of change and continuity in families of disabled children. Such understanding should build on a recognition of the special tasks, crises, and goals that characterize each family with a disabled child. It should also lead to the provision of support directed at these elements of change and continuity. Support may then be seen to take the form of some of the activities calibrated to reflect the unique needs of each family.

The provision of support activities should be based on relevant models of family functioning and take into account the resources of the family. The importance of recognizing the involvement of families and the assessment of their unique needs and resources has been central to the early intervention initiative (Black, 1991). There is thus a growing effort to document family strengths in a systematic manner to better understand the family in context as well as to identify targets for intervention (McCubbin & Huang, 1989). Working within a typology model, Failla and Jones (1991) have shown that family hardiness constitutes a significant factor in adaptation of families with developmentally disabled children.

While major emphasis has been placed on the value of theoretical frameworks, there is also a need to consider identified or potential resources for providing support for families. Parents do look to helping professions for the provision of effective and efficient services that reduce the stress of living with a disabled child (Lonsdale, 1978). An important purpose of early intervention is to promote attachment and parent adjustment to the child.

Complementing the value of assessing resources and strengths is the assessment of the functional needs of parents. Realistic information regarding the abilities and skills of a child can contribute positively to parental expectations. There is an increased emphasis on actively involving parents in the services and programs provided for their children and themselves (Deitchman, Newman, & Walsh, 1977). Such levels of family involvement may range from very limited contact with available services to thoroughgoing engagement of the family (Simeonsson & Bailey, 1991). In some instances, for example, this may involve shared responsibilities with professionals, whereas in other contexts parents may limit their involvement to other parents. Different types of involvement may have different values for parents, as illustrated in a study contrasting involvement with voluntary organizations against involvement with organized professional services. Parents saw involvement with the former as providing emotional support and practical advice (relief) and involvement with the latter as providing care (replacement) (Bradshaw, Glendinning, & Hatch, 1977). The opportunity to share with others and to learn from others in parent organizations may serve to reinforce the family in its tasks.

In addition to the available services, support, and sense of identification parent organizations offer, there is the informal and perhaps essential form of support provided by relatives and friends. A wide array of studies have documented that family coping is directly associated with the adequacy of social support systems. Careful attention to identifying sources of support is central to intervention efforts for families and their children. Informal support networks may be uniquely beneficial to families in that not only are friends and relatives strongly committed to the family, but they can also provide support that is qualitatively different from, but complementary to, that of professionals.

## Summary

This chapter has presented information about families of disabled children to facilitate an understanding of their needs. The information reviewed has been drawn from conceptual models, research, and clinical findings. The personal side of these issues can be placed in context with the poignant first-person accounts provided by Sondra Diamond in Chapter 3 and by several families in Chapter 4. The collective picture that emerges is that families with disabled children, like all families, seek to realize their expectations for their children. At the same time, however, families with disabled children often face additional and ongoing tasks of raising children with special needs. A developmental approach, encompassing the concepts of developmental tasks and developmental stages, seems consistent with the common as well as the unique coping demands experienced over time by families with disabled children.

Within a developmental perspective the child's own development influences and is influenced by the family system of parents, siblings, and other primary caregivers. Although empirical and clinical findings revealed that the stress and crises of parenting children with disabilities may result in maladjustment in some families, there is also evidence that many, if not most, families are remarkably resilient, drawing on resources and experiencing growth.

These findings underscore the complex interaction of factors determining the adaptation of families with disabled children. They also support the consideration of the family as a unit or system encountering individual and shared tasks in its development. The triaxial model was presented as a way in which to conceptualize the structural, functional, and developmental characteristics of families. The use of frameworks is proposed as a means to improve services to families with disabled children and enhance the quality of research conducted on family adaptation and coping.

We conclude with the premise that strengthening the family strengthens society (Novak, 1976, April). This premise is based on the belief that "the family is potentially the most effective social institution for rearing healthy children. From this it follows that the defense of the family is the first line of defense of the child" (Eisenberg, 1975, p. 801). This position translates into a challenge to develop interventions reflective of the dynamic nature of the family system. Given the inevitability of societal change, it is of particular importance to draw on enduring principles and values that can guide the development and provision of supportive services for families. In this regard, there is a need for principles that endorse fundamental values of nurturance, caring, and trust, with individuality finding its best expression in shared commitment. More than 20 years ago, Hobbs (1966) advanced a set of principles to address a major intervention priority, namely mental health services for children. These principles, embodying the Re-Ed model of services for children, are as timely today as they were when first proposed. Expanding their scope to the family, these principles can serve as a basic, yet encompassing frame to guide interventions for families (Table 2–1). In that they reflect universally shared and shareable values, principles of this nature may transcend specific service approaches and variability among families as a function of social class, culture, and changing family forms. As such, the principles speak to the centrality of mutual regard and trust as the basis for supporting relationships. They also acknowledge the benefits afforded by time as well as social systems in promoting child and family competence. Finally intervention efforts and priorities are placed in perspective in recognizing the centrality of the existential nature of human experience.

If families with disabled children are to be supported in their roles, there is a need not only to clarify principles but also to clarify the task for helping pro-

TABLE 2–1

## SUPPORTING CHILDREN WITH DISABILITIES AND THEIR FAMILIES: GUIDING PRINCIPLES

1. Life is to be lived now, not in the past, and lived in the future only as a present challenge . . .
2. Time is an ally, facilitating the development of child and family in a life phase of significant forward thrust . . .
3. Trust between child and caregiver, between family and helper is essential; the base on which all other relationships rest . . .
4. Competence makes a difference; children and families should be helped to be good at something . . .
5. Needs and problems can and should be addressed directly . . .
6. Skills can be taught and children and families helped to be in control . . .
7. Feelings should be nurtured and respected . . .
8. "Family" is of primary importance . . .
9. Values, beliefs, ceremony, and ritual give order, stability, and confidence to children and families . . .
10. Physical well-being is the foundation of psychological well-being . . .
11. "Community" is important for children and families, offering resources and support . . .
12. Children and families should know joy . . .

(Adapted from Hobbs, 1966)

fessions. In reference to the disabled child, Holt (1979) has proposed that a "disability is not a . . . problem to be treated, trained or counseled, but a burden which is impeding a child's development. Our task is to ease this burden and so provide for the development of the person" (p. 161). By extension, our task as helping professionals is to ease the demands faced by the family and to promote its development and function. The theories and findings reviewed in this chapter have indicated that a variety of factors act to increase or decrease demands on families. The manner in which any one of these factors influence the family's adaptation may be a function of the unique ways in which we can provide supportive and protective resources and minimize stresses and demands.

Although specific services may be required to meet the different needs of individual families, helping professions can also support families by affirming their commitment to families in general. The dignity of the family needs to be affirmed through official policies, standards, and laws to ensure that the family is recognized and supported as an essential component of society. In regard to families with disabled children, additional commitments can be identified.

Of importance is a need for ongoing assessment of the implications of contemporary service forms to ensure they do not place undue demands on family life (Cirillo & Sorrentino, 1986) or conflict with family priorities. The current popularity of an intervention form or strategy among professionals does not mean that it is inherently positive for families. We need to be aware that our programs might professionalize parents (Allen & Hudd, 1987). First and foremost, it is essential that the priorities and values of the family are reflected in a personalized supportive program of services.

Finally, there is a need to recognize that the roles and investment of families and their children as consumers, and professionals as providers, may be quite different. Perspectives on the helping process are not likely to be congruent (Carter, 1976), and the validity of information from families may vary substantially as a function of the manner in which it is obtained (West, 1990). The lives of most professionals have not included the personal demands and adjustments associated with raising a child with a disability. A critical task for professionals, therefore, is to adopt the perspective of families in order to more fully comprehend their unique views and feelings (Black, 1978). The importance of perspective-taking is that it may reduce professional egocentrism and clarify family needs and priorities. Such perspective-taking in relationships with families may foster a deeper understanding of challenges faced by families raising children with disabilities and, in so doing, transform in a simple but profound way a supporting activity into a sharing activity.

## BIBLIOGRAPHY

Allen, D. A., & Hudd, S. S. (1987). Are we professionalizing parents? Weighing the benefits and pitfalls. *Mental Retardation, 25*(3), 133–139.

Bailey, D. B., & Simeonsson, R. J. (1988). Assessing the needs of families with handi-capped infants. *Journal of Special Education, 22*, 117–127.

Bailey, D. B., Simeonsson, R. J., Winton, P. J., Huntington, G. S., Comfort, M., Isbell, P., Helm, J. M., & O'Donnell, K. J. (1986). Family-focused intervention: A func-tional model for planning, implementing, and evaluating individualized family serv-ices in early iantervention. *Journal of the Division for Early Childhood, 10*(2), 156–171.

Battle, C. V. (1974). Disruptions in the socialization of a young severely handicapped child. *Rehabilitation Literature, 35*, 130–140.

Bijou, S. W. (1963). Theory and research in mental (developmental) retardation. *Psy-chological Record, 13*, 95–110.

Black, J. M. (1978). Families with handicapped children—who helps whom and how? *Child: Care, Health, and Development, 4*, 239–245.

Black, M. M. (1991). Early intervention services for infants and toddlers: A focus on families. *Journal of Clinical Child Psychology, 20*(1), 51–57.

Bradshaw, J., Glendinning, C., & Hatch, S. (1977). Voluntary organizations for handi-capped children and their families: The meaning of membership. *Child: Care, Health, and Development, 3*, 247–260.

Carter, J. (1976). Parents' meetings in a hospital day center. *Child: Care, Health, and Development, 2*, 203–212.

Cirillo, S., & Sorrentino, A. M. (1986). Handicap and rehabilitation: Two types of in-formation upsetting family organization. *Family Process, 26*, 295–308.

Copley, M. F., & Bodenstein, J. B. (1987). Chronic sorrow in families of disabled children. *Journal of Child Neurology, 2*, 67–70.

Cunningham, C. C., & Sloper, T. (1973). Parents of Down's syndrome babies: Their early needs. *Child: Care, Health, and Development, 3*, 325–347.

Davis, R. (1975). Family of physically disabled child. Family reaction and deductive rea-soning. *New York State Journal of Medicine, 75*, 1039–1041.

Deitchman, R., Newman, I., & Walsh, K. (1977). Dimensions of parental involvement in preschool programs. *Child: Care, Health, and Development, 3*, 213–224.

Doherty, W. J., & Burge, S. K. (1987). Attending to the context of family treatment: Pitfalls and prospects. *Journal of Marital and Family Therapy, 13*(1), 37–47.

Dorner, S. (1973). Psychological and social problems of families of adolescent spina bifida patients: A preliminary report. *Developmental Medicine and Child Neurology, 14*, 24–26.

Drotar, D., Baskiewicz, A., Irvin, N., Kennell, J., & Klaus, M. (1975). The adaptation of parents to the birth of an infant with congenital malformation: A hypothetical model. *Pediatrics, 56*, 710–717.

Dunlap, W. R. (1976). Services for families of the developmentally disabled. *Social Work*, 220–223.

Dunst, C. J., Trivette, C. M., & Deal, A. G. (1988). *Enabling and empowering families: Principles and guidelines for practices.* Cambridge, MA: Brookline.

Eisenberg, L. (1975). The ethics of intervention: Acting amidst ambiguity. *Journal of Child Psychology and Psychiatry, 16*, 93–104.

Erikson, E. (1963). *Child and society.* New York: Norton.

Failla, S., & Jones, L. C. (1991). Families of children with developmental disabilities: An examination of family hardiness. *Research in Nursing & Health, 14*, 41–50.

Ford, F. R., & Herrick, J. (1974). Family rules: Family life styles: *American Journal of Orthopsychiatry, 44*, 61–69.

Fostel, C. (1978). Chronic illness and handicapping conditions: Coping patterns. In P. Brandt, P. Chinn, V. Aunt, & M. E. Smith, (Eds.), *Current practice in pediatric nursing* (Vol. 2) (pp. 53–67). Saint Louis: Mosby, 1978.

Fraiberg, S. (1976). Blind infants and their mothers. In M. Lewis & L. Rosenblum (Eds.), *The effects of the infant on its caregiver* (pp. 215–232). New York: Wiley.

Freeman, C. (1976). The family as a system: Fact or fancy. *Comprehensive Psychiatry, 17,* 735–749.

Gallagher, J. J., Haskins, R., & Farran, D. (1979). Poverty and public policy. In T. B. Brazelton & V. C. Vaughn (Eds.), *The family: Setting priorities* (pp. 239–268). New York: Science & Medicine.

Gath, A. (1973). The school age sibling of mongol children. *British Journal of Psychiatry, 123,* 161–167.

Gayton, W. F., & Walker, L. (1974). Down syndrome: Informing the parents. *American Journal of Diseases of Children, 127,* 510–512.

Goodyer, I. M. (1986). Family therapy and the handicapped child. *Developmental Medical Child Neurology, 127,* 510–512.

Gordon, N. (1972). Parent counselling. *Developmental Medicine and Child Neurology, 14,* 657–659.

Greenspan, S. (1978). Operational and preoperational parenting: A Piagetian view of discipline. In R. Weizmann, R. Brown, P. J. Levinson, & P. A. Taylor (Eds.), *Piagetian theory and the helping professions* (Vol. 1) (pp. 51–57). Los Angeles: University of Southern California.

Hancock, K., Wilgosh, L., & McDonald, L. (1990). Parenting a visually impaired child: The mother's perspective. *Journal of Visual Impairment and Blindness,* 411–413.

Havighurst, R. I. (1972). *Developmental tasks and education* (3rd ed.). New York: McKay.

Hobbs, N. (1966). Helping disturbed children: Psychological and ecological strategies. *American Psychologist, 21,* 1105–1115.

Holt, K. S. (1979). Assessment of handicap in childhood. *Child: Care, Health, and Development, 5,* 151–162.

Israelstam, K. (1988). Contrasting four major family therapy paradigms: Implications for family therapy training. *Journal of Family Therapy, 10,* 179–196.

Jaffe-Ruiz, M. (1984). A family systems look at the developmentally disabled. *Perspectives in Psychiatric Care, 22,* 65–71.

Kanfl, K. A., & Deatrick, J. A. (1987). Conceptualizing family response to a child's illness or disability. *Family Relations, 36,* 300–304.

Kodadek, S. M., & Haylor, M. J. (1990). Using interpretive methods to understand family caregiving when a child is blind. *Journal of Pediatric Nursing, 5*(1), 42–49.

Lloyd-Bostock, S. (1976). Parents' experiences of official help and guidance in caring for a mentally handicapped child. *Child: Care, Health, and Development, 2,* 325–338.

Lonsdale, G. (1978). Family life with a handicapped child: The parents speak. *Child: Care, Health, and Development, 4,* 99–120.

Lowit, I. M. (1973). Social and psychological consequences of chronic illness in children. *Developmental Medicine and Child Neurology, 15,* 75–77.

MacKeith, R. (1973). The feelings and behavior of parents of handicapped children. *Developmental Medicine and Child Neurology, 15,* 524–527.

Maier, H. W. (1965). *Three theories of child development.* New York: Harper & Row.

Marcus, L. M. (1977). Patterns of coping in families of psychotic children. *American Journal of Orthopsychiatry, 47,* 388–398.

Martin, P. (1975). Parental response to handicapped children. *Developmental Medicine and Child Neurology, 17,* 251–252.

McAllister, R., Butler, R., & Lei, T. J. (1973). Patterns of social interaction among families of behaviorally retarded children. *Journal of Marriage and the Family, 35,* 93–100.

McAndrew, I. (1976). Children with a handicap and their families. *Child: Care, Health, and Development, 12,* 213–237.

McCubbin, M. A., & Huang, S. T. T. (1989). Family strengths in the care of handicapped children: Targets for intervention. *Family Relations, 38,* 436–443.

McMillan, M. F., & Henao, S. (1977). *Child psychiatry treatment and research.* New York: Brunner/Mazel.

Melito, R., (1985). Adaptation in family systems: A developmental perspective. *Family Process, 24,* 89–100.

Minde, K., Hackett, J., Killou, D., & Silver, S. (1972). How they grow up: Forty-one physically handicapped children and their families. *American Journal of Psychiatry, 12,* 1554–1560.

Minuchin, S. (1974). *Families and family therapy.* Cambridge, MA: Harvard University Press.

Novak, M. (1976, April). The family out of favor. *Harper's 252,* No. 1511, pp. 37–46.

Olshansky, S. (1962). Chronic sorrow: A response to having a mentally defective child. *Social Casework,* 13–15.

Piaget, J. (1970). Piaget's theory. In P. H. Mussen (Ed.), *Carmichael's manual of child psychology* (3rd ed.) (Vol. 1) (pp. 703–732). New York: Wiley.

Pless, I. B., Satterwhite, B., & Van Vechten, D. (1978). Division, duplication, and neglect patterns of care for children with chronic disorders. *Child: Care, Health, and Development, 4,* 9–19.

Pollner, M., & McDonald-Wikler, L. (1985). The social construction of unreality: A case study of a family's attribution of competence to a severely retarded child. *Family Process, 24,* 241–254.

Poznanski, E. (1973). Emotional issues in raising handicapped children. *Rehabilitation Literature, 34,* 322–326.

Richards, I., & McIntosh, H. T. (1973). Spina bifida survivors and their parents: A study of problems and services. *Developmental Medicine and Child Neurology, 15,* 292–304.

Rollins, N., Lord, J. P., Walsh, E., & Weil, G. (1973). Some roles children play in their families: Scapegoat, baby, pet, and peacemaker. *Journal of the American Academy of Child Psychiatry, 12,* 511–530.

Rossi, A. S. (1977). A biosocial perspective on parenting. *Daedalus, 106,* 1–31.

Sameroff, A. J. (1975, July). *The mother's construction of the child.* Paper presented at the meeting of the International Society for the Study of Behavioral Development, Guilford, England.

Sameroff, A. J., & Chandler, M. J. (1975). Reproductive risk and the continuum of caretaking casualty. In F.D. Horowitz (Ed.), *Review of child development research* (Vol. 4) (pp. 187–244). Chicago: University of Chicago Press.

Sameroff, A. J., & Fiese, B. H. (1990). Transactional regulation and early intervention. In S. J. Meiself & J. P. Shonkoff (Eds.), *Handbook of early childhood intervention* (pp. 428–444). Cambridge: Cambridge University Press.

Sandow, S., & Clarke, A. D. B. (1978). Home intervention with parents of severely subnormal preschool children: An interim report. *Child: Care, Health, and Development, 4,* 29–39.

Schulman, S. (1988). The family of the severely handicapped child: The sibling perspective. *Journal of Family Therapy, 10,* 125–134.

Schwab, L. O. (1989). Strengths of families having a member with a disability. *Journal of the Multihandicapped Person, 2*(2), 105–117.

Shelton, T. L., Jeppson, E. S., & Johnson, B. H. (1987). *Family-centered care for children with special health needs.* Washington, DC: Association for the Care of Children's Health.

Simeonsson, R. J., & Bailey, D. B. (1986). Siblings of handicapped children. In J. J. Gallagher & P. Vietze (Eds.), *Families of handicapped persons* (pp. 67–77). Baltimore: Brookes.

Simeonsson, R. J., Bailey, D. B., Huntington, G. S., & Comfort, M. (1986). Testing the concept of goodness of fit in early intervention. *Infant Mental Health Journal, 7*(1), 81–93.

Simeonsson, R. J., & Bailey, D. B. (1991). Family-focused intervention: Clinical, research and training implications. In K. Marfo (Ed.), *Early intervention in transition* (pp. 91–108).

Sluzki, C. E. (1983). Process, structure, and world views: Toward an integrated view of systemic models of family therapy. *Family Process, 22,* 469–476.

Solnit, A. J., & Stark, M. H. (1961). Mourning and the birth of a defective child. In K. J. Eissler et al. (Eds.), *Psychoanalytic study of the child* (pp. 523–537). New York: International University Press.

Solomon, M. A. (1973). A developmental conceptual premise for family therapy. *Family Process, 12,* 179–188.

Steinhauer, P. D. (1985). Beyond family therapy: Toward a systemic and integrated view. *Psychiatric Clinics of North America,* 8(4), 923–943.

Stratton, P. (1988). Spirals and circles: Potential contributions of developmental psychology to family therapy. *Journal of Family Therapy, 10,* 207–231.

Tew, B., & Laurence, K. M. (1973). Mothers, brothers, and sisters of patients with spina bifida. *Developmental Medicine and Child Neurology, 15,* 69–76.

Textor, M. R. (1989). The healthy family. *Journal of Family Therapy, 11,* 59–75.

Tisza, V. B., Irwin, E., & Scheide, E. (1973). Children with oral-facial clefts. *Journal of the American Academy of Child Psychiatry, 12,* 292–313.

Travis, G. (1976). *Chronic illness: Its impact on child and family.* Stanford, CA: Stanford University Press.

Tseng, W. S., & McDermott, J. F., Jr. (1979). Triaxial family classifications: A proposal. *Journal of the American Academy of Child Psychiatry, 18,* 22–43.

Wallander, J. L., Hubert, N. C., & Varni, J. W. (1988). Child and maternal temperament characteristics, goodness of fit, and adjustment in physically handicapped children. *Journal of Clinical Child Psychology, 17*(4), 336–344.

West, P. (1990). The status and validity of accounts obtained at interview: A contrast between two studies of families with disabled children. *Social Sciences Medicine, 30*(11), 1229–1239.

Wing, L. (1969). A handicapped child in the family. *Developmental Medicine and Child Neurology, 11,* 643–644.

Worthington, R. C. (1992). Family support networks: Help for families of children with special needs. *Family Medicine, 24,* 41–44.

Zolko, M. E. (1991). Counseling parents of children with disabilities: A review of the literature and implications for practice. *Journal of Rehabilitation,* April/May/June, 29–34.

# FAMILY CONTEXTS

The importance assigned to family involvement in special education in general, and early intervention in particular, has been a major priority in recent years. Part II examines the dynamics of family life reflected in first-person accounts as well as in the perspectives of others such as parents and siblings. Case studies and reviews of pertinent research and clinical literature document the typical as well as unique adaptation patterns of family life in which there is a member with a disability. In addition to the functional and psychological aspects of family adaptation, there are often personal and existential dimensions. These are examined with specific reference to the role of religion in family life, both in terms of the search for answers as well as a source of personal strength and support.

# 3

# GROWING UP WITH PARENTS OF A CHILD WITH A DISABILITY: AN INDIVIDUAL ACCOUNT

*Sondra Diamond\**

## INTRODUCTION

My Mother
In age, her face as polished oak—grained and shined,
The shell of a walnut, furrowed, browned, lined,
Leather, rich and scented, well-tanned;
But soft, expressive, Divinely planned.

A smile scarcely hidden when sternness is feigned,
But readily visible when body be pained.
A laugh, strong and lusty, for a joke or a quip;
Her own wit quick, fast as a whip.

Wheat, bent in the wind, steady, strong:
leaning toward a sunset I yearn to prolong.
Wind as life, blustery, constant, never a slack;
Trying, but never breaking a sturdy back.

My Father
Experimenter, adventurer, teacher, friend. Marshmallows, white bread, and
velvet. My mother was the law-maker and disciplinarian. My father was forever
whisking me off to a new adventure, helping me to see, hear, and taste life.
Always introspective; at the age of seventy, he spoke to me about the guilt
feelings that a parent has as a result of having a disabled child under his care. He
said that for the first time in his life he understood his own guilt. It is not guilt

*The late Ms. Diamond was a psychologist who was an articulate spokesperson for the needs of the handicapped. She was herself severely disabled from cerebral palsy. She prepared this chapter specifically with parents in mind, looking back on her experiences in a family with her own parents and two brothers. Her personal account has value to the teacher who would consider education through the eyes of a family with a disabled child. This chapter was retained in its original form from the first edition with minimal editing.

*over having done something wrong by bearing or siring a disabled child, but, rather, guilt in terms of not having done the best for the child. He used examples such as feeling that he could have gone to more doctors to get help for me, feeling he could have explored other possible therapy treatments, and feeling he could have smoothed more of the hurt that I was exposed to as a result of being disabled.*

## SHARING FEELINGS

That my father could speak so openly with me about his feelings is indicative of the open and honest way in which my parents dealt with their feelings. It further shows how they were able to share their feelings with their disabled child. The importance of parents sharing these feelings—both negative and positive—is necessary for the healthy development of the disabled child.

When the parent shares his or her feelings with the disabled child, there are three major results: (1) the child feels secure; (2) the child feels accepted; (3) the child has a clear perception of his or her effect on others. On many a hot summer evening (more summertimes than I care to admit) my father would say to me, "I'm sorry to have to tell you this, Sondra, but you need a shower." No pussy-footing around! Straight talk. How did it make me feel? This man loves me, he accepts me—a budding young woman, and his statement makes me aware of how my body odor affects others. So many times I have encountered disabled adults with body odor. Everyone, including parents, has been too "polite" to tell them about it. What are some of the ramifications of this closed, dishonest politeness? The disabled adult has fewer friends, poor chances of being hired for and maintaining a job, and has never experienced the emotional connection that comes from caring and being cared about.

"I love you," "I'm really proud of you," and "You look pretty today." Simple, obvious statements that most parents say to their children all the time. Parents have these feelings about their children—whether able-bodied or disabled—and express them freely to the able-bodied children. But when parents relate to a disabled child, there are invisible walls between them and the child. A parent thinks, "I don't like the disability, so how can I say I love you?" "How can I say you're pretty, if your contorted body turns me off?" A child's beauty goes beyond the disability. We love our able-bodied children even when they're covered with mud. We laugh at the foolish antics of able-bodied children all the time. A hug and an "I love you," breaks down the walls between parent and child. It says, "I know you're disabled, but I love you anyway." To say "You look pretty in that dress," says, "I know you wear braces, but you're my little girl, and to me you're as pretty as any other little girl." A kid doesn't feel disabled. Sure, it gets in the way of what she wants to do, but it doesn't constantly impact her the way it does the parent. A disabled kid feels pretty in a new outfit. When the parent doesn't let her know that she is perceived as pretty, the kid learns that all the parents can see is the disability.

Parents of disabled children tend only to compliment the child on something related to the disability, such as: "You're really sitting up nicely these days," or, "You're doing much better on the crutches." To mention only these things is the same as praising an able-bodied child just for his or her athletic achievements. The disabled child feels that "getting better"—a minimization of the disability— is all that is important to the parent.

Saying "I love you," or "You need a shower" is, in essence, saying the same thing. It's true, one sounds positive and one sounds negative, but they are neither. They actually are verbal expressions of a parent's feelings. They are not denials of the child's disability, rather, they are both expressions of love for the child, who has a disability in only one of his or her many parts.

It should be apparent to the reader thus far that our present chapter will not be an intellectual exercise. Rather, we will be running barefoot through the psyches of parents of a disabled child. Throughout our journey, we will take sidetrips through the psyche of the disabled child, itself, and the people who touch the lives of both parent and child.

As the author, I would like to acknowledge that, in revealing the experiences of my journey, there lies within me a feeling of emotional risk, but I assuage this feeling of vulnerability with the knowledge that this is the best way to teach, and I am ever-mindful of the beneficiaries of these teachings.

My greatest comfort lies in the knowledge that the disabled child will be the ultimate beneficiary, through the mentors and advocates of the child, reading and digesting this book. This is not to say that the mentors and advocates will not themselves be beneficiaries, but our primary goal is to provide them with the tools to be effective benefactors.

Who are these mentors and advocates? They are parents, teachers, and all other professionals who work with and for the child.

## IMPORTANCE OF TEACHERS

Next to the parent, you, the teacher, will be the most important person in a child's life. This intimate relationship, second only to that of the parent, will have a profound effect on the child through the "lessons" you teach, the role model you present, and your sensitivity and understanding of the disabled child's personhood.

As you read this chapter and discover the components of the parent/child relationship that I feel are important, keep in mind that these also apply to the teacher/child relationship. As the person whose intimate interaction with a disabled child will have such a profound effect on its life, you, the teacher, must also maintain openness and honesty, foster healthy peer relationships, and place expectations on the child. As you read about the feelings and perceptions of the parent concerning his or her disabled child, be aware of and examine your feelings and perceptions of disabled children. As you read about the skills that I feel are important for the parents of a disabled child to impart to the child, appreciate the important role you have in the development of these skills.

The child will look to you for information, guidance, and affirmation. The parent will turn to you for these same three things. Your impact will be great! Your responsibility is awesome! The parent will view you as an "expert" on their child! It is my opinion that both parent and teacher should be partners, rather than seeing each other as "experts," for each has much to learn from the other. In helping a child, the parent is the best natural resource a teacher has—and the least used.

Unfortunately, throughout my growing up years, my parents and teachers were adversaries. My parents encouraged my creative writing urges while my teachers pejoratively called me a "dreamer" and "poet." My parents constantly spoke of and encouraged me to strive toward a successful future amidst "cheerful" remarks from teachers, such as "Don't get your hopes up too high" or "Be realistic." When my parents attempted to speak to my teachers about my going to college, they were faced with "Well, if you want to throw away your money. . . ." No dialogue, just searching parents and "omnipotent" teachers making pronouncements from "on high."

I thank the *real* Omnipotence that my parents rarely, if ever, took their words as gospel. But I, the child, *heard* their words, and I was constantly in turmoil. Questions gnawed at me, "Why are my teachers always putting me down? Why, when I look up to my teachers so much, do they disappoint me time after time? I try so hard to please them!" I was always so happy at home and so miserable at school. Many mornings, while waiting for the school bus, I would "get sick" or "fall" out of my wheelchair and get a bloody nose, just to avoid another ego-deflating, anxiety-filled day in school.

So, teachers, as you can see, my school history is not a happy one. However, I would like to change that for other disabled children. Throughout this chapter, like Alice-In-Wonderland, you will get to see another world—the world of the parent. Further, you will be privileged to hear the parent/child dialogue. You will experience, firsthand, a living source of knowledge—the parent.

This new knowledge will be acquired through a feeling experience. Rather than a didactic, textbook style, my material is written in a way that will allow you to feel the anguish, tears, and laughter of the parents of a disabled child. As a result of the acquisition of this knowledge, you will have a deeper understanding of the parent and, therefore, added depth of your effectiveness as a teacher. Additionally, I feel I have made it easier for you to bridge the gap in your parent/ teacher relationships. Rather than walking in blindly, you will be able to enter into a parent/teacher partnership with some insight and sensitivity.

## PARENTING DISABLED CHILDREN

If you step back a few feet and look at the parents of a disabled child, what you will see will be two individuals who, by chance, have acquired a disabled child.

Two ordinary people with hopes and dreams and fears of their own. The institutional process of marriage asks them to submerge or set aside some of their individuality and become a couple. Parenting asks them to compromise more of their individual identities. And here we are, asking these two ordinary people to become extraordinary people and parent a disabled child. We are asking them to feel good about themselves, to be in touch with their feelings, to relate well to each other, and to sensitively and competently raise a disabled child, difficult task, but not the unpleasant burden that the world says it is. The stresses on marriage are numerous: sex, money, parental interference, personality differences. The introduction of a disabled child into a marriage has the potential of an additional stress, if, as with any stress, open communication and healthy struggle does not prevail.

As parents in the process of raising a disabled child, you will be confronted with many issues that will cause conflicts within you as individuals, and between you as a couple.

Should I/we:

- Send our child to a regular school or a special school for disabled kids?
- Consent to the surgery that one doctor recommends, or consult with others?
- Place our child in a residential facility or keep him or her at home with us?
- Have more children after having a disabled child or focus all of our attention on the one child?
- At what point, and to what extent, foster independence—both physical and emotional—or offer to help the child?

These are issues which people feel dare not be said aloud. And yet, these are the very issues that a parent struggles over within himself and about which couples fight. Space does not allow for elaboration on all of these conflict-producing questions, so I will focus in on the one that plagued my parents the most. Should I/we, and at what point and to what extent, foster independence—both physical and emotional—or offer help to the child? This triggered two conflicts, one of which was *between* my parents and the other was *within* each of them as individuals. These conflicts were born out of the fact that my father was very protective of me and my mother, on the other hand, wanted me to be as independent as possible. I recall the first time I used a Kotex. My mother handed me the sanitary belt and Kotex, and said, "It's time you learned to put this on yourself." I was on the toilet for three hours, struggling, sweating, and swearing. Every few minutes, I heard my father yelling at my mother, "Rose, go in there and give her a hand." Since it was the weekend, the usual flow of neighbors and friends were coming in and out of the house. Noticing my absence, they asked what I was doing in the bathroom so long. I remember hearing her explain, and hearing each of them say, in different ways, "Rose, how can you be so cruel?" My father was in a rage. The neighbors were outraged by my mother's treatment of me. My mother never wavered. Amid this commotion, I learned how to use a Kotex, secretly admiring my mother's fortitude, and getting a kick out of the fuss that was being made over me.

A delicate and fragile balance always prevailed. Here were two people wanting to achieve the same end—my happiness and well-being. Two people diverse in personality and technique, but unified in intent. Their personality differences and marital tensions were heightened and charged more often in dealing with their disabled child than when they dealt with their two able-bodied children. My parents as individual people were constantly asking themselves, "Am I doing the right thing?" Each of them questioned themselves, asking, "Am I doing the right thing for Sondra by taking this stand, and to what extent is the stand that I'm taking on Sondra's behalf causing conflict between my spouse and me?" This was further compounded by the question, "Which is more important at the moment, my disabled child's need, my need, or my spouse's need?" What are the effects of these conflicts on each parent, on the marriage, and on the disabled child? The potential effects are myriad. Confused adults, an alienated couple, and an egocentric child, to name just a few.

People have a limited amount of psychic energy (mental as opposed to physical energy that is expended while dealing with issues on the feeling level). If we are forced to juggle this psychic energy for a sustained length of time in such a way as to spread it around "equitably" (between self, spouse, and child), we feel frustrated, exhausted, and ultimately confused. In this fog-like state, disintegration takes place: disintegration of one's own personality and disintegration of interpersonal relationships. To avoid this bleak forecast, it is imperative that a parent of a disabled child finds a comfortable level at which to function. Anger is okay, conflict is okay, disappointment is okay, pride is okay. It's all okay as long as there is not the feeling of "constant compromise." I can hear my father saying to my mother and me, "I don't give a damn what you say, this is how it's gonna be!" I learned from him, in my adulthood, that even though in his heart he questioned whether or not he was right, this is the way he maintained his own sanity as well as preventing my mother and me from running amuck. No psychic suffering, just straight management.

## THE CHILD'S VIEW

As a child, I did not feel disabled. I was aware that I could not *do* the same things that other children did, but I did not feel inferior because of this and I did not feel that my parents treated me differently from the way they treated my two older brothers.

There is an important question here, probably an unanswerable one, but nevertheless one that should be explored. Was my perception of myself formed as a result of the way my parents treated me, or did my parents treat me as a normal child because of the way I perceived myself. I know that my parents did not see me as a normal child. It's true that they saw me as their "child" first, but they also saw me as their disabled child, with many of the negative connotations that the word disabled implies—imperfect and limited in many aspects. The paradox of their perception of me is twofold. One, they did not treat me as if I were imperfect or limited, and two, I never perceived myself as imperfect or limited. My athetosis (the involuntary movements of my body) never seemed gross or ugly to me—an inconvenience when I reached for a glass of milk and knocked it over instead of picking it up—but not repulsive. It was something I didn't like but not something that made me feel negative toward myself.

The nature of my disability makes it impossible for me to have the normal pincer grasp (picking up objects with thumb and forefinger) so, as a child, I developed my now comfortable and unique grasp with the pinky and ring finger. I was aware that it was different, but I was enormously pleased with its functionality. One day, while I was mindlessly eating potato chips, my father asked me why I didn't pick them up the "right" way. He had intruded on my kid-like, blissful state, and I was taken aback by his comment and bewildered by his question. He grabbed the potato chip out of my fingers and while demonstrating the "correct" grasp, angrily said, "This is how people are supposed to eat potato chips!" I tried his way and smashed several chips. He had me repeat this for quite a while. I finally said, "What's the difference? They're getting into my mouth, and I'm having a good time." His concern was not that of a parent worried that his child would eat too many potato chips and get sick. Rather his concern was that the way I ate the chips didn't look normal. Something happens in a parent when relating to his disabled child; he forgets that they're a kid first. I used to think about that a lot when I was a kid. I would be off in a euphoric state, drawing or coloring or cutting out paper dolls, and as often as not the activity would be turned into an occupational therapy session. "You're not holding the scissors right," "Sit up straight so your curvature doesn't get worse." That era ended when I finally let loose a long and exhaustive tirade. "I'm just a kid! You can't therapize me all the time! I get enough therapy in school every day! I don't think about my handicap all the time like you do!"

I'm not sure that my parent's deep-seated attitudes actually changed after this episode, but I think they got a clear view of how I saw myself. In later years, my father told me he was always bewildered by my perception of myself.

I first became aware that other people saw me differently from the way I saw myself at a very young age. One afternoon, while being carried off the school bus, a woman was standing on the sidewalk, staring, at what to me was an everyday occurrence. My mother turned to her and said, "You know, lady, we charge a quarter for this." I was puzzled by my mother's comment. When I came into the house, I asked my father what this was all about. My father helped me to recall the many times I had been to the circus. "You know how we stared at the freaks?" he asked. Apprehensively, I asked, "Am I a freak?" "No," he said. "Some kids walk, some kids wear braces, and others don't. There's nothing wrong with you. You just have special problems and special needs." There I was realizing, for the first time, that what I had accepted as a natural part of me was viewed as freakish. With the sensivity that children possess, I promised myself that I would never go to another freak show again. I realized that the fat lady, and Mr. Sealo (a man with flippers in place of hands and feet), were like me in that they were different—not to be stared at or put on display. This shows the fertile groundwork that was laid down by my parents in order for me to experience feelings that confront a disabled child, and convey those feelings to my parents. A parent needs the courage to "tell it like it is." Firstly, a child responds best to frankness, openness, and honesty. Secondly, the parents' honest approach lays the foundation for the child's ability to deal with reality, not just in childhood, but throughout his adult life.

## THE DEVELOPMENT OF SELF-PERCEPTION IN THE CHILD

How is a child's perception of himself formed? Partially by how society perceives it and reacts to it, and partially by independently formed and self-generated self-concepts. The interplay between the two is unmeasurable. It is important for a parent to remember that his disabled child's self-perception is not necessarily a reflection of anyone else's perception. Look back into your own childhood and recall having played in the mud. After playing for a while, you proudly present yourself to your mother to show her the evidence of what a good time you had. The layers of mud to you, the child, were evidence of pleasure, to your mother they were a bothersome mess. All she saw was a dirty child.

It is vital that you, the parent, do not assume that the child perceives himself/herself the way that you perceive him/her. If you make this assumption, you may contribute to the development of a distorted self-image in the child.

If your disabled child tells you that he spit a distance of 3 feet today, do not look at it as a useless waste of time in this "poor crippled kid's" life. The disabled child, like any other child, sees it as an accomplishment. If your disabled child tells you that she saw a dead bird today, don't look at it as an insignificant incident in a "suffering chid's" life. To the child it is a new experience, an awakening to compassionate feelings, and an eagerness to share this with you, the parent. Don't react as if dead birds and spitting are of no importance to "crippled kids," or as if "the only real important things are learning how to walk and feed themselves." If you react negatively each time the child relates something "important" to you, the child will inevitably close himself off from you. Interest, praise, excitement are the "do's" for strengthening the child's self-image and maintaining the trust between parent and child.

## HANDLING FEELINGS

A feeling is a fragile and delicate thing. You can experience it, examine it, and understand it. It is forever in danger of being hurt, stifled, and thwarted. The feelings of others as well as our own must always be carefully handled. My parents understood this, but they were very practical people. Once they understood the feelings, pragmatic solutions were immediately sought and implemented. Feelings were to be understood and resolved—not wallowed in. There were many times, in my younger days, when I would be wallowing in a pool of feelings. One of my parents would "grab me by the neck," figuratively speaking, and insist that I find some resolution for what I was dealing with. They would not invalidate the feelings for they encouraged me to feel freely. Rather, they felt that a feeling was only as good as what it accomplished. A means to an end, not the end in itself. Anger and frustration were catalysts for constructive change, rejection and defeat were motivating forces to try harder—feelings were viewed as building blocks for creativity.

An illustration of this, that, in retrospect, is humorous, glaringly points out the way my mother orchestrated a resolution. My mother had accompanied me to a convention in Washington, D.C. For the first two days of a four-day conference I was being unwillingly pursued by an eccentric young man (we'll call him Oswald) whom I had known prior to the conference. I was finding his constant attentions smothering and "cramping my style." Amidst this annoying, if flattering, attention, I was invited out to dinner by another gentleman (we'll call him Bill) whom I found to be charming. Returning to my hotel room, I was bathed in the flood of my own tears and a mixture of feelings: guilt over not wanting to insult Oswald, trapped, angry because I *felt* trapped, afraid of making the wrong decision, and attracted to a member of the opposite sex. In my mother's absence, an acquaintance tried to be helpful. When I described to her how I felt, she said, "You shouldn't feel that way." She advised that I go out with Oswald and not Bill. Her feeble advice succeeded only in increasing my guilt. My mother came back to the room and listened to my tale of woe. While drying my tears, she made me feel that she really understood my plight. In this very special "mother and daughter" moment, a solution was found for, what seemed to me, an insurmountable problem. My mother said, "I think you should go to dinner with Bill and I'll sneak you out the back door so that Oswald doesn't see you." A practical, romantic woman, my mother. She understood the feelings of a nubile, 21-year-old (remembering her own youth) and guided me to action.

The following illustration demonstrates that, even in my parents' absence, the "cope, don't panic" philosophy works.

It was 2 o'clock in the morning. Alone in a Chicago hotel room, feeling no pain as a result of too many drinks, Mother Nature was insistently making me aware that my bladder was full. Not a unique or unsolvable problem under ordinary circumstances, but I could not get my wheelchair into the bathroom; the door was too narrow.

I had been sent to this Chicago convention by the United Cerebral Palsy Association. As this was the first day, I had been busy with meetings and conferences, using the bathroom facilities everywhere except my hotel room. It hadn't occurred to me to see if I could manage the facilities in my room; not until 2 A.M., that is.

Of course, I had written to the hotel weeks in advance, explaining my disability and describing my needs in terms of the dimensions of the room and bathroom. I had received a letter of confirmation stating that I would have what I'd requested.

Tears of pain and frustration were streaming down my face. I was too embarrassed, both over my drunkenness and my inability to attend to my personal needs to call another conventioneer. It occurred to me that there must be a hotel service for such a problem. There's a bar, a hairdresser, a restaurant, somebody must be available in this hotel to help relieve my bodily need!

I wheeled myself to the phone and looked at the outer dial around the numbers. Corresponding with each number on the dial there was a hotel service. As I frantically glanced around the dial, "Housekeeper," "Laundry," "Doctor," flashed before my eyes, but none of these was what I was looking for. I looked again and "Carpenter" stood out in vibrating three dimension.

I dialed the number and this is what transpired: "This is Miss Diamond in room 809, and I am in a wheelchair and would like to go to the bathroom; however, I cannot fit through the door." The deep male voice at the other end said, "Are you drunk, lady?"

"Yes, I am, but that's not relevant at the moment. The point is, I want you to come up to my room and remove the bathroom door." The faceless carpenter said, "You mean remove the door from its hinges?" "Exactly," said I, "Now we're understanding each other!"

I had come a long way in my struggle for independence. The man at the other end of the phone was to decide whether or not I would overcome this obstacle and be independent this night. "It's 2 A.M. lady! You want me to come up now?" "Either you come or I'll have to call the housekeeping department to repair the consequences of your absence!" I was beginning to picture a maid with a mop and bucket coming up to my room in 15 minutes. That was my only alternative, if this carpenter wouldn't cooperate.

The carpenter said, "Okay, lady," and abruptly hung up. I didn't know whether he was coming or not, but I decided to give him a few minutes to digest our conversation. My pride and fate were in his hands.

Fifteen minutes later, there was a heavy knock at the door. As I opened it, a man, dressed in overalls and carrying a toolbox asked, "You wanted your toilet door removed, lady?" "Yes, please come in!"

Within five minutes the door was off its hinges and the carpenter stood before me asking, "Where shall I put it, lady?" He had called me a lady, so I choked down my impulse to tell him "where to put it" and suggested that he stand it in the corner.

Before I could hand the carpenter a tip for his services, he packed up his tools and was halfway out the door. I tried to give him something, but he waved my hand way and quickly retreated, slamming the door behind him.

My parents always confirmed (never negated) their children's feelings. At the same time, they expected us to utilize our feelings to develop a plan of action and to implement that plan. This expectation, as well as all their expectations, was the same for their two able-bodied children as it was for their disabled child.

# OTHER CHILDREN IN THE FAMILY ▐█████████████████▌ ▐████████▌

In all phases of their relationships with their children, there was no distinction made among "disabled and able-bodied." They were open and honest with all their children. They shared their feelings *with* and accepted the feelings *of* all of their children. It was in this atmosphere that three children—my brothers and I—learned to interact.

When there are other children in the family, the parents of a disabled child experience a particular dilemma: "Should I foster sibling interaction among my disabled child and able-bodied children? And, if so, to what extent?" An absurd question! One that is never raised when dealing with able-bodied children. We expect siblings to interact and we expect them to be supportive—both physically and emotionally—of each other. As a professional, I am frequently asked by parents of disabled children how to handle sibling interaction among disabled and able-bodied children. Perhaps the issue arises because disabled children are less mobile and a natural physical interaction is less likely to take place. Perhaps the question of "Who's to be responsible for the future of the disabled child?" is another part of the puzzle. I have found that parents utilize either of the following extreme techniques. Some parents place a great deal of responsibility for the physical care and socialization of the disabled child on the able-bodied siblings. Their primary concern seems to be "Who will take care of my child when I die?" They feel that putting the responsibility, at an early stage, on the other children will ensure built-in guardians. In many instances, this embitters the able-bodied children—robbing them of their childhood and burdening them with responsibilities that are inappropriate before adulthood. At the other end of the spectrum, parents discourage *all* interaction among disabled and able-bodied children, justifying this by the guilt-ridden thought "I don't want to put *my* responsibility onto innocent children." As a result of this method, the disabled child is seen as an alienated member of the family and the able-bodied children see the disabled child (and all disabled people) as separate and disparate from themselves.

Neither of these extremes lead to healthy sibling interaction. Why is it acceptable to expect an 8-year-old able-bodied child to dress his or her 2-year-old sibling and not acceptable to expect him or her to dress a 2-year-old disabled child? Obviously, there are more difficulties to be overcome but these can be surmounted if the 8-year-old has been involved (even as an observer) in the dressing process. We expect siblings to "play nicely together." Why don't we expect disabled and able-bodied siblings to play together? It is true that adaptations to the game may have to be made to accommodate the disabled child's limitations, but a child who has not been kept separate from his or her disabled sibling will understand the limitations and, not only be willing to accommodate for them, but will initiate unique accommodating techniques.

If a parent does not impose his or her anxieties on the able-bodied children, there will be a natural interaction process. Children fight. It is part of the honing of socialization skills. Parents know this. Why then are they so quick to intervene when a disabled and able-bodied child are fighting? By this premature intervention, they are depriving both of the children of learning about each other in a healthy way. An able-bodied child will perceive his or her disabled sibling as an equal if they fight together. Further, the parent is depriving the disabled child of skills that he or she will need in handling the challenges that lie ahead.

The parent who is relaxed and has a laissez-faire attitude will find that his or her children—able-bodied and disabled—will interact in a relaxed natural fashion. When you are dressing or feeding your disabled child, let your able-bodied children observe or help. When you are helping your able-bodied child with homework, encourage your disabled child to sit nearby and become part of the process. This mutual inclusion nurtures a healthy atmosphere.

Looking back, I recall when my older brother (by 11 years) used to tease me. My first reaction was always to yell for my mother, "Ma, he's bothering me!" and my mother would always shout back at me, "Fight your own battles."

When an able-bodied and disabled child are fighting, rather than come to the defense of the disabled child, which would put him or her in an unfavorable light, a neutral and equalizing statement such as: "The *two* of you are driving me crazy," would help to foster the sibling relationship.

## RELATING TO PROFESSIONALS

The development of the disabled child depends on the quality of many different relationships: siblings, parents, peers, and adults other than parents. In a disabled child's world, there are many such adults: doctors, teachers, and therapists who, as professionals, assume authoritative roles in the child's life. There are times when the decisions or actions of these adults are physically or emotionally hurtful to the child. It is natural that the parent of a disabled child feels that these people are "experts," and know what is best for the child. In view of their professional status, the parents perceive these "experts" as having more knowledge of the rehabilitation program that is appropriate for their child. The parent feels helpless and in awe of these people. Throughout the development of the child from diagnosis to program implementation, the parent is fearful that, if he or she disagrees with the actions or decisions of the professional, the services to the child will be curtailed or denied. By my parents' admission, their feelings of helplessness, awe, and fear of the professional stood in the way of their clear judgment. They view this as their major mistake in raising their disabled child. There were many instances when their gut feelings and good sense totally contradicted what they heard or were advised to do by the professionals, but they opted to heed the professionals. My father often berated himself for not saying, "I know what's best for my kid, I live with her, I understand her, I know her abilities as well as her limitations." It is important to note here that nowhere, in any of the professionals' agendas, was there a place for my parents' input. They were never asked, "What do you think?" Rather, they were told, "This is what's best for your child."

From my perspective, my parents were not as weak in this area as they thought they were. I will discuss their "failures" in questioning professional decisions, but first I must tell of an incident where they trusted their own judgment. (In my opinion, there were many instances like this one, but my parents feel it more important that you know of the times that they kept their mouths shut.)

At the age of 12, I developed a lump on my eyelid. My parents took me to a specialist who diagnosed it as a "harmless cyst that would probably go away by itself in time." After making this benign diagnosis, the doctor turned to the subject of my disability. He told my parents that if he surgically severed the tendons in my hips, knees, and heels, he could have me up and walking in no time. Excitedly, and in great detail, the doctor told my parents of the miraculous outcome that this procedure would have. My mother turned to me and asked, "Well, Sondra, what do you think?" Before I could answer, with a shocked expression, and a shrill voice that was slightly out of control, the doctor exclaimed, "What do you mean, what does she think? What does she have to do with it?" My mother turned to the doctor and in a very calm voice said, "It's her body!" I said, "I think we ought to go home and talk about this." The doctor, red with anger, shook his fist at my parents and said, "Don't you want her to walk? She's only a child, what does she know?" My parents had heard this "miracle cure" talk many times. As parents of a disabled child, their hearts told them to grab every miracle cure there was; this is real and natural. Firstly, turning to me in the doctor's office to ask what I thought somehow lifted the burden of my parents having to given an immediate answer. As I said earlier in this chapter, my parents saw my disability in a much worse light than I did, and they realized this. Secondly, asking me what I want done with my body says, "We agonize for you because you're disabled, but you're the one that really has to live with it." My parents consulted with my orthopedist about the proposed surgery a few days later. He said the same thing he always said when my parents consulted him about another "cure." "As long as Sondra functions at a level comfortable to herself, don't experiment with her."

# SCHOOL

The instances when my parents were silent or passive, are what, in later years, plagued them. The most numerous examples concern my school days. I attended a "special" public school for disabled children. These were difficult years. Scholastically I did not belong in this school, but the school also provided physical, occupational, and speech therapy during the school day. I was not scholastically challenged, and I wanted to go to a "regular" school. When my parents suggested to the administration of the "special" school, that I would be better off in a "regular" school, they were threatened by the fact that they would have to take me to a clinic after school for the necessary therapies. My parents had the energy and the willingness to do this, but were further frightened by statements such as, "Your child is really secure in this environment. You know how cruel normal children can be." I knew that I would have to face the "normal" world eventually. I felt that I should begin in grade school. I also knew that I wanted to go to college and I was not being scholastically prepared for this. My parents acceded to the school's opinion. This issue came up again when I began high school at the same "special" school. I was no longer getting therapy; thus, I felt that I could now go to "regular" school. My parents, once again, consulted the administration, and the same rhetoric was repeated. I completed high school in the same place in which I had been entombed for a total of 13 years—kindergarten through high school.

I was bused to and from school each day. By bus, the trip took an hour-and-a-half each way; by car, 15 minutes. In addition to the time consumed in travel, there were other factors that contributed to the trip's unpleasantness: I was very fatigued after each hour-and-a-half trip; I frequently got sick and vomited on the bus, and, as a Jewish kid, I was constantly emotionally tortured by an anti-Semitic bus matron. My father was self-employed and had the time to drive me back and forth to school. Periodically, I would ask him to do this. He was willing, but felt that he had to consult with the school. The answer was always the same: "It's against school policy." My father didn't want his daughter to suffer 3 hours a day, but because this "highly acclaimed institution" that supposedly "knew" how to care for disabled children was unwaveringly rigid, my father felt impotent. It troubles me to relate this bus incident, for it makes my father sound stupid, and he was not a stupid man. He wanted the best for his daughter, and was told by many "experts" that this school was the "best." He felt that any independent action on his part would jeopardize his daughter's future. "If I take my daughter out of this school, I am depriving her of the education and therapy that the school says she needs. If I try to bend the rules, and insist that I be permitted to drive my daughter to and from school, she may be ejected from the school." What a contradiction! And what a bind for my father to be in! The school says it's the best place for me, but if you don't conform, we're going to throw you out.

When my father and I looked back and reminisced about my childhood school days, it was interesting to him that I described the horrifying experiences the same way I had described them as a child; for, he confessed to me that he was never quite sure whether or not my tales were childish exaggerations. It had been hard for him to believe that all of what I said was true. Painfully, he admitted that perhaps he didn't want to believe that what I was saying was true. It wasn't that my father thought me dishonest; rather it was that he found it hard to believe that such a prestigious institution would hurt me in so many ways. My father said that had he allowed himself to believe fully what I was relating to him, he would have put more energy into changing things and making my school life more pleasant for me.

There came a time, probably in the beginning of my adolescence, when I began to realize my parents' frustrations and feelings of helplessness on matters concerning my school. I began to see that if things were to get better at school, *I* would have to find my own ways of coping. (Considering my parents' pattern of "nonintervention," I had probably been doing this for a long time without realizing it.) The first time I consciously tried to solve a major school problem for myself was when I was about 13 years old.

It was September, the beginning of a new term. In my "special" school, we had therapy intermittently throughout the day. I went to my first session of physical therapy and I was assigned to a new therapist, a male. I found this to be a highly sexually stimulating experience—not particularly enjoyable, for it was hard for me to keep my mind on the physical therapy. I asked the chief physical therapist, who was female, if I could have a female physical therapist. She asked me why, and I, feeling very embarrassed, tried to explain. I barely understood these new sexual stirrings that were growing in me *myself*. How was I going to put them into words, let alone tell an adult, an adult who obviously was not sensitive to a 13-year-old girl's needs, about them. I was not given permission to change therapists. Between my own frustration and my frustration over my parents' impotence, I realized that, no matter what they did or didn't do or what I tried to do, the school would not change, and for me, this was a lesson in itself.

How does a parent know when a child is perceiving what he says he is perceiving, especially when the child is saying something negative about the education or therapeutic system that is supposed to be helping him? I know that a parent *feels* powerless but, in my professional experience, the parent is perceived by the institution to have power. There are options through which a parent can exercise this power, options which will lead to implementing change.

1.    Talk to other parents. Are their children having the same difficulty that your child is having? How have they solved the problem? Would the other parents be willing to align with you in forming a "Parents' Pressure Group" to implement change?

2.    Talk to other children in your child's peer group. Talk to older children who were formerly in your child's present situation (school, bus, class, teacher, etc.). Are the other children in your child's peer group having the same problems? When the older children were in your child's peer group, did they encounter similar difficulties? Children are candid, and basically very honest.

3.    Observe. Spend a day at school, as inconspicuously as possible (perhaps as a volunteer), and look for the problems your child has described. Ride the school bus a couple of days. Be present wherever the problem area lies. You will accomplish two things: (a) seeing the problems as they occur; and (b) being present, which will demonstrate to the "problem initiator" that you are interested in your child and that you will not tolerate the continuation of the problem.

4.    Talk to someone in the situation (school, clinic, hospital, day-care center). Speaking to the head of an institution can often be your best bet. However, keep in mind that they frequently feel defensive about their institution and loathe to see their institution in a negative light.

Further, they will be uncomfortable speaking about an employee (teacher, etc.) in a critical way. Often it is best, initially, to begin a dialogue with someone with whom you have already established a comfortable relationship. This might be a therapist, a teacher, or a child-care worker.

As a parent, you are the child's primary advocate and a powerful one at that!

## ADOLESCENCE

My maternal grandmother had a saying: "Little children, little problems; big children, big problems."

In the life of a child, the most difficult years are the adolescent years. In the life of a parent, the most difficult years are his or her child's adolescent years. This is true for all children but, because of limited mobility for the disabled child, the problems are magnified 10 times over!

When a disabled child is small, the concentration of energy goes into the child's education and therapy. As the child grows and enters adolescence, there are more numerous areas that require attention: socialization, sexuality, and plans for the child's adult life. For the disabled child, the adolescent period requires a great deal more energy on the part of the parent than for the able-bodied child. Because of the disabled child's lack of mobility, he or she does not experience the normal socialization process. The kid can't hang out on the corner with friends, or jump in the car and go to a rock concert, or sneak down to the woods and neck.

The disabled adolescent child, despite his or her physical limitations, begins to feel the same need for independence as does the able-bodied child. Conflict begins because the parent of the disabled child is frightened. "How can I let my child be more independent, if she is so physically dependent?" "I feel as if I can't even let my child venture outside alone. He won't know how to handle himself, if a problem arises." At some point the parent realizes that the child has led a sheltered life and has not been able to acquire the "street shells" that other children began acquiring at the age of 5. Parents also equate physical dependence with emotional dependence. Parents of a disabled child also get caught up in paradoxical thinking; "If my child can't dress herself, or toilet herself, she is also incapable of making decisions for herself or protecting herself."

It's difficult to make the transition in thought and deed from "this is my little child who needs schooling and therapy and so much of my time and energy," to, "my child who wants to assert herself and become emotionally independent from me." It's especially hard, because the child in one moment makes an attempt at being independent, comes up against a problem, and runs back to the parent for safety and guidance in the next moment. The parent then thinks, "He's still a child after all, not yet ready to venture out." It's important to keep in mind that this is a fluctuating process. This child/adult is flexing and developing "independence" muscles. It's a difficult period; the parent feels schizophrenic—"One minute he wants me to let him go, the next minute he needs Mommy." A parent has to learn to step back and let the process happen.

I remember the first time I wanted to travel alone, I had just turned 16. Some friends had invited me to stay with them in Baltimore. I sat down and discussed this with my parents. I said that I wanted to go by train, and that my friends would meet me in Baltimore at the train station. My parents were frightened and said so openly. They expressed their fears of my physical safety, of the fact that I couldn't help myself in case of an emergency, of possible physical attack by a strange man. We talked and argued and cried for hours. The decision was that I was to go. It was difficult for my parents. I understood that. But I had a need to try my wings and they understood that. I'll never forget that day. My mother did not go the train station with my father and me. She said she could give her permission for this to happen, but she couldn't watch it. My father settled me in a train seat and stood on the platform waving goodbye. I was trying not to cry and so was he. Blinking back tears, I waved goodbye to my father from the train window. He was also vigorously waving goodbye with one hand—for his other was resting on the arm of my wheelchair. The train began pulling out of the station and a panic gripped me. "My God! He still has my wheelchair." I had to forget how bad I was feeling about my first unescorted trip away from home. I yelled to a conductor who was passing my seat, "Stop this train!" By this time we were a few blocks out of the station. What a ridiculous scene this must have appeared, this wriggly little kid (I always looked young for my age) screaming at the top of her lungs to stop the train. Thank goodness the conductor had seen my father carry me onto the train, making him realize the seriousness of my plea. He pulled the emergency cord and stopped the train. The words stuck in my throat as I looked up at this towering man. What a big question this little kid was about to ask, "Would you please back up the train so that I can get my wheelchair?" As the train backed up to the platform, there was my poor father still standing there waving goodbye with one hand and holding my wheelchair with the other, unaware of anything but his departing daughter. He was shocked out of his numb pose only when the conductor jumped off the train and wrenched the chair from his hand.

Look back on your own youth and remember your struggle for independence, and how you had to fight your parents every inch of the way to gain more and more freedom. You weren't disabled, and your parents feared for you. But you got through it and became an adult.

In order for a child, disabled or able-bodied, to develop and grow, he or she must take risks. Trial-and-error learning, with the right to fail as well as the right to succeed, is important. Adolescence is the time in a child's life when the trial-and-error process is most vigorously practiced: a tug of war within the child, within the parent, and between parent and child.

# EXPECTING ENOUGH

We place few expectations on the disabled child but life places many on the disabled adult. Rather than thrust a disabled adult into the world unarmed and unaware of life's expectations, we must begin in early childhood to place expectations on him or her. The parent of a disabled child does not want to think about his or her child's adulthood. They fear for his or her future; therefore, they prefer not to think of the future. The result is a disabled adult who is unprepared for adulthood—socially unsophisticated and self-centered.

As a consultant at a residential school for disabled children, a parent jubilantly told me that her 13-year-old daughter had sent her a birthday card. "Wasn't that wonderful? Here she is, living at this school, and she was able to get someone to go out and buy a card to send to me! How thoughtful of her to remember my birthday! And she's so severely disabled!"

I was shocked to hear this verbalized so clearly. I had been aware that parents don't expect thoughtful, "non-self-centered" behavior from their disabled children as they do from their able-bodied children. But my awareness came primarily from working with disabled adults who lacked this quality. To hear it articulated by a parent made it vividly clear to me the origin of the process that results in a self-centered adult. My mind went back to my own childhood, a time when there were numerous expectations placed on me.

My parents expected all three of their children to formally remember the birthdays and anniversaries of family members and friends. It was expected that at least a card would be sent. If you couldn't get out to buy one, materials were always readily available for making one. It was the same when an occasion called for a gift—if you didn't have the money or opportunity to buy one, you made one. Holidays were likewise to be remembered with cards and gifts. A calendar, with all dates of special occasions circled, and the name of the celebrant written in, was kept hanging in the kitchen. As each special day approached, a gentle reminder was forthcoming from either my mother or father. About two weeks before my father's birthday, my mother would say, "Your father's birthday is coming up." I always felt annoyed being reminded of an occasion for someone to whom I was close. Who could forget such a thing? I had already begun making something "very special" weeks in advance. It was a different story for a more distant relative or for a family acquaintance. A little nudge ended my procrastination. In addition, if someone remembered us with a gift, our parents expected us to promptly write a thank-you note. Kids will be kids, so, frequently, we had to be reminded a few times.

There were many other expectations placed on us, too numerous to include a complete list, but to name just a few: We were expected to telephone and/or visit someone who was sick; keep in frequent contact with our grandparents; be punctual if we were invited somewhere. All of these expectations made us aware that there were people in the world other than ourselves—people with feelings and needs just like our own.

A parent of a disabled child is fearful of placing too many expectations on the child. "After all, doesn't my child have enough of a burden just handling the disability?" To the contrary. The more expectations that are placed on the child, the more he will expect from himself and the more the child will expect to gain from the world. As expectations are placed on a child by the parent, a process evolves whereby the child begins to place his *own* expectations on himself. Not for reward or approval by the parent, as was the fulfillment of the parent's expectations, but rather for internal intrinsic rewards.

The pleasure, esteem, and self-respect that a child derives from helping his or her parent is important to the growth and development of any child. It is more important for the disabled child. We expect our children to help with household chores—taking out the trash, drying the dishes, and so on. We don't expect this from our disabled children. This is unfortunate because for the disabled child the benefits of family participation and helping multiply in their effect. Because of physical and/or mental limitations, the setting in which a disabled child will be able to help a parent may have to be highly structured. For example, in order for a disabled child to help dry the dishes, Mother may have to complicate an otherwise simple task. The parent feels two things: (1) it's easier to do it myself; and (2) the child has enough problems coping with his or her disability. Psychologically speaking, this is contradictory. We have a disabled child whose self-image is distorted, damaged, and fragile, and a perfect opportunity to change this in a natural, nonclinical setting. In my family, we were all expected to pitch in. After dinner my mother would nonchalantly say, "It's time to do the dishes." She would spread a towel on the kitchen table, enabling me to reach the dishes while sitting in my wheelchair and hand me another towel for drying. As she washed each dish, she would place it on the towel in front of me. I recall many wonderful feelings: She didn't worry abut my breaking a dish (despite my involuntary motions); she had the confidence that I would get the job done and do it well (she never dried one after I had done it); she made me feel needed and a worthwhile part of the family. It's true that doing the dishes took three times longer than it would have without my participation. It's also true that my mother had to make repeated trips across the kitchen, to and from the sink and table. But look at the results: a kid who felt good about herself and the adult who is writing this chapter and who chose a career in a helping profession—I'm sure the direct result of being afforded the privilege (and the right) of being a full participant.

Obviously, the greater the severity of the disability, the more creativity will be needed to involve the child as a helper. Just as, without effort or ceremony, we move things out of the reach of infants and toddlers, we must put things *within* the reach of disabled children. Further, to involve the disabled child may require adaptations such as: taping a dish towel or dust cloth to the child's hand in order to prevent the towel or cloth from dropping; devising a board with nails in it to hold potatoes or other objects to be peeled (the potato is impaled on the nail); protecting the child's clothing with a smock or Daddy's old shirt so that a mess is of no consequence; or securing to the child's head (with tape or a strap) a spoon for stirring fudge, cookie dough, etc. A severely disabled child can be very helpful when you need to have the contents of a pot watched so that it doesn't boil over. The child can let you know when it's at the boiling point by a vocal signal (a grunt or a squeal will do), or by knocking over a dinner bell with a handle that is standing on the child's wheelchair tray table. For sure, a parent needs to exercise patience, understanding, and perseverance. In involving the disabled child in the helping process, one's frame of reference concerning time limits must be altered. Expect the job to take longer, expect to expend more energy. In order for the experience to be more pleasurable for both you and the child, as well as relieving the feeling of being pressured, *start earlier*. A disabled child is aware that he or she is slower than other children. He or she is also aware of how this inconveniences people—two painful awarenesses that a child lives with (and shouldn't have to). When eliciting a child's help, don't add to this painful awareness by watching the clock.

Space doesn't allow me to describe the joy I felt while helping my mother in the kitchen and helping my father in his sign shop. A covering of fudge or a covering of paint was a sign that I was being loved and that I was being allowed to love back. Soap and water would never wash away my feelings of accomplishment, productivity, and usefulness.

## FEELINGS OF PARENTS

We have discussed the fact that society, as well as many parents, perceive raising a disabled child as a burden. We have alluded to the many parental strengths that are needed in rearing the child: patience, understanding, creativity, and so on. Although implied, we have not specifically enumerated the pleasures that can be derived. There are many, some of which I'm sure you have experienced. Being a parent of a disabled child is not a one-way street—giving all and receiving nothing. There is one pleasure of which my father often spoke.

My father was plagued by the feeling that he was an inadequate parent. He was far from that, but that is how he saw himself, and he often told me so. He hoped that his children did not view him as harshly as he viewed himself, but he was never sure. It is important to note here that his children never saw him as an inadequate parent—quite the contrary. It always amazed me that we couldn't reassure him of his adequacy, for each time I asked him for help, he said it gave him a great deal of pleasure and made him feel worthwhile and less inadequate. Even after I reached the age of 40 (he died during the writing of this chapter, shortly before my 41st birthday; his death lent a keen edge to the task and brought into focus memories that might otherwise have been left dormant) and would ask my father for advice, an opinion, or help to do something, his face would light up and he would immediately become involved. As he grew older, I hesitated to tax his energy, but I never got away with it. For as soon as he perceived that I needed something, my father would willingly volunteer his time and energy. Helping me, as he said, "is what keeps me alive." I would be hunched over the kitchen table, clumsily working on some project or another, and he would casually saunter into the kitchen (not wanting to appear as if he were imposing) and subtly offer his help. He was always sensitive to my stubborn streak of independence, but knew when I had reached my frustration threshold. How ironic, that he would hold back his impulse to help me (the thing that gave him so much pleasure) in deference to my need to be self-sufficient. I never wanted to thwart his attempts to help but I always felt an obligation to struggle it out alone, first. He knew this and didn't offer help until I had struggled to my limit. I smile as I think about how I *knew* what he was doing. He needed to help, I knew he needed to help. I needed his help, and he knew that too! What a complex, respectful, and wonderful relationship.

Many parents tend to see all of the help their disabled children need as nothing but drudgery. To be sure much of the everyday ritual, such as the dressing, feeding, toileting, feels like drudgery. Let us visualize a straight line with drudgery at one end or extreme, and pleasure at the other

"HOW I FEEL ABOUT HELPING MY CHILD"

DRUDGERY ------------------------------------------------------------ PLEASURE

At different times, depending on differing conditions, we will be at different points on the line. If we are tired or in a hurry, helping the child will feel more like drudgery. If we've had a good day at work, or hit the lottery, helping the child will be a much more pleasurable experience. It is the rare person who will see assisting one's disabled child as drudgery all of the time or pleasure all of the time. In my professional experience, I have found that parents "set themselves up" in such a way that the feeling of drudgery can be the only consequence. They "booby-trap" themselves by helping the child at times that, for the parent, are unfavorable or inconvenient, thus ensuring, in a predetermined way, the tasks will be burdensome. My father, knowing that I was going to need his help (usually for one of my many "peabrained" projects) would say, "I'm going to take a nap for an hour, so I'll be in better shape to help you." As humorous as this sounds (and it usually was), a nap, and sometimes maybe even a tranquilizer, is a damn good idea. I was never insulted by my father's need to "gird his loins" (as he put it) before helping me. For there was little pleasure in it for either of us if he helped me when he was overly tired. The pleasure that a parent will derive from helping his or her disabled child is measured by the eagerness and enthusiasm that the parent brings to the experience.

## SKILLS PARENTS TEACH

The disabled child's world is limited. The disabled child's educational experiences are limited. In my opinion the skills that the disabled child will need, in order to survive in the world, can only be taught by his or her parents. The following is a partial list, and explanation, of skills that a parent must help the disabled child to develop:

1.  *An Awareness and Use of Psychological (Private) Space.* Private space is the unseen boundary around our body which we do not want invaded by touch or look, unless we give our tacit approval. It is vital to an individual's mental health to prevent one's private space from being

violated. The disabled child's private space is constantly violated. People stare at him or her in the street, and people feel free to touch or move the child without gaining his or her approval. Further, privacy, an extension of private space, is denied the disabled child—for fear that the child's safety will be in jeopardy. The deprivation of private space as well as privacy leads to a distorted self-image. The disabled child must be made aware that he or she is entitled to this private space, for, unlike his or her able-bodied peer, he or she does not learn of this concept and entitlement through a natural socialization process.

2. *Acceptance and Ability to Deal With One's Disability.* It is incumbent upon the parent to help the child accept his or her disability. In other spheres of the child's life, this will not occur. The physical, occupational, and speech therapists, by the very nature of their habilitative roles, will work at minimizing the disability. The child will interpret this to mean that the disability is something to be "cured" (gotten rid of). Teachers in the child's life will concentrate on academic ability; unfortunately, with little integration of the disability in the process. Well-meaning relatives and friends will "ignore" the disability or cater to it in a pitying way. The child needs a solid base or frame of reference from which to view the disability. The disability is a fact, not good, not bad, just a fact. It imposes limitations. Society imposes limitations that make the disability more burdensome than it need be. The child must know this about himself and his disability, and the parent must teach this.

3. *Decision Making.* Decision making is acquired as a result of having varied social experiences. By the time one gets to be an adult, needing to choose a career or a mate, hopefully, the decision-making skill has been finely honed to the degree that appropriate decisions can be made. The able-bodied child, on a sunny Saturday morning, is faced with the decision of what to do: "Shall I go to the park, visit a friend, or play with my new erector set?" He weighs, in his mind, the advantages and disadvantages of each activity, chooses the one which seems most appealing, and gets up and does it. Lack of mobility, and limited understanding or freedom of choice (which will be discussed further on) hampers the disabled child from initiating and/or following through in this decision-making process. Imparting this skill to the child can be done in many ways: At breakfast, offer the child his choice of three cold cereals; before repainting the child's room, show her three appropriate colors and have the child choose the one she wants. Decision making is learning to make a choice from a given set within a given universe. As adults, the universe from which we can choose is wider than that for a child. A child must learn that there is a finite universe from which he or she must choose. The parents' role is to define this universe (giving three choices), and allowing the child to choose within the given universe.

4. *Risk Taking.* Learning, growing, and developing requires taking many risks. Falling, while learning to walk, is an important part of the learning process for it teaches the child what mistakes not to make again.

Wrongly, we view the falling as something negative, but this component of walking is just as positive as is the importance of head position in learning to walk. Risk taking holds within it the possibility of making mistakes, failure, and disappointment. How many times have we heard the old adage, "We learn by our mistakes?" The parent always wants to protect the disabled child from failure. In doing so, the parent stunts the child's growth and fails to teach the value of risk taking. For, after all, the true value of risk taking is learning how to succeed. We learn how to avoid the pitfalls, for we have experienced them and know how they feel both physically and emotionally. We know that an able-bodied child while learning to ride a bicycle will probably fall off and get a bloody nose or a cut arm. We learn to accept this as inevitable. We may not like it, but we close an eye to it and grit our teeth for we know that after a few falls, he will be proficient at bike riding. It is just as important to the development of the disabled child to allow this to occur, but we don't do it. We are reluctant to let our disabled children socialize with able-bodied children in the neighborhood for fear that the other children will make fun of him, or in some way physically harm him. We are denying the disabled child the opportunity to learn vital social skills: self-defense, maintaining one's ego strength, selling one's personality to others, being a survivor.

5. *Freedom of Choice.* Closely allied with risk-taking and decision making is freedom of choice. A disabled child learns, quite early in life, that in many areas their choices are limited. A child in a wheelchair will not grow up to be a professional boxer, a child with intellectual limitations will not grow up to be a biophysicist. A result of knowing that his choices are limited, in some areas, generalizes to a feeling that he lacks the freedom of choice in *all* areas of life. The child in a wheelchair can aspire to be a scientist or a translator. But if he has not learned that he has this freedom of choice, he will be emotionally handicapped when it comes time to choose a career. Either he will make no choice or, at best, he will make an inappropriate one. Equally as important as knowing how to choose, is knowing that one has the right to choose. A child has the right to say, "I don't want to go to physical therapy today." We can gently attempt to persuade him of the benefits of going, but we must respect his right not to go. He may be tired, or emotionally down, or just feel unmotivated. If he knows that he is not trapped—having the freedom of choice—he will be more willing to participate in subsequent therapy sessions. He is part of the action, not just being acted upon.

In teaching these skills, the parent can use any or a combination of these techniques: example, practical application, experimentation, and direct verbal instruction.

The important thing to remember is that, as a parent, you must be comfortable with the skill you are teaching and the technique that you are using to teach it. Further, you must be comfortable with the child and with yourself.

Growing up with parents of a disabled child has been a joy, and a struggle; complex, but always alive, always enriching. I know this has been true for the disabled child. It is my greatest hope that it has also been true for the parents.

## SUMMARY

In this chapter I have described my experiences growing up in a family and the issues my family and I faced related to the fact that I have a disability. I have extracted from these personal experiences some principles that I believe can be generalized and will, hopefully, be useful to parents of disabled children and to teachers who work with disabled children and their parents.

# 4

## PARENT AND SIBLING PERSPECTIVES

*James L. Paul, Paula Beckman, R. Lee Smith*

## INTRODUCTION

The changing views of professionals toward families is evidenced through the increased valuing of parent perceptions apparent in federal policy. Federal legislation now emphasizes the importance of family on the child's development and the importance of addressing family priorities and concerns. Further evidence of a changing attitude is contained in the literature on the effects of a family member with disabilities on parents and siblings (Powell & Ogle, 1985; Rosenberg & Robinson, 1988).

This chapter addresses the issues of family interactions and effects of a family member with a disability. Information concerned with such effects was gathered from two sources. First, we discuss briefly some historical and contemporary research about children with disabilities and their families. Second, we present personal perspectives gathered from interviews and writings of parents and siblings with family members with disabilities.

## ISSUES IN PARENTING A CHILD WITH A DISABILITY

As indicated throughout this book, professionals working with children who have disabilities recognize the contributions the parents and families of these children can make in the many aspects of service delivery. In PL 94-142, and as reaffirmed by IDEA, the role of the parent has become increasingly evident. With the passage and implementation of PL 99-457, the importance of the family has been emphasized. Whereas PL 94-142 affirmed the right of the parent to participate in the child's public school education, PL 99-457 stresses the role of the family as a system, in which the child with a disability is a part. The individual family service plan (IFSP) recognizes the need for outcomes to be achieved with both the family and the child. Services to be provided in an IFSP may be broad-based, such as respite care, or specific, such as those of an individual education plan. The family focus of PL 99-457 requires professionals to restructure instructional practices so parents play a substantial role in their child's education (Mahoney, O'Sullivan, & Fors, 1989).

Historically, research has concluded that the parental involvement was crucial to maintain the effects of intervention (Bronfenbrenner, 1974). An issue emphasized in developmental psychology in the late 1960s and mid-1970s was the direction of effects (Bell, 1968). During this period a substantial literature concerned with parent-child interaction focused on the parent as the agent who produces behaviors in the child (Bell, 1968; Harper, 1971, 1975; Marcus, 1977; Parke & Collmer 1975; Sameroff & Chandler, 1975). Such descriptions were increasingly found unsatisfactory as evidence accumulated suggesting that children's characteristics also influence their parents (Bell, 1968, 1971, 1974, 1977; Harper, 1975).

In the late 1980s the directions of effects issue received attention from special educators and others working with these families. Several variables that may affect family interaction have been studied. Stress to parents resulting from the birth of a child with a disability and the subsequent demands on the family has received particular attention; with both child variables and parent variables being addressed. The child variables that have been studied include birth order, severity of the disability, caregiver needs, responsiveness to parents, and the quality and quantity of child-parent interaction (Beckman, 1983). Family variables studied include education and socioeconomic level, parental attitudes toward the disabilities of their child, age, family size, number of parents in the home, and systems of support to the family (McDonald, Kysela, & Reddon, 1988).

Additional studies have addressed other areas of parent and family involvement with professionals (Heifetz, 1977, 1980; Wilson, 1979). Yet, despite the increased attention to family-professional interaction, not all the literature reflects the development of family intervention practices. Mahoney, O'Sullivan, and Fors (1989) surveyed teachers of children with disabilities, aged birth to 6 years old, about a variety of interactions, including time spent interacting with the family. These researchers found more of the service professional's time is devoted to direct intervention with the child with a disability. Although evidence of family intervention was also reported, the time spent in this aspect of professional service was significantly less than that providing services directly to the child.

With the current emphasis on the family's contributions to the developmental outcomes and education of their children, professionals have become increasingly aware of the particular demands of parenting a child with disabilities. Parental and professional interactions have increased dramatically with the initiatives and legal implications of PL 99-457. Professionals realize that the reality of interacting with a child with disabilities on a day-to-day basis may be much different from the interactions that occur in professional practice. The collaborative role between professionals and families in dealing with the challenges of raising and educating children with disabilities is now emphasized. Traditional roles of professionals as experts who assign activities and dictate to the parent the best intervention are fading and being redefined. More and more often, daily interactions between family members and the child who is disabled, lifelong planning, and the decision-making processes are considered by families and professionals together (Brotherson et al., 1988; Dunlap, Robbins, Morelli, & Dollman, 1987).

## Interactions With the Caregiver

There is some evidence suggesting that even a young infant with disabilities may influence the direct interactions with her parents. One area of research identifies characteristics of the interactions that may vary as a function of a specific disability. For example, there is some evidence that children with neurological impairments may show differences in such behaviors as duration and frequency of crying, ease of soothing (Fisichelli & Karelitz, 1963; Karelitz & Fisichelli, 1962; Pretchl, 1961), and other similar traits. Other authors (Beckman, 1983; Frey, Greenberg, & Fewell, 1989) have found that the severity of the child's disability and child's communication ability affect the reported experiences of mothers and fathers.

Other studies address the implications for family life of the different disabling conditions children may face. In the care of children with disabilities, even routine child-care tasks are often stressful (Beckman, 1983; Flynt & Wood, 1989; Frey, Greenburg, & Fewell, 1989; Harris & McHale, 1989). Parents who have not found a way to structure common behaviors of their child routinely, such as toileting times, mealtimes, or bedtime, may be unable to find a willing, trustworthy babysitter. Inviting friends to visit may become a problem when a child has a behavior disorder.

Harris and McHale (1989) have found that providing leisure time activities for children who have mental disabilities may be as demanding as caregiving tasks. Beckman (1983) found there were increased caregiving and time demands of children with disabilities. Robson and Moss (1970) found the ease of handling and feeding the child can have an influence on the attachment of the primary caregiver to the child. Also, the mother's feelings of competence (Battle, 1974) and the general behavior of the mother (Ofosky, 1975) may be affected by the ease of handling and feeding the child. Such activities may be further influenced by the child's particular disability (Wolf, Noh, Fisman, & Speechley, 1989).

Freedman, Fox-Kolenda, and Brown (1970), in reporting a case study of a baby with multiple disabilities caused by rubella, noted that babies with this condition are often physically ill and difficult to handle and feed. They noted that the particular child they studied ate poorly and had to be fed every 3 hours around the clock. In cases where the baby is considered contagious by relatives, responsibility for caregiving activities may fall exclusively on the mother.

Cerebral palsy is a disability that may also affect handling and feeding. Battle (1974) found that children with cerebral palsy often have poor sucking and swallowing mechanisms, which may interfere with a mother's ability to feed her child. Battle points to the importance of successful feeding in the mother's feelings about her competence and notes that often some other, less emotionally involved family member may be more successful feeding the child.

Shere and Kastenbaum (1966) studied mother-child interactions in families with 2-to-4-year old children with cerebral palsy. These mothers noted that the child often had to be fed, changed, and dressed because they were unable to do so themselves. Other difficulties noted were the child's need or desire to be held and carried a great deal of the time.

Blasco, Hrncir, and Blasco (1990), in a study of interaction comparing infants without disabilities and infants with cerebral palsy, examined the mastery behavior of these two groups and the mother's adaptation to the characteristics of the disability. (Mastery behavior is the ability of an infant to engage in a task until the infant has it mastered.) Mothers were able to match their interactions to the needs of their children with cerebral palsy. Blasco, Hrncir, and Blasco (1990) indicated that the mothers of infants with disabilities made functional adaptations in their interactions as required because of their children's disability, and that these adaptations may contribute to the infant's pursuit of mastery.

Differential caregiving needs have also been noted among families having infants who are blind. Fraiberg, Smith, and Adelson (1969) found that blind infants frequently remain passive participants in the feeding process for relatively long periods of time. They attribute this to the difficulty on the part of the child in recognizing the series of activities that precede his receiving food. Fraiberg and his colleagues (1969) indicate that many mothers of children with blindness neglect to initiate self-feeding until later than if their child had no disabilities, perhaps because of the absence of demands from the child. The authors also noted the resistance on the part of some blind infants to being cuddled, which may have resulted in decreased holding and physical contact from the caregiver, even during feeding. It should be noted that the infants with blindness who resisted physical contact were also premature. The reasons for this lack of cuddliness are unclear, as the degree of desire for physical contact may vary among all infants, including those with disabilities.

Stress factors in parenting a child with disabilities have been studied. Salisbury (1987) investigated stressors of parents with young children with disabilities and of children with no disabilities. She found there were no differences between the groups on overall levels of stress. She discovered higher levels of stress among single parents of such children, however, than among coupled parents. Salisbury believes the increased stress may be due to the reduced caretaking and support networks available to single-parent families.

Stress and support in families of preterm and full-term infants have also been studied (Beckman, Pokorni, Maza, & Blazer-Martin, 1987). These researchers found that mothers of preterm infants experienced more parent, child, and family problems than mothers of full-term babies. Although child problems decreased over time, family and parent problems remained consistent over the 12 months of the study. Beckman and her colleagues also discovered that mothers of babies born preterm had more social support than mothers of full-term babies, and the difference persisted throughout the year of the study. In addition, families of preterm infants who reported increased stress from the beginning to the end of the study also reported less formal support in the preceding measured time period, again indicating a possible link to stress and available support networks. These results should be viewed tentatively due to the relatively short length of the study.

Haldy and Hanzlik (1990) surveyed 131 mothers of children with Down syndrome and 222 mothers of children with no developmental delays about their self-perception of competence in child rearing. The authors found both groups of mothers similar in many respects. Mothers of infants with Down syndrome felt more competent than mothers of infants with no delays; at school ages, however, the mothers of children with Down syndrome felt less competent than the mothers of children with no delays. There was a decrease in the self-perception of competency in child rearing for mothers of children with Down syndrome as the children aged.

Busch and Peters (1979) studied parental development in firsttime mothers of children with two types of conditions: children at risk of developmental delay and children without disabilities and not at risk of developmental delay. Differences in maternal variables of anxiety, self-sentiment, home parental sentiment, superego, knowledge, and expectations were exhibited across time. The researchers found that differences in some variables may have been due to socioeconomic levels. Mothers of children with disabilities and mothers of children without disabilities and not at risk of delays also differed in development in the area of career sentiment.

The cultural, ethnic, and socioeconomic background of the family may also affect interactions among family members and society. Gartner, Lipsky, and Turnbull (1991), as well as several contributors to this book, have addressed some of these issues. A cultural conception of the degree to which a disability is viewed as a positive or negative occurrence in the family may affect the family's interaction with the child or children with disabilities. Gallegos and Gallegos (1988) have addressed issues in the interaction of Hispanic families with disabled children and the schools. Among the problems cited was a lack of understanding between the school and parents of the cultural implications concerning a disability. This was particularly true of the more severe disabilities.

Other characteristics that may influence caregiver behaviors are a lack of verbal and nonverbal communication skills, physical appearance and characteristics, and, sometimes, a need for frequent hospitalization. At the present time, evidence regarding the influence of caregiver behaviors is being synthesized. Additional research will be needed to help professionals fully comprehend the extent and variety of demands of families with disabled children.

## Impact on Siblings

In the past few years, researchers have begun to address the effects of children with disabilities on siblings. Researchers in this area have studied the quality of relationships formed between siblings, the effect of sibling relationships within the families, and siblings as caregivers. Studies have also examined sibling relationships in the life cycle of the child. Researchers have recently begun to identify some differences in psychological characteristics of siblings of children with disabilities and siblings of children without disabilities.

Powell and Ogle (1985) have produced a key work in the area of siblings of children with disabilities. They state that the impact of a child with a disability on siblings may vary a great deal from family to family, and from child to child (p. 33). Factors such as family size, religious involvement and orientation, and socioeconomic status may influence the degree of impact of the disabled child on the family. Powell and Ogle (1985) believe that birth order and gender of the nondisabled sibling may be two important factors that contribute to their adjustment. The severity of the disability, type of disability, and age of the children may also greatly influence the sibling relationship.

Begun (1989) studied 46 sisters of individuals with profound disabilities and their relationship with their siblings and compared their results to sisters of persons without disabilities. The relationships between the sisters and disabled siblings were found to be positive but less intimate than between sisters with nondisabled siblings. Relationships were less competitive than those of sisters with nondisabled siblings. Also, subjects closer in age, within 3 years, tended to have rated conflict variables higher than individuals more widely disparate in age. Begun states that the relationships may not be more negative but more neutral; this may be due to the difficulty in relating to a person with limited social and language skills. The author cautions against generalizing the results of this study due to nonrepresentative sampling procedures.

Gunn and Berry (1985) studied the temperament of toddlers with Down syndrome and their siblings. Thirty-seven children with Down syndrome and their 13 siblings were rated using the Toddler Temperament Scale (TTS). The scores for the children with Down syndrome supported the stereotype of the so-called easy child. When compared with their siblings the only dimension which differed was that of persistence, with the siblings without disabilities being more persistent. However, the easy range was not portrayed by all the children with Down syndrome and a range of descriptive behaviors was present.

Dyson, Edgar, and Crnic (1989) studied psychological predictors of adjustment in siblings of children with developmental disabilities. One hundred and ten siblings under age 7 and their families participated; half had older siblings with developmental disabilities, and half had older siblings without developmental disabilities. Instruments measuring self-concept, family support, family environment, and behavior were administered. The results showed a general relationship between the child's adjustment and certain family factors. Psychological factors in siblings of children with disabilities contributed to all measures of adjustment. For siblings of children without disabilities, psychological factors contributed only to social competence, and the relationship was not as strong.

Dyson, Edgar, and Crnic (1989) also found that behavior problems of siblings of children with disabilities were best predicted by the type of family relationship. Few behavior problems were found in more supportive families. In homes where moral-religious beliefs, independence, and cultural-recreational activities were emphasized, siblings of children with disabilities scored higher in the area of social competence. The authors' hypothesis that there are specific psychological predictors which exist for the adjustment of siblings of children with disabilities was supported. To a lesser degree, similar factors also predicted adjustment of siblings of children without disabilities.

## Family Support

Many of the studies just cited support and emphasize the importance of approaching the family as a unit rather than as individuals related to the child with disabilities. The impact of a disabled child may vary with differences in family structures, ethnic and cultural background, religious orientation, and socioeconomic status. Siblings of children with disabilities also vary in their psychological characteristics, which may affect their ability to adapt to their brother's and sister's unique behaviors. With the recognition that both individual and family traits may affect family interactions, professionals are beginning to address all facets of the family.

This impetus has led to the examination of systems and methods that serve families of children with disabilities. Weissbourd and Patrick (1988) address the wide spectrum of programs that are labeled as family support. Historically, these authors note that family resource programs may have roots in the parent informational and educational system. Dunst, Johanson, Trivette, and Hamby (1991) have enumerated the practice indicators for four family-oriented program paradigms: family centered, family focused, family allied, and professional centered. These researchers are strong proponents of a family-centered approach to service.

Flynn and McCollum (1989) have reviewed strategies and support systems for children in neonatal intensive hospital care from a parent's perspective as well as a professional's. Services were examined from the time of entry into a neonatal intensive care unit to discharge from the hospital. These authors conclude that specific disciplines within hospital settings approach the parents' needs and demands somewhat differently. They further explain that the integration of education, social services, and medicine has the "capacity to rectify some obvious weak points in services to high-risk infants and their families" (Flynn & McCollum, 1989, p. 180).

Labato (1985) discusses a support and training program for 3- to 7-year old siblings of children with disabilities. She found that the participants became more accurate in their definitions of common disabilities, such as deafness, blindness, and mentally disability. Participants in the program also began making more positive verbalizations about their families and siblings.

## Parents and Professionals

When a child with severe disabilities enters public school, the parents and family already have an intensive history with social service and educational agencies. They may be concerned with issues of labeling, classification, and placement.

They may already have a number of mechanisms in place to assist them with their interactions with professionals.

Families with children who have disabilities do not constitute a homogeneous group. There is a considerable range in the feelings and abilities present in different families and family members. Even among other parents with disabled children, some parents may feel isolated from other parents because their child has special needs. The psychosocial consequences of this isolation can be a problem for the families and misleading to professionals. The combination of the attributes of the family, coupled with the economic, cultural, and social characteristics with which the family lives, and the variety of values the family may hold, require that professionals individualize approaches to families.

Issues that must be considered in the parent-professional relationship are many and varied. Despite the best intent of legislation and practice, the quality and types of services available varies considerably depending on the nature of the child's disabilities and the community's resources. For example, the availability of services needed may be limited. Services that are provided may not be effective or successful. There may be differences of opinion regarding the effectiveness and need for services. Parents and professionals together must determine how to best use the available services. They must explore all sources of potential help and build programs together that will benefit both the child and the family.

Professionals must be sensitive to the feelings and concerns of the family. They must relate to parents the complex and technical vocabulary that is used. Explanations may have to be given about certain methodologies or instructional procedures. Professionals must recognize that families may have different values, and attempt to affirm the parent's value system.

Despite the unique nature of problems faced by families of children with disabilities, most families of these children have some feelings in common: joy at the accomplishments of their children; concerns about safety, participating in activities with peers, having friends; and worry in times of ill health.

Many families have found that support and advocacy groups provide an understanding forum for their unique concerns and needs. In the case of parents with children with severe behavioral problems, for example, information on respite care may be available. Advocacy and support groups may sometimes help parents come to grips with the view of some professionals that parents are *part of the problem*.

Although parents of children with disabilities may need technical and professional services, they frequently report that the most important aspect of their encounter with professionals is the extent to which the professional is sensitive to the needs of their family and to the needs of their child. The personal and professional quality of the encounter may well be more important in the immediate situation than the professional and technical services that are provided to the child and family. The professional who sees the long-term benefit of a service such as physical therapy but neglects the need to be sensitive to the feelings and perspective of the parents and family is indeed shortsighted.

Sensitivity and empathy from professionals may bring dignity and integrity to the moments of contact with the family. Both are a condition and prerequisite for effective professional interaction. Parents remember the quality of the relationship in their encounters with professionals, the feelings of respect, and the feeling of contributing to the process in a unique and useful way.

## PARENT AND SIBLING PERSPECTIVES

In the preceding pages some important issues regarding families with disabled children have been discussed. Now we turn to the specific experiences and perspectives of parents of children with disabilities.

We asked several parents, brothers, and sisters of disabled children to respond to questions about the impact of their child or sibling on them, their family, and their community. They were asked to describe their experiences with professionals, the public school system, and other service agencies.

What is reported here is not necessarily representative of what most families with children with disabilities may think or feel. It is, however, a direct and honest account of several parents who were kind enough to share their thoughts, feelings, perceptions, and views about parenting children with disabilities.

### Impact on Self

Social, physical, and economic impacts on parents of a child with a disability can be great. Like all parents, many of these issues affect their families' day-to-day functioning. The following comments demonstrate some issues that may influence parents' feelings.

### Case Study: MRS. A

On the positive side, I have certainly been made more sensitive to persons of all sorts of abilities and disabilities as the result of having a child with disabilities in my family. I am also much more aware of the difficulties and complexities of communication, even among so-called normal people, and especially with the communication disabled. Certainly being the mother of a child with disabilities has made me aware of the human condition—its frailty, its vulnerability.

On the negative side, there is the guilt. Intellectually—especially now that research indicates almost beyond a shadow of a doubt that childhood schizophrenia is the result of genetic and/or physical causes—I accept the fact that Amy's condition was not my fault. Emotionally, however, I am still fighting the notions of responsibility. I was already a person prone to taking too much responsibility. I became a mother in the middle of the *mother-is-to-blame-for-everything* school of thought; and what the popular press and Bruno Bettelheim didn't do for making mothers guilty, my social worker did. I suppose I'll be fighting this the rest of my life.

There is also always the feeling that if-I-did-just-one-more-thing: tried one more psychiatrist, one more drug, one more method of treatment—maybe the miracle would happen. That's the *Reader's Digest* success story effect. I have a hard time fighting that one, too—especially when I read *Karen* or hear of *Son-Rise* [a television movie], which I deliberately decided not to watch.

Getting back to the vulnerability, I feel more at the mercy of everything: genes, incompetent or insensitive professionals, big and sometimes uncaring agencies, economic whirlwinds. And I feel less competent. Feeling incompetent to deal with Amy has made me hesitant about dealing with the other children (and has caused unnecessary conflict with them). It has also made me less assertive in other areas of my life, for I have always felt that if one could not handle his or her own personal relationships, well, he or she had no right to claim authority in a wider field. I realize now—again intellectually—that feeling is incorrectly based; but it is still there.

# Case Study: MRS. B

I have worked as a professional in the area of developmental disabilities since before I had my son. My son's disabilities have helped me to avoid the behavior I have been critical of in others. It has led me to feel that the service delivery system must be bent, changed, or even destroyed, if necessary, to adequately serve persons with developmental disabilities. This, unfortunately, has kept me constantly on the edge of controversy and probably affected others' perceptions of me as a member of the team.

I have become militant in working for the rights of the disabled. I am particularly concerned that the persons with mental disabilities receive the dignity and respect they deserve as citizens of our country. I am afraid that I have also become very cynical of institutions and agencies which offer services to persons with disabilities. They are too often seen as the raw material which keeps the agencies going and treated as material rather than as individual human beings.

## Impact on Marriage and Family

Many times marriages and families are affected by the birth of a child with disabilities. The following brief stories suggest the effects that disabled children may have on families and extended families.

## Case Study: MRS. D

Our two elder daughters have been influenced by Sara's birth in a positive way. We never treated Sara differently except as was necessary. Mary, aged 4, was disappointed that "she can't do anything" when we first came home from the hospital. While Sara was still a baby, Mary had her dressed in a holster, gun, and cowboy hat, trying to play cowboys and Indians with her.

Mary, Nell, and Sara all have degrees in social work and are active in those professions. We always shared with the three all we knew of Sara's condition that we felt they could accept. Sara was 12 when she asked with amazement, after a March of Dimes ad on TV, "Do I have a major disability?" She had not thought of it as such.

Sara's birth strengthened our marriage, although it was already strong. We have shared so many tears and decisions that only we could make together. Since I was home during most of Sara's younger years, I had most of the responsibility; but my husband gave me tremendous support, such as taking all three for a ride or a meal out so I could have some time alone.

We have always had fun as a family. Once, after a long stay in surgery, we surprised Sara when we picked her up for a trip to the World's Fair in New York. We first got into one of those long lines, but an attendant saw the wheelchair and came to us, took us to the front of the line, and said that at each show there was a special wheelchair entrance. Mary said to Sara, "Well, it's not so bad after all to have you as a sister."

## Case Study: BROTHER F

George has CP [cerebral palsy]—spastic diplegia—a disability but not real bad. I don't mind it, but people always ask me about it. I am five years older than he is. He is 4.

We are best buddies sometimes and not at other times. When I do things for him that he likes and when I like to play with him, we are best buddies. Whenever he does something wrong and he won't stop and I tell Mom, he gets mad. My sister picks on George because he is not as good at some things so I have to stop her. But I don't think it's because he's disabled. I think it's because he's only 4.

We can't do all the things that other families do, like go certain places. The beach isn't as much fun, because we have to watch out for George. Sometimes I want to go where I want to go, but we have to go where George has to go. We even moved to this city from another state because of George. But that was okay.

## Case Study: MRS. G

The relationship with my parents is very supportive. I know other people who have children with disabilities who have problems with their own parents. Mine have helped financially, but also emotionally. Before I knew the extent of the disabilities and when I found out Barbara didn't see that well, it bothered me. Me, being an artist and all; [the visual disability bothered me] more than the physical and the mental aspects. I didn't know how to deal with someone who didn't live through what they saw. My parents always showed caring and concern—it made it easier.

## Case Study: MRS. H

Sam has two sisters, they are identical twins, and they are almost 11 years old. They tolerate him—for the most part they don't like him. One is more vocal right now than the other one about disliking him tremendously and that he ruins her life—to put it bluntly. The other one is a little bit more tolerant. He can come up and touch the back of her hair. Sam adores the twins. He likes to have them around because they bring a lot of excitement into the house. He kind of likes that. He teases them, too.

They bring other kids over, but we can't relax. They love to play the piano when they have people over, but Sam has very sensitive ears and he throws a fit. They die of embarrassment and have to quit. It's like that when they have friends over. We just can't relax.

[Having Sam] has taught me to be more tolerant with the girls. One of my goals is to keep an even pace in our home—you could have a high stress level in a home with a kid with autism. You can live on such a thin wire that the family could fall apart. I decided that we were going to have a peaceful happy home no matter what it took. And if means looking the other way sometimes, we're going to do it and we're not going to worry.

### Impact on Relationships in the Social Community

Relationships with relatives, friends, neighbors, the church, and the general public give the family identity and status in the community. The family is a part of a network of social relationships in the community. The child with disabilities becomes a part of those relationships.

The parent stories that follow describe various aspects of their family and community interactions.

## Case Study: MRS. H

An overall picture of the people around me, from my viewpoint, is that the general public is certainly uninformed and really don't have the picture of what this child is really like. Some feel sorry for me, which I resent; that really shows ignorance.

Most enjoy getting to know Kent because they become educated in an unknown. I like having people ask questions. Kent is such a delight that he gives people a new image of a person with mental disabilities. The family treats him normally, so it teaches people that he is not a disaster happening to us. He is an accepted, loved person like everyone else.

## Case Study: MRS. C

Some relatives and friends reacted to the news by avoiding discussing it, treating it as an unmentionable shame. Others, after initial shock and sadness, responded with, "Well, thank God it's not worse. She'll do fine. Be thankful." Or often, "No one would ever guess it. You can't tell when she has a seizure."

Friends of my faith responded with hope and comfort and have been the most supportive. My mother was deeply sympathetic, and I have felt the most compassion from her.

## Case Study: MR. E

Parents need to talk with other parents who are going through the same sorts of problems. Often other parents can give the troubled and self-incriminating parent a new perspective by sharing common concerns and feelings.

Teachers and other helping professionals can make appropriate referrals to other parents, especially when help is first indicated, which also may ease the pain of seeking professional help. A supportive group of parents can be extremely helpful and usually find the time to share information, support, and comfort with new parents who are seeking professional help for the first time.

## Case Study: MRS. A

We have been very fortunate in having friends and neighbors who have taken an interest in Amy—including her in invitations, and made special events for her. In fact, they have been more helpful than relatives, who by and large have viewed Amy as a puzzle.

On the other hand, we have been fortunate not to have had grandparents who denied the possibility of having a [child with a disability] in the family—an experience a number of parents of children with disabilities have undergone.

The youth fellowship at our local Methodist church and a Girl Scout troop were both very helpful. In each case the leaders saw Amy as an opportunity for both service and to sensitize other members of the groups.

They included her in everything in as normal a way as possible. This furthered her socialization a great deal.

# Case Study: BROTHER F

My friends ask me about my brother's disability. Sometimes some kids think I'm kind of weird because I have a brother with CP, but it also helps me because I got interviewed on TV because of George. It was a puppet show; all the fourth graders went to see the show.

New people treat George so tenderly. They're afraid to hurt him and so nice—I don't like that. Sometimes he gets away with things, but not at our house.

## Interactions With the Schools

The school is a vital force in the life of a child. School is also important to parents because this is the proving ground for their children. Parents of children with disabilities have a special relationship with the school. Since the passage of PL 94-142 in 1975, parents have been guaranteed the right to participate in deciding the nature of the educational program their child will receive. What follows is a direct account of some of those experiences.

# Case Study: MR. E

The emotional problems with our child began to show up in his performance in the public school classroom. In working with school personnel, there was a distinct contrast in teacher reaction: (a) those teachers who were trained in and aware of emotional problems were quite supportive and helpful; (b) those teachers without prior training and/or awareness seemed only to offer complaints about our child's behavior.

One teacher in particular, who seemed to be able to relate to our child when he was in the process of withdrawing from friends, school responsibilities, and other teachers, was especially supportive and helpful. It was this special teacher who had prior experience with the emotional problems of children, who offered support, suggestions in getting professional help, and eased the pain of dealing with our child's problem by her understanding nature.

This teacher made us feel like our child was not a bad boy, but that he had problems and that we were not failing as parents but needed professional help for him.

## Case Study: MR. B

Professionals, including school personnel, have most often seemed to me to be primarily concerned with the comfort and safety of the organizations they serve. Many such professionals told me they could not serve my son because he would not fit within their program. In addition, there seemed to be an unwillingness of staff to accept the parent as a partner in working with a child with developmental disabilities.

I often felt that my son and I were seen as enemies of the system, so that certain tactical maneuvers had to be executed in order to deal with us. I think that over the years there has been some improvement, particularly in the amount of secrecy around professional decisions, but the problem is still there.

There were a few professionals who were very supportive, sometimes to the extent of conflict with their supervisors, in helping my son. I owe them a great deal.

## Case Study: MRS. A

Teachers (kindergarten and the first two grades) were very supportive, worked hard with Amy, accepted her, disabilities and all. So did her first two teachers where we currently live. Then she hit a fourth grade teacher who had no patience with even a minor deviance, much less major.

In fact that year she got two of them, one of whom spanked her—not for misbehavior, not for not doing her homework—but *for doing the wrong homework*. I still hate myself that I did not sue.

That year the principal told us that the public schools didn't have to keep Amy as a student. Of course they couldn't say that now.

## Case Study: MRS. D

As to school personnel we have had excellent experiences. We moved here when Sara was half through the first grade. She had been well accepted and her printing with hands or feet was displayed on the board and was beautiful. You could tell no difference.

I took Sara and Mary to the local school on a Thursday. The principal received us beautifully. I told her all about Sara, and she made one request— that she be given one day, Friday, to prepare the children for Sara's coming.

On Friday she went to the room and told the children about Sara, how she would walk (without braces then), how many operations she had and would have in the future, etc.

On Monday, when Sara and Mary went to school the children showered them with Valentines (which was on a Sunday that year).

# Case Study: BROTHER F

My brother is doing real good in school. I think he is accepted at his school because at his class there are other kids who have CP. . . . My parents say that the law is supposed to give therapy for these children, but they don't go by what the doctors say. George needs three hours per week, but the schools will give only one hour, so they only give a small part of it. We had to pay $1,400 for a stroller Mike needs. The stores take advantage of people with disabilities because they have to pay.

## Interactions With Professionals

Children with disabilities often require professional services that are available in social service agencies or through a private therapist. Parents, therefore, are nec-essarily in contact with professional service providers besides those provided by the schools. Both public and private practitioners in mental health, the medical fields, and the state social service agencies may be providing services to families with disabled children. Each may have its own set of special rules, forms, lan-guage, and procedures. Following are the parents' reflections about their contacts with some professional.

# Case Study: MR. E

In one of several referrals in our situation, we were assigned a social worker with whom we could not communicate effectively. The first reaction we had was that this was our problem (and that there must certainly be something wrong with us).

Since the social worker didn't question our lack of progress, we finally raised this issue. When the lack of progress was identified and it was decided to change social workers, the result was highly successful and, with another social worker, the communication problems disappeared.

Parents are often feeling extremely guilty at these times, and an understanding professional—with the parents' knowledge that there can be a lack of fit with helping professionals—gives everyone the opportunity to look more objectively at the basic family needs being addressed.

## Case Study: MRS. C

It seemed to me that the neurologists were solely interested in the physiological symptoms of Beth's epilepsy and completely excluded any reference to mental, emotional, or social implications, which were mainly my concern. Both specialists we contacted concentrated on the effect of medication only, and I was too ignorant to ask questions. I wish I had.

The only school representative I've talked with so far was a busy counselor. She was sympathetic but also ignorant and uninformed, as I was. Her referring to the seizures as "fits" was disturbing to me and I became defensive and apologetic, for which I was later resentful. She relayed the information I gave her to the teachers and the principal, but I noticed no improvement in teacher-Beth relationships or signs of support. However, neither was I aware of any negative repercussions or stigma.

The psychiatrist we visited in family sessions was immensely supportive and helpful in easing tensions and difficulty in discussing the epilepsy. His approach was point blank with all of us, and his openness and spiritual orientation were healing for us. The most negative experience for Beth has been a lengthy and courageous delay and possible denial of her learner's permit to drive. This might lead us to our first painful confrontation with bureaucracy through the courts.

## Case Study: MR. B

Generally, I would like to say that the service system for the development of the disabled is rigid, unfeeling, and strangled by politics and red tape. Its major focus is on meeting the political needs of those elected and nonelected people who run it.

However, I have had contact with many professionals in this system who are able to function well in spite of this. These individuals deserve a great deal of credit from me and other parents, because they often do not get it from the system.

## SUMMARY

Professionals have become much more aware and accepting of the realities facing families of children with disabilities. Our research is just beginning to help us understand the complexity of family functioning and the variability of effects, both positive and negative, of a child with a disability on his or her family. Listening to stories about the experiences of families deepens our understanding of both celebration and struggle in these families. This chapter affirms the importance of the perspectives of families in planning and developing programs for children with disabilities.

## REFERENCES

Battle, C. V. (1974). Disruptions in the socialization of a young severely handicapped child. *Rehabilitation Literature, 34,* 134–140.

Beckman, P. J. (1983). Influence of selected child characteristics on stress in families of handicapped infants. *American Journal of Mental Deficiency,* 88(2), 150–156.

Beckman, P. J., Pokorni, J. L., Maza, E. A., & Blazer-Martin, L. (1987). A longitudinal study of stress and support in families of preterm and full-term infants. *Journal of the Division of Early Childhood,* 11(1), 2–9.

Begun, A. L. (1989). Sibling relationships involving developmental disabled people. *American Journal on Mental Retardation,* 93(5), 566–574.

Bell, R. Q. (1968). A reinterpretation of the direction of effect in studies of socialization. *Psychological Review, 75,* 81–95.

Bell, R. Q. (1971). Stimulus control of a parent or caretaker behavior of offspring. *Developmental Psychology, 4,* 63–72.

Bell, R. Q. (1974). Contributions of human infants to caregiving and social interaction. In M. Lewis and L. Rosenblum (Eds.), *The effect of the infant on its caregiver* (pp. 1–20). New York: Wiley.

Bell, R. Q. (1977). Socialization findings re-examined. In R. Q. Bell and L. V. Harper, (Eds.), *Child effects on adults* (pp. 53–84). New York: Wiley.

Blasco, P. M., Hrncir, E. J., & Blasco, P. A. (1990). The contribution of maternal involvement to mastery performance in infants with cerebral palsy. *Journal of Early Intervention,* 14(2), 161–174.

Brofenbrenner, U. (1974). *Is early intervention effective?* Washington, DC: Department of Health, Education, and Welfare, Publication Number OHD 74–25.

Brotherson, M. J., Turnbull, A. P., Bronecki, G. J., Houghton, J., Roeder-Gordon, C., Summers, J. A., & Turnbull, H. R. (1988). Transition into adulthood: Parental planning for sons and daughters with disabilities. *Education and Training in Mental Retardation,* 23(3), 165–174.

Busch, N. A. and Peters, D. A. (1979). *Parental development in first time mothers of handicapped, at-risk, and normal children: Final report.* Washington, DC: Department of Health, Education, and Welfare.

Dunlap, G., Robbins, F. R., Morelli, M. A., & Dollman, C. (1987). Team training for young children with autism: A regional model for service delivery. *Journal of the Division of Early Childhood, 12*(2), 147–158.

Dunst, C. J., Johanson, C., Trivette, C. M., & Hamby, D. (1991). Family-oriented early intervention policies and practices: Family-centered or not? *Exceptional Children, 58*(2), 115–127.

Dyson, L., Edgar, E., & Crnic, K. (1989). Psychological predictors of adjustment by siblings of developmentally delayed children. *American Journal on Mental Retardation, 94*(3), 292–202.

Fisichelli, V. R., & Karelitz, S. (1963). The cry latencies of normal infants and those with brain damage. *Journal of Pediatrics, 62,* 724–734.

Flynn, L. L., & McCollum, J. (1989). Support systems: Strategies and implications for hospitalized newborns and families. *Journal of Early Intervention, 13*(2), 173–182.

Flynt, S. M., & Wood, T. A. (1989). Stress and coping of mothers of children with moderate mental retardation. *American Journal on Mental Retardation, 94*(3), 278–283.

Fraiberg, S., Smith, M., & Adelson, E. (1969). An educational program for blind infants. *Journal of Special Education, 3,* 121–139.

Freedman, D. A., Fox-Kolenda, B. J., & Brown, S. L. (1970). A multihandicapped rubella baby: The first eighteen months. *Journal of the American Academy of Child Psychiatry, 9,* 298–317.

Frey, K. S., Greenberg, M. T., & Fewell, R. R. (1989). Stress and coping among parents of handicapped children: A multidimensional approach. *American Journal on Mental Retardation, 94*(3), 240–249.

Gallegos, A., & Gallegos, R. (1988). The interaction between families of culturally diverse handicapped children and the school. In H. S. Garcia and R. Chavez (Eds.), *Ethnolinguistic issues in education* (pp. 125–132). (ERIC Document Reproduction Service No. ED 309 002)

Gallagher, J. J., Trohanis, P. L., & Clifford, R. M. (1985). *Policy implementation and PL 99-457: Planning for young children with special needs.* Baltimore: Brookes.

Gartner, A., Lipsky, D. K., & Turnbull, A. (1991). *Supporting families with a child with a disability: An international outlook.* Baltimore: Brookes.

Gunn, P., & Berry, P. (1985). The temperament of Down's syndrome toddlers and their siblings. *Journal of Child Psychology and Psychiatry and Allied Disabilities, 26*(6), 973–979.

Haldy, M. B., & Hanzlik, J. R. (1990). A comparison of perceived competence in child-rearing between mothers of children with Down syndrome and mothers of children without delays. *Education and Training in Mental Retardation, 25*(2), 132–141.

Harper, L. V. (1971). The young as a source of stimuli controlling caretaker behavior. *Development Psychology, 4,* 73–88.

Harper, L. V. (1975). The scope of offspring effects: From caregiver to culture. *Psychological Bulletin, 82,* 784–801.

Harris, V. S., & McHale, S. M. (1989). Family life problems, daily caregiving activities, and the psychological well-being of mothers of mentally retarded children. *American Journal on Mental Retardation, 94*(3), 231–239.

Heifetz, L. J. (1977). Behavioral training for parents of retarded children. *American Journal of Mental Deficiency, 82*(2), 194–203.

Heifetz, L. J. (1980). From consumer to middleman: Emerging roles for parents in the network of services for retarded children. In Abidin, R.R. (Ed.), *Parent education and intervention handbook* (pp. 349–394). Springfield, IL: Thomas.

Karelitz, S., & Fisichelli, V. R. (1962). The cry thresholds of normal infants and those with brain damage. *Journal of Pediatrics, 61,* 979–685.

Labato, D. (1985). Brief report: Preschool siblings of handicapped children—impact of peer support and training. *Journal of Autism and Developmental Disorders, 15*(3), 345–350.

Mahoney, G., O'Sullivan, P., & Fors, S. (1989). Special education practices with young children. *Journal of Early Intervention, 13*(3), 261–268.

Marcus, L. M. (1977). Patterns of coping in families of psychotic children. *American Journal of Orthopsychiatry, 47,* 388–398.

McDonald, L., Kysela, G. M., & Reddon, J. (1988). Stress and support to families with a handicapped child. In D. Baine (Ed.), *Alternative futures for the education of students with severe disabilities* (pp. 192–200). Edmonton, Canada: Conference Paper.

Ofosky, J. D. (1975). *Neonatal characteristics and directional effects in mother-infant interaction.* Paper presented at the meeting of the Society for Research in Child Development, Denver, CO.

Parke, R. D., & Collmer, C. W. (1975). Child abuse: A interdisciplinary analysis. *Review of Child Development Research, 5.*

Paul, J. L., & Beckman-Bell, P. J. (1981). Parent perspectives. In J. L. Paul (Ed.), *Understanding and working with parents of children with special needs* (pp. 119–154). New York: Holt.

Powell, T. H., & Ogle, P.A. (1985). *Brothers and sisters—A special part of exceptional families.* Baltimore: Brookes.

Pretchl, H. F. R. (1961). The mother-child interaction in babies with minimal brain damage (a follow-up study). In B. M. Foss (Ed.), *The terminance of infant behavior* (pp. 53–59). New York: Wiley.

Robson, K. S., & Moss, H. A. (1970). Patterns and determinants of maternal attachments. *Journal of Pediatrics, 77,* 976–985.

Rosenberg, S. A., & Robinson C. C. (1988). Interactions of parents with their young handicapped children. In S. L. Odom & M. B. Karnes (Eds.), *Early intervention for infants and children with handicaps* (pp. 159–178). Baltimore: Brookes.

Salisbury, C. (1987). Stressors of parents with young handicapped and nonhandicapped children. *Journal of the Division for Early Childhood, 11*(2), 154–160.

Sameroff, A. J., & Chandler, M. J. (1975). Reproductive risk and the continuum of caretaking causalty. In F. D. Horowitz (Ed.), *Review of child development research* (Vol. 4) (pp. 187–224). Chicago: University of Chicago Press.

Shere, E., & Kastenbaum, R. (1966). Mother-child interaction in cerbral palsy: Environmental and psychological obstacles to cognitive development. *Genetic Psychology Monographs, 73,* 255–335.

Weissbourd, B., & Patrick, M. (1988). In the best interest of the family: The emergence of family resource programs. *Infants and Young Children, 1*(2), 46–54.

Wilson, W. (1979). Parent training: Some observations. *Academic Therapy, 15*(1), 45–51.

Wolf, L. C., Noh, S., Fisman, S. N., & Speechley, M. (1989). Brief report: Psychological effects of parenting stress on parents of autistic children. *Journal of Autism and Developmental Disorders, 19*(1), 157–166.

# 5

# HOPE IN DESPAIR: THE IMPORTANCE OF RELIGIOUS STORIES FOR FAMILIES WITH CHILDREN WITH DISABILITIES

*The Rev. Brett Webb-Mitchell*

## INTRODUCTION: A STORY OF HOPE

It has been said that families who have children with disabilities are more intensely invested in being a family. These families demonstrate to others what it means to be a parent or parents, and be committed to children, no matter what the child may look like, sound like, act like, or be like as these parents embrace the child who is far different than what society would describe as normal (Hauerwas, 1986). Clara Park, the mother of an autistic child, wrote that when considering the life of a child with autism, if the child is to be helped, we must consider the needs, wants, and desires of the whole family. For if the child is to be helped, then it is important that the parents and the other members of the family do not fall apart. If they go under, then the child goes too (Park, 1982).

This chapter focuses on the religious stories or narratives that guide each religious community, the sacred stories that give people meaning in their lives. The religious stories shape the parents' perceptions of their child with a disability, influencing how they interact with the child and shaping their expectations for the child. The significance of these religious stories often emerge in the cry of many parents: "Why, God, is this happening to us?", a question that has no easy answers nor is easily resolved, but has meaning because of the religious story in which the fearful question is asked.

An example of how religious stories shape and nurture the very lives of parents with children who are disabled is in this story of a family in the state of Washington who have a daughter, Annie, a 12-year-old autistic girl who lives at home. The primary storyteller in this story is Patty,[1] the mother, who is in her 30s. The setting is a small rural house, set off of a dirt road, near the Washington-Idaho border, where five children live with their mother and father.

The house itself is hot inside during the winter with a wood-burning stove pumping out the heat. The house, inside and outside, looks a bit battle worn. It

---

[1]All names have been changed for matters of confidentiality.

could use a coat of paint or two outside. Inside, the walls are scarred and the rug is dirty, because it has been wet all too often from an autistic child's fascination with shampoo and water. Many of the doors are locked with high-tech electronic computer locks, and even the refrigerator and cabinets in the kitchen have special locks. There are few pictures on the walls. Instead there are holes in the wall, and places where Sheetrock has been ripped off. This is because Annie picks up many household items and throws them around the house. Patty said there are days when the house appears to be flying inside.

As I came into the house to talk with Patty and meet Annie, Annie was taking the hand of her younger brother, leading him off into the kitchen so that he could get her some food. She grunted as she passed me while the rest of the family greeted the stranger. Soon Don, a part of the transportation team for Annie and a member of Patty's church, came to take Annie to the nearby institution for what Patty's family calls a "weekend of normality." Annie goes away to respite care, and the other children can invite their friends over without explaining the bizarre behavior of their autistic sister. Another member of the church works doing in-home care when Annie is at home.

As I sat down on the slightly wet couch, Patty started to tell me about the preceding weekend with Annie at home for the Easter holiday, which was quite exciting. It was a warm Saturday afternoon of Easter weekend when Annie suddenly was nowhere to be found around the house: She had simply vanished into the heavily wooded forest that annexed their backyard! Her parents quickly called the nearest and most logical helpers: the members of their church's prayer chain. All 50 members showed up within an hour and began searching for Annie. Patty was scared as she heard the coyotes in the surrounding wilderness.

Patty's mother in Spokane was asked to have her church's prayer chain pray to find the child. Her mother-in-law's job was to call the nearest neighbor. By mistake, in calling someone else to come and help search, Patty called the sheriff at his home, and he, too, came out for the search on his own time.

What made this search so difficult was the fact that Annie was autistic. Unlike many children who can and will respond to the normal calling of their name, Annie's response to vocal commands is silence. She would rather be in an activity that is self-stimulating than obeying someone else's dictums.

Patty was busy taking care of feeding the 50 people who were there to help find her daughter. One friend asked if she had been praying, but Patty said that she had been too busy feeding the 50 that suddenly descended upon her house. When she did get a chance to pray, she told God that, even though there were times she would be more than glad to let go of her daughter with autism, this was not the time. Her prayer was, "Please, God, I'm not ready to give her up yet. The state has just started providing services for my daughter; you can't take her yet!" Then Patty was suddenly reminded of God's loss of his son on Good Friday: "That's what I did; I lost my Son for you." This put Patty's mind and heart to rest: God knew what it was like to lose one's most precious child.

Before they needed to call the search and rescue squad, Patty was met with the good news that her daughter had been found, innocently playing in the forest. Her child had not been taken by God to heaven. Patty adamantly claims it was her belief in God, and the dependability and commitment of her church that has been invaluable in its support of both Patty and her family, helping them move from times of despair to bright moments of hope.

When I asked Patty what are some of the lessons she has learned in living with Annie, discovering who she is, Patty was quite prepared with answers, quoting constantly from the Bible, which is the record of her religious community's story of faith. First, she quoted the passage in First Corinthians, where the apostle Paul talks about the refining fire that burns off the excess material until only precious gold is revealed (1 Cor. 3:13). Patty feels she is being refined through the fire, and that she's waiting for the gold to come out of this experience.

Second, when she is asked, "What do I expect in heaven? I just tell them, 'Rest.' That's all: rest." The state of Washington knows Patty because she has had to do so much of the advocacy work on behalf of her daughter.

Third, Patty understands that Annie is a blessing in disguise. Patty claims that the blessing is truly going to come from God in the end because Annie is so unlike other children, even children with Down syndrome: "At least kids with Down's can *show* you love. Annie can't even show love like normal kids can. But I know God will pay me back in the end for taking good care of Annie."

Fourth, Patty truly believes that God is using her family to make it possible for other families with autistic children to find services more readily available in that part of the state:

> God is using me and Annie. She's this way so that I can blaze a new trail or path for her and others. God is using me, and us, for opening up a lot of doors for others to use.
>
> For example, there's PAVE, Parent Advocates for Vocational Education, and the director, when I ask for help, says that they listen to me because I'm 10 steps ahead of them. You've got to think as a Christian. I want to know what to do. If God wants it done, then God will get it done. I couldn't get to where I am today without God.

Finally, Patty said that they have gone through so many things; so much has happened:

> But it's how we live. Annie is just part of our life. We've gone past the "Oh my God!" part of grief, and now we are onto the business at hand. It happened, and I can't make it go away. But I can be responsible from this moment on. If she dies, then I'll at least know I did the best I could do; I couldn't do anymore.

Patty freely volunteers that her faith has been shaped by her experiences in life. Patty, herself, was an adopted child, brought up in an abusive home, has had to deal with many personal tragedies, including filing for bankruptcy and her youngest child who was born with meningitis. A sixth child is on the way.

What has helped Patty and the family live and grow with a daughter and sister who is autistic has been the church. Not all churches have welcomed Annie. The pastor of one church quietly told Patty that she and her family would have to leave because the congregation just didn't like Annie coming to church.

The church where they now attend has worked hard in accepting Annie as she is, with all her limitations and abilities. This small rural church that Patty says "doesn't speak in tongues" accept Annie's random babbling in the back of the church. For a church where no one dances in worship, they now accept Annie's running around in the front of the sanctuary during the sermon. Even when Annie has gone to the basement of the church, to the nursery, and stripped off her clothes, the members of the church shield their eyes and just say, "Yep, we see Annie's here," and walk on. The church has become the compassionate, understanding community that the family needed in searching for a daughter lost in the woods, and for a family who has needed an understanding community in living with a child whose very presence is a theological question about God's creation (Webb-Mitchell, 1992).

## FINDING HOPE IN DESPAIR

In Patty's final statement of her story about losing Annie there is that cry of despair that she eludes to: "Oh my God!" This is a familiar cry among many families when they find out that the child, a symbol of hope born anew in religious communities, is born with a disabling condition. At the moment when a family finds out a child has a disability, many parents feel very vulnerable, fearing the unknown. All the emotions are naked in front of the doctors and the medical staff, other family members, and friends, as all they can do is watch the parents and the immediate family try to sort out what has just happened (Ikeler, 1986). The once bright future appears shattered as the family struggles to put together the tattered pieces of life, looking for some meaning in their now disturbed lives.

Theologians and philosophers alike would call this cry of "Why, God, is this happening?" the theodicy question. It is this question that pushes philosophers, theologians, and parents with children who are disabled to ponder, reflect, and ask for some pattern, some systematic, logical response from God or a community of believers. The families hope that God can make sense of what appears senseless, without meaning (Bernstein, 1983).

In many stories of what happens in the lives of families when they first hear the news that their child has a disabling condition like mental retardation, a sensory impairment, or a physical disability, many are shocked, in grief and bitterness, full of disappointment, fury, horror, and anger. Pat Vyas, a mother with a son who has Down syndrome, wrote that as she and her husband learned to love their son, the grief and fear didn't go away. Instead, these emotions came in "great, overwhelming waves. I felt a deep need to cry it out—cry and cry until I had worked this immense sorrow up from the center of my being and out into the open. Maybe then it would go away" (Dougan, Isbell, & Vyas, 1983).

Along with this grief comes the pointed question to God, "Why is this happening to us?" For the writer Bern Ikeler, born with cerebral palsy, his birth was the dream child's death to his parents. But unlike the physical death of a child, a disabling condition is a death that happens hundreds of times during the day as the child is unable to do what "normal" children could do. Many turn to God as the "source for our amazing potential for surviving anguish and then going on to live affirmatively" (Ikeler, 1986).

The educator Helen Featherstone writes that when a child with a disabling condition is born, people feel not only like shaking a fist at life, but directly challenging God. For many religious people they feel that "If a healthy child is a perfect miracle of God, who created the imperfect child? Why would God create imperfection? Especially in a child? Especially in our child?" (Massie in Featherstone, 1981). God alone is to be blamed for this chaos in the midst of the cosmos:

> From the time Michelle was old enough to question her birth defects, we have always answered, "You were born this way. God made you." And the answer was sufficient.
>
> But recently she asked, "Why did God make me with no feet and two fingers?"
>
> "We don't always know why God does things, Michelle."
>
> "Well, I wish I was like everyone else. Anyway, God is not like this. How would He like it?" (Ouellett, 1976 in Featherstone, 1981).

The Irish writer Christy Brown, subject of the Academy Award-winning film *My Left Foot*, writes that his mother found having a child with cerebral palsy who seemed "an idiot and beyond help" before they knew his intellectual abilities, a test of faith:

"Inwardly, she prayed God would give her some proof of her faith. She knew it was one thing to believe but quite another thing to prove" (Brown, 1990).

The book *Under the Eye of the Clock* by Christopher Nolan, a young man with cerebral palsy, is the writer's autobiography that asks questions of God. Nolan asks God what is the meaning and purpose of putting his life in the body of a "spastic?" His questions are raw: "Is faith too pat a consolation in the circumstances? How could it endure such a pitiless doom? How can you forgive a God who has put you into a spastic's body?"

In one scene in the book, the fictional character Joseph, who is really Nolan, wheels himself up to a great crucifix in St. John the Baptist's Church in order to swing his arm in a grand defiant arc and then raise two fingers to the hanging Christ, which in Britain and Ireland means "fuck off." The blasphemous act is followed by the statement of absurdity: "Imagine telling God to fuck off" (Nolan, 1987).

When medical services didn't seem to be the "cure-all" for Clara Park's autistic daughter, Park writes about people who shared with her the power of prayer in helping children with disabilities. Friends said they knew of a man in Philadelphia who prayed with the parents of children with disabilities and had success. Another Catholic friend prayed for her daughter and the family, since Park claims she didn't pray. Park writes that in a "desperate case one thinks carefully before one rejects any course of action that responsible people think holds out some hope" (1982). Faith in God holds out some hope.

The naturalist Annie Dillard writes about a young girl whose body is covered with third-degree burns from a plane crash. No drugs can ease the pain of the burns that destroy the skin as the drugs simply leak into the sheets. Dillard searches for some understanding or reason for this tragedy and cites the story found in the Gospel of John where Jesus and his disciples find a blind man on the road. The disciples ask Jesus if his blindness was caused by the man's sins or the sins of the parents. Jesus, spitting on the ground, making clay that he put over the man's eyes and healed, giving him sight, said,

> *Neither this man nor his parents sinned; he was born blind so that God's works might be revealed in him. (John 9:3)*

Dillard writes that we do need reminding not of what God can do, but of what God cannot do, or will not do:

> *To catch time in its free fall and stick a nickel's worth of sense into our days. And we need reminding of what time can do, must only do; churn out enormity at random and beat it, with God's blessing, into our head: that we are created, created, sojourners in a land we did not make, a land with no meaning of itself and no meaning we can make for it alone. Who are we to demand explanations of God. There is no such thing as a freak accident. "God is at home," says Meister Eckhart, "We are in the far country." (Dillard, 1984)*

In a book of stories told by women with disabling conditions, Susan Campling, the editor of the stories, includes Barbara's narrative. Barbara, who is 31 years old and an Oxford graduate, was in a car accident when she swerved to avoid hitting a dog and broke her back. At first, she felt thankful she was alive. But this mood of gratitude collapsed as she dealt with her disabling condition; soon, anger was the new mood: "A feeling that my body was now flawed, no longer as God meant it to be—and frustration succeeded. I hadn't been *made* like this, why should I be expected to live like it?" (Campling, 1981).

The common thread of all these stories is the belief among people that maybe, hopefully, probably, God alone understands the apparent cruelty of the situation. Having a child with a disability, or being a person with a disabling condition in a society of able-bodied people that fears differences rather than accepting them, raises questions that ask the larger question of "Why?" Each parent and sibling wants to know why their baby, their brother or sister, was born with a disability. Why did God take what should have been a normal child and, instead, create a child who is deformed? Or people who have tragic accidents that make them disabled, limited in ways that the great majority of people cannot understand, ask God the theodicy question, "If God is good and powerful, then why is there evil and a sense of powerlessness in this world?" Living with a disabling condition or living with a person who has a disabling condition is really *living with* the theodicy question. One's worst fear is that they are either a creation of a lesser God, or, as a person with a disabling condition, they are "an off duty image of God" (Thielicke in Moltmann, 1985).

Not only do these questions reveal poignant, insightful thinking about the very nature of God, but these stories from life assume the following about the faith of the very questioners: Each person who asks God these questions about the meaning of life does so out of faith in God. It is the task of their faith in God to search for, seek out reasons, and gain some understanding for what appears, in all likelihood, to be a grand mistake. Feeling free to ask God questions, to sign off on God, yelling and blaming God, assumes that these people believe in God, and that God's love is able to withstand the insults and lamentations coming his way.

Yet these faithful questions of God also assume there is a religious community guided by a religious narrative where these families find meaning for their lives. Each one of the human narratives told by parents and the people with disabling conditions reflects the upbringing and nurturance of a religious context that informs the family members, including the disabled individual, that God exists, that God is the creator of all living things, and that, in a crisis such as the birth of a child with a disabling condition or an accident, it is primarily God, and God alone, who can answer the "Why, God?" question.

These questions of God assume these three characteristics of the religious narratives. First, people are their stories. In reading and listening to these stories it is essential that those who work and live with these families take in the importance of the individual narratives or stories. Second, there is the belief in the primacy of a larger, sacred story that, metaphorically speaking, is being told by God. In the Jewish and Christian faith, the sacred story is revealed, in part, in the Bible. In looking and listening to the sacred story, the family and the person with a disabling condition can find meaning, explore possible answers to life's questions, and sometimes find the hope to journey on in life with the questions of life still dangling. Third, the religious community is a community of people who essentially share the same truths as revealed and described by the larger, sacred story. The religious community gathers together to shape and nurture each other's image and perception of the very nature of God and humankind's relationship with God.

In the sections to follow, we discuss the role and function of the personal stories of families with disabilities, the place of the sacred story, and the importance of the religious community. Following this description we show briefly how these three characteristics of the religious context enable families with children who are disabled to give voice and name the anger, hurt, loneliness, surprise, hope, joy, and challenge in living with a child's disabilities.

## CHARACTERISTICS OF THE RELIGIOUS COMMUNITY'S STORY

What individuals, families, and religious communities have in common are stories. The scientist Daniel Dennett writes that while it is natural for spiders to weave webs, and beavers to build dams, so it is natural for human beings to tell stories (Dennett, 1991). Stories, the novelist Barry Lopez writes, hold everything and everyone together: "Everything is held together with stories . . . that is all that is holding us together, stories and compassion" (1981). Each person, regardless of their abilities and limitations, has his or her story that explains who they are and whose they are. Each religious community is based on and depends on a sacred story that guides the gathering into the future. Our stories reveal something about our past, that therefore help to explain our current situation, giving people perspective on life issues which, in turn, help shape future decisions and actions. It is essentially our collective stories that help to sustain the life of our religious communities, stories that are recognized in celebrations and rituals throughout the year.

This section discusses the importance of stories and how stories shape us, how we add on and shape the ongoing stories of our families, and the nature of stories in communities. Knowledge of the primary role and function of stories in the lives of families, especially religious narratives, lends a vital perspective that professionals in the health-care community could use in knowing how best to work with and care for families with children who are disabled.

## Our Personal Story

Each religious community is composed of individuals who each have their own unique, changing narrative or story. This means that each family, and each member within the family, including the child with a disability, is born into and lives within a family that is a unique story unto itself. In truth, we are all born into families as story listeners who, later in life, are storytellers. Thus a child with a disability is not just his or her disabling condition. The child is a person with a story to tell, to sing, to laugh, to dance, to paint, and to live and act out in this world.

Seeing each person as an ongoing story is a perspective shared by the physician and poet William Carlos Williams, who saw his patients, young sick children, as stories being lived out and wanting to be told and to be heard. Treating the child without listening and knowing essential parts of the life story is treating the condition and not the whole child (Coles, 1989). The medical ethicist Daniel Callahan writes that professionals in fields like medicine, psychology, and special education must understand there is a biographical vantage point we need to consider in working with a person who has a disability (Callahan in Hauerwas, 1990). In other words, when we are working with and teaching a child, for example in a special education classroom, we are not only working with an individual in that time and place. We are working with a child who is part of a larger collective past and future, whose life, for this brief moment, is intersecting and interacting with the life of the special educator's story.

Who a child with a disability is and how he or she interacts with the world is shaped and nurtured by the child's family. Knowledge of who the child is gives the caregiver some essential information about how best to engage the child's attention and imagination.

Talking about our personal stories means that each person is born into and inherits the life story of a family, whether a child is disabled or not. For example, a milestone event like birth is marked by the parents' naming the child with the family's surname. Being born as a "Smith," "Jones," or "Webb-Mitchell" means that the child is not born as an isolated individual, an atomistic bit in a patternless universe. Instead, the child is born as someone's child, into a family that has had a past, a present, and now a future.

To demonstrate the power of the family in the life of a child, consider one of the favorite activities of educators and therapists working with children and adults with disabling conditions when first meeting the disabled individual's parents. Time and again, even if the child has Down syndrome, with the common characteristic of a short stature, small round head, and certain facial characteristics, the child still resembles his or her genetic heritage. Then, watching the mannerisms of the other family members, we begin to understand that some of the "unusual mannerisms" of the child with Down syndrome are now "usual mannerisms" when understood in the context of a specific family.

## The Sacred Story

The second important part of understanding the role and function of the story is what the theologian Stephen Crites calls the sacred story (Crites in Hauerwas & Jones, 1989). For example, the Koran is a sacred story of the Islamic community. The Bible is a sacred story, shared in part by both the Jewish and the Christian religious communities. What Christians refer to as the Old Testament is the Hebrew Bible for the Jewish community, while the Christians also include what they call the New Testament. In these religious communities the sacred story may also be understood as God's story.

Crites writes that the sacred story is a fundamental narrative where our personal and collective sense of who we are and our knowledge of the world is fashioned through the dialogue of our personal ordinary stories with the sacred story. The place where this dialogue occurs is in the context of the religious community.

The sacred story serves these three functions: first, it provides for our understanding of where we are coming from and what we have been born into. Not only does our personal family have a collective past, but the family's collective story inherits a tradition, a basis of hope for the present, and faith in the future when placed within the context of the sacred story. The sacred story tells those who believe in this story whose they are.

The family's knowledge of whose they are gives the personal and family story some sense of unity, some sense of meaning within the framework of the sacred story. Thus the second function of the sacred story is that, knowing whose we are, we are empowered to discover who we are in terms of a collective identity, and what is our place in this ongoing story.

The third function of the sacred story is not only to hold one's personal and family story together, becoming a story that one may find meaning in. The story also holds together or gives some sense of unity to the collection of personal stories gathered by the individuals of a community (MacIntyre, 1984). In a sense, the sacred story reveals to people who gather together not only their collective identity, but it excites the imagination of the gathering as they begin to understand the collective goal, or *telos* for the community.

From the interaction or interplay between our personal story, the family's story, and the sacred story, we discover meaning in our life as we see ourselves as actors within the context of a sacred story (Howard, 1991). In this interaction, we find out whose we are, who we are, where we are, and where we are going in life. One's story and the sacred story is told, listened to, and lived out and continually expanding in this world, where good and evil are played out, justice and injustice is debated, and people with real differences in terms of abilities and limitations are part of the human family.

## THE PROMINENCE OF THE RELIGIOUS COMMUNITY

Where does the interaction or interplay of our personal story and the sacred story happen? Within and among the people who compose or find themselves as members of a religious community, who share in the traditions and rituals that highlight significant events within the story.

What identifies a community as "religious" is the sacred story that it is based on, which is capable of ordering its existence so that it resembles and is appropriate with the nature of the sacred story (Hauerwas, 1983). What makes a Jewish community Jewish is the community's very beliefs, which are found in the Hebrew Bible. What makes a Christian community Christian is the community's beliefs in the sacred story as told in the Old and New Testament.

What identifies a gathering as a *community* are its common characteristics. Communities are gatherings of people who share a common reliance in a common good based on a common ground (Berry, 1987). What communities share is a common reliance on the commitment and the good works of the other members of the gathering and, in the case of religious communities, on the blessings of God. Communities strive for what is good for the community: the common good. In other words, what is good for one is good for all. Communities express their reliance on one another and God, their support and commitment to the greater good of the gathering in a common place. A community cannot be separated by place. Be it in a fellowship hall, a meeting house, a home, a sanctuary, or a temple, it is in these physical places, where the physical selves meet that the community is real.

What makes the community stay together are the traditions and rituals of events in our personal and family story, the events in the community's story, and the important moments in the sacred story. Through and in the rituals of a religious community, celebrating the important dates of a gathering's collective story in the larger sacred story, the religious community is recognizing and celebrating the transcendent bond with the community's creator. In the Jewish community's celebration of Passover, they celebrate God's miracle of salvation during the Israelites' slavery in Egypt. At Christmas, the Christian community is celebrating the gift of the Christ child.

Thus a family's understanding of a child's disabling condition is shaped by the religious stories of their respective religious communities. The family with a child who is disabled is, itself, a story that has a past, lives on in the present, and has a future. Some key insights into the meaning of what may be considered a chaotic life experience may be discovered in the context of a sacred story, a story that is listened to and repeatedly told within the context of a religious community.

# A CASE IN POINT: THE RELIGIOUS CONTEXT AND PATTY'S FAMILY ▮▮▮▮▮▮▮

Dr. William Carlos Williams instructed the young psychiatrist and storyteller Robert Coles to "stay with your patients long enough, through thick and thin, and you'll learn a hell of a lot more than you ever expected" (Coles, 1990). In some sense, listening to the story of the families with children who are disabled, many families have come to see how those labeled "disabled" have taught the family and others in these religious contexts much about the meaning and value of life. The story of these children with disabilities become the young masters teaching the older disciples, their own parents, about life and God.

The following brief description about the role and function of the religious community serves as a vehicle for gaining some understanding of what may be happening in Patty and Annie's family. We break down our discussion into the three characteristics of the religious context, where the personal story interacts with the sacred story in the context of a religious community.

To begin with, Patty, as the storyteller in this family, has a personal story to share that has a beginning, a middle, and, we assume, an end point in the future. What has helped Patty struggle with being a full-time mother with five children, one who is autistic, has been the other traumatic experiences in her past. Given her personal story with a past that includes abuse, bankruptcy, and serious illnesses, Patty's ability to weather the turbulent times with Annie is buffered by her history. Her personal experiences in life that have become her story have shaped Patty to such a degree that she has learned how not to be stopped by these moments but to work through them. She has learned from her life experiences to embrace these dark moments of life rather than run away from them. In this embrace, the result has been the very richness of her character, displayed in the depth of her commitment and willingness to fight the state and the church who, legally and theologically, should provide the services that will enable Annie to live a richer, fuller life.

The sacred story has been invaluable for Patty and her family. There are three occasions in the interview with Patty that she refers back to Christian Scriptures, the New Testament of the Bible, which is the sacred story of her religious community. In each case, Patty gains some understanding about the ordinary and extraordinary moments of her life by placing these moments in the context of the sacred story. In a way, Patty has spent much time, both alone, with other family members, and with members of her congregation, searching for answers to the questions and paradoxes of her life.

For example, when asked how she would summarize her experiences with Annie, as mentioned earlier, Patty cites a passage from First Corinthians 3:13, where the apostle Paul is writing about the refinement that those who believe in Jesus will go through in their journey of faith. This refinement will, in the end, bring out the jewel, the essence of the Christian experiences as the dross in one's life will be burned away until only the gold of life appears. In a metaphorical sense, Patty believes Annie is a fire that is burning some of the excess matter, and in the process, Patty is becoming more as God wants her to be in this world.

In the last place, the very religious context or community, in this case the community Christian church that Patty and the family attend, has been of great support and nurturance for the family as they have all learned to live life with an autistic child. In its actions, the community has expressed to Patty and her family their belief that this Christian community is held together by their common reliance on the common good in this common place. It has been out of the congregation's understanding that since God called them together they need one another, need to be able to commonly rely on one another in emergencies. This is what brought these people together and provided them with the necessary care of turning out when Annie was lost in the surrounding woods. It has been the congregation's belief that, for the sake of the common good, all should be free to attend worship. They have been willing to stretch their understanding of worship and their courage to reform the rituals of the worship service that has made it possible for Annie not only to attend the church potlucks but also worship. And it is because of the common place that they share in this rural part of Washington that they have been available to be part of a transportation team, and provide help with in-home care.

## SUMMARY: IMPLICATIONS FOR ALL WHO CARE

The claim of some 20th-century philosophers like Alisdair MacIntyre and theologians like Stanley Hauerwas is that we can know more about one another, about our families, and about our religious communities through the stories or narratives that we live by in this world. MacIntyre writes that our very sense of self, the knowledge of who we are and whose we are, resides in the unity of the story or narrative that links birth to life to death, just like a story has a beginning, a middle, and an end (MacIntyre, 1984). All that goes on in our life between birth and death are episodes or chapters in the ongoing narrative of our lives.

Yet our mundane lives alone cannot give us the perspective we need in order to discover or gain some meaning and understanding of what is happening in our lives. The opportunity to discover or find some perspective on what is happening in our lives occurs when our ordinary stories of life are interactive and placed within the context of the sacred story a community of people believe in and worship. Hauerwas writes that, in the Jewish and Christian tradition, the sacred story provides a much needed perspective and serves the role and function of continually guiding the actions and shaping the attitudes of those who believe in the primacy of the story (Hauerwas, 1981).

Where does the interaction of our stories and the sacred story occur? Within the context of a religious community. The religious community is a story-formed community about a people who are on a journey of faith. The community is comprised of other people who share the experiences of their common lives, and worship together by expressing their beliefs and celebrating their story through rituals (Westerhoff, 1985).

In conclusion, there are three important lessons we can learn in considering the religious context of families with children who are disabled. First, the individual child we work with who has a disabling condition is, first and foremost, a person, a child, with his or her own biography or story. The disabled child is not his or her individualized education plan (IEP), a series of behavioral incidents, an object that one does therapy with or provides education. The child is best understood as a person who has an ongoing life story within which he or she has a disabling condition. It is only within this context, looking at a disabled child as a life story, that his or her disabling condition has meaning in one's community of meaning (Barnard in Hauerwas, 1990).

Second, this individual child's ongoing story is impacted and shaped by the larger family story. A child, whether one is disabled or not, is greatly influenced by the cultural context of his or her family (Howard, 1991). We understand the primacy of the family's influence upon the young life of a child through the work by the psychiatrist Alice Miller. She has helped many professionals and families to see that, in working with adults, knowing the story of a child's life is an important key in perceiving a person's entire life. Becoming sensitive to not only the story of the child but also the powerful story of the family, we begin to understand the power of the family in shaping the beliefs, attitudes, thoughts, feelings, and actions of the members of the family (Miller, 1986). Knowing the personal story of a child with a disability as well as the story of the family is important in working and living with children who are disabled.

Third, we need to be aware that many of the families we work with and encounter in our daily lives are often part of a greater religious community. One of the keys to knowing how to work with families who have children with disabilities is knowing the sacred story of the religious community where they are active. For the sacred story that binds the members of these religious communities together helps in large part to shape the perspective of how the members of the family understand and thus influence the hopes and goals that the family has for the current and future life of the child with a disabling condition. By becoming aware of and sensitive to the religious community and the sacred story that binds this gathering together, we gain some important insights and a better understanding of the situation of the child with a disabling condition.

For example, if the members of a religious community see disabling conditions as a sign of some sin, a result of divine retribution, then this understanding of the sacred story will many times shape the families' reaction to the disabling condition with the questions "Why us, God? What did we do wrong?" Or the religious community may understand that people with disabling conditions are part of God's kingdom as acknowledged within the sacred story, like in Patty's family. If this is the case, then the family may understand a disabling condition as another brick in the road or the path of faith. In the case of Patty's family, they may take a child like Annie more in stride.

Finally, not only do individuals, families, and religious communities have a personal story and sacred story that they live by: Individuals, families, and religious communities are their stories. These stories are being lived out each day of the week in this active, changing world. That is all that keeps us together yet keeps us apart, enabling us to see the world more fully yet restricting our vision. We are the stories we tell, the stories we listen to, and the stories we live by. Knowing another person's story, the family's story, and the sacred story lends invaluable insight in knowing not only who is the child but, more important, whose the child is as the very foundation of one's being.

# REFERENCES

Bernstein, R. (1983). *Beyond objectivism and relativism: Science, hermeneutics, and praxis*. Philadelphia: University of Pennsylvania Press.

Berry, W. (1987). *Home economics*. San Francisco: North Pointe Press.

Brown, C. (1990). *My left foot*. London: Mandarin.

Campling, S. (1981). *Images of ourselves*. New York: Routledge & Kegan Paul.

Coles, R. (1989). *The Call of Stories*. Boston: Houghton Mifflin.

Coles, R. (1990). *The spiritual life of children*. Boston: Houghton Mifflin.

Dennett, D. (1991). *Consciousness explained*. Boston: Little, Brown.

Dillard, A. (1977). *Holy the firm*. New York: Harper & Row.

Dougan, T., Isbell, L., & Vyas, P. (1983). *We have been there: Families share the joys and struggles of living with mental retardation*. Nashville: Abingdon Press.

Featherstone, H. (1981). *A difference in the family: Living with a disabled child*. New York: Penguin Press.

Hauerwas, S. (1981). *A community of character: Toward a constructive Christian social ethic*. Notre Dame: University of Notre Dame Press.

Hauerwas, S. (1986). *Suffering presence*. Notre Dame: University of Notre Dame Press.

Hauerwas, S. (1990). *Naming the silences: God, medicine, and the problem of suffering*. Grand Rapids, MI: Wm. Eerdmans Press.

Hauerwas, S., & Jones, G. L. (1989). *Why narrative? Readings in narrative theology*. Grand Rapids, MI: Wm. Eerdmans Press.

Howard, G. (1991). "Culture tales: A narrative approach to thinking, cross-cultural psychology, and psychotherapy." *American Psychologist, 46*(3), 187–197.

Ikeler, B. (1986). *Parenting your disabled child*. Philadelphia: Westminster Press.

Katz, R. (1982). Education as transformation. *Harvard Educational Review*.

MacIntyre, A. (1984). *After virtue* (2nd ed). Notre Dame: University of Notre Dame Press.

Miller, A. (1986). *Thou shalt not be aware: Society's betrayal of the child*. New York: Meridan.

Moltmann, J. (1985). *God in creation: A new theology of creation and the spirit of God*. New York: Harper & Row.

Nolan, C. (1987). *Under the eye of the clock: The life story of Christopher Nolan*. New York: St. Martin's Press.

Park, C. (1982). *The siege: The first eight years of an autistic child*. Boston: Atlantic-Little Brown.

Webb-Mitchell, B. (1992). "The prophetic voice of parents." *New Oxford Review*. To be published.

Westerhoff, J. (1985). *Living the faith community*. Minneapolis: Winston Press.

# CULTURAL CONTEXTS

There can be little doubt that much of the variability in how children and parents adapt to childhood disability is accounted for by individual differences in families. Cultural factors, however, are also likely to play a key role in defining the nature and form of a family's response. Although we often recognize the significant role of culture in family life, our consideration of unique as well as common dimensions across cultures has been less detailed.

Part III defines variability of cultural contexts with particular reference to the issue of disability in childhood. As an introductory frame, Chapter 6 describes the diversity of cultures in North America in terms of a cultural mosaic characterized by majority as well as minority cultures. Of particular importance in developing and providing appropriate supports for families is a recognition of perspectives and needs that may be unique to these minority cultures. To this end, contributors describe features that are shared as well as differ in First Nation, African-American, and Hispanic families. Extending a cross-cultural frame, chapters focusing on Europe, Africa, and Asia not only provide perspectives on family adaptation specific to a country, but also clarify national origins as sources of diversity to the cultural mosaic found in North America.

# 6

# CULTURAL SENSITIVITY IN WORKING WITH CHILDREN AND FAMILIES

*Cathleen Smith*

## INTRODUCTION

For 500 years, immigrants have poured onto the North American continent. People of dozens of cultures, races, and religions meet here and join what is called in Canada the "cultural mosaic." Historically, North American Anglo attitudes toward persons of other cultural backgrounds were blatantly ethnocentric and patronizing. Other cultures were judged against the perceived correct standards of the Anglo way of doing things. This led to both subtle and explicit racism and discrimination. Current work with children and families of many heritages is very much concerned with sensitizing society to the ways of becoming supportive to people from *all* cultures.

Professionals are now becoming more aware of the many injustices, and there is a growing appreciation of a cultural positive approach. This is a welcome shift, and is becoming imperative in places like Vancouver where half of our school-age population has English as a second language and includes a multitude of ethnic groups.

Caregivers need to be especially sensitive to people from First Nation families, whose values have been systematically undermined for generations. This is reflected in grave problems such as low self-esteem among adults who, as children, came from families who were forced to send them to residential schools. North American society is left with a shameful legacy of social problems among individuals who had the experience of having their cultural and family values systematically crushed. This was an extreme example of public policy based on an ethnocentric Anglo view of other cultures. It has happened over and over to people from many groups, for example, Japanese Canadians and Americans interned during World War II.

The year 1992 is being celebrated in Barcelona as the anniversary of a discovery made by Columbus. It is also the occasion for indigenous peoples around the world to speak out and declare, "enough is enough." Canada is presently undergoing a profound identity crisis regarding the relationship between Quebec and the rest of the country. The French-English struggle has now receded in importance as aboriginal leaders speak eloquently and demonstrate that First

Nation peoples have enduring social values which can contribute a great deal to the major issues of family, spiritual values, social justice, and environmental attitudes confronting the whole hemisphere. This is the first time in Canadian history that native Canadians have been allowed to take their rightful places at the bargaining tables of the nation.

## HISTORY

For hundreds of years, the dominant culture in North America has compelled dispossessed native people to live under its power. As native people now patiently educate, it is imperative that the bulk of the population carefully examine and figure out ways to change their attitudes, which exhibit profound ignorance and lack of sensitivity. These ideas have been acquired and entrenched over many generations of ethnocentric indoctrination and need to be systematically enlightened in ways such as those proposed by such native social service innovators as Terry Cross (1988). He describes the process of teaching cultural competence as a continuum that involves stages of understanding and putting enlightened attitudes into practice. These are ethical and moral decisions requiring deep personal commitment to listening, and relearning ways to serve and work with people.

The Columbus celebrations have been the occasion for the publication of excellent original source materials that debunk the myths perpetuated by ethnocentric historians who have convinced us that their official manipulated fictions are true. Ronald Wright's *Stolen Continents* (1991) details how official versions of historical events are in total contradiction to eyewitness accounts of dispossession and the deaths of 90 million aboriginal people. Accounts of what really happened to indigenous people need to be read to appreciate the wonder of how native values managed to survive at all.

## CURRENT PRACTICES FOR CAREGIVERS

The current shift from institutional and program-centered services to neighborhood, mainstreamed, and family-focused support requires radical changes and reevaluation of the cultural awareness, behavior, and attitudes of early childhood educators and other service providers in the helping professions. The complex challenges of providing culturally competent care for children and families of our diverse communities require more positive and authentic interpersonal relations (Hanson, 1990).

In settings that mainstream special needs children, there is another big change happening: the shift from specialized child-centered care to community-based family-centered programs (McGonigel et al., 1992). In the past, families were virtually excluded from important decision making and planning for their special needs children. For culturally diverse families with special needs children, the alienation was exacerbated by communication problems. An even more devastating issue has been professionals' lack of knowledge, respect, and appreciation of the families' values. The new inclusive models that involve participation of families from many backgrounds will need staff who are aware of ethnocentric pitfalls and issues concerning acculturation.

# DEFINITIONS AND LEVELS OF CULTURAL SENSITIVITY

First let's define the key concepts of cultural group, acculturation, and ethnocentrism. *Cultural group* refers to people with common customs, identity, language, history, religious and ethnic beliefs, and values. *Acculturation* means the extent to which people from one culture adapt to and display behaviors of the dominant group. This usually increases over generations, particularly if there is a lot of contact at schools, in the workplace, and in social activities. For first generation immigrants, and for First Nation families, acculturation may be very stressful to the relationships among grandparents, parents, and children. As we learn about specific cultural characteristics, it is important to be conscious of the possibility of stereotyping when we begin attributing certain values and characteristics to a cultural group. Every individual develops his or her own variation of beliefs and behaviors. Generalization about cultural groups can be very misleading and oversimplify complex relationships.

Ethnocentrism refers to viewing one's own group as doing things the "right" way. It means not understanding or respecting the ways of other cultural groups, and often leads to discrimination, racism, and prejudice.

There are levels of cultural awareness including recognition of *cultural diversity*, that is, noting differences and expressing interest in various ways of doing things. Another level is *cultural competence*, which means understanding the differences and having the experience to know how to help. *Cultural sensitivity* means honestly accepting the other person's beliefs and values and showing understanding and respect. If you are culturally sensitive, you genuinely feel you can try to support or help without imposing your own agenda for change.

# THE NATURE OF CULTURAL DIVERSITY

Folk sayings can reflect cultural beliefs and values and help clarify some aspects of cultural diversity (see Table 6–1). An example is the difference between belief in personal control over one's life rather than believing in fate as the determining factor. If you believe you can control things, being active and doing things early and quickly is indicated. Some cultures accept things as they are. They may, to outsiders, be onlookers and seem detached from what happens to their child. An appreciation of these kinds of differences in cultural beliefs provides a framework for understanding how families approach such central issues as parenting and family relationships. In this regard we now look at the major areas of concern for persons working with culturally diverse families who have a child with disabilities. These topics include child-rearing practices and family roles, views on disabiity, and views of medicine, sickness, and sexuality.

## Child Rearing and Family Roles

A major area in which perspectives differ is that of child rearing practices. North Americans tend to feel very certain of their methods of ensuring independence and self-sufficiency. Babies sleep by themselves from day 1. In other cultures, there may be a great deal more attention and nurturing for infants. Babies often sleep with the parents. In some cultures, young children are encouraged to be assertive and to challenge authority until a certain age. Other cultures believe in more stern methods of control. In some societies, toddlers are cared for by older siblings—a practice that some North Americans might view as neglectful. Family roles are equally important to understand. The stereotypical nuclear family is not at all familiar to many cultures, in which major roles are played by grandparents, siblings, and other extended family members. Multiple or extended families often live in one household and, in the case of a special child, collaborate in the care and nurturing which, for families, can be a great stress release. For those reasons, persons from cultures that usually rely on extended family for support may have difficulties if they are living far from family and can't find relief from the extra chores of raising a special child. In some families it may seem that a child is rejected and/or neglected, especially if the family is isolated and not able to find support. Special attention needs to be given to refugee families whose

TABLE 6-1

| ANGLO | OTHER |
| --- | --- |
| "The early bird gets the worm." | "The wise owl watches." |
| "He who hesitates is lost." | "The fool rushes in and forgets why he went there." |
| "The squeaky wheel gets the grease." | "The nail that stands up gets pounded down." |
| "God helps those who help themselves." | "It's the will of God." |

members have experienced physical and/or psychological trauma as well as dislocation.

## Views on Disability

North Americans tend to expect that people who face challenges can "pull themselves up by their bootstraps." Therefore, they advocate rigorous early intervention and early childhood programs for children with disabilities: the earlier the better, and the more the better. In a culture that views a disability as ordained by fate, the goal may be to attain harmony with nature. People in this group might either accept the child's disability without concern or believe that the child's problem is a result of misfortune or bad luck. In such cases, entry by an outsider into the family circle may not be acceptable. If the family feels it wants help, it will usually be sought from the extended family or a cultural network. Families may be trying to save face and find the North American Anglo openness and directness to be very intrusive. In general, it appears that helping professionals need to carefully develop ways to bridge cultural competence in order to establish trust. The family may have its own resources or may only want to be put in touch with agencies that can provide specific services, such as physiotherapy.

## Views on Medicine, Sickness, and Sexuality

The Anglo view on sickness as a matter for health-care professionals, drugs, surgery and equipment, and on disabilities as needing Western technological education and training, run counter to cultural values that connect body and spirit. Such families often consult both modern and traditional practitioners at once. Many cultures turn to healers, elders, herbs, massage, and traditional medicines as their natural response to a disability. Traditional healers in other cultures have years of studying and training. They incorporate the healing in a holistic, integrative, and preventative way. These important resources for the family need to be respected by authorities who are providing social services, health care, and education.

Communication and language are basic issues, and nonverbal gestures such as pointing, beckoning, and patting a child on the head may be inappropriate. In some cultures, real information will only be exchanged after many trusting interactions, so the helping professionals will need patience and should not give up trying if it seems like slow going. They may need help from a person who can interpret the culture. Or they may need to back off.

Sexuality is treated very casually in some societies, and is a completely private matter in others. We have to learn those values for the cultural groups we work with and show families we appreciate their way.

As a way of illustrating cultural diversity and the importance of sensitivity, let's review a case in terms of the broad issues just covered.

## Case Study: MARITZA AND ERIC

Maritza is a Chilean refugee, the mother of Eric, a multihandicapped 4½-year-old pleasant, nonverbal boy. He had been enrolled in a segregated treatment center program and was recently mainstreamed into his 3½-year-old brother Alfonso's day care at the community college where his mother attends. English classes. What follows is a description of some ways the day-care staff provided culturally sensitive care. Eric and his family became involved in this mainstream day care because his mother needed both school and child care. As a single parent on social assistance, she was struggling to educate herself and become self-supporting while meeting her children's needs. The early intervention she wanted was a normalized care situation for both sons.

### CULTURAL VALUES/HISPANIC-LATINO

1.  Child-Rearing Practices
    - Family is central. Mainstreaming in the college day care supported the family's desire to remain together and be supportive to a disabled member. Maritza says Eric will always live at home, and he needs to learn appropriate behavior so he can function positively in his family. Family focus was central in determining how Eric's needs were met.
    - Pride in personal appearance. Eric's handsome clothing, which his mother sewed, was appreciated by the staff. They also complimented her on how beautifully the boys were groomed. Lots of photos were taken and copies given to Maritza. The boys' personal appearance was a matter of self-esteem for the whole family.
    - Explicit physical affection. Staff encouraged the mother's frequent visits to the day care at lunch and breaks. She maintained a close relationship with both sons throughout the school year.
    - Expectations for children to be polite. Staff supported the mother in her efforts to teach both of her sons to be appreciative and well mannered. The boys were expected to be respectful to adults and children. Staff spent extra effort in teaching the children to show consideration for others.

2.  Communication and Language Issues
    - Although Maritza spoke good English, at times there needed to be a person to bridge between cultures, so a translator was provided for critical meetings to give assistance filling out forms and to interpret at hospital assessment sessions. (When using an interpreter it was important to remind the doctors and therapists to speak directly to the mother; it is easy in such situations to begin speaking to the translator and leave the mother out.)
    - Staff members were responsive to family members' tendencies for physical closeness, but taught Eric to be respectful of other chil-

dren's personal space. This involved training him to control some of his tendencies to become intrusive.

- Communication issue based on informality-formality level: staff intervened for the mother when she visited a new center upon completing her college training. This new center had a standing policy of home visits, about which the mother was not comfortable. In many cultures, visiting the home and disclosing personal or family information to strangers is not appropriate. The new center needed to establish trust before the mother would feel comfortable with a home visit.

- Another very sensitive area is that of relationships with officials or authorities. Many immigrant families have suffered both physical and psychological traumas. They may feel very unsure in situations with government or bureaucratic authority figures.

3. Roles of Individual Family Members: Dreams and Expectations
   - *Alfonso:* The younger brother was aware of his brother Eric's needs, and would comfort him if he was distressed. Generally, Alfonso played independently, keeping track of Eric visually. Having Eric mainstreamed gave Alfonso a realistic picture of his brother's disability. The mother sought guidance from the staff in explaining Eric's differences to his younger brother. She appreciated this support.

   - *Mother:* As is appropriate in her culture, Maritza took on a strong nurturing and teaching role. Day-care staff made extra efforts to collaborate with her on goals for Eric. The mother was very keen to pursue a career that might enable her to include her disabled son, specifically, horticulture. Staff encouraged her to try out preschool gardening experiences at the day-care center. This gave *her* a chance to contribute.

4. Views on Sexuality
   - Staff showed utmost respect and privacy when changing Eric. Although Eric used diapers, he was treated respectfully for his age and changed privately. In cases where children asked questions about Eric, the staff usually said, "Eric is still learning how to do that."

   - Great sensitivity was needed when discussing a sexual abuse program with Maritza because this is not a subject that is spoken about publicly in the Latino culture. This was a very successful intervention for the entire family. None of the strategies was very dramatic or difficult. Mostly, they involved the day-care staff being knowledgeable about the family's cultural values, and finding times to express support for the very caring and well-functioning family. Maritza expressed gratitude that this service enabled her to qualify for the job training to make her an independent breadwinner. The younger brother, Alfonso, thrived in the mainstream day care and learned to be alert to his brother Eric's needs but still enjoy his independence and peer friendships. Although Eric was very delayed in all areas, he seemed much more motivated in the mainstream day care than he was in the rather quiet specialized treatment center. The brothers' play skills carried over to the apartment complex where they were able to establish friendly relationships with neighboring children.

# IMPLICATIONS

As we become more knowledgeable of the general cultural values of various groups, we need to take great care not to stereotype individuals. Persons within a given community have wide-ranging particular personal values, interests, and traits, as well as varying levels of acculturation. Although cultures share common goals of nurturing their developing child, they have a wide variety of ways to express their love and caring.

Lorna Williams, a native storyteller, who is a First Nation education specialist for the Vancouver school board is among the many native people who are gently but firmly speaking to us and helping us understand that comparing cultures in oversimplified we/they terms does not really help us to become more sensitive. In fact, this method may inadvertently support notions of inherent differences that can be used to actually entrench negative feelings.

We need to try to understand how native cultures view values such as respect for nature and the environment, the connections between children and youth and their elders, the concept of time as fluid and continuous, and ways in which people living in crowded circumstances can find an interior privacy.

For example, Lorna explains very carefully that it is not accurate to think of native people as being noncompetitive. Her brother is an excellent hunter and is able to bring home large amounts of meat when others have not succeeded. He is acknowledged in their community as a superior marksman when he brings home the food they need. It is then shared with all who are hungry. So, skill levels are acknowledged but the results are shared with everyone.

Lorna acknowledged the great pain and loss by the whole generation of people who were ripped out of their cultural environments and sent to residential schools. They were actually robbed of the experience of being parented by their natural extended families.

She expresses a deep sense of sorrow that there are now no elders left who did not suffer that indignity. It is a wonder that the values survived at all. At the same time, Lorna expresses empathy for any person who suffers a childhood trauma and is very aware of the long-term effects on people when family life is disrupted.

The implications of culturally sensitive care with families are that while families see their role as nurturing and caregiving, they want to see *their* way as having as much validity as any other. We need to show we are trying to understand the values of their culture, and that we value and honor their ways. The families need to see professionals as supportive in ways to help them and their child realize their dreams.

Culturally sensitive care includes recognition of cultural diversity, understanding cultural values, and accepting and respecting the wide variety of ways families care for each other. It is recommended that all training programs and agencies include cultural competence education and policies to assure that professionals are informed, respectful, and supportive to *all* families.

## REFERENCES

Cross, T. L. (1988). Cultural competence continuum. *Focal Point, 3*(1), 1–4.

Hanson, M. J. (1990). Honouring the cultural diversities of families when gathering data. *Topics in Early Childhood Education, 10*(1), 112–131.

McGonigel, M., Kaufmann, R., & Johnson, B. (1992). *Guidelines and recommended practices for the indiviudalized family service plan* (2nd ed.). Bethesda, Maryland; Association for the Care of Children's Health.

Wright, R. (1991). *Stolen Continents*. Toronto: Viking.

# 7

# MINORITIES IN NORTH AMERICA: AFRICAN-AMERICAN FAMILIES

*Daphne D. Thomas*

## INTRODUCTION

Changing demographic patterns have emphasized the need for greater awareness and understanding of cultural and ethnic diversity in minority populations. Recognition of this need is evident in a growing literature on the nature and expression of cultural diversity and the implications of such diversity for clinical sensitivity in the provision of social, health, and educational services (Banks, 1991; Nieto, 1992; Tiedt & Tiedt, 1990). Given the fact that minority children are disproportionately represented in interventions and special educational programs for children with disabilities, appreciation and respect for cultural diversity among professionals becomes an important priority. Responses to this priority have taken the form of recommendations to understand cultural diversity (Anderson, 1991) and to develop cross-cultural competencies in working with families with Native American, African-American, Hispanic, Asian, Middle Eastern, and Pacific Islander roots (Baca & Cervantes,1989; Harry, 1992; Lee, 1989; Marfo, 1991; Lynch & Hanson, 1992). Complementing such recommendations has been research to explore the conceptualization of childhood disability across minority groups. Representation of such research are studies examining reactions of Chinese-Americans families to services with disabilities (Smith & Ryan, 1987) and comparison of feelings and adjustment to child disability in African-American, Caucasian, and Hispanic families (Mary, 1990). Although it is clear that each minority group differs in important ways from majority culture, there are also some features likely to be common to the experience of minority status. This chapter focuses on African-American families as a representative group and addresses specifically the variability found within this group.

## AFRICAN-AMERICAN FAMILIES WITH DISABLED CHILDREN

Although African-American families compose a distinct cultural group, it is a group characterized by significant diversity (Allen, 1978; Billingsley, 1968; Boyd-

Franklin, 1989; Hines & Boyd-Franklin, 1982; McAdoo, 1981). This chapter explores the nature of some of the factors contributing to the variability found within African-American families, particularly as such variability relates to the delivery of early intervention and special education services. Specifically, we focus on the variability within the African-American families in terms of socioeconomic status, family structure, and social support. These are critical dimensions along which African-American families have been found to differ from their Anglo-American counterparts but have often been overlooked in the formulation of research questions and public policy as well the development of intervention programs.

The importance of bringing a within-culture variability framework to the study of African-American families with disabled children is based on a recognition of the limitations of earlier studies, which focused on between-culture variability. Central to such limitations is the need to explore fundamental aspects of the life of African-American families. These limitations include the following:

- The number of children with disabilities served in early intervention and special education programs come disproportionately from minority families;
- Special education programs lack an appropriate conceptual framework in which to approach minority families, specifically African-American families;
- Prevailing concepts in the modal culture are inadequate to encompass variability in minorities;
- Prior conceptual approaches to minority families are rooted in an orientation of family functioning rather than an orientation based on sociocultural differences;
- African-American culture is assumed to be homogeneous.

Special education has traditionally served disproportionately high numbers of minority children (Mercer, 1973; Reschley, 1989). This overrepresentation has been attributed to a range of child-specific variables (behavior problems, motivation, respect for authority), which are often inconsistent with both the traditional classroom experience and the established norms of the school environment. The school's expectations run counter to the cultural and behavioral experiences of many minority children (Ogbu, 1985). The extent to which the educational experience for many of these children can be successful is contingent on a better understanding of linguistic and sociocultural differences (Vasquez, 1990), and the incorporation of a more culturally sensitive perspective in the school's curriculum, instruction, and assessment practices.

Some researchers have perceived children who deviate from the norms of the modal culture as deviant or deficient and thus prime candidates for special education programs. Comparative studies that have employed these perceptions have fostered a knowledge base rooted in a deficit orientation. This knowledge base has resulted in policies and practices that seek to remediate or compensate for perceived deficits. Variability within a minority group has thus often been viewed as unidimensional pathology. Alternatively, such intragroup variability could be understood as the "creative adaptations to life-course discontinuities required of minority families in their efforts to survive and thrive amid unacknowledged societal inconsistencies" (Chestang, 1972).

The need to approach intragroup variability in an alternative manner is increasingly being recognized. In a special issue of child development on minority children, McLoyd (1990a) critiques the traditional approaches that have compared minority children (specifically African American) with Anglo-American children. According to McLoyd, the problem with this comparative approach is that it

- impedes the development of a rich, meaningful, and culturally anchored knowledge base about African-American children, by documenting how African-American children do not behave, rather than how they do behave;
- fosters a tendency to ignore intragroup variability, which minimizes the individual differences among African-American children or the sources of deviation from the norms of development within that population;
- fails to delineate the discrete variables that explain intragroup differences and that are different from those variables that explain intergroup differences;
- fosters the view that African-American children are abnormal, incompetent, and not change-worthy and draws attention away from the structural forces that undermine their development;
- emphasizes the race of subjects (which is often confounded with social class) or personal characteristics associated with race, thereby promoting person-blame interpretations of social problems rather than promoting thoughtful analyses of the roles of situational and systemic factors. (p. 264)

McLoyd (1990a) encourages the study of minority children and their families in their own right, without the need for a "control" group of Anglo-American children and families in order to derive and interpret an adequate research base on minority children. This approach forms the basis for an emerging line of inquiry that seeks to examine the variability within African-American children, drawing on established as well as experimental approaches such as multigenerational influences in child rearing, ethnic identity, life course, and cultural competencies (McLoyd & Spencer, 1990; Spencer, Brookins, & Allen, 1985).

The school-family partnership identified in PL 94-142 and expanded in PL 99-457 provides a mechanism by which schools can gain a fuller understanding of the linguistic and cultural experiences of all children served, including minority children. The function of families is to transmit and shape cultural attitudes, behaviors, and patterns (Bacca-Zinn and Eitzen, 1990). Families also provide information with which we can better understand the diversity of behaviors, learning styles, and interactional patterns of children in schools today. The importance of exploring within cultural diversity is thus to challenge the myth of a monolithic American family and the accompanying expectations for uniformity in family characteristics, structure, and functioning.

## DIVERSE CHARACTERISTICS OF AFRICAN-AMERICAN FAMILIES ▬▬▬▬

Given the within-cultural variability of African-American families , what are the implications for social and educational services? In order for early intervention and school programs to provide more culturally sensitive and effective educational experiences and support services to disabled children of African Americans, the nature of these families must be more fully explored. The need for a systematic comprehensive analysis of characteristics of African-American families with particular reference to family functioning and caregiving is critical to the effective delivery of culturally sensitive services to at-risk and disabled children. How researchers have explained the variability in African-American families is due in part to how they operationalize African-American culture (Boyd-Franklin, 1989; Hines & Boyd-Franklin, 1982). Different perceptions of the cultural context have resulted in different emphases when examining these families. Some researchers have suggested that the African-American culture is merely the result of an uneven distribution of economic and political resources and power (Scanzoni, 1971). Such conclusions have led to research questions focusing on socioeconomic issues. Other researchers (Mbiti, 1969; Nobles, 1981) have suggested that remnants of African society have been intergenerationally preserved through family traditions and practices and manifest themselves in current family functioning. This framework has resulted in research questions centering on the unique African-American family lifestyle.

A more eclectic view such as that proposed by McAdoo (1981) has attempted to explain African-American culture as the combination of a number of factors. These factors include the experiences of slavery and reconstruction (McAdoo, 1978), the economic hardships that followed, and the adaptation made in response to racism and discrimination, which combined explain the uniqueness of the African-American experience. This eclectic view suggests that the uniqueness of the African-American experience can be explained as the combination of several factors.

Drawing on this eclectic perspective, it may be useful to examine the multiple factors which account for some of the variability within African-American families. Of primary interest in this regard are the factors of socioeconomic status, family structure and social support, and the role of religion and spirituality.

## Socioeconomic Status

Socioeconomic status (SES) has been one of the variables most frequently used to define the role of African-American families in society (Allen, 1985; Frazier,

1966; Gibbs, 1989; McLoyd, 1990b; Patterson, 1990; Rupersmidts & Vaden, 1990). The disproportionate number of African-Americans historically living in poverty has led to a persistent focus in the literature on lower socioeconomic status often to the neglect of African-American families of other SES levels. This approach has drawn many to conclude that little class variability exists within this ethnic group. As a result there is limited information about African-American middle-class families and the level and type of variability in style and function.

The rise of black graduates of universities and professional schools (U.S. Bureau of the Census, 1990) and the inherent upward mobility that follows indicates an accelerated growth in the numbers of African-American middle-class families. However, the African-American middle class is unique and does not necessarily conform to the definition of the Anglo-American middle class nor display all its characteristics. Middle-class status in this group is often more fragile due to limited opportunities for educational advancement and upward mobility afforded other ethnic groups. The nature of upward mobility in African-American families was explained in a study by McAdoo (1981), who examined SES status in four generations of 128 African-American families. The study was based on subjects, all of whom were born middle class, traced back to the subject's grandparents' generation. McAdoo identified four patterns of African-American middle-class families.

### Pattern I: Born Working Class, Newly Mobile

This group (62% included individuals who were born into working class families) was poor but self-sufficient. Through higher education and professional degrees (79%) they secured high-status jobs. They were the first generation of the middle class, and the majority of mothers were generally better educated than the fathers. Their grandparents, in general, had grade school education; however, 17% of them did attend some college. Both the parents and grandparents were able to secure solid working class jobs within the community.

### Pattern II: Upward Mobility in Each Generation

This group (23%) represented upward mobility across three generations. Their grandparents had been reared in lower class poor families, the parents had moved to working class, and the subjects were mobile in the middle class. Subjects in this group had the highest academic training; almost all had college or advanced degrees. Their fathers had high school educations. The mothers of this group were also better educated: 14% had college degrees and 24% had some college training.

### Pattern III: Upward Mobility in Parent's Generation

In this group (6%) the subjects were born into middle-class status and their grandparents were born into working class families. The mobility in this group occurred in their parent's generation. Only 29% of the subjects had graduate or professional degrees as compared to

63% of their fathers and 50% of their mothers. The second generation in this group was better educated than any of the other three patterns. In the paternal grandparent line one-third of each sex had high school training. In the maternal line, the males had grade school, the females finished high school, and 14% of the maternal grandmothers graduated from college.

### Pattern IV: Middle Class Over Three Generations

This group (9%) included families with three generations of middle-class status. A unique characteristic of this group was the low level of education: 33% had college and only 9% had advanced professional degrees. The parent's generation had the same education as the subjects (fathers, 42%; mothers, 25%). The grandfathers, however, were very well educated for that period, in that 60% of the paternal grandfathers and 20% of the maternal grandfathers had college and advanced degrees (McAdoo, 1981)

Boyd-Franklin (1989) suggests that the SES assigned to contemporary African-American middle-class families, characterized by higher education and upward mobility, may not necessarily be reflected in previous and future generations. She noted that the shift that has occurred in African-American middle-class status is the result of the lack of a historically stable "level of financial security that could provide a cushion for a subsequent generation that does not achieve higher education or career level. The maintenance of a middle-class lifestyle in these families is dependent upon an inherited wealth that must be sufficiently large to afford the non-achieving generation the same opportunities of education and social standing that would otherwise require that generation's own concerted efforts" (Boyd-Franklin, 1989). African-American middle-class families are particularly affected by unemployment due to the lack of a financially secure extended family to provide relief.

## Family Structure

Family structure is the second variable often considered when examining African-American families. Much of previous research has focused on the disproportionate number of families living in female-headed, single-parent households, the many stressors associated with solo parenting, and the coping mechanisms employed by these families (Reichle, 1987; Schilling, Kirkham, Snow, & Schinke, 1986). Such families are often defined as dysfunctional on the basis of marital status alone. It is clear that the single-parent family structure in itself does not constitute dysfunctionality among African Americans or any other group. In this regard, Bristol (1987) lists several methodological caveats that should be considered in determining the functionality of these families as well as providing interventions for them:

1. The absence of a father from a single parent home should not be assumed to reflect a lack of involvement. Father involvement in one-parent and two-parent families of exceptional children is a continuum, not a dichotomy.

2. Persons other than parents contribute to child rearing in single-parent families.

3. Socioeconomic differences between one-parent and two-parent families of exceptional children are important in interpreting research results and designing interventions.

4. Single-parent families are a heterogeneous group. All single-parent families are not alike. The basis for single parenthood is a key variable, that is, death of a spouse, desertion, separation or divorce, or never having been married. To treat single mothers as a distinct group and attribute any of the child's deficits to the absence of a father in the home reflects a failure to recognize the heterogeneity of single-parent families.

5. Single parenting of a child with disabilities is a coping process that changes over time. Negative assumptions about these families that are formed at the time of family dissolution may lead to a serious underestimation of the family's long-term strengths and viability. Repeated assessment of these families over time is critical to understanding the process of parenting.

6. The deficit model of single parenting as a broken home fails to advance understanding of how to serve these families. It is not useful to assume that outcomes for all single parent families will be unfavorable any more than to assume that outcomes for all two parents will be favorable (Bristol, 1987).

The rapid growth in African-American single-parent families in recent years has caused providers of special education services to examine the assumptions that have guided our interventions with these families. Many of these assumptions were derived from earlier contributions (Moynihan, 1965) which described the African-American single-parent family as a dysfunctional matriarchal structure whose major deficit was the absence of a male as the head of the household. Such assumptions need to be examined in historical as well as contextual grounds.

The African-American single parent is an alternate family structure in which family members have adapted roles and responsibilities in response to their unique circumstances and needs (Flaherty, 1983). Considerable variations exist within this group of families, which may include never married, separated, divorced, and widowed. The socioeconomic status and level of social support are critical factors to consider in determining the functionality of these families (Bristol, Reichle, & Thomas 1987; Reichle, 1987; Thomas, 1989). To view these families as dysfunctional based solely on the mother's marital status without considering the degree of success they may have attained in areas such as communication, household management, and child rearing, as well as the level of family cohesion and adaptability, does not reflect a true multisystems view of these families but rather is an unjust reliance on a unidimensional view of family functioning based solely on marital status (Bailey and Simeonsson, 1988; Minushin, 1974; Turnbull & Turnbull, 1990). These single-parent families have been often misunderstood in the assessment and intervention process, primarily because of the limitation of the instruments and intervention strategies in capturing the diverse lifestyles they represent. Epps (1985) cautions us:

> *Each group must be understood from the context of its historical experience and current circumstances. The influence of race, ethnicity, and class on socialization patterns and family style must be viewed from a variety of perspectives, free of the implicit ethnocentrism that idealized the middle class Anglo European life styles. (Epps, 1985)*

Although the single-parent family does explain some variability in African-American family structures, more focus is needed on the wider range of family constellations sometimes adopted by African-American families (Bristol, Reichle, & Thomas, 1987; Thomas, 1989). The constellation might include both individuals with biological or nonbiological ties to the immediate family.

The extended family is one such constellation. Kinship networks have a major historical significance for African-American families. The tribal experience of West Africa was grounded in a shared sense of connectedness. A commitment to the well-being of the total group, including both biological and nonbiological relationships, was paramount to survival (Nobles, 1981). Although slavery caused a great disruption in the tribal life for many transplanted Africans in America, it created its own theme of interconnectedness among these individuals. It was fostered by a system that separated biological kin, in which fathers were often separated from their families for breeding purposes often never to be reunited with their biological families. This, in turn, placed women and children in situations where they had to "make family" among people who shared a common life experience and were committed to child rearing and survival. These displaced families never lost hope of one day uniting with their lost biological kin. Referring to the current context, Hines and Boyd-Franklin (1982) conclude, "The reliance on a kin network, not necessarily drawn along 'blood lines,' remains a major mode for coping with the pressures of an oppressive society" (p. 87).

African-American families have historically maintained strong alliances with their kin networks (Billingsley, 1968; Dobson, 1988; Hale-Benson; 1982; Hill, 1972; Wilson, 1986). This has been due in part to the economic hardship many of these families have faced as well as their shared experiences associated with racism and discrimination. Extended families have traditionally provided support to adolescent and other never-married mothers, as well as nuclear families in crisis with problems such as incarceration, drug and alcohol dependency, and spousal abuse (Flaherty, 1983; Jackson, McCullough, & Gurin, 1988; Martin & Martin, 1978; Stevens, 1984). More recently, extended families have emerged as alternate structures for families whose members are pursuing higher education, saving to purchase housing, or encountering serious elder- and child-care difficulties.

There is thus considerable variation within the extended family structure among African-American families. Unlike the traditional nuclear family, extended families are not dependent on domicile, biological ties, or male presence for definition. Billingsley (1968) has provided a framework categorizing extended families into four types: (1) subfamilies; (2) families with secondary members;

(3) augmented families; (4) nonblood relatives. Subfamilies are composed of two or more individuals and may take on any of the following forms:

- *The incipient extended family*, which consists of a married couple with no children of their own who take in other relatives;
- *The simple extended family*, which consists of a married couple with their own children who take in other relatives;
- *The attenuated extended family*, which consists of a single, abandoned, legally separated, divorced, or widowed mother or father living with his or her children, who take other relatives into the household.

Families with secondary members "take in" relatives and kin (primarily children and elderly persons) to provide refuge during a family crisis or during transition in the family life cycle (Hill, 1972). They include "minor relatives" (nieces, nephews, cousins, grandchildren, and younger siblings); relatives close in age to the primary parent; elders of the primary parent (aunts, uncles); and parents of the primary family (p. 34).

Augmented extended families are an important part of the African-American kin network. In these families children are cared for in homes where they have no biological relationship to the head of the household, nor are they related by marriage, ancestry, or adoption (Hill, 1972). These children are often neighbors, church members, students, or playmates who are thought to need a better home. Extended families often "make room" for these children in their homes and augment their families to include these children.

The nonblood extended family, a structure unique to African-American families, is characterized by a series of individuals who are respected as family members but have no biological ties to the family. Stack (1974) refers to these members of the African-American extended family as "fictive kin." This network includes "play mama," "godmothers and godfathers," neighbors, and church members. These fictive kin play a major role in the family network, but they are often inappropriately labeled as friends by service providers unfamiliar with African-American extended family structures.

Shifts in nuclear family structure, social class, and mobility patterns have also influenced the extended family functioning of single parents. Many single- and two-parent black families operate independently along nuclear lines, due in part to the restricted geographic proximity to extended family members. These families may have less frequent direct contact with extended family members as a group. They rely on frequent telephone contact and reserve direct contact for the major family events and holidays, but still consider themselves very much a part of their extended families.

Some researchers have examined the role of extended family members in African-American middle-class families (Billingsley, 1968; Boyd-Franklin, 1989; McAdoo, 1981; McQueen, 1971; Stack, 1974). Their work suggests that the success of the black middle class is related to the level of support provided by the black extended family and support network that surrounds it. Some authors, however, have described extended family support as a positive outcome but not without some cost. McQueen (1971) and Stack (1974) suggest that the fragile nature of the black middle class can only be protected when members recognize they cannot pursue their goals of upward mobility and personally eradicate the poverty that oftentimes continues to surround their extended family members. McAdoo (1978) argues that this detachment does not preclude black middle-class families from maintaining close ties with extended family members and that economic stability and cultural and familiar ties are compatible.

The level of formal and informal social support available to families has also been studied. Many of these studies have examined the role social support has played in stress reduction (Goldfarb, Brotherson, Summers, & Turnbull, 1986) and in the adjustment to the presence of a handicapped child (Friedrich, 1979). Few of the studies, however, have attempted to examine the belief systems surrounding social support from varied cultural reference points. The need for a culturally sensitive construct of social support is particularly important in light of the large number of African-American families that still reside in racially segregated communities and gain a large amount of their social support from racially segregated religious and social institutions (Martin & Martin, 1985; Stack, 1974). For some, the educational and social service network may well be the only formal support system outside their communities. It is important that helping professionals seek to understand the belief systems of these families in order to develop culturally sensitive social support services (Harry, 1992).

## Religion and the Church

The spiritual belief systems of many African-American families has historically been a major source of social support (Frazier, 1963; Lincoln, 1990). During slavery, spiritual gatherings provided strength and sustenance away from the wrenching controls imposed by the institution of slavery. These gatherings were filled with hymns and spiritual songs. Traditional African customs and rituals of food, dance, preaching, and witnessing were also practiced. In these gatherings, plans for survival, mutual support, and caregiving were formulated. Strategies for escape were oftentimes conveyed through songs.

During Reconstruction the church continued to be the glue that held together displaced freed slaves as well as blacks who were free before the Civil War through the formation of mutual aid groups. One group, the Free African Society, was established in Philadelphia in 1787 to provide medical support and aid to widows with young children. Churches provided the impetus for many contemporary civil rights organizations such as the National Association for the Advancement of Colored People and the National Urban League. Many of the present-day historically black colleges and universities (HBCs) were founded by African-American churches. Combined, HBCs continue to produce the largest number of African-American college graduates in spite of the increased enrollment of African-American students in majority colleges and universities. C. Eric Lincoln (1990) suggests,

> *The Black Church has no challenger as the cultural womb of the black community. Not only did it give birth to new institutions such as schools, banks,*

*insurance companies, and low income housing, it also provided an academy and an arena for political activities, and it nurtured young talent for musical, dramatic, and artistic development.*

Religion and spirituality is a major source of social support in many African-American families. Boyd-Franklin (1989) has identified the following five key areas in which the church functions as a social support system:

1.  Churches are a major source of help for families in crisis. They function as an additional extended family and provide spiritual guidance and counsel in time of need. Their networks of clergy and elder church members (often called trustees) and benevolent aid societies support families through hard times, when more formal sources of help might appear intrusive.
2.  Through Sunday School and Bible study (Baptist Training Union), children are cared for and guided in the traditions of the faith. Parents may or may not participate in these activities but often insist on their children's participation.
3.  Traditionally, black ministers have aroused strong emotions in congregations during services. Their preaching often conveys a message of hope, the route to salvation, and the capacity for survival as a people.
4.  Black churches often function as surrogate families for many isolated and overwhelmed families. Many mothers have reported they "raised their children in the church" and see certain church members as partners in the parenting process.
5.  The church functions as a role model for many young people through its Boy Scout troops, youth groups, junior choir, and basketball teams. The leaders of these groups are often church members who are familiar with the youth's family and can establish trusting relationships over time and provide support and guidance in their development. (Boyd-Franklin, 1989).

African Americans are affiliated with many different denominations and religious organizations. They include the African Methodist Episcopal (AME), Black and American Baptist, Church of God in Christ, Seventh Day Adventist, Roman Catholic, Lutheran, Episcopal, Presbyterian, Jehovah's Witness, and the Nation of Islam. The largest numbers of African Americans are affiliated with the National Baptist Convention, USA (the umbrella organization of the Black Baptist Church) and the African Methodist Episcopal (AME) Church. Boyd-Franklin (1989) describes these church groups as:

*the sole institutions that belonged to the black community.*

*They were, and still are, one of the few places where black men and women could feel that they were respected for their own talents and abilities. A black man or woman who might have a job as a domestic worker during the week could achieve status in the church as a deacon or deaconess. The community church became one of the most important sources of leadership experience and development in the black community. (p. 81)*

Although African Americans have traditionally held strong religious beliefs, there is considerable variability in affiliations and practices. In addition to the wide range of denominations observed by African Americans, they also differ in the manner in which they observe their faith.

Brisbane and Womble (1985–86) distinguished church attendance or participation from spirituality among African-American families. They suggest that church affiliation among these families has not always entailed attendance at worship services. Many individuals assert a very strong belief in God and in fact "grew up in the church." They continue to see their faith as fundamental to their daily existence and may often refer to the protection they are provided as believers, but do not participate on a regular basis in any organized religious service (p. 250). However a spiritual bond or "personal relationship" with a "God" is often referred to when these African-American families discuss their spiritual beliefs. These beliefs are often evident during problem solving and decision making when family members may refer to the "partnership" they have established with God.

# SUMMARY

The research cited is of great utility for those designing and providing clinical and educational intervention for African-American families with disabled children. Key implications for work with these families are summarized in Table 7–1. However, policymakers and providers should be ever cognizant of the within-group variability factor when working with these families.

The myth of homogeneity in these families has often been based on SES factors. It is important to remember when designing service that the lower SES status is not universal in African-American families. Service delivery systems should reflect the multiple class levels represented by these families with particular focus directed toward the growing middle class.

Single-parent families are often embedded in extended families in which maternal grandmothers share household and child-care responsibilities. Service providers should avoid the traditional deficit view of these families and attempt to understand the structural adaptations as manifested.

Some African-American families have extensive kinship networks including biological and nonbiological members. These networks should be recognized as legitimate components of the family system, and, when indicated by the family members, included as part of the intervention plan. Additionally, the large network of self-help groups in some African-American communities may be an appropriate culturally sensitive avenue for family support. Service organizations, social clubs, and church groups have provided support for families since slavery and continue to be a major mainstay for many African-American families.

The African-American church is a major educational, economic, social, and political institution in many communities. Many families rely on the church as

TABLE 7-1

# IMPLICATIONS FOR FAMILY SUPPORT IN AFRICAN-AMERICAN FAMILIES

| KEY ISSUE | FAMILY SUPPORT IMPLICATIONS |
|---|---|
| *SES* | |
| ■ Myth of universal low SES | ■ Do not assume uniform SES status |
| ■ Growing African-American middle class | ■ Structure service options to reflect SES |
| ■ Fragile nature of middle-class status | ■ Be sensitive to the transient nature of some African-American families |
| ■ Intergenerational changes in SES | ■ Recognize the family member's economic responsibilities to prior and future generations |
| *Family Structure* | |
| ■ Single parenting as an alternate family structure | ■ Avoid the deficit view of these families |
| ■ Variable father involvement | ■ Father involvement may not take typical expression |
| ■ Centrality of maternal grandmothers | ■ Recognize and build on the strong influence of maternal grandmothers in child rearing |
| *Personal Support* | |
| ■ Fictive and nonbiological kin | ■ Incorporate nonbiological relationships when designing social support systems |
| ■ Significance of spirituality | ■ Respect the personal expression of worship, prayer, and church involvement |
| ■ Traditions of self-help | ■ Gain an understanding of African-American support organizations and enlist their support |
| *Religion and Church* | |
| ■ The church as the cultural womb | ■ Take into account that the family and community life may be embedded in the church |
| ■ Surrogate child rearing | ■ Where indicated, work through the church in providing child-care services |
| ■ Context and definitions for life | ■ Look to the church for a basic understanding of the family's definition of life |

the major transmitter of African-American culture and look to the church for a basic definition of life. This combination makes the church critical to family life and particularly child rearing. In designing interventions and educational services providers should take into account the role of religion/spirituality in family life.

Intervention and education services for children with disabilities are particularly concerned with the transactions between children and their caregivers (Sameroff & Chandler, 1975). A significant component of the caregiving unit is the cultural/ethnic context. The effective delivery of special education can only occur in an atmosphere of cultural sensitivity to the uniqueness of family constellations. There is a growing need for approaches that are sensitive to the wide range of family characteristics and structures present in culturally diverse groups as well as their caretaking patterns and practices.

# REFERENCES

Allen, W. R. (1978). Black family research in the United States: A review, assessment, and extension. *Journal of Comparative Family Studies, 10,* 167–189.

Allen, W. R., & Farley, R. (1985). The shifting social and economic tides of Black America, 1950–1980. *Annual Review of Sociology, 12,* 277–306.

Anderson, N. B. (1991). Understanding cultural diversity. *American Journal of Speech Language Pathology.*

Bacca L., & Cervnates, H. (1989). *The billingual special education interface* (2nd ed.). Columbus, Ohio: Merrill.

Bacca-Zinn, M., & Eitzen, D. (1990). *Diversity in families* (2nd ed.). New York; HarperCollins.

Bailey, D., & Simeonsson, R. (1988). *Family assessment in early intervention.* Columbus: Merrill.

Banks, J. A. (1991). Multicultural Education: For freedom's sake. *Educational Leadership, 49*(4), 32–36.

Benson, Hale, J. (1989). *The culture, roots and learning styles of black children* (2nd ed.). Baltimore: John Hopkins University Press.

Billingsley, A. (1968). *Black families in white America.* Englewood Cliffs, NJ: Prentice-Hall.

Boyd-Franklin, N. (1989). *Black families in therapy: A multisystems approach.* New York: Guilford Press.

Brisbane, F., & Womble, M. (1985–86). Treatment of black alcoholics. *Alcoholism Treatment Quarterly, 2,* 3/4.

Bristol, M. M. (1987). Methodological caveats in the assessment of single-parent families. *Journal of the Division for Early Childhood, 11,* 135–142.

Bristol, M. M., Reichle, N. C., & Thomas, D. C. (1987). Changing demographics of the American family: Implications for single-parent families of young handicapped children. *Journal of Division for Early Childhood, 12,* 56–69.

Chestang, L. W. (1972). Character development in a hostile environment. *Occasional Paper No. 3.* Chicago: University of Chicago.

Dobson, J. (1988). Conceptualization of black families. In H. McAdoo (Ed.), *Black Families* (2nd ed., pp. 77–90). Beverly Hills: Sage.

Epps, E., (1985). Foreward. In M. Spencer, G. Brookins, & W. Allen (Eds.), *Beginnings: The social and affective development of black children* (pp. xiii–xv). Hillsdale, NJ: Lawrence Erlbaum.

Flaherty, M. J. (1983). Seven caring functions of black grandmothers in adolescent mothering. *Maternal-Child Nursing Journal.* Catholic University: Washington, DC. 191–207.

Frazier, E., (1963). *The Negro church in America.* New York: Schocken.

Frazier, E. (1966). *The Negro family in the United States.* Chicago: University of Chicago Press.

Freidrich, W. (1979). Predictors of coping behaviors of mothers of handicapped children. *Journal of Consulting and Clinical Psychology, 47,* 1140–1141.

Gibbs, J. (1989). Black American adolescents. In J. Gibbs, L. Huang, & Associates (Eds.), *Children of color: Psychological interventions with minority youths.* (pp. 179–223). San Francisco: JosseyBass.

Goldfarb, L., Brotherson, M., Summers, J., & Turnbull, A. (1986). *Meeting the challenge of disability and chronic illness.* Baltimore: Brooks.

Goldnick, D., & Chinn, P. (1990). *Multicultural education in a pluralistic society.* Columbus, Ohio: Merrill.

Hale-Benson, J. (1982). *Black children, their roots, culture, and learning style.* Provo, Utah: Brigham Young University Press.

Harry, B. (1992). *Cultural diversity, families, and the special education system: Communication and empowerment.* New York: Teacher's College Press.

Helms, J. E. (Ed.). (1990). *Black and white racial identity: Theory, research, and practice.* New York: Greenwood Press.

Hill, R. (1972). *Strengths of black families.* New York: Emerson Hall.

Hines, P., & Boyd-Franklin, N. (1982). Black families. In M. McGoldrick, J. McPearce, & J. Giordano (Eds.), *Ethnicity in family therapy* (pp. 84–107). New York: Guilford.

Jackson, J. J. (1983). Contemporary relationships between black families and churches in the United States: A speculative inquiry. In W. D. Antonio & J. Aldous (Eds.), *Families and religion: Conflict and change in modern society.* (pp.). Beverly Hills: Sage.

Jackson, J., McCullough, W., & Gurin, G. (1988). Family, socialization, environment, and identity in black Americans. In H. McAdoo (Ed.), *Black families* (2nd ed., pp. 252–263). Beverly Hills: Sage.

Johnson, R. (1981). Cultural heritage and parenting in black families. In J. McAdoo, H. McAdoo, & W. E. Cross (Eds.), *Fifth conference on empirical research in black psychology.* Washington, DC: NIMH.

Lee, A. (1989). A socio-cultural framework for the assessment of Chinese children with special needs. *Topics in Language Disorders, 9*(3), 38–44.

Lincoln, C. E., & Mamiya, L. H. (1990). *The black church in the African American experience.* Durham, NC: Duke Univeristy Press.

Lynch, E. W., & Hanson, M. J. (1992). *Developing cross-cultural competence: A guide for working with young children and their families.* Baltimore: Brooks.

Marfo, K. (1991). *Early intervention in transition: Current perspectives on programs for handicapped children.* New York: Praeger.

Martin, E., & Martin, J. (1978). *The black extended family.* Chicago: University of Chicago Press.

Martin, J., & Martin, M. (1985). *The helping traditions in the black family and community.* Silver Springs, MD: The National Association of Black Social Workers.

Mary, N. L. (1990). Reactions of black, hispanic, and white mothers to having a child with handicaps. *Mental Retardation, 28*(1), 1–5.

Mbiti, J. (1969). *African religions and philosophies.* New York: Anchor Books.

McAdoo, H. (1978). Factors related to stability in upwardly mobile black families. *Journal of Marriage and the Family, 40,* 761–776.

McAdoo, H. (Ed.). (1981). *Black families.* Beverly Hills: Sage.

McAdoo, H., & McAdoo, J. (Eds.). (1985). *Black children: Social, educational, parental environments.* Beverly Hills: Sage.

McLoyd, V. (1990a). Minority children: Introduction to the special issue. *Child Development, 61,* 263–266.

McLoyd, V. (1990b). The impact of economic hardship on Black families and children: Psychological distress, parenting, and socio-emotional development. *Child Development, 61,* 311–346.

McLoyd, V., & Spencer, M. (Eds.). (1990). Special issue on minority children. *Child Development, 61,* 263–589.

McQueen, A. (1971). *Incipient social mobility among poor black urban families.* Presentation at a Howard Univeristy Research Seminar. Washington D.C. at Howard University.

Mercer, J. (1973). *Labeling the mentally retarded child.* Berkeley: University of California Press.

Minuchin, S. (1974). *Families and family therapy.* Cambridge: Harvard University Press.

Moynihan, D., (1965). *The Negro family: The case for national action.* U.S. Department of Labor: Office of Planning and Research.

Nieto, S. (1992). *Affirming diveristy: The socio-political context of multi-cultural education.* White Plains, New York: Longman Press.

Nobles, W. W. (1981). African-American family life: An instrument of culture. In H. McAdoo (Ed.), *Black families.* (pp. 77–86). Beverly Hills: Sage.

Ogbu, J. (1985). A cultural ecology of competence among inner-city blacks. In M. Spencer, G. Brookins, & W. Allen (Eds.), *Beginnings: The social and affective development of Black children* (pp. 45–66). Hillsdale, New Jersey: Lawrence Erlbaum.

Oyemade, U. J., & Rosser, P. L. (1980). Development in black children. *Advances in Behavioral Pediatrics, 1,* 153–179.

Patterson, C., Kupersmidt, J., & Vaden, N. (1990). Income level, gender, ethnicity, and household composition as predictors of children's school-based competence. *Child Development, 61,* 485–492.

Peters, M. F. (1981). Parenting in black families with young children. In H. McAdoo (Ed.), *Black families.* (pp. 211–224). Beverly Hills: Sage.

Raver, S. A. (1991). *Strategies for teaching at-risk and handicapped infants and toddlers: A transdisciplinary approach.* New York: Merrill.

Reichle, N. (1987). Stress, support, and quality of parenting: Comparison of black, never-married and previously-married mothers of handicapped children. *Unpublished dissertation.* Chapel Hill, North Carolina: The University of North Carolina at Chapel Hill.

Reschley, D. (1989). Minority over representation and special education. *Exceptional Children, 54,* 316–323.

Rosser, P. L., & Randolph, S. M. (1989). Black American infants: The Howard University normative study. In K. Nugent, B. Lester, & T. B. Brazelton (Eds.), *The cultural context of infancy.* Norwood, NJ: Ablex.

Rosser, P. L., Randolph, S. M., & Gaiter, J. L. (1985). An ethnomethodological approach to the development of black infants. In A. J. Franklin (Ed.), *The eighth conference on empirical research in black psychology.* Washington, DC: NIMH.

Sameroff, A. J., & Chandler, M. J. (1975). Reproductive risk and the continuum of caretaking casuality. In F. D. Horowitz (Ed.), *Review of child development research,* (pp. 187–244). Chicago: University of Chicago Press.

Scanzoni, J. (1971). *The Black family in modern society.* Boston: Allyn and Bacon.

Schillings, R., Kirkham, M., Snow, W., & Schinke, S. (1986). Single mothers with handicapped children: Different from their married counterparts? *Family Relations, 35,* 69–78.

Smith, M. J., & Ryan, A. S. (1987). Chinese-American families of children with developmental disabilities: An exploratory study of reactions to service providers. *Mental Retardation,* 345–350.

Spencer, M. B., Brookins, G. K., & Allen, W. R. (Eds.). (1985). *Beginnings: The social and affective development of black children.* Hillsdale, New Jersey: Erlbaun.

Stack, C. B. (1974). *All our kin: Strategies for survival in a black community.* New York: Harper & Row.

Staples, R. (1986). *The black family.* Belmont, California: Wadsworth.

Stevens, J. (1984). Black grandmother's and black adolescent mothers' knowledge about parenting. *Developmental Psychology, 20,* 1017–1025.

Thomas, D. (1989). Focus on families: Assessing young black children with handicapping conditions within the context of their families. *SANGA, 1,* 18–23.

Tiedt, P., & Tiedt, I. (1990). *Multicultural teaching: A handbook of activities, information, and resources.* Needham Heights, Massachusetts: Allyn and Bacon.

Turnbull, A., & Turnbull H. (1990). *Families, professionals and exceptionality: A special partnership.* Columbus, Ohio: Merrill.

Vasquez, J. (1990). Teaching to the distinctive traits of minority students. *The Clearing House, 63,* 299–304.

Washington, M. H. (Ed.). (1991). *Memory of kin: Stories about family by black writers.* New York: Doubleday.

Wilson, M. (1986). The black extended family: An analytical consideration. *Developmental Psychology, 44,* 246–258.

Zinn, M. B., & Eitzen, D. S. (1990). *Diversity in families.* (2nd ed.). New York: Harper-Collins.

# 8

# FAMILIES IN WESTERN CULTURES: SWEDEN AS A CASE EXAMPLE

*Agneta Hellstrom*

## INTRODUCTION

Like other modern Western industrial countries, Sweden has undergone great changes during the last century, changes that have had an important impact on the role and function of the family. Many social tasks that were previously the family's responsibility have now become the responsibility of society. The tasks and functions of the family have been reduced to a question of mainly satisfying emotional needs among its members. Families are small, and the network around the family is often small as well. In general, parents are regarded as very important for their children and their becoming competent. This attitude has had a great impact on the way we have formed our services for families, such as preschool education, child health care, habilitation, services and so on. It is strongly emphasized that each service input must be provided and formed according to parents' own conditions, with great respect for their ability to know what is best for their children and a focus on the entire family. Most parents in Sweden expect this attitude from the professionals within these services. They are also very conscious of their rights to demand these services and that they can expect high quality.

Attitudes about children and child rearing have also undergone great changes. To beat a child is forbidden by law. Sweden was one of the first nations to ratify the UN convention of children's rights. Parents are very ambitious, anxious to do right, and very afraid of not "doing all" for their children. Childhood appears to be organized and viewed as a "project," which has to be successful, an investment for the future. Especially middle-class parents have "plans" for their children. Their children take part in many organized activities at an early age. Attitudes toward children are very protective, and safety and security are viewed as very important.

Attitudes toward children with disabilities have changed a lot as a result of the normalization and integration process and in general can be said to be very tolerant and open. We view it as natural and normal to see children with different kinds of disabilities in our preschools and schools and treat them as equals.

# CHILDREN WITH SPECIAL NEEDS

The concept of *children with special needs* is not very clearly defined. We use it, however, to describe children with different kinds of disabilities such as mental retardation, physical disability (such as cerebral palsy and spina bifida), deaf and impaired hearing, blind and impaired vision, children with asthma, diabetes, and other chronic illnesses. The term *special needs* also denotes children with emotional and behavior problems, children who are abused or neglected, children with learning difficulties and attention deficit disorders, children with autism, speech/language and communication problems, and other developmental deficits. Immigrant and refugee children are also sometimes described as children with special needs.

There are different opinions about whether the number of children with special needs has increased or whether the character of problems has changed. Most of our children are very healthy physically. The large number of professionals in the field of early childhood means that the majority of our children are also in very good psychological and social condition. However, a minority may have a harder situation than previously thought. Many children are said to show more or less severe attention deficit disorders and hyperactivity. Some child psychologists also feel that children with early attachment disturbances have become a more common problem. The increasing number of refugee children, especially in certain areas, creates specific problems. Almost all children with disabilities grow up in their own families. These factors create demands for better services to the families.

Six concepts, typical for our society's basis of evaluation, can be said to have formed our early intervention services: *Justice,* that all citizens, regardless of economy and social class should be entitled to good services; *solidarity,* that we have certain responsibility for weaker groups who have special needs; *integration,* that we try to include all citizens in our regular services rather than providing segregated services for certain groups; *responsibility,* that we believe it is a responsibility for society to provide services for all its citizens; *influence,* that the individuals addressed should have the greatest possible influence on the forming of the services; and *prevention,* that regular services addressed to all members in a population have a preventive impact and reduce the need for specialized services for treatment and care.

A powerful tradition in Swedish social welfare programs is that various social supportive inputs, such as health service, medical care, and education are viewed as something to which all members of society should be entitled. The "good" society should be for everyone independent of social class and income. We try to avoid singling out certain groups or individuals. Instead, we try to give them most of the support they need within the regular service systems.

In keeping with this philosophy, support for families with children with disabilities/special needs has been augmented in recent years (Hellstrom, 1988). Children with special needs and their families are entitled to our regular family service programs, such as child-care/preschool education, parental insurance services, mother and child health care, basic child allowance, and national housing allowance for families. There are also specific programs for children with special needs and their families such as assessment, the provision of special treatment, and parental support.

The trend during recent years has been to transfer much of the responsibility for children with special needs to the regular service system, increasing the need for service coordination. Early intervention services are very family focused, with the parents' role and importance strongly emphasized. As we see it, it is important to provide support to the child from an early age and from a holistic view, including medical, psychological, social, and educational support.

The responsibility for social welfare programs is shared among three administrative levels: (1) national government (the state); (2) municipalities, which are local units and; (3) county councils, which are regional units. The national government (state) is responsible for laws, ordinances, and supervisory functions and also for direct grants aimed at achieving uniformity of accessibility. The municipalities are responsible for basic social services, primary and secondary education, culture, leisure time activities, technical services, and other basic services for their inhabitants. On the local authority level, there are 284 municipalities across the country. In Sweden there are 23 county councils and 3 large municipalities. County councils are responsible for providing health services and medical care. Maternal and child health care is regulated by this act, as are the child psychiatric services and habilitation services for disabled children. Specialized services for children with mental retardation, however, are provided on the basis of the special Mental Welfare Act. In recent years, services have become more and more decentralized on the local level.

Every effort is made to meet the needs of families of children with disabilities/special needs within the regular service systems even if there is also a supplementary need for specialized services. These services are provided as preventive and early intervention measures for children from birth to 7 years of age, when they start their compulsary schooling.

## THE PARENTAL INSURANCE SYSTEM

The parental insurance system provides different forms of financial compensation to all parents when they stay at home to care for their children. In general, this compensation corresponds to 90% of the parent's earned income. Parental insurance also includes compensation of income when one of the parents stays at home to care for a sick child, 120 days annually per child. This compensation also give parents the opportunity to visit child health services and preschool and school for two days annually. Considering disabled children's increased tendency for illness, and also their prolonged dependency on their parents, parents are entitled to stay at home when the child is ill or join the child at treatment and hospital care up to a higher age (age 16).

## PRESCHOOL EDUCATION/CHILD CARE

Along with the parental insurance system, public child care is a cornerstone in Swedish family policy (Swedish Institute, 1987). Public child care in Sweden includes care of preschoolers and children in their early years of compulsory schooling (7 to 12 years). Child care services for children under 7 take a number of different forms. Preschool denotes group activities in the day-care centers (full time) and part-time groups (3 hours per day). Day-care centers are engaged in activities for children from birth to 6 years whose parents work or study. Family day care means that the municipality employs child-care providers who work in their own homes, caring for children while the parents are at work or school. In day-care centers, infant groups (1 to 3 years) and sibling groups (3 to 6 years) are the most common arrangements, but mixed age groups (1 to 6, 9, or even 12) are also increasing.

### Children With Special Needs

Like the parental insurance system, public child care/preschool education can be regarded as a form of prevention and early intervention. Children with special needs and their families are unconditionally entitled to attend preschool and receive the special support they need. Among the disabled children, 70% now attend preschool in one form or another with the great majority attending ordinary preschool groups. An important aim of preschool placement is to provide the child with developmental stimulation through natural play and socialization with other children. Staffing ratios are relatively high by international standards, and we look on preschool placement as social support for the entire family. Parents need to meet and to feel like "ordinary" parents, and they need relief in looking after their child with special needs.

The rationale for preschool placement of a child with special needs is not defined in terms of the deficits of the parents or the child but rather on the normal and healthy needs common to all families and children. The purpose of preschool placement thus is no different from that for normal children and is based on the same principles.

## PRIMARY HEALTH CARE SERVICES FOR CHILDREN AGE BIRTH TO 7

Practically all children in Sweden are born at a hospital and examined by a pediatrician during the newborn period. Services for mothers and children before school age (age 7) is a part of the primary health-care system (Jakobsson & Kohler, 1991). One of the most important tasks for the child health services is health surveillance for all children from birth up to 7 years of age (when the school health services takes over responsibility). Health surveillance includes vaccination and regular health control of the child at certain so-called key ages. The nurse has the major responsibility for health supervision and sees mother (or father) and child about 20 times during the preschool year. Normally the child is examined by a physician 6 to 7 times during this same period.

One purpose of health surveillance is to discover disability, illness, or developmental deficits at an early age. If a delay or disability is discovered, the child is referred to a pediatric clinic or other specialist clinic for further examination and diagnosis and appropriate treatment from specialists. Increased attention along with reinforced health surveillance is being used to identify children with disabilities or other developmental problems, for example, perceptual, attentional, and communication problems. About 10% to 25% of the children need such an intensified contact because of disability, illness, and psychological or social problems.

## Parental Support and Education

During recent years we have been paying increased attention to the psychological and social aspects of the child's development and environment. Support to parents can be given either by advice to individuals or in the form of parental education groups. The latter exists mainly for parents before the child's birth and during the first year of the child's life. Parental education does not mean traditional instruction, telling parents how to educate the child, but is rather aimed at reinforcing their capacity and their own resources. Psychological and social work with families is assumed to be a key function of child health care, especially since the medical problems among children have declined.

## SERVICES FOR CHILDREN WITH SPECIAL NEEDS AND THEIR FAMILIES

Although disabled children and their families are entitled to obtain basic support and assistance within regular services, specialized care and treatment may be indicated. Enabling every child to grow up in his or her own family circle may place added burdens on the family. Demands for various types of relief services for families with disabled children have risen steeply in recent years. Relief services can take the form of attendants in the home, "backup families," and short-term residential homes.

It has become rather common for attendants to come to the home and look after the child so that the parents can take time off and devote time to other activities. In addition to home relief, municipalities offer "backup families" (support families) to whom the family can entrust their children over a weekend, for the night, or when they are going away. Small homelike settings for temporary accommodation, known as short-term homes, also provide a form of parental relief, above all for severely retarded children with secondary disabilities. Relief services must be introduced into the life of the family at an early stage so that from the very outset parents find it natural to demand and accept help without any feelings of guilt or anxiety.

## Habilitation Services

Disabled children and their families also require qualified support and treatment by medical, educational, and psychosocial specialists. The aim is a habilitation organization open to all categories of disabled children and their parents. Habilitation services are mostly organized on an outpatient basis. The organization is extensively decentralized and involves mobile therapeutic teams comprising professionals such as physiotherapists, occupational therapists, preschool teachers, speech therapists, psychologists, and social workers. These teams frequently operate on a community team basis in the child's natural surroundings, for example, home and preschool settings, to provide counseling and guidance for parents and staff. Medical specialists act as consultants to the team. In recent years, parents have become increasingly eager to take part in therapy conferences and design individual habilitation plans for the child. This reflects a distinct change of attitude in recent years, in that experts used to occupy a much more dominant position.

Extensive efforts are made to integrate stimulation and training into the child's everyday life. Toy and equipment lending services, concerned above all with parental counseling and also with the supply of suitable educational play materials, deserve special mention in this connection. One of the big challenges involving intervention services in Sweden today concerns cooperation and collaboration between habilitation and general services of preschool education, social services, child health care, and schools.

The psychiatric services for children and youth is a responsibility for the county councils and is organized as both hospital and outpatient care. The task for the psychiatric services for children and youth is to discover, cure, mitigate, and prevent emotional disturbances and psychiatric illness among children. The aim is to support and facilitate developmental potential and to help the child find and use resources and cope with traumatic experiences. Working with the entire family has become more common in recent years and parents are encouraged to be involved in the child's treatment. Through family therapy sessions, parents and other family members get the opportunity to work through their relationships and patterns of communication that may be associated with the child's problems.

Psychiatric services for children are sometimes criticized for being isolated from other services, waiting for parents to come to them. Many children in preschools and schools treating severe emotional disturbance are left without adequate psychiatric help and treatment because of inadequate cooperation with the psychiatric services. There is undoubtedly a need to change the structure and aim of these services to make them more accessible and outreaching.

# SUMMARY: MAIN ISSUES FOR THE FUTURE

The major trend in services for children with special needs and their families has been a significant shift of responsibility from specialized agencies to regular service systems. Key factors reflecting this shift have been normalization, integration, decentralization, local independence, decreased influence from central authorities, and the increased role of the consumer. Western European countries, including Sweden, are facing a new shortage of resources. We have to use our resources more efficiently, evaluate results and effects, and consider what priority decisions we have to make in the future without abandoning our ideology and value system. We also have to be more creative in forming new systems for services, including private ones.

The problems today have to do with these changes in societal structure and the economic conditions, but also with changed attitudes, like higher demands from families to influence the services provided. The challenge for the future is to create high-quality services for all families that are sensitive to their wishes and needs. Those with children with disabilities and other needs should have full access to these services. A great deal needs to be done to make intervention services more effective. Important challenges to be faced in the future include the following:

1. Increase our efforts to define distinct, concrete, and realistic aims for services for the individual child and family. Our tradition is to be more general and ideological than concrete.

2. Develop better methods and strategies to evaluate impact and effectiveness. We have no strong tradition in this regard. In situations where financial resources are limited, there are increasing demands from politicians and service authorities to evaluate the results and effects.

3. Develop specialized competence of staff in the regular services, such as preschool and child health services, as well as in habilitative, psychiatric, and social services. The need for high professional competence and specialized knowledge is not fully acknowledged.

4. Define areas of responsibility and tasks and develop better collaboration between different professional groups as well as between service agencies. The process toward normalization has created confusion concerning these issues.

5. Provide qualified and specialized care within the regular services and in the child's normal environment. This can be done if professionals increase their efforts to work through parents and caregivers as consultants, rather than directly with the child.

6. Increase efforts to involve parents: regard them as real assets, seek their opinions, and recognize their competencies in the development of services. We always must keep in mind that the parents know the child best and never exclude their input.

7.  Given a shortage of resources, discuss options and criteria for how to determine priorities. Can we, for instance, afford to keep our ideology of universal services or do we have to prioritize certain "at-risk groups"? Are some services more important than others? Are some groups more important?

8.  Promote greater coordination of services. Today responsibility is scattered across different areas, which causes significant problems for parents and children and is an obstacle for efficient, holistic care.

9.  Balance the advantages and disadvantages of decentralization and centralization in providing care. There is a risk that extreme decentralization of services can reduce the availability of highly specialized programs that require centralization.

## REFERENCES

*Child care in Sweden.* (1987). Fact sheets on Sweden. The Swedish Institute.

Hellstrom, A. (1988). *Early supportive measures in Sweden for families with disabled children aged up to 7 years.* Stockholm: Reports OECD.

Jakobsson, G., & Kohler, L. (1991). *Children's health in Sweden.* Information from the Swedish National Board of Health and Welfare.

# 9

# FAMILIES IN NON-WESTERN CULTURES: AFRICA AS A CASE EXAMPLE

*Kofi Marfo*

## INTRODUCTION

Cross-cultural considerations in the design and delivery of services for children with disabilities and their families should be of interest to practitioners and researchers in the United States for a variety of reasons, two of which are highlighted here. First, it is important for American professionals in the fields of special education and rehabilitation to understand that the impact of their work often goes significantly beyond the borders of the United States. Hayes (1991), Marfo (1991), and Sturmey (1991) illustrate this point quite succinctly in their extensive discussions of the manner in which developments in the early intervention field in the United States have influenced the delivery of services in Australia, Canada, and the United Kingdom, respectively. In a similar vein, Marigold Thorburn's work in Jamaica and other parts of the Caribbean (see Thorburn, 1986; Thorburn & Marfo, 1990) provides a vivid example of how programs in the United States have shaped the development of services for young children and their families in the developing world.

Among the more direct mechanisms by which this influence occurs, two are particularly worth noting in the context of the present discussion. Through consultations and various forms of exchange programs, professionals from the United States provide direct assistance in the design and delivery of services for children with disabilities and their families around the world. In addition, many nations around the world depend on American institutions of higher learning for the preparation of their special education and rehabilitation personnel. Given this position of significant influence, a good understanding of other cultures is necessary if American professionals and institutions of higher learning are to be optimally helpful to foreign nations that depend on them for the development of appropriate expertise.

A second and equally compelling reason why cross-cultural considerations should be of interest to professionals in the United States is that there are important lessons to be learned about how cultural variables influence services in other societies. In other words, because the United States is a multicultural society, cross-cultural knowledge and experiences on the part of American professionals can contribute significantly to the design and delivery of culturally appropriate services. Services developed around assumptions regarding child development and family functioning among white middle-class Anglo Americans can no longer be deemed universally appropriate for all Americans.

This chapter has a dual purpose. First, through a focused study of one region of the world, it seeks to delineate some of the major challenges posed by the transfer of technologies of intervention from Western industrialized societies to developing nations. The selected region is Africa, with which I have ample familiarity, and the technology of focus is that of *early intervention*, a field in which I have had specialized interest over the past decade. Second, the chapter seeks to underscore the relevance of knowledge about other cultures to the delivery of services in the United States. Specifically, it draws implications for working with immigrant families of African descent in the United States. We begin with a brief overview of some of the forces behind the globalization of early intervention services, with particular reference to the Third World.

## EARLY INTERVENTION "ARRIVES" IN THE THIRD WORLD

Of the many factors that are responsible for the emergence and increasing popularity of early intervention programs in the developing world during the 1980s, three strike me as key forces. The first has to do with the commitment of individual professionals who sought to take advantage of early intervention strategies and resources developed in North America and elsewhere to help Third World communities improve the developmental and learning potential of children with disabilities. For example, in 1975 Marigold J. Thorburn, a medical doctor, set up one of the first early intervention programs in the Third World—the Jamaican Early Stimulation Project. Designed along the lines of the Portage Model, which was developed in Wisconsin in 1969, the aims of the Jamaica project were (1) to mobilize parents of preschool children to become teachers of their own children in their own homes; (2) to improve significantly the rate of development of such children; and (3) to demonstrate that such a service can be provided at low cost by previously untrained community workers (Thorburn, 1976, 1981, 1986). Over the past 15 years, the service originally established in Jamaica has served as the hub from which programs have been established for other Caribbean nations (see Thorburn, 1986; Thorburn & Marfo, 1990).

The second factor has to do with the role of local voluntary and nongovernmental funding organizations. For example, in Zimbabwe, the Zimcare Trust, which provides services to people with mental handicaps, delivers home-based early intervention services for children as young as 6 months of age. Employing the video training procedures developed in Ireland by Roy McConkey and his associates (see McConkey, 1988), Zimcare has recently produced the Home Operated Program of Education (HOPE) package consisting of 14 short video programs focusing on how the development of children with disabilities can be enhanced with the help of family members (see McConkey, 1990). In Bangladesh, the Protibondhi Foundation has been providing early intervention services for children with disabilities under 5 years of age since 1984 (Zaman, 1986; Zaman & Munir, 1990).

The third factor has to do with the role of international organizations with specialized interest in educational and rehabilitation services worldwide. Beginning in the late 1970s, several major international organizations began to place greater emphasis on disability prevention, early detection, and early habilitation in developing countries. The World Health Organization, for example, has convened several "expert working group" meetings devoted solely to these issues over the last decade (e.g., WHO, 1980, 1981). WHO teamed up with UNICEF and UNDP to launch IMPACT, the United Nations interagency program for disability prevention; this program has focused much of its attention on the developing world. In 1981, Rehabilitation International published its *Charter for the 80s*, in which it committed itself to launching in each country a program to prevent as many impairments as possible and to ensure that the necessary preventive services reached every family. The leadership of these organizations has helped to raise awareness about the need for early developmental intervention programs. Indeed, in some of its working group reports, WHO has directly addressed such key early intervention themes as parent involvement, psychological counseling, and multidisciplinary team work (e.g., WHO, 1980).

The World Health Organization's Community-Based Rehabilitation (CBR) initiative, in particular, has become one of the strongest catalysts for the proliferation of early intervention services in developing countries. The CBR approach is not an early intervention model because it targets individuals with disabilities across the life span; however, by virtue of the fact that its central attribute of home-based service delivery through working with family members is congruent with current approaches to early intervention, the CBR movement has opened a wider door for professionals interested in developing early intervention services in the Third World. Since CBR represents the World Health Organization's key strategy for popularizing low-cost habilitation and rehabilitation services, the endorsement of the CBR approach by indigenous governments often means accessibility to international funding. Thus professionals seeking to establish early intervention services in Third World countries are much more likely to obtain funding from both internal and external sources now than was the case prior to the launching of the CBR movement.

O'Toole's work in Guyana provides an excellent example of the link between the CBR movement and the development of early intervention services in a Third World country. Using the CBR manpower training model, O'Toole implemented and evaluated a home-based early intervention program for 53 children with disabilities and their families (O'Toole, 1989a, 1989b, 1989c, 1990). Thorburn's early intervention work in the Caribbean, which began long before the launching of the CBR approach, now incorporates CBR concepts and strategies (see Thorburn & Marfo, 1990), a move that has resulted in the upward extension of intervention services beyond the early childhood years.

The promotion of early intervention outside the medical model has perhaps been undertaken more directly by UNESCO and UNICEF. Since the early 1980s, both UNICEF and UNESCO have been encouraging and supporting early intervention work in developing countries. The expertise of Western researchers and practitioners has been used to develop guidelines and resources to help stimulate early intervention services in the Third World (e.g., Kristensen, Baine, & Thorburn, 1987). In Africa, the burgeoning work of the UNESCO Sub-Regional Special Education Project for Eastern and Southern Africa (see Kisanji's introduction to Kristensen, Baine, & Thorburn, 1987) provides a good example of the increasing commitment to the promotion of early intervention through the development of early detection and assessment services.

The introduction of Western-style early intervention services into many developing countries during the course of the past decade and a half is a major landmark in the history of the early intervention movement. However, while this development may be a blessing, it also presents some complex challenges for the professionals who will be engaged in personnel preparation, program development, and service delivery. In the next section, some insights from cross-cultural research are presented to underscore these challenges.

## EARLY INTERVENTION AS APPLIED DEVELOPMENTAL PSYCHOLOGY: LESSONS FROM CROSS-CULTURAL RESEARCH

The proliferation of Western-style early intervention services in non-Western societies increases the relevance of cross-cultural developmental psychology to the early intervention field. As cross-cultural research has firmly established (see Levine, 1989, for a discussion), there are remarkable differences in the conditions of early development in Western and non-Western societies. Levine's discussion of three salient dimensions of the developmental environment—material, social, and cultural—sheds some light on the specific ways in which the conditions of early development in Western and non-Western societies vary. There are clear differences in material conditions, such as access to medical care, nutrition, playthings, and physical surroundings. There are perhaps even more marked differences in the social conditions under which Western and non-Western children develop. Compared to a Western child, a typical African child grows up with more siblings in an extended family setting where parents are not the only adults of the household. Levine (1989) underscores the significance of this difference quite succinctly:

> *The social experience of a child who is part of of a multi-age group of siblings from the early years and whose routine interaction includes grandparents and parents' siblings is quite different from the nuclear family experience of a child in a modern low-fertility industrial society. There are many possible ways of characterizing the difference*, but it is not implausible to claim that the

agrarian experience is a richer one in terms of opportunities for easily acquiring a variety of social skills useful in adulthood (my emphasis). *(p. 59)*

Even under circumstances where Western influence has significantly reduced the discrepancy in material conditions, such as is the case in the affluent homes of many transitional societies—where children play with Western toys, sleep in their own rooms, and receive Western-style medical care—indigenous cultural codes and practices interact with material conditions to produce a unique developmental environment for the non-Western child. It is for these reasons that cross-cultural psychologists have often cautioned against generalizing developmental findings on Western children to children in non-Western cultures.

For any intervention curricula and/or strategies to address the developmental needs of children and their families effectively, they must necessarily be founded on knowledge of normal and atypical child development within the given culture. From the recognition of culture-specific differences in the conditions that influence early child development, it is axiomatic that intervention procedures designed to facilitate development or remediate developmental deficits in children from one culture cannot be applied indiscriminately to children of another culture. Experience shows, however, that this cross-cultural developmental maxim has often not been upheld in applied settings. The reason for this can be found in what Levine (1989) has depicted as the *optimality assumption* underlying generalizations of developmental research. Levine describes this assumption as follows:

> *Many child development specialists implicitly assume that the conditions of infants and children among educated middle-class Anglo-Americans represent, or at least approximate, the optimal environment for individual development in humans. . . .* Deviations from this pattern are interpreted not as alternative pathways for normal child development but as conditions of deficit or deprivation, representing less adequate environments in which to raise children . . . (my emphasis) *(p. 54)*

Disregard for the fact that different cultures provide alternative pathways for normal development manifests itself in many intriguing ways, among them (1) the indiscriminate use in other cultures of Western screening and assessment tests; and (2) the blind implementation in non-Western contexts of curricular goals and targets determined on the basis of developmental milestones established for Western children. Baine (1988, 1990) has presented extensive discussions of the dangers of adopting Western tests in developing countries. In one commentary, Baine (1990) notes;

> *Many of the adopted tests are not ecologically valid. Adopted tests may assess knowledge and skills that are not required in developing countries and fail to test knowledge and skills that are required. Frequently children are tested on tasks that they have not had the opportunity to learn, while equivalent tasks that are familiar to them are not tested. (p. 200)*

As early intervention professionals transport the best practices in North America and Europe to Third World countries, they need to be aware of the assumptions that underlie the *transport model*. Parenthetically, it must be pointed out that the *optimality assumption* is as much a challenge to early interventionists operating within the United States as it is to those applying advances in American research and intervention practice in non-Western cultures.

## AFRICA AS A CASE EXAMPLE

Africa is certainly one of the regions of the world where early intervention services are least developed. Operating under the premise that Western-style early intervention services are appropriate for Africa only to the extent that they are adapted to the unique material, social, and cultural conditions of child development, we now examine the various forces that will likely influence the viability of services, determine the choice of models for working with children and their families, and shape decisions regarding personnel preparation.

We begin with a comment on the pluralistic nature of African "culture." Contrary to conventional connotations, there is no one African culture. Across the continent, many major cultures and subcultures can be identified. To complicate matters further, cultures are not necessarily defined by national borders. Contemporary national borders are not reliable demarcators of cultural boundaries, largely because of the arbitrariness with which the European colonial powers apportioned the continent among themselves. To take one example, the border between Ghana and Togo in West Africa has split one ethnic group (the Ewe) between two independent countries, with families on one side of the border having kin on the other side. Thus different cultural boundaries can be drawn depending on whether the criterion for demarcation is ethnicity, linguistic identity, historical heritage, or religious identity.

One immediate implication of the cultural diversity suggested in the preceding paragraph is that no single formula for intervention can be conceived of as an African solution or model. Also, for those who rightly and laudably advocate sensitivity to cultural diversity in the provision of services to families with African heritage in the Diaspora (e.g., within the United States), an extension of the foregoing implication is that there is no uniform African culture against which to assess the unique needs, strengths, and weaknesses of individual families targeted for intervention services.

Notwithstanding the diversity just noted, there are commonalities that sometimes make it legitimate to talk of African culture as if it were homogeneous. For example, the structure of the family in much of Africa is the extended type. Family size generally tends to be much larger than it is in Western cultures. There tends to be greater respect for older people and people in authority generally, resulting in more acquiescence to and less questioning of authority. Child rearing occurs in a much broader communalistic milieu, and beliefs about the causes of disabling/handicapping conditions tend predominantly to reflect so-called prescientific thinking. It is on these and other common attributes that an African perspective on intervention may be conceptualized. The value of such a composite perspective lies in its potential as a basis for developing a service delivery framework or model that can be modified to suit the needs and orientations of families from specific subcultures.

In the remaining sections of the chapter, we discuss a number of themes of direct relevance to the development and delivery of services in African communities. These are followed by a discussion of some key challenges with which prospective program developers must come to terms. The chapter concludes with a summary of some practical tips for interventionists who work within an African context as well as for those who serve immigrant African families in Western contexts.

## Theme 1: Understanding African Traditional Beliefs and Superstitions Regarding the Causes of Disability

As a conceptual framework for understanding the basis of African traditional belief systems and superstitions, let us consider, from a sociocultural perspective, the two fundamental modes by which human civilizations have sought to comprehend the universe and its constituents. The two modes, as revealed in the writings of numerous scholars on African religious, cultural, and medical systems (e.g., Assimeng, 1987; Marfo, 1978; Parrinder, 1969; Twumasi, 1972a, 1972b, 1974, 1975), are the *secular* and the *sacred*. The secular mode is empirical, and is employed to explain day-to-day matter-of-fact experiences and events with objectively verifiable cause-effect relationships. As Assimeng (1987) points out, knowledge in the secular mode (which we may also call *scientific knowledge*) tends to be limited in the early phases of social and cultural development within all civilizations. The sacred mode, on the other hand, deals with knowledge that cannot be readily verified through objective means. Matters pertaining to the nature of the universe—the nature of human beings, the mission of human beings on earth and beyond, and so on—fall largely in the domain of sacred knowledge. Generally, "the range of what is regarded knowable empirically and what is not knowable empirically differs from culture to culture" (Assimeng, 1987, p. 2) and varies largely as a function of the degree of technological advancement within the culture.

In transitional societies, such as Africa and other technologically less developed regions of the world, the sacred mode of knowing tends to feature dominantly. Africans have been depicted as being incurably or notoriously religious (Marfo, 1978; Mbiti, 1969; Parrinder, 1969) because of the strong inclination to place even obviously secular events and experiences in the context of the sacred. As far as disease and disability are concerned, Walker (1978) reviews research indicating that even when natural etiology is recognized, the traditional African has the tendency to consider the supernatural as the original precipitating cause. Geoffrey Parrinder, a Western authority on West African traditional religion, once commented that in Africa "students may peer through microscopes to study the apparent causes of diseases, but they may still retain their conviction that the *spiritual part* of the disease comes from a witch" (cited by Assimeng, 1987, p. 1). In a similar vein, the Ghanaian medical sociologist, P. A. Twumasi (1974), made the following observation regarding traditional beliefs about the role of physical (scientific) and supernatural factors in the causation of illness and disability:

> *Traditional cosmology has no room for a purely naturalistic notion of illness, because in traditional society . . . there is no clear-cut conceptual separation of the natural or physical from the supernatural.* (p. 97)

Indeed, in one empirical study of traditional concepts of disease and medical practice carried out in Ghana (Pappoe, 1973), 73% of the respondents expressed belief that supernatural powers have more control over people's lives than can be explained scientifically.

### Beliefs Regarding Childhood Disability and Handicap

The preceding discussion should help to place beliefs regarding childhood disability and handicap in traditional Africa in a broader epistemological perspective. Despite the advances that have taken place in medicine and science in general, childhood disability in African societies is often attributed to a wide range of supernatural forces. Children may be born with a physical or mental disability because the gods are angry with a parent for some kind of wrongdoing, such as breaking a taboo. In many traditional societies, the consequence of breaking a taboo is some form of a supernatural penalty. Disease and disability may also represent the workings of evil forces, juju and witchcraft being two of the most frequently cited evil forces in this connection.

Walker (1978) reviews a Ghanaian study on the perceived causes of mental retardation (Danquah, 1977) that sheds some light not only on the pervasiveness of the supernatural belief system but also on how little difference level of education makes in the expression of these beliefs among rural dwellers. Danquah's study was a survey of 306 parents of children with mental retardation and 800 relatives and neighbors of these parents. Educated and uneducated respondents alike attributed mental retardation to supernatural causation: God's punishment to the child or parent or the work of juju and witchcraft. There were even instances when the willful use of supernatural powers by parents to impose disability on their own children was suggested. Some nonparent respondents indicated that rich and prosperous parents of children with severe handicaps attained their wealth by supernaturally giving up the joy and ease of bringing up an able-bodied child in exchange for material prosperity.

Danquah found that a sizable percentage of even well-educated parents living in cities seemed to take personal responsibility for giving birth to a child with a handicap; these parents ascribed the outcome of their pregnancy to their possible nonobservance of some kind of a taboo in the past. Many of the fathers, regardless of educational background, blamed their child's disability on their wives. To parents, relatives, and neighbors alike, mental retardation was significantly associated with supernatural forces.

**Implications for Intervention** The general tendency to view childhood disability as a "predestined" outcome or act of fate, over which humans have little control, has profound implications not only for routine parenting of children with handicaps but also for intervention services. Whether a child's disability is seen as a punishment to the parents for displeasing the gods or as punishment to the child for "sins" in an earlier life (see Werner, 1987), one immediate implication of this belief system is the accompanying belief that to attempt to alter or correct the child's condition is to go against the wishes of the gods (Werner, 1987).

In areas where traditional cultural modes of thinking are still very strong, the belief in disability as a predestined phenomenon will likely manifest itself in several ways that could constitute a major challenge to the delivery of intervention services. First, parents and/or relatives may not actively seek help, even when they are aware that some kind of help exists. Second, some families will likely resist enrollment in an intervention program openly. A third possible manifestation is reluctant participation, which would likely result in a less than faithful adherence to suggested intervention routines. All three possibilities underscore the importance of viewing basic education about the physical factors in developmental disabilities as a key component of the intervention service.

# Theme 2: The Influence of Religion

Family dynamics in Africa are strongly influenced by religion. Before the arrival of the two main foreign religions (Christianity and Islam), the nature of African family life was determined in part by traditional religious belief systems and practices. For example, many ethnic groups manifested remarkably strong relationships between living family and kin members and the ancestors. Elaborate ceremonies were performed at various stages of the family life cycle to enable "the living to maintain ties with non-living family and kin members" (Kayongo-Male & Onyango, 1984, p. 45). The following observation by Kayongo-Male and Onyango provides one illustration of the influence of traditional religion on African family life:

> When misfortunes arose, people often atoned to the dead, assuming that the dead were angered by some behavior of their living relatives. Maintenance of family shrines was believed to be crucial to the peaceful continuance of family life. Ancestors were believed to discipline family members if these members neglected familial duties or acted disrespectfully to older members. (p. 45)

With the arrival of Christianity and Islam, some traditional beliefs and practices have been lost, while others have been blended with practices and beliefs from the newer religions. Of the three dominant religions, however, perhaps Islam imposes the most profound practices with direct implications for family-professional relationships in the context of Western-style early intervention services. For example, Islamic law requires that women be secluded from male non-family members. While some aspects of Islamic law have received statutory recognition in some countries (e.g., Kenya and Uganda), the extent to which specific rules, such as seclusion, have been enforced varies from one subculture to another. For example, while Hausa women from the ruling class were completely secluded at some point, Baganda Muslim women were seldom veiled and secluded (Kayongo-Male & Onyago, 1984).

Comparisons of families from the various religious traditions on a variety of social, economic, and health indicators reveal one finding that is particularly pertinent to the present discussion. A study of fertility and infant mortality among the Yoruba of western Nigeria found higher rates of child mortality among Muslims than among other religious groups (Sembajwe, 1981). Kayongo-Male and Onyango (1984, p. 46) suggest that "the higher rates of mortality are probably due to less access to modern medical knowledge, reluctance to use medical services, or *seclusion rules which make it difficult for women to attend public clinics*" (emphasis mine). It appears that the limitations Islamic laws place on women could be a potential source of problems for early intervention program delivery. To take an example from outside Africa, Jaffer and Jaffer (1990) found, in their analysis of factors associated with the failure of a WHO-sponsored community-based rehabilitation program in Pakistan, that the use of unmarried female local supervisors with home-visiting responsibilities was problematic because of the conservative nature of the Islamic society. Thus religious beliefs and practices have profound implications even for the choice of early intervention personnel.

## Theme 3: African Family/Community Dynamics and the Socialization of Children

Among the well-known distinguishing attributes of African societies are the extended family system, the relatively large size of the component nuclear families, and the overall communal atmosphere in towns and villages. One of the striking attributes of the socialization of an African child is that it involves a larger number of socialization agents. Biological parents are not the sole or even the main socializers of children. Socialization is a shared process among parents, siblings, grandparents, peers, and adults in the community at large.

### The Communal Dimension
Traditionally, the entire community plays a role in every child's socialization. Any adult member of an African community, whether he or she is a relative, a neighbor, a friend, or an ordinary member of the community, may correct or punish a child's misbehavior. Such punishment may even be corporal, and parental permission may not be necessary. Similarly, any adult could instruct a child to perform a whole host of duties/tasks without first consulting with the child's parents. In return, every adult had a responsibility to protect every child in the community. Adults would generally come to the aid of any child in trouble.

### The Unique Role of Siblings and Grandparents
In many African societies, older siblings and grandparents play a key role in the upbringing of young children. In

some cases older siblings and grandparents are closer to or more responsible for the day-to-day interactions between the child and the person world than the child's actual parents. The multiple agents of socialization to which the African child is exposed play a functional role in the psychological well-being of parents. Parenting is rendered significantly less stressful, even for parents who may not be economically well off.

From the point of view of designing and implementing early intervention, the communal spirit and the extended family structures of African communities constitute unique assets. Program planners must come up with innovative ways of taking advantage of these attributes instead of imposing the Western-style parent-as-teacher model.

# KEY CHALLENGES TO PROVIDING INTERVENTION SERVICES IN AFRICA

Any attempt to develop appropriate and effective intervention services in an African community must take into consideration not only the many assets that communal life and the extended family structure offer but also the broad variety of obstacles that need to be overcome. Beside more obvious obstacles, such as (1) the absence of culturally appropriate screening and assessment instruments; and (2) the limited developmental knowledge base on which to build appropriate curricula, there are other key challenges. Three of these are discussed briefly in the following section.

## Childhood Disability, Socioeconomic Well-Being of the Family, and Early Intervention

Where poverty is extreme and the standard and quality of life are generally low, a child's disability assumes little importance in the broader scheme of family needs and priorities. Werner (1987) underscores this point with an anecdote involving an Asian family. When a family in Sri Lanka was asked about their disabled child, the mother responded that her biggest worry was the leak in the roof of their hut. Werner reports that as part of the basic steps in helping this family to participate in providing help for the child, the village rehabilitation workers organized neighbors to help build a new roof. This episode, which typifies the dilemma of competing needs and priorities around the developing world, underscores the importance of an integrated approach to the delivery of human services.

## Defining Handicap and Developmental Delay in the African Context

The early interventionist working in an African context has to contend with the challenges of defining handicap or developmental delay within the indigenous sociocultural context. The way these two concepts are defined has profound implications for ascertaining the size of the population to be served as well as for determining the kinds of developmental tasks and milestones to be targeted in the intervention process. If Western standards are applied, very large numbers of children will likely be identified as being handicapped or developmentally delayed. Yet it is a fact of life in many African communities that many children who would be labeled mildly retarded or handicapped in Western society are very actively integrated into the daily activities of family and community. In the words of Hughes (1986);

> . . . *in the rural communities of developing countries varying degrees of mental retardation can easily pass unnoticed because the degree of retardation does not inconvenience the "affected" person and does not ostracize him from the social group. In other words, the person may not be regarded as "mentally retarded" or unusual in some way in the rural community because even though his level of intellectual functioning (assuming one is able to meaure it) is well below average, in his own rural community, he is "socially competent" and "socially acceptable." He merges imperceptibly with his fellow villagers and is able to cope quite well with the incidents and hazards that might arise in his lifetime.* (p. 166)

As these children reach school age, however, their handicaps become more obvious as they are unable to cope with the demands of Western-style schooling. This scenario constitutes a major dilemma for the interventionist who decides to tie intervention targets to local norms of competence. While respecting indigenous standards for defining normality, the interventionist also has to worry about children's future life in school, where the standards of average performance and competence continue to be based on Western norms. Indeed, the interventionist has to worry about the child's ultimate place in a society that is increasingly becoming industrialized and Westernized.

## The Challenges of Parent Training and Family Involvement

There are good intuitive reasons for involving parents in the intervention process. However, the extent to which such involvement is possible or necessary depends on a host of other factors. A guide I find useful is that whenever possible, it is important that the provision of a service does not become a mechanism for disrupting natural family processes and routines. For very young children, especially, this principle alone will suggest the necessity of a programming choice in which parents or other family members are involved. However, in many African communities, the nature of economic and subsistence activity may be such that only minimal levels of parental involvement make practical sense. In particular, the traditional, didactic *parent-as-teacher* model, which has been the dominant approach in Portage-type programs in the United States and the United Kingdom, does not appear to be a realistic model for the rural communities of Africa. As O'Toole (1989c) points out, active parent involvement in early intervention programs in the West is premised on an "orderly, controlled lifestyle" (p. 334), which is uncharacteristic of family life in rural Africa.

It appears instructive to propose a two-tiered system of intervention. Under this system, the more intensive programming for the child will be undertaken by trained teams of community workers in center-type settings. Not only will this approach be time-efficient but also it will provide parents much needed respite to carry on with the hectic routines of rural life. In addition, however, parents and other family members—particularly mothers, older siblings, and grandparents—will be offered information sessions at conveniently arranged times. Such sessions, to be designed after the adult and mass education programs that government departments of rural development and social welfare used to run in the 1950s and 1960s, will aim at providing parents and significant others with as much information as they need to (1) understand the nature of the child's disability; (2) know what kinds of facilities and services are available for children with special needs; (3) gain a realistic understanding of the child's weaknesses and potential strengths; (4) come to terms with the additional responsibilities that the care of a child with a disability entails; and (5) learn ways of interacting more effectively with the child and involving him or her in the day-to-day routines of the family and community.

## WORKING WITH FAMILIES IN AFRICA AND THE DIASPORA: SOME PRACTICAL TIPS FOR THE INTERVENTIONIST

It is important that those who develop or deliver programs understand some of the cultural dynamics that may influence the response of families to the "culture" of intervention. This response can significantly impact the relationship between the intervenor and the primary adult(s) with whom the intervenor is in direct contact. To extend the relevance of this discussion for professionals in the United States and other Western countries, our discussion includes tips for those who work with African immigrant families in Western contexts.

### Utilization of Services

In an earlier section, we noted how traditional cultural beliefs about the causation of disability can prevent active seeking of intervention services or produce reluctant participation when services are offered. Added to this cultural dimension is the commonsense consideration that resistance or indifference may stem purely from the fact that because the service is alien to the culture, its utilization requires significant adjustment, especially on the part of less educated, rural people.

The interventionist who works with an African immigrant family in the United States may also notice some degree of reluctance or resistance to accessing the service, despite the fact that immigrants are generally better educated and hold values and belief systems that place them in the transition between traditional African culture and Western culture. Among the factors that may explain this difficulty, the following two are particularly worth noting. First, African immigrants will generally not be used to universal provision of developmental and psychoeducational intervention services in their respective countries of origin. Indeed, they may even have the tendency to view the service as a privilege rather than as a right. Second, failure to access services, especially among the relatively less educated, may reflect a desire to avoid appearing a social burden, especially in light of their knowledge that American immigration policy conspicuously seeks to exclude immigrants who do not demonstrate the potential to become independent.

## Difficulty in Disagreeing Openly with Professional Authority

It is not polite in some subcultures to disagree openly, especially with an older person or an authority figure. The early intervention worker is a professional authority figure. A parent may not agree with prescribed or suggested routines but may not show such disagreement because of this cultural orientation. A parent may therefore attempt to implement suggestions only to please the professional or may not implement them at all.

## Tendency Not to Request Clarification During Explanation or Communication of Vital Information

The extent to which this attribute is typical of most Africans is not clear. However, some Africans may have a greater tendency to receive information noninteractively, even when the information being conveyed may not be fully understood. Several potential explanations may be offered for this; first, this situation may represent the long-term effect of a culture of child rearing in which children are tacitly taught to listen more than to talk back. Second, this may be a reflection of the general tendency on the part of most humans to avoid appearing stupid. As new immigrants enter a new culture they find themselves increasingly ignorant and incompetent by the standards of the new culture. The greater the discrepancy between the levels of economic and social development in the two cultures, the more intense this feeling of ignorance and incompetence is likely to be. With increased exposure to situations that induce feelings of ignorance and incompetence, the new immigrant is forced to build psychological defense mechanisms to protect his or her psychological well-being. Feigning comprehension may be one such tool. According to this "theory," new African immigrants are much more likely to avoid appearing stupid than you would expect in the general population because of the huge sociocultural gap between the African and the American contexts. Regardless of how this attribute is explained, it has the potential to reduce the role of the parent in program decision making.

## Nonassertiveness

African parents may not be up front in voicing their concerns in a variety of situations. For example, if for some reason a parent finds it inconvenient for a scheduled visit to take place as planned, he or she will often find it difficult to call to cancel or reschedule. Africans are more than likely to inconvenience themselves than to appear to be offending or inconveniencing the other person. When the other person is an authority figure, such as a professional with acknowledged expertise, the likelihood of not being candid about concerns is even greater.

## The Importance of Informal Social Support

We noted earlier how the participation of siblings and grandparents in the child-rearing process serves as a potential buffer against parenting stress. Relocation to industrialized environments like the United States often means the loss of this important socialization and social support base. Used to a broad social support base, in the form of the extended family and the community at large (neighbors), the African parent discovers that bringing up a child with a handicap in the United States is more traumatic. Both the birth and rearing of the child and the loss of the social support base are psychologically stressful, largely because for many African parents the first place to turn for help is not some professional agency but relatives or friends. For some African families, then, helping to build social supports may be even more important than providing skills for working with the child. It is interesting to note that this problem is as true of families relocating to large commercial and industrial centers of their native country as it is of those migrating to the Western world.

## CONCLUDING COMMENTS

It is important that the issues raised here be understood in the broader context of both cross- and intracultural variability. As we implied at the outset, while the universals of a culture enable us to understand and address the needs of its members more appropriately, they can also become the basis for naive overgeneralizations. The extent to which any client manifests any of the attributes presented in the preceding section, for example, will depend as much on cultural beliefs as it does on other factors like individual personality, educational background, socioeconomic status, or even experience with other cultures. It is important, then, that the suggestions offered here be seen purely as rough guides rather than as golden rules of thumb for relating to African families professionally.

The discussion in this chapter has obviously been limited to issues pertaining to the delivery of services to African children and their families in two different contexts: the indigenous African context and the context of the Diaspora (e.g., immigrant African families in the United States). Nevertheless, the underlying theme has implications beyond working with families of African descent. American society is a mosaic of cultural and ethnic groups, each with unique attributes that profoundly influence child development and family functioning. For this reason, the design of services for all families of children with disabilities must take into account not only those common attributes of the mosaic which give it the quality of an entity but also those unique differences that are the very essence of the mosaic.

# REFERENCES

Assimeng, J. M. (1987). Sacred and secular classification among Ghanaian children. In P. A. Twumasi (Ed.), *Problems and aspirations of Ghanaian children: Implications for policy and action.* (pp. 1–37). Accra: Ghana National Commission on Children.

Baine, D. (1988). *Handicapped children in developing countries: Assessment, curriculum and instruction.* Edmonton, Canada: Vector.

Baine, D. (1990). Guide to the development, evaluation, and/or adoption and modification of tests for early childhood education in developing countries. In M. J. Thorburn & K. Marfo (Eds.), *Practical approaches to childhood disability in developing countries: Insights from experience and research* (pp. 199–225). St. John's, Canada: Project SER-EDEC, Memorial University of Newfoundland.

Danquah, S. A. (1977, July). *A preliminary survey of beliefs about severely and moderately retarded children in Ghana.* Paper presented at the meeting of the First International Training Workshop in the Education and Rehabilitation of the Disabled, Cape Coast, Ghana.

Hayes, A. (1991). *The changing face of early intervention in Australia: Following foreign fads and fashions?* In K. Marfo (Ed.), *Early intervention in transition: Current perspectives on programs for handicapped children* (pp. 271–298). New York: Praeger.

Hughes, J. M. (1986). Educational services for the mentally retarded in developing countries. In K. Marfo, S. Walker, & B. Charles (Eds.), *Childhood disability in developing countries: Issues in habilitation and special education* (pp. 165–176). New York: Praeger.

Jaffer, R., & Jaffer, R. (1990). The WHO CBR approach—program or ideology: Some lessons from the CBR experience in Punjab, Pakistan. In M. J. Thorburn & K. Marfo (Eds.), *Practical approaches to childhood disability in developing countries: Insights from experience and research* (pp. 277–292). St. John's, Canada: Project SEREDEC, Memorial University of Newfoundland.

Kayongo-Male, D., & Onyango, P. (1984). *The sociology of the African family.* London: Longman.

Kristensen, K., Baine, D., & Thorburn, M. J. (1987). *Educational assessment and early intervention for handicapped children in developing countries* (Digest 22). Paris: Unesco-Unicef Cooperative Program.

Levine, R. A. (1989). Cultural environments in child development. In W. Damon (Ed.), *Child development today and tomorrow* (pp. 52–68). San Francisco: Jossey-Bass.

Marfo, K. (1978). *Essays in West African traditional religion for G.C.E. 'A' Level and Higher School Certificate aspirants.* Cape Coast: University of Cape Coast Press.

Marfo, K. (1991). The evolution and current status of early intervention in Canada. In K. Marfo (Ed.), *Early intervention in transition: Current perspectives on programs for handicapped children* (pp. 235–270). New York: Praeger.

Mbiti, J. S. (1969). *African religions and philosophy.* London: Heinemann.

McConkey, R. (1988). Educating parents: An approach based on video. In K. Marfo (Ed.), *Parent-child interaction and developmental disabilities: Theory, research, and intervention* (pp. 253–272). New York: Praeger.

McConkey, R. (1990). Using video as a teaching aid. In M. J. Thorburn & K. Marfo (Eds.), *Practical approaches to childhood disability in developing countries: Insights from experience and research* (pp. 115–132). St. John's, Canada: Project SEREDEC, Memorial University of Newfoundland.

O'Toole, B. (1989a). The relevance of parental involvement programs in developing countries. *Child: Care, Health, and Development, 15,* 329–342.

O'Toole, B. (1989b). One response to the challenge of special education in the 1990s. *International Journal of Special Education, 4*(2), 129–140.

O'Toole, B. (1989c). The relevance of parental involvement program with pre-school disabled children in Guyana. *International Journal of Special Education, 4*(2), 173–181.

O'Toole, B. (1990). Community-based rehabilitation: The Guyana evaluation project. In M. J. Thorburn & K. Marfo (Eds.), *Practical approaches to childhood disability in developing countries: Insights from experience and research* (pp. 293–316). St. John's, Canada: Project SEREDEC, Memorial University of Newfoundland.

Pappoe, V. L. (1973). *Ghanaian traditional concepts of disease and medical practices.* Unpublished doctoral dissertation, Yale University Medical School, New Haven, CT.

Parrinder, G. (1969). *West African religion.* London: Epworth Press.

Sembajwe, I.S. (1981). *Fertility and infant mortality amongst the Yoruba in Western Nigeria.* Canberra: Australian National University.

Sturmey, P. (1991). Early intervention in the United Kingdom: Historical perspectives and current provision. In K. Marfo (Ed.), *Early intervention in transition: Current perspectives on programs for handicapped children* (pp. 299–324). New York: Praeger.

Thorburn, M. J. (1976). Working with handicapped children in Jamaica. *Family Involvement, 8,* 11–19.

Thorburn, M. J. (1981). In Jamaica, community aides for disabled preschool children. *Assignment Children, 53/53,* 117–134.

Thorburn, M. J. (1986). Early intervention for disabled children in the Caribbean. In K. Marfo, S. Walker, & B. Charles (Eds.), *Childhood disability in developing countries: Issues in habilitation and special education* (pp. 63–72). New York: Praeger.

Thorburn, M. J., & Marfo, K. (1990). *Practical approaches to childhood disability in developing countries: Insights from experience and research.* St. John's, Canada: Project SEREDEC, Memorial University of Newfoundland.

Twumasi, P. A. (1972a). Ashanti traditional medicine and its relation to present day psychiatry. *Transition, 41,* 50–62.

Twumasi, P. A. (1972b). Medicine: Traditional and modern. *Insight and Opinion, 7*(1), 20–50.

Twumasi, P. A. (1974). The sick role cycle: A sociological perspective on the problems of adapting modern scientific medicine to the needs of a developing country. *Universitas, 3*(3), 96–102.

Twumasi, P. A. (1975). *Medical systems in Ghana: A study in medical sociology.* Accra: Ghana Publishing Corporation.

WHO (1980). *Early detection of handicap in children: Report on a WHO working group* (EURO Reports and Studies No. 30). Copenhagen: World Health Organization Regional Office for Europe.

WHO (1981). *Disability prevention and rehabilitation: Report of the WHO expert committee on disability prevention and rehabilitation* (Technical Report Series No. 668). Geneva: World Health Organization.

Walker, S. (1978). *The disabled in Ghana: Status and change in information and attitude.* Unpublished doctoral dissertation, Teachers College, Columbia University, New York.

Werner, D. (1987). *Disabled village children: A guide for community health workers, rehabilitation workers, and families.* Palo Alto, CA: Hesperian Foundation.

Zaman, S. S. (1986). The care and education of disabled children in Bangladesh. In K. Marfo, S. Walker, & B. Charles (Eds.), *Childhood disability in developing countries: Issues in habilitation and special education* (pp. 177–190). New York: Praeger.

Zaman, S. S., & Munir, S. Z. (1990). Meeting the challenge of implementing services for handicapped children in Bangladesh. In M. J. Thorburn & K. Marfo (Eds.), *Practical approaches to childhood disability in developing countries: Insights from experience and research* (pp. 133–145). St. John's, Canada: Project SEREDEC, Memorial University of Newfoundland.

# 10

# FAMILIES IN ASIAN CULTURES: TAIWAN AS A CASE EXAMPLE

*Tien-Miau Wang*

## INTRODUCTION

This chapter uses the Chinese family and society in Taiwan, the Republic of China, to discuss the effect of cultural beliefs and family practices on the delivery of early intervention services for young disabled children and their families. The traditional features of patri-blood memberships, authoritarianism, sentimentality, and intrafamily relationships in the Chinese family are first identified as the salient factors affecting family practices. With the birth of a disabled child, the family usually experiences much stress and frustration particularly because of the traditionally high expectations on offspring and limited public support, resources, and services in the Chinese society of Taiwan. However, the close intrafamily relationship plays an important role in assisting parents to adapt to this stressful situation. Professionals who deliver intervention services to the Chinese family with disabled children need to be sensitive not only to unique needs of individual families but also to the variety of family practices resulting from the social and economic changes in contemporary Chinese society. The family benefits the most from intervention services that are delivered in a relationship of trust between parents and professionals. Involving the extended family and facilitating the family's sense of power are also strongly recommended.

In the Western world, the last decade has seen a dramatic increase in research, programs, and policies designed specifically to examine and improve the family's ability to cope with the presence of a disabled child (Bricker, 1987; Gallagher & Vietze, 1986; Turnbull & Turnbull, 1986). Researchers have strongly emphasized parent involvement and family dimensions in delivering early intervention. The importance of individualized family support and service has also been highlighted (Bailey et al., 1986; Bronfenbrenner, 1974; Dunst, Trivette, & Deal, 1988; Rosenberg, Robinson, & Beckman, 1984). A comprehensive assessment of family strengths and needs is suggested as a necessary prerequisite for individualized services in which unique characteristics of each family with young handicapped children are identified (Bailey & Simeonsson, 1988).

Professionals who work with the family from a different cultural background must recognize both cultural beliefs and family practices in addition to individual family needs related to the birth of a disabled child (Rogow, 1985). Before planning or delivering services to such a family, professionals need to ask questions such as, How are family roles defined in a specific culture? What family beliefs and attitudes related to child rearing can be expected? How do these family beliefs and attitudes affect child-rearing practices in the family?

The cultural issue also appears critical when professionals in less advanced countries try to adopt the theoretical and empirical models developed by those in other countries. For example, in Asia, professionals have continually adopted service models developed in North America and Europe or even actively involved professionals from the United Kingdom or the United States in planning intervention programs or directly working with young disabled children. However, adopting service models developed in the Western world with only minimal modifications based on the family structure, family roles, and child-rearing practices in Eastern society could be problematic. Differences are believed to be greater between the East and the West because of their respective political, social, and economic systems. A similar problem could arise even for countries or districts in Asia when models from other countries or districts in the same region are adopted because they may differ from each other in their societal or structural characteristics and their patterns of response to Western-style industrialization (Lin, 1988).

In addition to the cultural difference in family beliefs and child-rearing practices, social resources and services may complicate the difficulties the family confronts with the birth of a disabled child. For example, in most of the Asian countries, a very high proportion of the families with very young disabled children receive limited or no services and resources (Wang, 1991b). As a consequence, parents may experience significant stress associated with trying to meet their child's needs. Disabled youngsters are thus also likely to be exposed to less stimulating learning environments (Nihira, Webster, Tomiyasu, & Oshio, 1988; Wang, 1989; Wu, Wang, & Retish, 1987).

In this chapter, we first discuss family features in the Chinese culture and their relation to child-rearing beliefs and practices. Second, we review the current status of special education and early intervention services in Taiwan. Third, we identify the problems or special needs of the Chinese family with a young handicapped child. Finally, we make recommendations for the planning and delivery of educational and intervention programs in this particular cultural context. A broader review of family beliefs and practices in other countries in Asia is also included in order to highlight some important areas of concern for the discussion.

## FEATURES AND PRACTICES OF THE CHINESE FAMILY

The word *family* in Chinese can have the double meaning of "the smallest and fundamental unit" in the sociological sense and "the kin group and kinship system" in a broader sense (Wong, 1981). The kinship system is made up of families and a large group of households belonging to the same ancestry and linked together by common blood relationships. Traditionally, *family* refers to the broader definition, a small but "deep or core structure" in Chinese society

(Lin, 1988). The features of the traditional Chinese family dictate the practice and behavior of the society and the Chinese.

In addition to the important role the family plays in society, *centrality* appears in some unique features of the traditional Chinese family. These features include (1) the emphasis on the succession of the patrilineal line; (2) authority-oriented but cohesive functioning as a small social unit around elders; (3) the supremacy of sentiment over instrumentality; and (4) a clear distinction between insiders (familial members) and outsiders (nonfamily members) (Hsu, 1953; Lee, 1988; Lin, 1988). The traditional features of the Chinese family and their effects on family practices are summarized in Figure 10-1.

## Patri-Blood Memberships

The traditional Chinese family functions primarily to ensure the continuity of the patrilineal line. Having a male offspring with patrilineal blood, therefore, is traditionally preferred. The blood line not only defines who can inherit in the transfer of authority and property, but also sets the boundary of potential memberships within the family (Lin, 1988). As a consequence, while male offspring are required to remain loyal and committed to the family lineage, female offspring have less power or lower status in the family. Thus caretaking is the primary responsibility of the mother or the female offspring. On the other hand, in order to transfer authority and property to the next generation properly, parents frequently have high expectations about the child's performance, particularly academically.

## Authoritarianism

Traditionally, the family operates under the elders in the patrilineal line or the father in the family in which a sense of "proper order" is required for every family member. Propriety based on filial piety, which is defined as "respect and formality to elders and authority figures," has enabled generations to live together with a minimum of overt conflicts. In the family, parents and elders represent authority figures and children are expected to behave in the right order and the right way. This formality toward authority also extends to relationships with outside authority figures. Full agreement with or dependence on professionals such as teachers is considered to be necessary even when a dispute occurs between professionals and parents.

## Sentimentality

Human sentiment has its place among members of the Chinese family and beyond the immediate family. Family members automatically assume and share the responsibilities and obligations of an emotional relationship in everyday life or particularly when one or more members in the family experience a crisis. These

FIGURE 10–1

*The Traditional Features of the Chinese Family and Their Effects on Family Practices.*

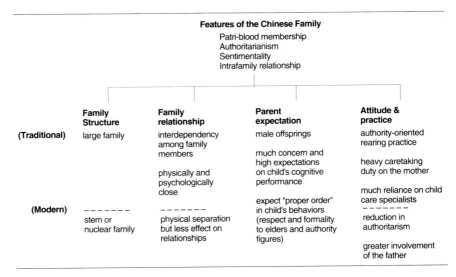

**Features of the Chinese Family**
Patri-blood membership
Authoritarianism
Sentimentality
Intrafamily relationship

| | Family Structure | Family relationship | Parent expectation | Attitude & practice |
|---|---|---|---|---|
| **(Traditional)** | large family | interdependency among family members | male offsprings | authority-oriented rearing practice |
| | | physically and psychologically close | much concern and high expectations on child's cognitive performance | heavy caretaking duty on the mother |
| | | | expect "proper order" in child's behaviors | much reliance on child care specialists |
| **(Modern)** | - - - - - - stem or nuclear family | - - - - - - physical separation but less effect on relationships | (respect and formality to elders and authority figures) | - - - - - - reduction in authoritarism |
| | | | | greater involvement of the father |

exchanges may include lending objects or money, helping to find jobs, tutoring, or even daily child care. For example, with a handicapped child in a family, all family members, including those in the extended family or close friends of the family, share caretaking work and offer help with no reservations or expectations of reimbursement.

## Intrafamily Relationships

The self and the family are intimately related in Chinese culture, but the demarcation between members of the family and the rest of the community, the country, or even the world is rigid. That is, the inside circle is tightly knit, based on a strong sense of sentiment, exchange, mutual indebtedness, and filial piety. A person's concerns are mostly for self and family. When a crisis arises, family members, including those in the extended family, frequently turn to each other instead of outsiders for comfort and help. A cross-cultural study reported that most of the Chinese families of handicapped children in Taiwan seek comfort within the family or among relatives, whereas American families look for help from outside resources (Wu, Wang, & Retish, 1987).

The traditional features of patri-blood memberships, authoritarism, sentimentality, and intrafamily relationships in the Chinese family are also reported in the family of other Asian cultures. For example, the tightness of family organization has also been found in the Japanese family. But in the Japanese family the socialization process aims toward interdependence among members; in the American family the process aims toward the individual's independence (Yamamoto & Kubota, 1983). In the *Handbook of Asian Child Development and Child Rearing Practices*, Suvannathat, Bhanthumnavin, Bhuapirom, and Keats (1985) reported that Asian children were brought up to have lifelong obligations to their family. The elder was also reported to play an authority role in Muslim and Hindu cultures.

Today, the revolutionary changes in political and social systems and the strong influences of Western ideas and practices have brought changes in the structure and characteristics of the traditional Chinese family as well as the family in other Asian countries. For example, even in the stem family, which includes parents, unmarried children, and married sons with their spouses and children, and is the primary family structure in Taiwan, there are increasing numbers of nuclear families replacing the large family units made up of several generations. In addition, like any other industrialized society, relocation for employment has made younger generations physically separate from their extended family. However, physical separation seems to have little effect on the traditional intrafamily relationship and, on the contrary, results in a higher degree of dependence on extended family members, such as grandparents, who have more time to take care of young children in the family (Lee, 1988; Wong, 1981).

Regarding the changes in family practices, Ho and Kang (1984) confirm a high degree of intergenerational commonality. Attitudes toward filial piety in Chinese patterns of child training is one of these examples. However, they also reported some important changes in child-rearing attitudes and practices. These changes include an orientation toward a reduction in authoritarianism and a greater involvement of the father in the early years of the child. Relations between both parents and their children are reported to be warm and affectionate in general. Younger fathers are becoming more involved in child care, reflecting a weakening of the traditional parent-role differentiation between the father and the mother.

Even so, a few problems of parenting practice still can be identified in the modern Chinese family (Suvannathat et al., 1985). Parents frequently fail to recognize individual differences among children by placing too much value on children's academic performance or demonstrating parent-centeredness in child care. A lack of balance between the roles of the mother and the father and an overestimation of the child care specialist's importance because of the respect given to authority figures are also problems in parenting.

# EARLY INTERVENTION AND EDUCATIONAL PROGRAMS FOR DISABLED CHILDREN IN TAIWAN

Next we discuss the current practices in special education for school-aged disabled children and efforts to provide early intervention services for the under-6 age group in Taiwan.

In Taiwan, *handicapped* refers to individuals who have at least one or more of the following handicap(s): mental retardation, visual impairments, auditory impairments, speech and language disorders, physical handicaps, chronic illness, emotional or behavioral disorders, learning disabilities, multiple handicaps, and other unclassified handicaps (Department of Education of the Republic of China, 1984). Under the Special Education Law, all eligible school-aged disabled children from 6 to 14 have equal rights like those of their nonhandicapped peers to receive free education and are entitled to special education services in regular classes, resource rooms, special classes, or special schools in the public school system. For school-aged children with severe, profound, or multiple disabling conditions, a referral for home training provided by itinerant teachers or for special education services in public or private institutions or training centers in the social welfare system may be considered.

No data on the prevalence of exceptional children have been reported at the present time. However, the data in Table 10-1 illustrate the different forms of educational placements, numbers of facilities, and numbers of school-aged handicapped children served in special education programs during the school year of 1990 (Wu & Chang, 1990). Until now, special education programs were provided in the form of resource rooms, special classes, special schools, and institutions or centers for those school-aged children who are mentally retarded, hearing impaired, physically disabled, visually impaired, learning disabled, and multiply handicapped. Even though there are trends to integrate disabled children in the regular schools, a higher proportion of disabled children served continue to be placed in institutions, centers, or in special schools. Fortunately, all the eligible school-aged disabled children, regardless of their placements, may be provided with related services of special devices (e.g., hearing aids, wheelchairs), transportation, and financial assistance once such needs are identified.

Special education services have also been expanded to disabled children at the senior high and the preschool levels. High school special education primarily is provided in special schools for mentally, visually, and auditorily disabled students who need vocational training. Any disabled student who completes the compulsory education and passes the entrance exam given to their nonhandicapped peers can continue advanced studies with special assistance.

Special education services in public schools are extended downward into the 3- or 4-to-5 age group. However, because all children under 6 are not entitled to free education, young children with special needs receive limited intervention services provided by the government. Fortunately, increasing attention and efforts have been given to early intervention for young handicapped children, especially with programs for children with mental handicaps, physical handicaps, and sensory impairments. This is evident from the increasing number of early intervention programs for handicapped children from birth to 6 years old from 1982 to 1990 (Wu & Chang, 1982, 1990). In 1982, there were only eight programs providing special classes in regular schools, special schools, and private and public institutions, but in 1990 there were 58 programs offering early intervention. Among the early intervention programs, approximately 17% of them (10 out of 58) provide services for handicapped children whose ages range from birth to 3 (see Table 10-2).

At the present time, children who receive intervention are mainly 3- to 6-year-olds. For most of the families with handicapped youngsters in Taiwan, medical care rather than educational or therapeutic consultation may be the only service they receive from professionals during the child's first three years. Children with visible and more severe disabilities receive earlier identification and medical or rehabilitation services, which are provided only on request by their parents. Limited preschool special education programs, especially integrated ones, are provided to those whose handicapping conditions are less severe. Most of the intervention programs are provided by private interest groups; only a very small number of them are government supported.

Limited services and traditional Chinese beliefs and child-rearing practices have made adjustment very difficult for the family with a disabled child. Furthermore, educational, medical, and social programs each providing separate services may compound the problems of the child and the family. Medical treatments or rehabilitations are provided without educational services. Educational pro-

FORMS OF EDUCATIONAL PLACEMENTS, NUMBER OF FACILITIES, AND NUMBER OF SCHOOL-AGED HANDICAPPED STUDENTS SERVED DURING THE SCHOOL YEAR OF 1990

TABLE 10-1

| | Mentally Retarded | Hearing Impaired | Physically Impaired | Visually Impaired | Learning Disabled | Multiple Disabilities | Total |
|---|---|---|---|---|---|---|---|
| **Special Schools** | | | | | | | |
| Number of classes | 88 | 184 | 26 | 75 | — | — | 373 |
| Number of students | 809 | 1948 | 272 | 729 | — | — | 3758 |
| **Special Classes** | | | | | | | |
| *Elementary Schools:* | | | | | | | |
| Number of schools | 314 | 33 | 3 | — | — | — | 386 |
| Number of classes | 601 | 89 | 8 | — | — | — | 742 |
| Number of students | 5798 | 749 | 82 | — | — | — | 7453 |
| *Secondary Schools:* | | | | | | | |
| Number of schools | 95 | 12 | 4 | — | — | — | 129 |
| Number of classes | 265 | 26 | 6 | — | — | — | 342 |
| Number of students | 2612 | 248 | 58 | — | — | — | 4047 |
| **Resource Rooms** | | | | | | | |
| *Elementary Schools:* | | | | | | | |
| Number of schools | — | — | — | — | 36 | — | 36 |
| Number of classes | — | — | — | — | 44 | — | 44 |
| Number of students | — | — | — | — | 824 | — | 824 |
| *Secondary Schools:* | | | | | | | |
| Number of schools | — | — | — | — | 18 | — | 18 |
| Number of classes | — | — | — | — | 45 | — | 45 |
| Number of students | — | — | — | — | 1129 | — | 1129 |
| **Institutions or Centers** | | | | | | | |
| Number of centers | 56 | 3 | 10 | 5 | — | 9 | 83 |
| Number of students | 3785 | 96 | 508 | 308 | — | 1072 | 5769 |

grams may likewise be offered without adequate attention to social or medical needs. Separate delivery systems operate under separate administrative structures in education, health, and social welfare (see Figure 10-2), which makes an integrated approach almost impossible.

In the educational system, only the preschool education for children aged 4 to 6 is under the administration of the Department of Education, at the different levels of the government. In the Taiwan area, there are a few preschool special education programs for 4- to 6-year-old disabled children in special schools, or special classes in the college-affiliated centers and regular elementary schools. Most of the mildly disabled children are unidentified and placed in regular kindergartens or nursery schools without special assistance. Children with disabilities who need medical care may receive medical or therapeutic services under the administration of the Health Department. These services of neurological or developmental diagnosis, medical treatment, follow-up service, or rehabilitation therapy, for example, are only provided when the cases are referred from medical professionals or are requested by parents of disabled or high-risk children. Children with disabilities under 4 or those with more severe conditions receive social welfare services under the auspices of the Department of Social Welfare. These children may be placed in public or private institutions or training centers. Social workers in the social welfare system mostly provide services to disabled children from poor families or those who have been abused.

The fragmentation of service delivery is confusing to families of handicapped children and forces them to use a lot of energy to "struggle" with professionals from different disciplines at different places and even at different times.

# PROBLEMS AND SPECIAL NEEDS OF THE FAMILY WITH DISABLED YOUNGSTERS

In Taiwan, limited resources and services delivered in a fragmented system compounded with traditional beliefs and child-rearing practices have caused parents

TABLE 10-2

## EARLY INTERVENTION PROGRAMS FOR HANDICAPPED CHILDREN AGED BIRTH TO 6 IN TAIWAN, 1982–1990

|  | Special Schools | Special Classes | Centers/ Institutions | Total |
|---|---|---|---|---|
| 1982 | 3(1) | 2(260) | 3(60) | 8(330) |
| 1985 | 3(10) | 2(369) | 31(62) | 36(441) |
| 1987 | 3(10) | 2(430) | 44(72) | 49(512) |
| 1990* | 3(11) | 8(515) | 47(83) | 58(609) |

*In 1990, there were only approximately 17% of the programs (10 out of 58) providing services for handicapped children ages birth to 3.

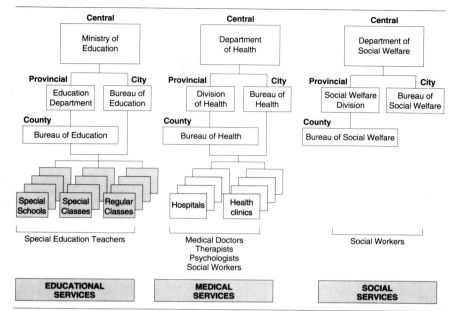

FIGURE 10–2

*The Array of Services from the Health, Education, and Social Welfare Systems in Taiwan, the Republic of China*

a great deal of frustration and stress following the birth of their disabled child. One study showed that Chinese families in Taiwan experienced more stress than American families of disabled children (Wu, Wang, & Retish, 1987). It was found that parents of Down syndrome toddlers ages 12 to 31 months perceived less satisfaction with their parenting, and had more difficulty in reading their child's cues than parents of nonhandicapped children (Wang, 1990).

The mother typically bears most of the stress because of the traditional care-giving role she plays in the Chinese family (Wang, 1985). High expectations and overemphasis on the child's academic performance may result in stereotypical negative attitudes toward the handicapped held by most of the Chinese public and also by the parents themselves.

To cope with the stress and difficult caretaking, parents, especially mothers, of the disabled child usually find inside support first before turning to someone outside the family because of the inside-outside distinction. Family members, including those in the extended family or very close friends of the family, are frequently the ones that offer "inside" support and comfort to the family with a young handicapped child. They usually offer their support and help by sharing the frustration and daily caretaking work for the disabled child or other sibling(s). Parents who experience less support from family members or close friends have more difficulty in adjusting and handling the heavy caretaking demands.

Traditional beliefs of fate in Chinese culture may prevent the family from seeking outside help, either from a family having similar problems or professionals who try to offer their assistance. "Disability" or "handicap" in the child with obvious handicaps may be accepted by the parents as manifestations of their own wrongful deeds, either in this life or in the previous cycle of incarnation. The sense of responsibility and guilt may compel them to shelter disabled children as much as possible from any interferences from the outside world. It is considered to be a serious "loss of face" or "failure of the family" when the disabled offspring is discovered by an outsider or stranger. Therefore, parents may be hesitant to share their difficulties with "the outsider," for example, a family with similar problems. A clinical observation in a mother-child interaction study gave evidence that approximately half of the mothers of children with disabilities had no idea about the existence of parent support groups in the city they lived, and only about 28% of the mothers actively participated in the monthly meetings of the parent group (Wang, 1989). Similar findings have been found in the Nihira et al. (1988) cross-cultural study, which reported that Japanese parents much less openly discussed the child's disability and had less idea of the child's health and educational needs than American parents.

Defensive reactions may also occur when professionals are trying to offer help to the family with a disabled child, especially in mild cases (Wang, 1985). However, professional assistance has been reported to be helpful for the parents who come from lower socioeconomic status families or whose child is more severely disabled (Wang, 1985). For those who receive help from professionals, parents may tend to rely more on professionals for training of their disabled child. Although there is no direct evidence provided in the Chinese literature, Japanese parents have been found to rely more on teachers and specialists than American parents (Nihira et al., 1988). As a result, parents may expend less effort to train the child than they should. The reliance of external control from professionals may be interpreted as a reaction of formality to authority figures.

It should be noted here that due to the revolutionary changes in the structure and characteristics of the Chinese family, a variety of family needs may be expected. Although traditional beliefs and family practices are still kept mostly within most of the family, there are families, particularly nuclear families in the urban area, that have adopted Western values and lifestyles. They experience stress and adjust to the crisis of having a disabled child differently than more traditional families. The family may lose support from the extended family because of physical separation. However, in the nuclear family, the father seems to share more and more caregiving work with the mother in the early years of their disabled child's life. In addition, these parents are more likely to seek outside support and resources when they are needed.

## SUMMARY: CHALLENGES AND RECOMMENDATIONS FOR INTERVENTION AND EDUCATIONAL PROGRAMS IN TAIWAN

Special education has been offered in Taiwan for over 30 years to mentally handicapped children and for about 50 years to hearing impaired, visually impaired, and physically impaired children. In the past 10 years, we have observed rapid changes, especially in the quantity of services. Administrators and professionals in Taiwan are facing not only the challenge of solving the problems in special education practices for school-aged children with disabilities, but also the challenge of expanding special education to the below-6 age group and those after the 9 years of free education. In terms of special education practices, shortages and lack of training of special education personnel have been identified as the main problems (Wang, 1991a). Special attention has been paid to the following issues for improvement: (1) train special education teachers in preservice programs rather than 20-credit inservice training programs; (2) expand services to those school-aged disabled children who have more severe *conditions;* (3) develop guidelines for practice; (4) eliminate the possibility of personal bias in assessing disabled children for placement purposes; (5) recruit certified personnel, develop teaching materials, and encourage special teachers to participate in training workshops to deliver services through area resource centers for ensuring quality of teaching; (6) initiate and develop early intervention programs for young children and their families (Wang, 1991a).

There are a number of challenges professionals and policymakers need to confront in planning for intervention as well as educational services. We may learn lessons from our own special education practices during the last 10 or 20 years or from the challenges confronted by professionals in other countries such as the United States. In order to ensure high quality service to young disabled or at-risk children and their families, our first challenge is to provide comprehensive and multidisciplinary early intervention in *a united or integrated administration and service delivery system* in which professionals from all related disciplines work and support each other. Only if an integrated service delivery model is adopted, can effective family support be delivered to decrease the possibility of family "shopping" for pieces of services.

Even though comprehensive and integrated early intervention services could be delivered to families with special needs youngsters, the quality of services is ultimately dependent on those who provide the service. Personnel quality has been identified as one of the prime indicators relating to the effectiveness of early intervention programs (Bryant & Graham, 1990). In Taiwan, no direct evidence of such an indicator can be found, but the lesson we have learned from our practices in special education may remind us of the importance of personnel competence. Rapid increases in the number of special education programs without better planning for special education teacher training have made the quality of teaching decline (Wang, 1991a). Tsai and Chuang (1985) also reported that the personnel issue would be the first concern if handicapped children were integrated in the preschool settings. Therefore, the second challenge for our policymakers is to have better planning for *personnel preparation* before the immense expansion of early intervention programs. To meet such a challenge, personnel training program designers may need to incorporate a number of areas into the curriculum to prepare personnel not only to work with young children with special needs and their families, but also to work with other professionals.

In planning intervention and educational services for handicapped children and their families, special educators face the third challenge: to design *programs that match our traditions and values.* Professionals in Taiwan have adopted the theoretical and empirical models that have been developed by professionals from North America and Japan where most of our professionals have received training. However, when theoretical and empirical models are adopted from other areas, professionals need to be sensitive to differences in traditions and the political, social, and economic situations unique to a particular culture.

Developed countries recently have emphasized providing broader family supports to address a variety of family needs for families of handicapped youngsters (Dunst, 1985; Kysela & Marfo, 1983). Therefore, the fourth challenge for professionals is to provide *family supports based on the particular needs* of the family within the Taiwanese cultural and societal context. However, to provide family support or to involve the parents, professionals in Taiwan may need to consider two critical issues suggested in Western literature. First, an intervention program should seek to create goals for family outcomes in their own right (Bristol, Reichle, & Thomas, 1987). Second, specific teaching functions that parents usually are asked to play can, in many instances, prevent the development of appropriate parent-child relationships (Affleck, McGrade, McQueeney, & Allen, 1982). Hence the primary role of professionals is to provide important information, counseling, or training and, at the same time, to foster natural, supportive, and reciprocal relationships between parents and the handicapped child.

In addition, although it is important to give support to families with the disabled youngster in early intervention programs, how to involve them is a more critical issue. Early intervention services for disabled children and their families are recommended to be delivered in the following ways:

1. *Establish a trusting parent-professional relationship before further family supports are delivered.* Professionals need to be sensitive to psychological adjustments or possible defensive reactions in parents of disabled youngsters. Family attitudes and conventions must be accepted and not openly challenged because critical attitudes are easily perceived and produce frustration on both sides. Unless the advice is provided by someone who is trusted, even well-informed advice may be ignored. It should be also noted that the trust may take a longer time to achieve and must be nurtured by consistency and continuity of the professional involved.

2. *Expect a variety of family structures and practices resulting from the changing situations in contemporary Chinese society.* In some cases, attitudes and practices oriented toward reduced authoritarianism and a greater involvement of the family, particularly the father, in child rearing have replaced traditional family practices. However, the traditional beliefs and family practices are still easily observed in modern Chinese society. Thus it is necessary to consider the family factors together with the unique needs of families with disabled children.

3. *Facilitate the sense of power for the family through different forms of intervention.* With the reaction of hiding their disabled child from the outside world and the traditional belief in fate, parents need to be encouraged to control and support their disabled child's development. Parents can learn strategies to promote the child's development, develop skills to cope with crises, and make good use of the needed resources. Different forms of intervention may involve providing information, parent training, family counseling, parent support groups, and community resources.

4. *Give support and actively involve both parents, especially the mother, and the extended family members in the intervention.* Because of the increasing caregiving role the father plays and supportive roles shared by extended

family members in the modern Chinese family, supports need to be given to both parents and extended family members, if necessary, in the intervention. However, the mother of the disabled child in the Chinese family may still be the person needing the most professional support.

The goal for families with disabled children in Taiwan is the same as in other countries; to develop effective coping strategies and draw on family support programs that consider the needs of individual families in particular cultural and societal contexts. This will ensure that a favorable quality of life for disabled youngsters and their families can be realized.

# REFERENCES

Affleck, G., McGrade, B. J., McQueeney, M., & Allen, D. (1982). Promise of relationship-focused early intervention in developmental disabilities. *Journal of Special Education*, *16*, 413–430.

Bailey, D., & Simeonsson, R. J. (1988). *Family assessment in early intervention*. Columbus: Merrill.

Bailey, D., Simeonsson, R. J., Winton, P., Huntington, G., Comfort, M., Isbell, P., O'Donnell, K., & Helm, J. (1986). Family-focused intervention: A functional model for planning, implementing and evaluating individual family services in early intervention. *Journal of the Division for Early Childhood*, *10*, 156–171.

Bricker, D. (1987). Impact of research on social policy for handicapped infants and children. *Journal of the Division for Early Childhood*, *11*(2), 98–105.

Bristol, M., Reichle, N., & Thomas, D. (1987). Changing demographics of the American family: Implications for single-parent families of young handicapped children. *Journal of the Division for Early Childhood*, *12*, 56–69.

Bronfenbrenner, U. (1974). Is early intervention effective? In M. Guttentag & E. Struening (Eds.), *Handbook of education and research* (pp. 519–603). Beverly Hills: Sage.

Bryant, D., & Graham, M. A. (1990). *Linking theory, research, and practices: quality indicators in early intervention*. Paper presented at the meeting of the International Early Childhood Conference on Children with Special Needs, Albuquerque, NM, October 20–24.

Department of Education of the Republic of China (1984). *Special Education Law of the Republic of China*. Taipei: Department of Education.

Dunst, C. J. (1985). Rethinking early intervention. *Analysis and Intervention in Developmental Disabilities*, *5*, 165–201.

Dunst, C., Trivette, C., & Deal, A. (1988). *Enabling and empowering families: Principles and guidelines for practice*. Cambridge, MA: Brookline.

Gallagher, J. J., & Vietze, P. (Eds.). (1986). *Families of handicapped persons*. Baltimore: Brooks.

Ho, D. Y. F., & Kang, T. K. (1984). Intergenerational comparisons of child-rearing attitudes and practices in Hong Kong. *Developmental Psychology*, *20*(6), 1004–1016.

Hsu, F. K. (1953). *Americans and Chinese: Two ways of life*. New York: H. Schuman.

Kysela, G., & Marfo, K. (1983). Mother-child interaction and early intervention programs for handicapped infants and young children. *Educational Psychology*, *3*, 201–212.

Lee, Y. Y. (1988). Chinese family and family culture. In C. Y. Weng & S. H. Shiau (Eds.), *Chinese: Concepts and behaviours* (pp. 113–128) (in Chinese). Taipei, Taiwan: Gi-Liu.

Lin, N. (1988). Chinese family structure and Chinese society. *Bulletin of the Institute of Ethnology Academia Sinica* (in Chinese), 65, 59–129.

Nihira, K., Webster, R., Tomiyasi, Y., & Oshio, C. (1988). Child-environment relationships: A cross-cultural study of educable mentally retarded children and their families. *Journal of Autism and Developmental Disorders*, 18 (3), 327–341.

Rogow, S. M. (1985). *Where service begins: Working with parents to provide early intervention: Considerations for the culturally different.* Paper presented at the meeting of the 63rd Annual Convention of the Council for Exceptional Children, Anaheim, CA, April 15–19.

Rosenberg, S., Robinson, C., & Beckman, P. (1984). Teaching skills inventory: A measure of parent performance. *Journal of the Division for Early Childhood*, 8, 107–113.

Suvannathat, C., Bhanthumnavin, D., Bhuapirom, L., & Keats, D. M. (Eds.) (1985). *Handbook of Asian child development and child rearing practices.* Behavioral Science Research Institute, Srinakharinwirot University, Thailand.

Tsai, C. M., & Chuang, M. J. (1985). A study of preschool special education problems (in Chinese). *Bulletin of Special Education*, 1, 45–64.

Turnbull, A., & Turnbull, H. (1986). *Families, professionals, and exceptionality.* Columbus, OH: Merrill.

Wang, T. M. (1985). The difference of parent-teacher viewpoints regarding the impact of a mentally retarded child on the family (in Chinese). *Bulletin of Special Education*, 1, 115–140.

Wang, T. M. (1989). *Interaction of Down syndrome toddlers and their mothers: A comparative study with a Chinese population.* University of North Carolina at Chapel Hill. Doctoral dissertation.

Wang, T. M. (1990). A study of parents' perceptions of parenting in Chinese families of children with and without Down syndrome. *Bulletin of Special Education*, 6, 151–162.

Wang, T. M. (1991a). Perceived problems and actions to promote the special education practice in the Taiwan area (in Chinese). *Bulletin of Special Education*, 7, 1–22.

Wang, T. M. (1991b). *Quality of life: The promise of early intervention programs for handicapped youngsters and their families in Asia.* Paper presented at the Tenth Asian Conference on Mental Retardation, Karachi, Pakistan, November 3–8.

Wong, C. K. J. (1981). *The changing Chinese family pattern in Taiwan* (in Chinese). Taipei, Taiwan: Southern Materials Center.

Wu, T. W., & Chang, C. F. (1982, 1990). *The directory of special education, rehabilitation, and welfare services in the Republic of China* (in Chinese). Taipei: Special Education Center, National Taiwan Normal University.

Wu, T. W., Wang, T. M., & Retish, P. (1987). The inter-impact of families and their handicapped children (in Chinese). *Bulletin of Special Education*, 3, 1–28.

Yamamoto, J., & Kubota, M. (1983). The Japanese-American family. In G. J. Powell (Ed.), *The psychosocial development of minority group children* (pp. 237–247). New York: Brunner/Mazel.

# SOCIETAL CONTEXTS

Part IV examines the nature and form of societal response to children with disabilities and their families. The response of a society is not only defined in terms of direct and indirect services to children and families but, perhaps more fundamentally, in the expressed philosophy and values within which such services are provided. Given the developmental focus adopted in this volume, primary services pertain to developmental and educational interventions for children and associated supports for families.

Family-centered intervention for preschool children is examined in detail as a service model, reflecting a clear statement about family involvement. The endorsement of the centrality of the family can be traced in earlier forms in legislation pertaining to the IEP and more recently in the greater detail of the IFSP. As families of children with disabilities progress from early intervention in the home to center- and school-based services for children and youth, it is clear their expectations and experience will contribute to the continued evolution of services that are family oriented.

The contributions in Part IV define the principles and practices of interventions for children and their families in two major developmental periods: the preschool years and the educational experience for children and youth. Recognizing that expectations of families may not be matched by societal provisions and perspectives on what is needed or appropriate for the family may not be provided, we also consider legal and ethical issues involving families and society.

# 11

# FAMILY-CENTERED CARE IN EARLY INTERVENTION: COMMUNITY AND HOSPITAL SETTINGS

*Elaine C. Meyer, Donald B. Bailey, Jr.*

## INTRODUCTION

The relationship between parents of children with special health or educational needs and the professionals who provide services has varied quantitatively and qualitatively. Professionals once were the ultimate decision makers, determining what information should be shared with families and what services or treatments would be provided for their children. Although this model still prevails in some settings, recent years have witnessed a dramatic shift in the relationship between parents and professionals. Current approaches recognize the centrality of the family and emphasize a philosophy of service provision that is responsive to family needs, priorities, values, and concerns.

Although the movement toward family-centered practices applies to children of all ages, it is especially evident today in the context of services for young children and their families. This chapter describes the rationale and principles of family-centered care as they pertain to young children. Drawing on the importance of ecological factors that influence service delivery, a special focus of the chapter is an analysis of the principles of family-centered care as applied in community-based early intervention programs compared with their application in hospital-based programs.

## ELEMENTS OF FAMILY-CENTERED CARE

What is family-centered care? This question is best answered by examining five factors that contributed to its evolution: (1) stories told by parents about their interactions with professionals; (2) data regarding family follow-through on professional recommendations; (3) concerns about the potentially negative effects of professional practices for families; (4) evolving theories about family coping and adaptation to stress; and (5) a rethinking of the goals for services with families.

## Parents' Stories

Perhaps the first indication of the inadequacy of a professionally dominated approach to services was found, not in the empirical or theoretical literature, but in the stories told and feelings expressed by parents of young children with special needs. Sometimes published (e.g., Dougans, Isbell, & Vyas, 1983; Featherstone, 1981; Turnbull & Turnbull, 1985a), but more often told, a general theme underlying these stories is a frustration with and anger at a system that did not listen to or respect the rights, feelings, and wishes of families. Familiar stories include the physician who conveyed information about a condition or disability in an insensitive fashion; the program that could not provide a desired service or admit a particular child because of agency rules and regulations; the report that included unexplained test scores, jargon, and negative statements; or the therapist or teacher who insisted that parents conduct lengthy and sometimes unpleasant therapeutic or educational activities with their child. From this literature and oral tradition came the message that many parents wanted a different kind of relationship with the professionals who provided services for them and their children.

## Parent Follow-Through on Professional Recommendations

A second factor contributing to the evolution of family-centered practices was accumulated data regarding parent follow-through on the recommendations made by professionals and participation in professionally planned activities. Rosenberg, Reppucci, and Linney (1983), for example, described their frustration at planning parent training groups for low-income, high-risk families, only to have one family keep their appointment. Other professionals have reported difficulty in getting parents to follow through on recommendations for home-based programming or health-care routines, and several reviews of the literature have suggested that generalization and maintenance of parent training activities and treatment effects often is minimal (Breiner & Beck, 1984; Gross, Eudy, & Drabman, 1982; Howlin, 1984; Snell & Beckman-Brindley, 1984).

In order to identify factors related to follow-through, Cadman, Shurvell, Davies, and Bradfield (1984) studied a regional consultation team in Canada that conducted comprehensive assessments of children and provided written recommendations to parents and professionals in the child's home community. They found that neither child characteristics, family characteristics, nor the type of recommendation were related to follow-through. Several characteristics of the *decision-making and consultation process*, however, were significant, including the following:

1. the care the consultant took in listening to the client at assessment;
2. the adequacy of the consultant's explanation of the reason for the therapy;
3. the amount of time taken for discussion of the recommendation;

4. belief in the efficacy of the prescribed therapy;
5. clarity of roles of other individuals working with the child;
6. the client's perception of his or her own adequacy at implementing the specific therapy;
7. the feasibility of the recommendation; and
8. overall agreement with the prescription. (p. 44)

The study suggests that a model of services that listens to families and responds to their unique perspective could ultimately be more successful than one in which professionals make decisions without such consultation and discussion.

## Concerns About the Negative Effects of Some Practices

Most professionals have a positive view of families and want to help them. Generally, professionals have assumed that most families want their help. When families do not wish professional intervention, professionals further assume that families ultimately will come to realize that what professionals have to offer is in their best interests. However, some have questioned whether imposing services on families, especially those families who do not perceive a need for them, may in fact have negative consequences.

This hypothesis was confirmed in a study by Affleck, Tennen, Rowe, Roscher, and Walker (1989). They examined the effects of a formal support program for mothers of high-risk infants who had been in the neonatal intensive care unit. The program consisted of an initial consultation session prior to discharge and 15 weekly home visits by a neonatal nurse. Six-month outcome data indicated that mothers' predischarge need for support and the severity of the infants' predischarge medical problems moderated program effects. Although numerous positive outcomes were documented, they were only observed for those mothers who, prior to discharge from the hospital, indicated a need for support. Mothers who did not feel a need for the program, but received it anyway, reported less competency, had a lowered sense of control, and were less responsive to their infants than prior to the program. The authors speculated that mothers with little need for support may have experienced threats to their adaptation due to information that disrupted their optimistic view of the child's condition and, ultimately, diminished their self-confidence. The findings highlight the importance of considering parents' needs and coping styles when designing and allocating formal support interventions. Moreover, this study suggests that trying to help persons who do not perceive a need for help could have negative consequences.

## Changing Models of Coping and Adaptation

A fourth factor influencing the emergence of family-centered practices is a gradual change in the way professionals have come to understand family adaptation and coping in the presence of childhood illness or disability. Knafl and Deatrick (1987) describe two models, one which views families as relatively passive respondents. This model predicts that families experience high levels of stress, and progress through a sequence of stages of coping until they finally "accept" their child's condition. Here, much of the interpretation of parental responses centers around the grief process. An alternative model, labeled as the subjective active process approach, maintains that "there is no single, objective meaning to chronic illness or disability" (p. 302). Each family interprets the illness or disability from a different perspective; thus the professional's job is not one of classifying parents according to the acceptance process but rather one of trying to understand the unique needs and perspectives that each family brings to the intervention context.

Bernheimer, Gallimore, and Weisner (1990) propose "ecocultural" theory as a basis for individualized work with families, arguing that families must be viewed within their cultural context, and professionals need to understand the process by which families construct meaning of circumstances and the events. Perspectives such as these have helped professionals realize that each family has unique needs and priorities requiring services that are consistent with family desires and expectations.

## Changing Views of the Goals for Services

Early intervention for children with disabilities focused historically on the needs of the children. Gradually, professionals have realized that children live in complex ecologies, requiring that services be expanded to include supporting families (Dunst, 1985). This perspective is reflected in Zigler and Black's (1989) review of America's family support movement, the ultimate goal of which is "to enable families to be independent by developing their own informal support networks" (p. 11).

## Current Status of Family-Centered Care in Early Intervention

Given this background, we can now begin to describe family-centered approaches in early intervention. Two sources are important in this context. First, PL 99-457 explicitly recognizes the importance of the family in the context of providing early intervention services for infants and toddlers. The law requires that instead of an individualized education plan (IEP), programs develop an individualized family service plan (IFSP). The IFSP is to include, in addition to the usual child goals and services, a statement of family needs and strengths, goals and services for the family, and case management services designed to help families gain access to services across multiple agencies. Thus there is a strong legal mandate for a family focus in early intervention services.

The legal imperative is based on changing views and philosophies that are important because they help shape the implementation of the law about work with families. Also, they are important because some settings that provide services for young children may not be required to abide by these regulations. Implementation of family-centered care in these settings must be based either on principle or on local policy statements. In this context, the Association for the Care of Children's Health (1990) has developed a set of eight principles, or elements of family-centered care (Shelton, Jeppson, & Johnson, 1987), displayed in Table 11–1. These principles have been widely discussed and their application to a variety of fields and settings has been advocated (e.g., Roberts & Magrab, 1991; Rushton, 1990).

This context, a law and a set of principles, provides an interesting opportunity to examine how these principles might be applied in two very different settings. Bronfenbrenner (1977) argues that behavior viewed out of context loses much of its meaning. This point is well illustrated in Gilkerson's (1990) comparison of institutional functioning style between community-based early intervention programs and hospital settings. Gilkerson describes hospitals as self-contained settings that establish the rules for how they will function, with physicians characteristically in charge. Hospitals have an acute, short-term

TABLE 11-1

## ELEMENTS OF FAMILY-CENTERED CARE

1.  Recognition that the family is the constant in the child's life while the service systems and personnel within those systems fluctuate.
2.  Facilitation of parent/professional collaboration at all levels of health care:
    - care of an individual child;
    - program development, implementation, and evaluation; and
    - policy formation.
3.  Sharing of unbaised and complete information with parents about their child's care on an ongoing basis in an appropriate and supportive manner.
4.  Implementation of appropriate policies and programs that are comprehensive and provide emotional and financial support to meet the needs of families.
5.  Recognition of family strengths and individuality and respect for different methods of coping.
6.  Understanding and incorporating the developmental needs of infants, children, and adolescents and their families into health-care delivery systems.
7.  Encouragement and facilitation of parent-to-parent support.
8.  Assurance that the design of health-care delivery systems is flexible, accessible, and responsive to family needs.

*Source:* Shelton, Jeppson, and Johnson (1987).

orientation to care, responding to immediate needs and focusing on the individual patient. Early intervention programs, in contrast, have a long-term approach to service delivery, focusing on the individual within the broader family context. Early intervention programs must work with multiple agencies and programs to coordinate services, and are based on a symmetrical relationship between professional and client.

How do the principles of family-centered care apply in these two settings? In the remainder of this chapter, we consider each of the eight principles mandated by PL 99-457 and their implications for community-based early intervention programs and hospital settings that typically have no such mandate but are rethinking practices and approaches.

# RECOGNITION THAT THE FAMILY IS THE CONSTANT IN THE CHILD'S LIFE WHILE THE SERVICE SYSTEMS AND PERSONNEL WITHIN THOSE SYSTEMS FLUCTUATE

This central tenet of family-centered care reminds professionals that the family as the child's consistent caregiving context holds the ultimate responsibility for managing the child's physical, social, and emotional needs (Shelton et al., 1987). Historically, parents have been recognized as their children's principal decision makers and care providers (Shelp, 1986; President's Commission, 1983). That is not to diminish the role professionals may play in a child's life, but rather to realign the role into proper perspective, highlighting the enduring, overarching role of the child's family and fostering a certain humility on the part of professionals in light of their circumscribed role in the child's life.

**Early Intervention Programs.**   Although community-based early intervention programs historically have had a strong family component, PL 99-457 further emphasizes and systematizes this family focus as evident in regulations for Part H:

> Part H recognizes the unique and critical role that families play in the development of infants and toddlers who are eligible under this Part. It is clear, both from the statute and the legislative history of the Act, that the Congress intended for families to play an active, collaborative role in the planning and provision of early intervention services. (Federal Register, 54(119), June 22, 1989, p. 26309)

The importance of recognizing the constancy of the family is evident when we realize the number of transitions a family and child may make during the first six years of life. During this period children may be hospitalized immediately after birth, following which they may be enrolled in a hospital-to-home transition program, staffed by professionals other than those who cared for the child in the hospital. Once at home, the child may be eligible for early intervention services, which will likely vary considerably depending on the child's condition or disability, special educational or therapeutic needs, and available services. Since the lead agency for programs may vary, families in one state may receive these services through the department of education, whereas in other states they may be provided by the department of human resources or the health department. During the infancy period, programs are likely to follow a home-based model of services. Once the child reaches age 3, however, the state's department of education must bear responsibility, and so another transition is likely. At age 5, yet another transition occurs when children enter kindergarten.

For many families, this represents a high number of stressful transition periods, many of which are unavoidable. Obviously the family is the constant caregiving context for the child while service systems and personnel fluctuate. This assumption is fundamental to the remaining eight.

**Hospital settings.**   Hospitalization can be an intimidating and stressful experience for children and their families (Harrison, 1983; Miles, 1979). Throughout hospitalization, parents have multiple demands placed on them including providing support to their ill child, integrating information about the child's illness and participating in decision making, caring for their other children, balancing finances and employment responsibilities, and minimizing disruption to family life (Harrison, 1983; Miles & Carter, 1982).

Parents must also grapple with a certain enforced passivity as the traditional parenting role is usurped by health-care professionals and monitoring equipment (Zeanah, 1989). Gorski (1984) highlights the uncertainty, lack of confidence, and self-consciousness that parents may experience amid bustling, technology-oriented intensive care nursery settings. Parent-child interactions may be compromised due to barriers created by life support equipment, sedating medications, policies designed to reduce the risk of infection (e.g., face masks), prolonged hospitalization, and visitation restrictions (Minde, 1984; Resnick, Eyler, Nelson, Eitzman, & Bucciarelli, 1987). Thus many aspects of hospitalization converge to make it a stressful experience for children and their families.

While families take for granted their usual control over children's lives, hospitalization and illness may threaten that sense of control and stability (Harrison, 1983). The posture of professionals toward families can serve to further threaten or to foster the parents' sense of control and competence within the unfamiliar health-care arena. The role of professionals as consultants and advisers to parents (Barnard, 1985) is consonant with the spirit of family-centered care as it preserves the authority and natural caregiving role of parents.

Hospitals are generally characterized by high-volume, short-term acute care, with preservation of life as the most critical function (Gilkerson, Gorski, & Panitz, 1990). Psychosocial care is generally assigned far less fanfare and expert attention than critical care (Hurt, 1984). Traditionally, nurses and social workers have been identified as the providers of psychosocial support to families. However, within increasingly technological hospital units, nurses have less time to devote to psychosocial aspects of care, and are less prepared to address the often highly charged emotional aspects of hospitalization (DiMario, 1988). Social workers devote a great percentage of their time to crisis intervention for children and families rather than to ongoing psychosocial support (Beres, 1988). This means that the family's role as advocate, comforter, and caregiver for their children becomes even more important.

From a young child's point of view, hospitalization represents a tremendous disruption in life (Campis, Pillemer, & DeMaso, 1990; Rutter, 1980). Upon hospitalization, the child may be in pain; the hospital environment is full of new sights, sounds, and smells; many unfamiliar people participate in the child's care; the child may be separated from parents; familiar routines (for example, getting dressed in the morning, going to school, mealtime, bedtime) are dismantled; and the language used by adults may be incomprehensible and bewildering. Perhaps most upsetting to children, and their parents, are necessary though painful procedures. While infants and children expect adults to protect them from pain and to care for them, this fundamental expectation is likely to be violated in the hospital. Parents report that perceiving their children to be in pain, and feeling helpless to intervene to comfort the child, are among the most stressful aspects of hospitalization (Meyer, 1991; Miles & Carter, 1982). Health-care professionals thus need to remember that, ultimately, it is the family who helps the child to understand, to cope with, and to make sense of the hospitalization experience.

## FACILITATION OF PARENT/PROFESSIONAL COLLABORATION AT ALL LEVELS OF HEALTH CARE

In both health-care and educational settings, there has historically been a distinct power differential with professionals having greater power than families. The power differential is multidetermined and has been attributed to situational dependency, in which families need services and situational authority and professionals have specialized knowledge and professional prestige (West, 1984). This situation implicitly calls for the equalization of parents' and professionals' relative status in order to enable productive collaboration (Vincent, 1985).

**Early Intervention Settings.**    The regulations for part H of PL 99-457 require the development of an individualized family service plan (IFSP) that must include information about the child's status, a statement of family strengths and needs, outcomes to be achieved for the child and the family, the early intervention services to be provided, a designated case manager, and a transition plan at age 3. The IFSP must be developed jointly by the family and professionals. Thus collaboration in the planning of early intervention goals and services is a necessary component of early intervention programs. From a legal perspective, families are the ultimate decision makers, since they must sign the IFSP (or the IEP for children over 36 months of age) before it can be implemented and have the right to require modification of service plans or to refuse services if they so desire.

**Hospital Settings.**  Family-centered care requires recognition that while professionals bring necessary skills and expertise to the situation, parents offer a broader perspective of the child's life based on their longitudinal experience across multiple settings. Edelbrock (personal communication, 1984) considers parental observations of their children as "unimpeachable" and the cornerstone of child assessment. Indeed, parents know their children best and should be enlisted to share their knowledge and insights in planning individualized care for their children.

The principle of parent-professional collaboration is relevant to direct health care of children, the development of community and hospital services, as well as policy-making (Shelton et al., 1987). In a survey compiled by the Association for the Care of Children's Health (Roberts, Maieron, & Collier, 1988), several parameters were evaluated as indicators of hospital commitment to psychosocial family-centered care. In 1988, 69% and 78% of general and pediatric hospitals, respectively, had written policies and/or philosophies that delineated a role for families, and 98% and 88%, respectively, had 24-hour visiting policies for pediatric patients admitted to general floors. With regard to parental access to children's medical records, 67% of general hospitals and 77% of pediatric hospitals permitted such access during and after hospitalization. However, only 6% of general hospitals and 20% of pediatric hospitals had established parent advisory boards.

The historical account of parents of preterm infants provides some insight into parent-professional relationships within a hospital setting. As recently as 25 years ago, hospital policies enforced parent-infant separation due to fears of introducing infections into the nursery (Wortis, 1960). These same restrictive policies precluded mothers from assuming any role in caring for their infants. It was not until it was empirically demonstrated that parental contact did not significantly increase the infection rate that hospital visiting policies permitted parental contact (Leiderman, Leifer, Seashore, Barnett, & Grobstein, 1973). Clearly, the role of parents in the intensive care nursery setting is attenuated amid the machinery, instability of the infant, and limited opportunities for caregiving. In a review of the role that parents have played traditionally in preventive intervention programs with preterm infants, Barrera and Rosenbaum (1986) concluded that parental involvement had varied widely, with parents often relegated to instrumental roles and enlisted as vehicles of intervention (e.g., doing motor development exercises with their infants). While many interventions have since addressed the broader issues of parent-infant relationships and psychosocial care (Als et al., 1986; Bromwich & Parmalee, 1979; Klaus & Kennell, 1982; Minde, Shosenberg, Marton, Thompson, Ripley, & Burns, 1980; Rauh, Achenbach, Nurcombe, Howell, & Tefi, 1988), most interventions address problems and needs as hypothesized by professionals rather than as identified by parents. While great strides have been made to view the infant in the context of the family, equal status partnership and collaboration between parents and professionals remains to be achieved.

## SHARING OF UNBIASED AND COMPLETE INFORMATION WITH PARENTS ABOUT THEIR CHILD'S CARE ON AN ONGOING BASIS IN AN APPROPRIATE AND SUPPORTIVE MANNER

The sharing of unbiased and complete information with parents lies at the very heart of family-centered care. Although many of the issues and strategies for sharing information are similar across early intervention and hospital settings, some differences between the two settings are important to note.

### Early Intervention Settings. For parents to participate in decision making, they must have access to all relevant information. This process has two fundamental components: (1) involving parents in the assessment process, and (2) involving parents in team meetings and decision making.

Involving parents in the assessment process may include several activities. The first is determining what information parents are seeking about their child. Often parents come to early intervention programs because their child is delayed in some aspect of development. They may want confirmation of a developmental delay, a diagnosis, or guidance for planning intervention activities. In some cases, parents may not want to participate in the assessment process at all, resenting the time it takes or worrying about what it might yield. Understanding parents' views of assessment helps shape the assessment activities and how assessment results are shared. Second, parents can share important information about how their child responds in various situations, helping to create a context in which optimal assessment information is obtained. Parents can also indicate the degree to which the child's behavior in the assessment context is representative of typical behavior. Third, parents can provide important information about a child's skills and behavior in an array of environments. Finally, some parents may want to participate in the information-gathering process themselves.

Involving parents in team meetings and decision making is another primary context for information sharing. By law, an IFSP meeting is to be held every six months, and an IEP meeting every year. In reality, every encounter between professionals and parents is an opportunity for sharing information and making decisions about future goals and activities. In this context, several points are worth noting. First, the way that information is shared is critical to how it is received. Murphy (1990) characterized the traditional informing conference as one involving authoritative professionals telling parents about their children. Effective informing requires good communication skills, a realization that parents and professionals have perspectives on child and family needs, a sensitivity to feelings, sharing information clearly and without jargon, and providing a variety of opportunities to discuss assessment results. Second, professionals need to recognize that team meetings are often threatening for parents and thus they should be organized in ways to maximize parent comfort and participation. Strategies might include working with families prior to the meeting by involving them in assessment and planning (Brinckerhoff & Vincent, 1986) and organizing the meeting around their goals and perceptions rather than professionals' summaries of their reports.

**Hospital Settings.** The likelihood of communication difficulties is increased in a hospital setting given the complexity of health-care issues, multiple professionals, and level of parental anxiety. Typically, a hospitalized child is assigned to a primary service depending on the child's presenting problems (e.g., pulmonary service, renal service). Additional services may be consulted as needed, thus increasing the number of professionals involved. The periodic rotation of residents and attending physicians further increases the number and complexity of the health-care provider network, and can make it difficult to establish parent-professional relationships (Meyer, 1991). Some parents worry about who is "in charge" of their child's care, particularly when staff rotation patterns are unexplained and unexpected. There may be only limited opportunities to convene parents and health-care providers for collaborative meetings due to the number of professionals involved, heavy clinical demands, crisis situations, time pressures, and limited privacy and space (Drotar, Benjamin, Chwast, Litt, & Vaner, 1982; Gilkerson, 1990; Gilkerson et al., 1990). In the hospital setting, it is understood that life-threatening situations and clinical needs take precedence over other activities, including meetings with families and supportive psychosocial interventions (Gilkerson et al., 1990; Meyer, 1991).

Parent-professional partnerships and collaboration are sacrificed when information is not freely and regularly exchanged. Unbiased and complete information empowers parents and enables parents to participate fully in decision making related to their children's health care (Shelton et al., 1987; Zaner & Bliton, 1991). Clear language that is not obscured by technical jargon facilitates parent-professional collaboration, as well as parental understanding and sense of control. On the other hand, information that is incomplete, biased, or otherwise non-understandable diminishes parents' status relative to professionals, and cripples parental participation in health-care decision making. Shelton et al. (1987) recommend that parents be provided with both layperson's terms and appropriate technical terminology to enable them to communicate with professionals and to research their children's conditions.

The literature is replete with strategies, advice, and opinions regarding what information to share with parents and how information should be shared. Shelton et al. (1987) summarize in a word: *everything* should be shared with parents including medical information, community resources, support groups, and the pros and cons of treatment choices. Similarly, parents of disabled and high-risk infants and children emphasize the importance of complete, honest communication between parents and professionals (Featherstone, 1980; Harrison, 1983; Nance, 1982; Weyhing, 1983). Rushton (1990) advocates honest, straightforward, timely discussions of a child's condition and prognosis, with recognition of the impact surrounding ambiguous diagnoses and uncertain outcomes. Bogdan, Brown, and Foster (1982) address the complexities of parent-professional communication in a neonatal intensive care unit, and advocate that professionals be "honest but not cruel." Others, however, believe that in situations of terminal illness, determination of the "appropriate level of care" represents a medical decision that should be discussed with the family, but without placing the burden of decision making on the family (Grenvik, Powner, Snyder, Jastremski, Babcock, & Loughhead, 1978; Safar & Winter, 1990; Wanzer et al., 1984).

Despite what may seem to be majority support for the sharing of unbiased, complete information with parents, there are many subtle, and not so subtle, obstacles to open exchange of information in the hospital setting. For example, it is not uncommon for health-care professionals to convene meetings without parents, prior to meeting with the parents, presumably to determine what and how information should be shared with parents, and to clarify what messages and conclusions the team wishes to communicate to the parents. This is not to say that there is no place for exclusive team meetings. However, there is the danger that, with the intention of delivering "consistent information" and edited versions of the child's situation, parents may be underinformed and, to a greater or lesser extent, excluded from the decision-making process for their children. In some cases, this may result in families not having the full range of treatment options for their children, which families have identified as essential to being full-fledged partners with health-care professionals and making informed choices (Domingue personal communication, 1989). Unfortunately, this process smacks of paternalism and undermines the spirit of family-centered care.

Zaner and Bliton (1991) provide an excellent review of issues related to medical discourse and parent-professional communication. The ambiguous nature of some diagnoses, inherent uncertainty in diagnostic categories, imprecision of prognostic estimates, and reluctance to deliver bad news converge to obscure communication between parents and professionals. The use of descriptors (e.g., "good baby"; "very sick baby"; "chronic baby") reflect formal diagnostic and prognostic information; however, the meaning may be unclear or ambiguous to parents. For example, "you have a very sick baby" may be understood contextually by professionals as there is a substantial possibility that the child might not survive, yet parents may merely interpret this to mean that their child requires additional hospitalization (Bogdan, Brown, & Foster, 1982). Clearly, parents and professionals need a common language and means of interpretation, forum, and time for candid discussion, and mechanism for clarification in order to communicate successfully.

A related issue has to do with the choice of vocabulary utilized by health-care professionals. The way in which language shapes people's perceptions of disabled or chronically ill children has long been recognized in the literature on severe disabilities (Goffman, 1963). Consider the classification of "nonsalvageable survivors" used to describe the population of pediatric trauma patients

(Jaimovich, Blostein, Rose, Stewart, Shabino, & Buechler, 1991). At first pass, "nonsalvageable" seems a clear means to communicate a grave prognosis. However, consider the usual context in which one is likely to hear such a term, most probably a scrapyard. To use terminology that typically describes junk cars and scrap metal in the context of explaining the condition of children with injuries or illnesses is not psychosocially sensitive, is likely to shape professionals' perceptions of the children with whom they work, and thus it is not acceptable (Zeanah, 1989).

# IMPLEMENTATION OF APPROPRIATE POLICIES AND PROGRAMS THAT ARE COMPREHENSIVE AND PROVIDE EMOTIONAL AND FINANCIAL SUPPORT TO MEET THE NEEDS OF FAMILIES

Generally, the presence of childhood chronic illness or disability within the family is perceived as an emotionally costly and stressful experience for the affected child and other family members (Featherstone, 1980; Gallagher, Beckman, & Cross, 1983; Pless & Pinkerton, 1975). This principle is grounded in the knowledge that childhood illness and disability can have far-reaching implications for the psychosocial adjustment of the child, parents, siblings, and extended family members; marriage; careers; family finances; and family lifestyle and opportunities (Shelton et al., 1987). Many parents have eloquently articulated their experiences and needs which, in turn, have guided service delivery models and legislation (Arango, 1990; Beckett, 1985; Featherstone, 1980; Oster, 1985; Turnbull & Turnbull, 1985b; Weyhing, 1983). The intent of such comprehensive emotional and financial support for families translates into a necessary scaffolding of services to help enable families to fulfill their natural caregiving roles.

**Early Intervention Settings.** Public Law 99-457, Part H, reinforces this principle through several aspects of the legislation. First, the legislation requires that programs have the capability of assessing family needs and strengths, if such an assessment is desired by the family. Personal interviews are to be used as one way of gathering this information. Second, programs are required to address family goals through an array of services provided directly by the early intervention program or coordinated with other agencies. Third, in order to facilitate access to services and resources for paying for those services, each family whose infant or toddler has a disability must be assigned a case manager.

These aspects of the legislation reflect an important principle of family-centered care, but have required a rethinking of goals and services provided by early intervention programs. Because most professionals have little training in work with families, care will need to be taken to ensure that family assessments are conducted in ways that are viewed by families as positive and facilitative, rather than intrusive or evaluative.

**Hospital Settings.**   Gilkerson et al. (1990) describe hospitals as having an individual approach that traditionally emphasizes the treatment of individuals in isolation from their broader family and sociocultural context. By contrast, family-centered care assumes a systems approach in which the child's illness is viewed contextually. Thus there are differences in the underlying assumptions of what should be the appropriate focus of intervention and how resources should be allocated when children are hospitalized.

Family-centered care advocates for the child and family as the appropriate focus of health-care intervention and for the commitment of necessary resources to support families properly. Successful family-centered care is individualized and creative, with the broad goal of humanizing health care. In implementing aspects of family-centered care, hospitals have been challenged to broaden their care perspective and traditional interventions.

The Association for the Care of Children's Health survey of hospital psychosocial policies and programs (Roberts et al., 1988) reviewed several means by which hospitals have demonstrated psychosocially sensitive, family-centered care. These include psychosocial policy statements, 24-hour visiting policies, accommodations for parents, parental involvement in children's care and procedures, access to medical records, parent and sibling support groups, child life programs and developmentally appropriate playrooms, hospital school programs, child and family educational material and programs, and family resource libraries. Special services provided by some hospitals illustrate a variety of innovative, creative approaches to making family-centered care a reality. Services available to families may include foreign language interpretation, interpretation for the hearing impaired, pediatric patient representatives, surgical liaison staff to communicate information and messages between operating room staff and families of children who are undergoing surgery, parent consultants, parent surrogate programs, home-care programs, respite care, hospice care, and day-care and recreational/educational camps for children with special health-care needs.

To be sure, there is considerable variability among hospitals in the range and quality of family-centered policies and programs. However, as a whole, hospitals have moved in the direction of providing psychosocially sensitive care to children and their families. Current challenges to hospitals include ongoing training of staff to understand and provide family-centered care, bridging the gap from theory to clinical reality, and examining the efficacy of family-centered care.

## RECOGNITION OF FAMILY STRENGTHS AND INDIVIDUALITY AND RESPECT FOR DIFFERENT METHODS OF COPING

Traditionally, ill and disabled children have been narrowly viewed in terms of their diagnoses, illness characteristics, and treatments. The focus is often skewed in the direction of what the team has to offer in the way of assessment and treatment. This principle encourages a more comprehensive view of the child and family and a consideration of both strengths as well as limitations. Moreover, it implies that the family's strengths and resources figure prominently into the intervention plan.

**Early Intervention Settings.**    Part H of PL 99-457 requires that a statement of family strengths be included in the IFSP (if desired by the family). Trivette, Dunst, Deal, Hamer, and Propst (1990) review the literature on assessing family strengths and conclude that five principles are necessary:

> First, it must be recognized that all families have strengths and that those strengths are unique. . . . Second, the failure of a family or individual family member to display competence must not be viewed as a deficit within the family system or family member, but rather the failure of social systems and institutions to create opportunities for competencies to be displayed or learned. . . . Third, work with families must be approached in ways that focus and build on the positive aspects of functioning, rather than families being seen as "broken" and "needing to be fixed." Fourth, a shift must be made away from the use of either treatment or prevention models and toward the adoption of promotion and enhancement models, because the latter are the only approaches consistent with strengthening family functioning. . . . Fifth, the goal of intervention must not be seen as "doing for people" but, rather, as the strengthening of functioning in ways that make families less and not more dependent upon professionals for help. (p. 21)

Implementation of these principles requires a recognition that strengths and resources are inevitably a function of the family's *perception*, and thus their view on available strengths and resources is preferable to the professional's evaluation of them.

**Hospital Settings.**    There is a growing body of knowledge in the areas of parental stress, family adaptation, and coping with childhood illness and hospitalization (Curley, 1988; Featherstone, 1980; Gallagher, Beckman, & Cross, 1983; Harrison, 1983; Kirschbaum, 1990; Lewandowski, 1980; Miles & Carter, 1982, 1983, 1985; Stein & Reissman, 1980). Common stressors have been identified during pediatric intensive care hospitalization including sights and sounds in the highly technical environment, the child's appearance and behavior, necessary painful procedures, communication difficulties between family and staff, and alterations in the natural parenting role (Miles & Carter, 1982, 1983). Clarification of such stressors and better understanding of the parents' experience of hospitalization have raised the overall consciousness of health-care providers and resulted in improvements in psychosocial services and policies.

Systematic investigations and parent accounts of coping with hospitalization have also led to an appreciation for the multiple strategies with which families cope with the stress inherent in hospitalization. The model proposed by Miles and Carter (1982, 1983) conceptualizes parental coping as multidetermined, complex, and individualized. Coping behaviors described include appraisal-focused coping that involves attempts to understand and make meaning of the situation; problem-focused coping that involves instrumental efforts to reduce stress; and emotion-focused coping that includes attempts to manage emotions and maintain emotional equilibrium. Zeanah (1989) emphasizes that parents vary in terms of strengths and resources, experience with authority figures, understanding of medical information, and styles of obtaining information, all of which influence how they cope with hospitalization.

From an anthropological perspective, Newman (1980) identified two primary coping styles between and within families as they adapted to their infants' preterm birth and hospitalization. "Coping through commitment" is an intense though variable approach in which parents essentially become a part of the team involved in their infant's care. "Coping through distance," on the other hand, is characterized by a slower, more tentative acquaintance with the infant in which parents seemed to rely more on directives from staff, and were described as expressing fear, anxiety, and perhaps denial before accepting their surviving infant.

Caution against overgeneralization and respect for family differences are urged when considering the issue of family adaptation to childhood chronic illness or disability (Blacher, 1984). Drotar, Baskiewicz, Irwin, Kennell, & Klaus, (1972) suggest a series of stages that parents experience on learning about their child's illness or disability. Featherstone (1980) cautions that stage models, while serving a useful conceptual function, fail to capture the nonlinear nature of adaptation as well as the diversity of family experiences. With insight born of her own experience as a mother of a multiply handicapped boy, Featherstone adds that rarely is the "promised land of acceptance" achieved on schedule, if at all. Wikler, Wasow, and Hatfield (1981) eloquently address the chronic nature of sorrow that parents may experience, postulating that unachieved developmental milestones on the part of the child serve to rekindle parental grief.

While "good" coping and family adaptation may seem quite straightforward to recognize, there is considerable variability even among health-care professionals as to what it constitutes (Williams & Anders, 1987). When asked to identify the parameters of good family adaptation to childhood chronic illness, health-care professionals differentially emphasized aspects of adaptation, largely according to disciplinary affiliation. For example, nurses emphasized proper administration of medications and compliance with treatment recommendations; social workers emphasized having integrated the child into the family system. Families, on the other hand, typically reported that successful adaptation had more to do with adopting a philosophy of family life such as "taking one day at a time" and "remembering to stop and smell the roses."

Thus good coping and adaptation are multifaceted concepts that are best not measured or judged by a unitary yardstick. The family's organization, sociocultural background, previous experience with illness and hospitalization and support network, as well as the nature and circumstances of the illness, all impact on the family's repertoire of coping capacities and strategies.

# UNDERSTANDING AND INCORPORATING THE DEVELOPMENTAL NEEDS OF INFANTS, CHILDREN, AND ADOLESCENTS AND THEIR FAMILIES INTO HEALTH-CARE DELIVERY SYSTEMS

Since developmental needs form the core of early intervention services, this principle is discussed here primarily as it pertains to hospital settings. This principle recommends health care that addresses not only the hospitalized child's condition, but also the child's inherent developmental challenges and strivings. In this way, the child's development serves to individualize care during the course of hospitalization. Fostering the child's development is viewed as an integral, overarching goal in family-centered care, beyond the limited focus on specific health-care problems. This principle also requires an appreciation for the family's developmental life cycle stage.

Increased health-care subspecialization has contributed to a compartmentalization of care and, in some cases, a fragmentation of service delivery (Shelton et al., 1987). Hospitalization is particularly ripe for such problems given the high number of subspecialties, the focus on the presenting problem, and the removal of the child from usual routines and activities. In the event of critical care hospitalization, the child's medical requirements may preclude optimal attention to developmental needs (Rushton, 1990). Similarly, the demands of prolonged hospitalization and technology dependence attenuate normal developmental experiences and challenge hospitalized children's successful negotiation of developmental tasks (Goldberger, 1988; Goldberger & Wolfer, 1991; Warner & Norwood, in press).

During general pediatric hospitalizations, the child's cognitive, social, and emotional development should be incorporated into health-care planning and considered a priority. Unfortunately, while the move in the field is toward more developmentally sensitive care, there remain instances in which the child's personhood and development are underemphasized. In the worst case, the child's illness remains the exclusive focus of intervention, decoupled from the child as a whole, developing person. For example, there is a vast difference between "the CFer in room 401" and "the toddler with cystic fibrosis in room 401." In the first example, the illness defines the child, whereas the latter example respects that the illness is merely one aspect of the child and provides some information about the child's developmental capacities.

The nature of hospitalization can compromise the opportunity to get to know the child and family and establish a trusting relationship. Consider the difference between having care provided by a trusted community pediatrician, and hospitalization, in which unfamiliar health-care professionals are assigned to treat health problems. Often, families find themselves in situations in which, at their greatest time of need, care must be provided by highly specialized health-care professionals who are strangers to them. To address this issue, some hospitals encourage parents to bring in photographs and meaningful objects of their previously healthy children and to share aspects of the child's development with staff. For example, the family of a young girl in the intensive care unit brought in photographs of her cheerleading with her friends. This exchange fostered the relationship between family and staff and, later, the cheerleading served as a common developmentally appropriate goal to work toward together.

A child's experience and psychosocial adjustment to illness and hospitalization is best understood from a developmental perspective (Rae, 1981; Shore & Goldston, 1978). It has been well established that infants and children experience illness and hospitalization differently depending on their conceptual (cognitive) understanding and level of psychological (emotional) development (Campis et al., 1990; Reissland, 1983; Simeonsson, Buckley, & Monson, 1979; Whitt, Dykstra, & Taylor, 1979). Health-care providers need a working knowledge of these developmental differences in order to recognize adjustment difficulties and have realistic expectations of children, to prepare children adequately for various procedures, to communicate and teach effectively, and to support children throughout the course of hospitalization. Medically fragile infants and children who remain technology dependent and require frequent and/or prolonged hospitalizations present special developmental needs and challenges (Daly, Rudy, Thompson, & Happ, 1991; Warner & Norwood, in press).

Hospital child life programs and school programs are very important in fostering the developmental capacities of hospitalized children. Such programs provide children with familiar experiences amid the largely unfamiliar, stressful hospital culture. The staffing, funding, and capacity of these programs are barometers of a hospital's psychosocial sensitivity and commitment to needs of children. Often, child life specialists, teachers, physical therapists, and child psychologists have the strongest backgrounds in normal child development within the hospital's multidisciplinary team.

Beyond formal child life and hospital school programs, numerous innovative projects have been instituted in hospital settings to address child development and family issues (Roberts et al., 1988; Shelton et al., 1987). For example, some nurseries combine administration of the Neonatal Behavioral Assessment Scale (Brazelton, 1984) and careful observations to assess infant development, teach parents about infant development, and modify environmental and caregiving elements to foster development (Als et al., 1986; Meyer, 1991; Rauh, Achenbach, Nurcombe, Howell, & Teti, 1988). Other examples include developmentally appropriate preadmission programs, preparation for and debriefing following procedures, and school/community reentry efforts to facilitate children's transition from hospital to home. Efforts to address the needs of family members include sibling workshops, parenting classes and groups, educational newsletters, and clinic camps and reunions that provide the opportunity for children and families to maintain contact over time.

## ENCOURAGEMENT AND FACILITATION OF PARENT-TO-PARENT SUPPORT

Thus health-care and early intervention professionals can provide considerable support to families in a variety of ways. There is, however, a qualitative difference between what professionals have to offer and what fellow parents have to offer (Oster, 1985). Parents who have had ill or disabled children bring an invaluable personal perspective to the situation. The support that parents can provide to each other, through individual relationships and parent organizations, has been highlighted as very important by parents themselves (Featherstone, 1980; Mariska, 1984; Oster, 1985; Weyhing, 1983). Similarly, the literature supports the utility and benefits of parent-to-parent groups for providing emotional support and education (Iscoe & Bordelon, 1985; Johnson, 1982; Perrin & Ireys, 1984; Rowland, 1983; Yoak & Chesler, 1983). Ideally, parents of hospitalized children should have a full range of formal and informal, professional and parent, resources available to them.

Nathanson (1986) outlines various functions that parent-to-parent support can provide including mutual support and friendship, information gathering and sharing, and improving the health-care delivery system. Parents emphasize the tremendous role parent-to-parent support can fulfill regarding the profound sense of isolation that some parents may experience. Gould and Moses (1985) distinguish between the empathy that fellow parents are able to share, and the sympathy that others, who have not lived with illness or disability, have to offer. Fellow parents are also able to provide practical suggestions and help that comes only from firsthand experience. With regard to health-care referrals and recommendations, parents can offer each other valuable opinions and relative rankings of services, programs, or service providers, whereas health-care professionals may feel uncomfortable offering such specific information. Organized parent groups can also identify systematic problems and make improvements in the health-care system. Shelton et al. (1987) emphasize that organized parent groups not only have "strength in numbers," but a certain leverage due to their parental experience and insight. Participation in such groups can provide parents with the opportunity to be heard and to make contributions in the larger sense by improving the quality of life for children and their families.

Parent-to-parent groups may be organized around specific medical conditions or disabilities, around specific issues related to illness (e.g., newly diagnosed diabetics, compassionate friends for parents who have experienced the death of a child), or around common issues related to coping and adaptation to childhood illness. In hospital settings, groups are typically led by professionals or jointly led by parents and professionals. Groups that have only professional leadership are less likely to result in a network of 1:1 parent contact, have less focus on changing the health-care delivery system, and organize fewer opportunities for socialization (Yoak & Chesler, 1983).

Hospital staff members have a role to play in facilitating and encouraging parent-to-parent support. First, the hospital often represents the family's entry point into the health-care system. Staff members have the opportunity to introduce the benefits of parent-to-parent support to parents early on, facilitate such referrals and networking among parents, and generally sanction the legitimacy and value of parent-to-parent support (Shelton et al., 1987). Second, staff members should suggest parent-to-parent support in a manner that supports the family rather than inadvertently conveys the impression that the family is not coping adequately (Poyadue, 1986). Third, hospitals can provide instrumental support (e.g., place to meet, secretarial services), inservice training, and educational training programs to facilitate parent-to-parent efforts. Finally, hospital staff members need to examine their own attitudes regarding parents and professionals as equals in the partnership of providing optimal health care.

# ASSURANCE THAT THE DESIGN OF HEALTH-CARE DELIVERY SYSTEMS IS FLEXIBLE, ACCESSIBLE, AND RESPONSIVE TO FAMILY NEEDS

The delivery systems in health and human services are extraordinarily complex and, at times, overwhelming for families to negotiate. Children with chronic illness or disabilities and their families characteristically require a myriad of services and interact with literally hundreds of professionals over time (Shelton et al., 1987). Thus programs need to be organized in ways that are accessible to families and help families gain access to services.

**Early Intervention Settings.** In recognition of the variety of agencies and services potentially available for families and young children with disabilities, three aspects of PL 99-457 should be noted. First, the law requires that each state assure the presence of a system of services that is statewide, coordinated, and interagency in focus. Second, states must maintain a central directory that includes a description of the available, early intervention services, a listing of other resources (including subject matter experts), and any demonstration projects in the state. The directory should be accessible to parents and professionals, updated regularly, and used to identify gaps in services as well as instances of service duplication (Mayfield-Smith, Yajnik, & Wiles, 1990). Third, every family of an infant or toddler with a disability has a right to *case management* services provided at no charge. According to the regulations, case managers are responsible for coordinating evaluations and assessments, facilitating and participating in the development and review of IFSPs, helping families identify available service providers, coordinating and monitoring the delivery of available services, and informing families of the availability of advocacy services. Research on case management suggests that it can be helpful to clients; however, most case managers find their work frustrating because of heavy caseloads and lack of authority or clout (Bailey, 1989).

Peterson (1991) suggests that five factors must be in place in order to ensure the presence of a coordinated system of interagency services. First, the agency that has been designated as responsible for services must establish a leadership style and operating procedures that promote collaboration. Each state is required to establish an interagency coordinating council, and the authority and leadership provided by this council is essential in establishing a collaborative philosophy. Second, a comprehensive child-find and referral system is needed to ensure that children can be identified for all relevant services. Third, case management and IFSP development procedures need to be established so that all children and families have equal access to services. Fourth, personnel policies need to be established to facilitate cross-agency collaboration. Finally, formal interagency agreements are needed in order to operationalize interagency collaboration.

**Hospital Settings.**   Hospitals are among the most complicated health-care settings to negotiate. To illustrate the point, a hospitalized girl with complicated chronic renal failure was documented to have some 314 different health-care providers who had entered notes into her chart (Lim, 1991). Clearly, management and coordination of health-care services within the hospital setting is of utmost necessity.

When a child requires hospitalization, the family requires an introduction to the hospital culture as well as specific information about their child's condition. The family needs to know who will be providing care, monitoring, and participating in health-care decisions. Given the large number of staff participating in their child's care, parents need to understand the usual means of communication among care providers including daily rounds, nursing shift reports, multidisciplinary care meetings, and chart documentation. Parents should also be provided with information regarding access to staff members who are responsible for their child.

In addition, parents need basic information about accommodations, parent lounges, shower and laundry facilities, food preparation areas and restaurants, child care, public transportation and parking, and telephones (Roberts et al., 1988). Architectural designs and the use of physical space in hospitals can facilitate or deter family-centered care (Olds & Daniel, 1987). For example, the provision of privacy for families is important be it to nurse a newborn, comfort an ill child, or mourn the death of an infant. Given the stress inherent in hospitalization and the great deal of information that parents will be required to integrate, written family orientation booklets and hospital maps are recommended.

To a great extent, families adjust their priorities and schedules when children are hospitalized. There is considerable variability among families, however, with some families staying at the hospital round-the-clock and other families integrating the hospitalization into the fabric of family life. Hospital staff members tend to view parents primarily as parents of a hospitalized child, with less than adequate recognition of the parents' broader family, employment, and community responsibilities. Problems may arise, for example, when hospital staff members assume that parents can be available during the day for meetings or care conferences. Similarly, convenient parent visiting times may conflict with unit rounds, teaching conferences, or nursing report time. Thus there needs to be a mutual respect and flexibility on the part of both health-care providers and families to enable the collaborative process.

The issue of flexibility within the hospital also has implications with respect to individual patient care. It is unfortunate, but not uncommon, that some patient care decisions are based more on staff issues than what is in the patient's best interest. For example, a sleeping child may be woken up at 10 P.M. for a blood sample that might have been drawn earlier had there been better communication between health-care providers. In another example, an intubated toddler, who is unable to speak and whose family can only visit on weekends, may be scheduled for multiple interventions (e.g., suctioning, wound care, medications) throughout the day and night based on staff availability, rather than according to a typical toddler's schedule. Rushton (1990) notes that psychosocially sensitive, family-centered care can begin with such clinical decision making in which staff members can make positive changes.

Families need to know what psychosocial services and programs are available within the hospital, their eligibility, and how to access such services (Shelton et al., 1987). Ideally, hospital staff members incorporate psychosocial assessment into hospital admission, continue to assess and address changing psychosocial needs over the course of hospitalization, and facilitate appropriate referrals. Staff members who have consistent involvement with the family over time, including social workers and primary nurses, are often in good positions to secure relevant services. However, this responsibility should not rest solely with these members of the team. Parent orientation booklets and other families can also be very useful resources. Similarly, parent surrogate programs, in which volunteers visit and establish relationships with hospitalized children whose families are unavailable, can be valuable referrals.

Responsiveness to families' needs and priorities is a hallmark of family-centered care. To the degree that health-care systems are responsive to the needs and priorities of families, parents and professionals approach collaborative partnership in the design and delivery of health care. Hospitals are encouraged to ask families directly about what types of services would be useful, and how to improve on existing programs (Shelton et al., 1987). This process can be formalized via parent advisory boards, parent consultants, and family consumer satisfaction questionnaires. Beyond providing families with a voice with which to articulate their needs and priorities, health-care professionals need to listen carefully.

## ISSUES IN IMPLEMENTING FAMILY-CENTERED PRACTICES

This chapter has provided an overview of the principles of family-centered care and described their application in both community-based early intervention programs as well as hospital settings. We must recognize, however, that despite the value attributed to these principles in the professional literature, full implementation of each is far from a reality in many settings.

What barriers stand in the way of implementing these principles and what is needed to facilitate change? Two major barriers are significant to full implementation of the principles of family-centered care. First, with the exception of a few disciplines, most professionals graduate from college or university programs that focus almost exclusively on the ill or disabled child as the primary focus of intervention. A recent survey of training programs across eight disciplines found very little coursework or experiences in working with families, with the exception of the disciplines of social work and nursing (Bailey, Simeonsson, Yoder, & Huntington, 1990). Because university training programs shape both professional skills and identity, changes are needed to ensure that all professionals have skills in working with families and recognize the importance of family-centered approaches.

Second, we must recognize that significant systems-level factors stand in the way of family-centered services. Recent surveys of early intervention professionals document that while professionals verify their belief in the importance of family-centered practices, administrative barriers such as time constraints, lack of administrative support, and concerns about how teams will work together to provide family-centered care are viewed as significant factors in limiting implementation (Bailey, Buysse, Edmondson, & Smith, 1992; Bailey, Palsha, & Simeonsson, 1991; Mahoney & O'Sullivan, 1990; Mahoney, O'Sullivan, & Fors, 1989). Also, in one study, many professionals expressed concerns about whether families wanted a family-centered approach or whether parents had the skills to participate fully in decision-making activities (Bailey, Buysse, Edmondson, & Smith, 1992).

Given these barriers, what can be done to facilitate the implementation of the principles of family-centered care? Three recommendations are offered here:

1. Modify college and university programs to ensure that every professional has some basic skills needed to work with families and a recognition of the critical importance of a family-centered approach.
2. Engage service delivery systems in a systematic process of examining practices and setting goals for family-centered change.
3. Seek family input in the evaluation of current practices and setting goals for change. A recent study by Bailey, Buysse, and Elam Smith-Bonahue (1992) documents that parent involvement in decisions about program practices is viewed positively by both parents and professionals, and substantially influences the outcomes of that process.

Finally, we must recognize that the principles of family-centered care represent a set of basic values about how families and children should be viewed and how care should be provided. At one level, the acceptance of the principle is philosophically based. This fact does not, however, preclude the responsibility to evaluate the effects of implementing the principles. The need for careful evaluation, including clarification of what intervention characteristics and family characteristics contribute to program efficacy, is especially important in light of evidence that not all parents benefit from well-intentioned intervention efforts (Affleck et al., 1989). Since they are, indeed, principles, they will be implemented in a variety of ways, only some of which are consistent with their intent. Thus systematic research on the efficacy, parental perceptions, and cost-benefit analyses of alternative implementation strategies is essential.

# REFERENCES

Affleck, G., Tennen, H., Rowe, J., Roscher, B., & Walker, L. (1989). Effects of formal support on mothers' adaptation to the hospital-to-home transition of high-risk infants: The benefits and costs of helping. *Child Development, 60,* 488–501.

Als, H., Lawhon, G., Brown, E., Gibes, R., Duffy, F. H., McAnulty, G., & Blickman, J. G. (1986). Individualized behavioral and environmental care for the very low birthweight preterm infant at high risk for bronchopulmonary dysplasia: Neonatal intensive care unit and developmental outcome. *Pediatrics, 78*(6), 1123–1132.

Arango, P. (1990). A parent's perspective. Family-centered care: Making it a reality. *Children's Health Care, 19*(1), 57–62.

Association for the Care of Children's Health. (1990). *Physician Education Forum Report.* Bethesda, MD: Association for the Care of Children's Health.

Bailey, D. B. (1989). Case management in early intervention. *Journal of Early Intervention, 13,* 120–134.

Bailey, D. B., Buysse, V., Edmondson, R., & Smith, T. M. (1992). Creating family–centered services in early intervention: Perceptions of professionals in four states. *Exceptional Children, 58*(4), 298–309.

Bailey, D. B., Buysse, V., Smith–Bonahue, T. M., & Elam, J. (1992). The effects and perceptions of parent involvement in program decisions about family–centered practices. *Evaluation and Program Planning, 15*(1), 23–32.

Bailey, D. B., Palsha, S. A., & Simeonsson, R. J. (1991). Professional skills, concerns, and perceived importance of work with families in early intervention. *Exceptional Children, 58*(2), 156–165.

Bailey, D. B., Simeonsson, R. J., Yoder, D. E., & Huntington, G. S. (1990). Preparing professionals to serve infants and toddlers with handicaps and their families: An integrative analysis across eight disciplines. *Exceptional Children, 57,* 26–35.

Barnard, K. (1985). Toward an era of family partnership. In *Equals in this partnership: Parents of disabled and high–risk infants and toddlers speak to professionals.* (pp.4–5). Washington, DC: National Center for Clinical Infant Programs.

Barrera, M., and Rosenbaum, P. (1986). The transactional model of early home intervention. *Infant Mental Health Journal, 7*(2), 112–131.

Beckett, J. (1985). Comprehensive care for medically vulnerable infants and toddlers. In *Equals in this partnership: Parents of disabled and at–risk infants and toddlers speak to professionals.* (pp.6–13). Washington, DC: National Center for Clinical Infant Programs.

Beres, E. A. (1988). *Discharge planning and community resources.* Presentations at the Assessment and Intervention Practicum of the Psychosocial Intervention with High Risk Infants Training Program, Women and Infants' Hospital, Providence, RI.

Bernheimer, L. P., Gallimore, R., & Weisner, T. S. (1990). Ecocultural theory as a context for the individual family service plan. *Journal of Early Intervention, 14,* 219–233.

Blacher, J. (1984). Sequential stages of parental adjustment to the birth of a child with handicaps: Fact or artifact? *Mental Retardation, 22,* 55–68.

Bogdan, R., Brown, M. A., & Foster, S. B. (1982). Be honest but not cruel: Staff/parent communication on a neonatal unit. *Human Organization, 41,* 6–16.

Brazelton, T. B. (1984). *Neonatal Behavioral Assessment Scale.* Philadelphia: Lippincott.

Breiner, J., & Beck, S. (1984). Parents as change agents in the management of their developmentally delayed children's noncompliant behaviors: A critical review. *Applied Research in Mental Retardation, 5,* 259–278.

Brinckerhoff, J. L., & Vincent, L. J. (1986). Increasing parental decision–making at the individualized educational program meeting. *Journal of the Division for Early Childhood, 11*, 46–58.

Bromwich, R. M., & Parmalee, A. H. (1979). An intervention program for preterm infants. In T. M. Field, A. M. Sostek, S. Goldberg, and H. H. Shuman (Eds.), *Infants Born at Risk: Behavior and Development*. (pp. 389–411). New York: S.P. Medical and Scientific Books.

Bronfenbrenner, U. (1977). Toward an experimental ecology of human development. *American Psychologist, 32*, 513–531.

Cadman, D., Shurvell, B., Davies, P., & Bradfield, S. (1984). Compliance in the community with consultant's recommendations for developmentally handicapped children. *Developmental Medicine and Child Neurology, 26*, 40–46.

Campis, L. K., Pillemer, F. G., & DeMaso, D. R. (1990). Psychological considerations in the pediatric surgical patient. In L. B. Kaban (Ed.), *Pediatric Oral and Maxillofacial Surgery* (pp. 21–29). Philadelphia: W. B. Saunders.

Curley, M. A. Q. (1988). Effects of nursing mutual participation model of care on parental stress in the pediatric intensive care unit. *Heart and Lung, 17*, 682–688.

Daly, B. J., Rudy, E. B., Thompson, K. S., & Happ, M. B. (1991). Development of a special care unit for chronically critically ill patients. *Heart and Lung, 20*(1), 45–51.

DiMario, P. (1988). *The role of the nurse in the special care nursery*. Presentation at the Assessment and Intervention Practicum of the Psychosocial Intervention with High Risk Infants and Their Families Training Program, Women and Infants' Hospital, Providence, RI.

Dougans, T., Isbell, L., & Vyas, P. (1983). *We have been there: A guidebook for parents of people with mental retardation*. Nashville: Abingdon Press.

Drotar, D., Baskiewicz, A., Irwin, N., Kennel, J., & Klaus, M. (1975). The adaption of parents to the birth of an infant with a congenital malformation: A hypothetical model. *Pediatrics, 56*, 710–717.

Drotar, D., Benjamin, P., Chwast, R., Litt, C., & Vajner, P. (1982). The role of the psychologist in pediatric outpatient and inpatient settings. In J. Tuma (Ed.), *Handbook for the practice of pediatric psychology* (pp. 228–250). New York: Wiley.

Dunst, C. J. (1985). Rethinking early intervention. *Analysis and Intervention in Developmental Disabilities, 5*, 165–201.

Featherstone, H. (1981). *A difference in the family: Life with a disabled child*. New York: Basic.

Gallagher, J. J., Beckman, P., & Cross, A. H. (1983). Families of handicapped children: Sources of stress and its amelioration. *Exceptional Children, 50*(1), 10–19.

Gilkerson, L. (1990). Understanding institutional functioning style: A resource for hospital and early intervention collaboration. *Infants and Young Children, 2*(3), 22–30.

Gilkerson, L., Gorski, P. A., & Panitz, P. (1990). Hospital–based intervention for preterm infants and their families. In S. J. Meisels and J. P. Shonkoff (Eds.), *Handbook of early childhood intervention* (pp. 445–468). Cambridge, England: Cambridge University Press.

Goffman, E. (1963). *Stigma*. Englewood Cliffs, NJ: Prentice–Hall.

Goldberger, J. (1988). Infants and toddlers in hospitals: Addressing developmental risks. *Zero to Three: Bulletin of the National Center for Clinical Infant Programs, 8*(3), 1–6.

Goldberger, J., and Wolfer, J. (1991). An approach for identifying potential threats to development in hospitalized toddlers. *Infants and Young Children, 3*(3), 74–83.

Gorski, P. A. (1984). Premature infant behavioral and physiological responses to caregiving interventions. In J. D. Call, E. Galenson, & R. L. Tyson (Eds.), *Frontiers of human psychiatry* (pp. 256–263). New York: Basic.

Gorski, P. A. (1989). *The effects of the NICU environment: Womb for improvement.* Presentation at the Prevention and Intervention Seminar of the Psychosocial Intervention with High Risk Infants and Their Families Training Program, Women and Infants' Hospital, Providence, RI.

Gould, P. T., & Moses, L. S. (1985). Mild developmental delays from a parent's perspective. In *Equals in this partnership: Parents of disabled infants and toddlers speak to professionals* (pp.14–17). Washington, DC: National Center for Clinical Infant Programs.

Grenvik, A., Powner, D. J., Snyder, J. V., Jastremski, M. S., Babcock, R. A., & Loughhead, M. G. (1978). Cessation of therapy in terminal illness and brain death. *Critical Care Medicine,* 6, (4) 284–291.

Gross, A. M., Eudy, C., & Drabman, R. S. (1982). Training parents to be physical therapists with their physically handicapped child. *Journal of Behavioral Medicine,* 5, 321–327.

Harrison, H. (1983). *The premature baby book: A parent's guide to coping and caring in the first years.* New York: St. Martin's Press.

Howlin, P. (1984). Parents as therapists: A critical review. In D. J. Miller (Ed.), *Remediating children's language: Behavioral and naturalistic approaches* (pp. 197–229). San Diego: College–Hill Press.

Hurt, H. (1984). Continuing care of the high–risk infant. *Clinics in Perinatology,* 11(1), 3–17.

Iscoe, L., & Bordelon, K. (1985). Pilot parents: Peer support for parents of handicapped children. *Children's Health Care,* 14(2), 103–109.

Jaimovich, D. G., Blostein, P. A., Rose, W. W., Stewart, D. P., Shabino, C. L., and Buechler, C. M. (1991). Functional outcome of pediatric trauma patients identified as 'non-salvageable survivors.' *Journal of Trauma,* 31(2), 196–199.

Johnson, M. (1982). Support groups for parents of chronically ill children. *Pediatric Nursing,* 8(3), 160–163.

Kirschbaum, M. S. (1990). Needs of parents of critically ill children. *Applied Research,* 9(6), 344–352.

Klaus, M. H., & Kennell, J. H. (1982). *Maternal–Infant Bonding.* St. Louis: C. V. Mosby.

Knafl, K. A., & Deatrick, J. A. (1987). Conceptualizing family response to a child's chronic illness or disability. *Family Relations,* 36, 300–304.

Leiderman, P. H., Leifer, A. D., Seashore, M. J., Barnett, C. R., & Grobstein, R. (1973). Mother–infant interaction: Effects of early deprivation, prior experience and sex of the infant. In J. I. Nurenberger (Ed.), *Biological and Environmental Determinants of Early Development,* ARNMD (Vol. 51). Baltimore: Williams & Williams.

Lewandowski, L. (1980). Stresses and coping styles of parents of children undergoing open–heart surgery. *Critical Care Quarterly,* 3, 75–84.

Lim, B. (1991). *Clinical case presentation: Chronic renal failure.* Pediatric Grand Rounds, University of North Carolina Hospitals, Chapel Hill.

Mahoney, G., & O'Sullivan, P. (1990). Early intervention practices with families of children with handicaps. *Mental Retardation,* 28, 169–176.

Mahoney, G., O'Sullivan, P. S., & Fors, S. (1989). The family practices of service providers for young handicapped children. *Infant Mental Health Journal,* 10(2), 75–83.

Mariska, J. (1984). *Acceptance is only the first battle: How some parents of young handicapped children have coped with common problems.* In S. Duffy, K. McGlynn, J. Mariska, & J. Murphy (Eds.). Missoula: Montana University Affiliated Program, University of Montana.

Mayfield–Smith, K. L., Yajnik, G. G., & Wiles, D. L. (1990). Information and referral for people with special needs: Implications for the Central Directory of Public Law 99–457. *Infants and Young Children,* 2(3), 69–78.

Meyer, E. C. (1991). Preventive psychosocial intervention with parents of very-low-birthweight infants, Ann Arbor, Michigan. (Doctoral dissertation, University of Rhode Island. *University Microfilms International,* 9106521.

Miles, M. S. (1979). Impact of the intensive care unit on parents. *Issues in Comprehensive Pediatric Nursing, 3*(7), 72–90.

Miles, M. S., and Carter, M. C. (1982). Sources of parental stress in pediatric intensive care units. *Children's Health Care, 11*(2), 65–69.

Miles, M. S., & Carter, M. C. (1983). Assessing parental stress in intensive care units. *Journal of Maternal Child Nursing, 8*(5), 354–360.

Miles, M. S., & Carter, M. C. (1985). Parental coping strategies during a child's admission to an intensive care unit. *Child Health Care, 14*(1), 14–21.

Minde, K. K. (1984). The impact of prematurity on the later behavior of children and their families. *Clinics in Perinatology, 11*(11), 227–244.

Minde, K., Shosenberg, N., Marton, P., Thompson, J., Ripley, J., & Burns, S. (1980). Self–help groups in a premature nursery: A controlled evaluation. *Journal of Pediatrics, 96*(5), 933–940.

Murphy, A. (1990). Communicating assessment findings to parents: Toward more effective informing. In E. D. Gibbs & D. M. Teti (Eds.), *Interdisciplinary assessment of infants* (pp. 299–307). Baltimore: Brookes.

Nance, S. (1982). *Premature babies.* New York: Arbor House.

Nathanson, M. N. (1986). *Organizing and maintaining support groups for parents of children with chronic illness and handicapping conditions.* Washington, DC: Association for the Care of Children's Health.

Newman, L. F. (1980). Parents' perceptions of low birthweight infants. *Pediatrician, 9*(3–4), 182–190.

Olds, A., & Daniel, P. (1987). *Child health care facilities: Design guidelines-Literature outline.* Washington, DC: Association for the Care of Children's Health.

Oster, A. (1985). Comprehensive care for medically vulnerable infants and toddlers: A parent's perspective. In *Equals in this partnership: Parents of disabled and at-risk infants and toddlers speak to professionals* (pp.26–32). Washington, DC: National Center for Clinical Infant Programs.

Perrin, J., & Ireys, H. (1984). The organization of services for chronically ill children and their families. *Pediatric Clinics of North America, 31,* 235–258.

Peterson, N. L. (1991). Interagency collaboration under Part H: The key to comprehensive, multidisciplinary, coordinated infant/toddler intervention services. *Journal of Early Intervention, 15,* 89–105.

Pless, I. B., & Pinkerton, P. (1975). *Chronic childhood disorder: Promoting patterns of adjustment.* Chicago: Year Book.

Poyadue, F. (1986). *Perspectives from selected innovative family-centered care projects.* Presented at the meeting of the Association for the Care of Children's Health Family–Centered Care Panel, Washington, DC.

President's Commission for the Study of Ethical Problems in Medicine and Biomedical and Behavioral Research (1983). *Deciding to forgo life-sustaining treatment: A report on the ethical, medical, and legal issues in treatment decisions.*

Rae, W. A. (1981). Hospitalized latency–age children: Implications for psychosocial care. *Children's Health Care, 9,* 59–63.

Rauh, V. A., Achenbach, T. M., Nurcombe, B., Howell, C. T., & Teti, D. M. (1988). Minimizing adverse effects of low birthweight: Four-year results of an early intervention. *Child Development, 59,* 544–553.

Reissland, N. (1983). Cognitive maturity and the experience of fear and pain in hospital. *Social Science Medicine, 17,* 1389–1395.

Resnick, M. B., Eyler, F. D., Nelson, R. M., Eitzman, D. V., & Bucciarelli, R. L. (1987). Developmental intervention for low birthweight infants: Improved early developmental outcome. *Pediatrics, 80*(1), 68–74.

Roberts, M. C., Maieron, M. J., & Collier, J. (1988). *Directory of hospital psychosocial policies and programs.* Washington, DC: Association for the Care of Children's Health.

Roberts, R. N., & Magrab, P. R. (1991). Psychologists' role in a family-centered approach to practice, training, and research with young children. *American Psychologist, 46,* 144–148.

Rosenberg, M. S., Reppucci, N. D., & Linney, J. A. (1983). Issues in the implementation of human service programs: Examples from a parent training project for high–risk families. *Analysis and Intervention in Developmental Disabilities, 3,* 215–225.

Rowland, T. (1983). Support groups for parents of children with heart disease—Boon or bane? *Clinical Pediatrics, 22*(4), 322–323.

Rushton, C. H. (1990). Family–centered care in the critical care setting: Myth or reality? *Children's Health Care, 19*(2), 68–78.

Rutter, M. (1980). Attachment and the development of social relationships. In M. Rutter (Ed.), *Scientific foundations of developmental psychiatry* (pp. 267–279). London: Heinemann.

Safar, P., & Winter, P. (1990). Helping to die. *Critical Care Medicine, 18*(7), 788–789.

Shelp, E. E. (1986). *Born to die? Deciding the fate of critically ill newborns.* New York: Free Press.

Shelton, T. L., Jeppson, E. S., & Johnson, B. H. (1987). *Family–centered care for children with special health care needs.* Washington, DC: Association for the Care of Children's Health.

Shore, M. F., & Goldston, S. E. (1978). Mental health aspects of pediatric care: Historical review and current status. In P. R. Magrab (Ed.), *Psychological management of pediatric problems (Vol. 1)* (pp. 15–31). Baltimore: University Park Press.

Snell, M. E., & Beckman–Brindley, S. (1984). Family involvement in intervention with children having severe handicaps. *Journal of the Association for Persons With Severe Handicaps, 9,* 213–230.

Simeonsson, R. J., Buckley, L., & Monson, L. (1979). Conceptions of illness causality in hospitalized children. *Journal of Pediatric Psychology, 4,* 77–84.

Stein, R. E. K., & Reissman, C. K. (1980). The development of an Impact-on-Family Scale: Preliminary findings. *Medical Care, 18* 465–472.

Trivette, C. M., Dunst, C. J., Deal, A. G., Hamer, A. W., & Propst, S. (1990). Assessing family strengths and family functioning style. *Topics in Early Childhood Special Education, 10*(1), 16–35.

Turnbull, A. P., & Turnbull, H. R. (1985a). *Parents speak out.* Columbus, OH: Merrill.

Turnbull, A. P., & Turnbull, H. R. (1985b). Personal testimony before the Select Committee on Children, Youth, and Families, U.S. House of Representatives. *Families With Disabled Children: Issues for the 1980's* (Publication No. 48–1370). Washington, DC: U.S. Government Printing Office.

Vincent, L. J. (1985). Family relationships. In *Equals in this partnership: Parents of disabled at at–risk infants and toddlers speak to professionals.* Washington, DC: National Maternal and Child Health Clearinghouse.

Wanzer, S. H., Adelstein, S. J., Cranford, R. E., Federman, D. D., Hook, E. D., Moeriel, C. G., Safar, P., Stone, A., Taussig, H. B., & van Eys, J. (1984). The physician's responsibility toward hopelessly ill patients. *New England Journal of Medicine, 310,* 955–959.

Warner, J., & Norwood, S. (1991). Psychosocial Concerns of the Ventilator-Dependent Child in the Pediatric Care Unit. AACN *Clinical Issues in Critical Care Nursing*, 2(3), 432–435.

West, C. (1984). *Routine complications*. Bloomington: Indiana University Press.

Weyhing, M. C. (1983). Parental reactions to handicapped children and familial adjustments to routines of care. In J. A. Mulick & S. M. Pueschel (Eds.) *Parent-professional partnerships in developmental disability services* (pp.125–138). Cambridge, MA: The Ware Press.

Whitt, J. K., Dykstra, W., & Taylor, C. A. (1979). Children's conceptions of illness and cognitive development: Implications for pediatric practitioners. *Clinical Pediatrics*, 18, 327–339.

Wikler, L., Wasow, M., & Hatfield, E. (1981). Chronic sorrow revisited: Attitude of parents and professionals about adjustment to mental retardation. *American Journal of Orthopsychiatry*, 51, 63–70.

Williams, J. R., & Anders, T. (1987). *Family adaptation to childhood chronic illness*. Final grant report submitted to the Maternal Child Health Service, U.S. Government.

Wortis, H. (1960). Discussion: Maternal reactions to premature birth. *American Journal of Orthopsychiatry*, 30, 547–552.

Yoak, M., & Chesler, M. (1983). Alternative professional roles in health care delivery: Leadership patterns in self-help groups. *Journal of Applied Behavioral Science*, 21(4), 427–441.

Zaner, R. M., & Bliton, M. J. (1991). Decisions in the NICU: The moral authority of parents. *Children's Health Care*, 20(1), 19–25.

Zeanah, C. (1989). *Parental perspectives of preterm birth and hospitalization*. Presentation at the Assessment and Intervention Practicum of the Psychosocial Intervention with High Risk Infants and Their Families Training Program, Women and Infants' Hospital, Providence, RI.

Zigler, E., & Black, K. B. (1989). America's family support movement: Strengths and limitations. *American Journal of Orthopsychiatry*, 59, 6–19.

# 12

# COMMUNICATING WITH FAMILIES: EXAMINING PRACTICES AND FACILITATING CHANGE

*Pamela J. Winton, Donald B. Bailey*

## INTRODUCTION

What does it mean to be family centered in the provision of early intervention services? This question can be asked and answered at any number of levels of specificity or formality. For example, some might define being family centered as meaning that a program assesses family needs and resources and writes an individualized family service plan (IFSP) instead of an individualized educational plan (IEP). Another program might offer its parent support group or parent-training services as evidence of a family-centered approach. When specific services, forms, assessment procedures, and the other trappings of professional practice are set aside, however, what is left of a family-centered approach is the extent to which professionals and families have been able to establish a *relationship* that is mutually respectful, supporting, trusting, and collaborative. At the heart of this relationship is effective communication (Winton, 1988a).

The skills needed for effective communication have been described by any number of authors (Benjamin, 1969; Gorden, 1969; Ivey, 1971; Weber, McKeever, & McDaniel, 1985). A framework for conducting focused interviews in the context of early intervention has been described (Winton & Bailey, 1988; Winton, 1988b), and workshops providing training in this interview format have been implemented and evaluated in selected sites (Bailey et al., 1988; Winton & Bailey, 1990). Data from these studies, coupled with personal experiences in conducting these workshops, have led us to the following observations about the development and application of communication skills in early intervention programs.

First, communication should be broadly defined as the messages that are sent to families by a program and the ways in which programs respond to messages sent by families. In this context, then, we must recognize that communication occurs at multiple levels that include specific parent-professional interactions as well as agency policies and procedures. In other words, simply being a skillful communicator may not ensure that a program is effectively communicating in a family-centered manner. We convey certain messages to families through policies and the timing and sequence of procedures, as well as through face-to-face interactions. Therefore, it is important to consider both communication skills and program practices when addressing how to translate principles into practice.

Second, an outgrowth of this broad view of communication is that changing communication patterns will necessitate training and decision making at both the individual and program level. Not only do findings from communication workshops support this assumption (Winton & Bailey, 1990), but the literature on the change process also challenges the idea that brief training experiences provided to individuals can be of lasting benefit (Fullan, 1982; Havelock & Havelock, 1973). Since building a set of effective communication practices is partly a program-level endeavor, the development and refinement of communication skills is likely to be enhanced if (1) teams make a program-level commitment to changing communication practices; (2) a needs assessment is conducted in order to identify areas in which change is needed; (3) specific goals for change are established and timelines for their achievement are set, and (4) at least some of the training activities involve all team members.

The purpose of this chapter is to demonstrate a potential application of this process in four domains of family-professional interaction: (1) intake and referral; (2) planning a family meeting; (3) identifying family resources and priorities; and (4) generating family outcomes. In each interaction context, issues and suggestions are provided regarding the purpose of the interaction, its place in the intervention process, and levels of family involvement. We describe traditional and alternative approaches to communication and sample ways of actually saying things to family members. Finally, we present some strategies for practicing communication skills.

Effective communication skills and practices might be defined as the extent to which professionals and programs engage in practices that achieve specific communication goals or outcomes. An explicit description of those goals is essential, however, because the goals will heavily influence the skills and practices needed. Suppose, for example, that Program A wants to communicate to families that its staff are highly knowledgeable professionals who can pinpoint children's needs and advise families on the precise goals and treatment for their child. Program B, on the other hand, wants to communicate to families a recognition that parents are knowledgeable about the needs of their children and an affirmation of their role as competent decision makers and team members. It is quite likely that the communication skills and practices needed by Program A would be different from those needed by Program B.

The chapter is based on certain values with respect to communication goals. To the extent that programs and individuals agree with these goals, we believe that the skills and practices described will be effective. In brief, it is our belief that the following messages are important for families to hear:

1. Your opinions and priorities are valued and respected;
2. You are or can be a competent advocate and decision maker about what is best for you and your child;
3. We are listening to you and acknowledge and respect what you are saying;

4. We have a team of experts that are available as resources for you; and
5. We want to provide services in a way that is consistent with your values and priorities.

The remainder of this chapter explores how these goals can be realized in the context of specific programmatic activities.

## INTAKE/REFERRAL

## What Is the Purpose of Intake?

How families are first referred to early intervention and special education services varies considerably. Referrals may come from a variety of agencies, professionals, or from parents themselves. The process for conducting intake for new referrals also varies across programs. However, most programs tend to have standard procedures whose major purpose is to determine if the child and family is eligible for the services of the program (Johnson, McGonigel, & Kaufman, 1989).

The first step in examining communication practices is to consider the purpose of intake. Historically intake has been viewed as the process of determining eligibility for services. Yet research with families suggests that transitions are difficult, especially those related to beginning new programs or locating services (Johnson, Chandler, Kerns, & Fowler, 1986; Winton, Turnbull, & Blacher, 1984). Descriptions from families of a fragmented, uncoordinated system in which there is no one person or place for accurate information about what is available in the community suggest ways that intake might better serve families. Rather than focusing narrowly on determining eligibility for the services of a single agency or program, intake might be seen as an opportunity to identify and match broad family concerns or interests with community resources that might best serve those interests. This approach reflects a philosophy that services be comprehensive, coordinated, and community based and that family needs rather than available services define the focus of intervention. Intake provides a logical point for beginning to implement that philosophy.

## How Are Families Involved in Intake?

One way of addressing how families are involved in intake is to ask what information is typically requested of families, how it is gathered, and what information is given to families. In many programs intake procedures are routinized, with a standard set of information requested from all families. This may also include lengthy family and social histories or other information of a personal nature. It may include information that has already been collected and is available from another agency or professional. It is important to consider how this information is used and whether it is necessary at this point. Upon reflection, professionals often say that much of the intake information they gather ends up unused in a file drawer. It is also important to consider the words we use. We sometimes start our initial contacts with families with phrases like, "How can I help you? What are your needs as a family? What kinds of problems are you having with your child?" These words immediately focus attention on what is going wrong and on a relationship based on the professional being in a position of power. If we truly believe in the family-centered ideas related to building on family and child strengths, identifying existing resources, and empowering families, we might consider using different words to begin our relationship. Simply asking, "What brings you here to our clinic or agency?" allows families to start with their story. The main theme of their story might not be needs and problems, but triumphs and challenges. The question, "What has happened so far?" is one that further encourages a family to share information about their child, previous contacts with professionals, and prior evaluations. This question lets the family know you are interested in their story but respectful of their right to provide the information that is relevant and important from their perspective.

In addition, it is important to consider what and how information is provided to families during intake. In the traditional approach, a description of the specific services of the agency or program is often one of the first pieces of information shared. This fits with the traditional purpose of intake, that is, determining if the family is eligible or desires the services of the particular agency. However, if a broader definition of intake is adopted, in which the purpose is to elicit family interests and link those interests with community resources, a description of particular agency services at the beginning of the process will likely limit how a family member defines family interests.

The major point to be made here is that a commitment to interagency coordination and a family-centered approach can be implemented in the context of first contacts with families. Often the "family" part of intervention is viewed as occurring after the intake and child assessment phases. A recognition that family intervention begins at the first point of contact may lead to the realization that intake communicates a different set of messages to families than those articulated in a program's philosophy.

# PLANNING TO MEET WITH FAMILIES

## What Is the Purpose for Planning a Family Meeting?

Family meetings traditionally have been planned for two primary purposes: (1) to provide families with diagnostic information ("the interpretative interview"); and (2) to involve families in the development of individualized education plans (IEPs, IHPs, IPPs). The current emphasis on giving families the opportunity to be involved in all aspects of the intervention process clearly challenges these traditional practices. If family interests are to guide intervention efforts, prompt planning of a family meeting for whatever purpose the family identifies as important emerges as an alternative to current practice.

## How Are Families Involved in Planning Meetings?

Typically family meetings take place at times and places that are determined by professionals. In order to respect family preferences and encourage participation by all interested family members, determining times and places for meeting that are convenient for the family is important. An implication of eliciting this information from families is that professional work schedules must permit evening, weekend, or lunchtime meetings. If this kind of flexibility is not possible, it is another way in which programmatic policies and practices convey unspoken messages to families. Turnbull, Turnbull, Summers, Brotherson, and Benson (1986) have provided suggestions for involving families in preconference planning and a format for eliciting parent preferences regarding location, time, persons in attendance, and ways of preparing for conferences.

The literature on effective interviewing suggests that anxiety is created when certain information is not clarified before an interview is held (Gorden, 1969). This includes the issues of purpose, time allotment, who will attend, and confidentiality. Confidentiality is often handled through signed consent forms or written agreements. Ensuring that all family members attending meetings are fully aware of policies related to confidentiality is important if candid, open communication is to occur.

## IDENTIFYING FAMILY RESOURCES AND PRIORITIES

## What Is the Purpose of Identifying Family Resources and Priorities?

When Part H of PL 99-457 was first passed in 1986, the component of the law that created the most controversy was the mandate that IFSPs should contain a statement of the family's needs and strengths related to enhancing the development of the infant with disabilities. Criticisms were leveled at the wording of this mandate. Dunst, Trivette, and Deal (1988) suggested that terms such as *projects* and *aspirations* might be substituted for *needs*. Research reported by Bailey and Blasco (1990) indicated that many parents do not like the word *need* used repeatedly in survey instruments. Dunst et al. (1988) suggested that there is danger in using the word *strengths* because of the implication of a continuum with *weakness* at the other end. Another concern was that well-intentioned professionals might invade a family's privacy in their attempts to gather family information. As a result of these concerns, the wording of the law was changed during the reauthorization of Part H in 1991, and the words *needs and strengths* were replaced with *resources and priorities*.

These concerns and the subsequent modifications of the law highlight the importance of being clear about our purposes in gathering family information. The primary purpose is that family priorities guide what happens in early intervention. Andrews and Andrews (1991) use the analogy of basil and spaghetti sauce in describing a family-centered approach. Family priorities should flavor every action that is taken, just as basil is used to season spaghetti sauce; gathering family information is not an activity to be added on at the end, just as you would never serve basil as a side dish to add to the sauce after it is cooked.

## How Are Families Involved in the Identification of Family Needs and Strengths?

Because a family-centered approach is relatively new, there is not a lengthy history or tradition related to gathering family information. In fact, this is an area in which professionals are searching for measures, strategies, and guidelines. Research studies by Summers et al. (1990) and Bailey and Blasco (1990) have provided guidance in this area. Bailey and Blasco (1990), in a survey of parents who filled out a family needs survey form, reported that parents feel strongly that choices should be available to family members regarding how they share information. Data gathered by Summers et al. (1990), through the use of focus groups comprised of professionals and family members, suggested that informal, unstructured conversations conducted in sensitive ways are the preferred method for gathering information related to family needs and strengths. This emphasis on family choice, and indications that a first choice for many families might be face-to-face conversations, presents a challenge to many professionals who feel uncertain about their communication skills. Another concern is how to translate the wealth of information that might be gathered into a written document that fulfills criteria for an IFSP.

Asking family members to simply identify their resources and priorities is likely to yield global responses that are minimal in length and not easily translated into our traditional notions about intervention goals. Truly understanding what a family hopes to achieve takes time and depends on the development of a trusting relationship. By listening to what families wish to share and by acknowledging and validating their experiences, points of view, and actions, we are likely to start building a relationship on a positive and supportive note. The way we acknowledge what families say is through nonverbal and verbal communication skills. Given the recent emphasis on this aspect of the intervention process and the significant interest that professionals have in what to say and do, we provide an extended description and illustration here of an approach to questioning relevant to gathering family information.

*Circular questioning* has been described within the family therapy literature (Tomm, 1987) as a useful strategy in helping professionals understand more about the family's situation. This approach emphasizes building on family's existing resources, eliciting natural competence, and helping families develop solutions to the problems they identify (O'Hanlon & Weiner-Davis, 1988; Weiner-Davis, 1990). The approach reflects a recognition that events are interrelated and is designed to gather information about the relationships among feelings, values, beliefs, contexts, events, and people. Rather than being investigative in nature, it conveys an attitude of exploration and curiosity about what is happening.

Circular questioning has been contrasted with linear questioning. Linear questions are investigative in nature and tend to focus on definitions and explanations of problems and events. This mode of questioning is associated with determining basic facts as a way of understanding the family.

What follows are two brief transcripts of the information-gathering phase of a family interview within an early intervention context that demonstrate linear and circular questioning approaches, respectively.

## LINEAR QUESTIONING

Interventionist:  What needs do you have as a family?

Father:  We need help getting Johnny to eat right.

Interventionist:  Who feeds Johnny?

Father:  My wife.

Interventionist:  What kinds of problems do you have with feedings?

Mother:  Getting him to feed himself.

Interventionist:  Are you using foods that he can easily pick up?

Mother:  Yes.

Interventionist:  Have you had this problem evaluated?

Mother:  Evaluated? Well, I've talked to the pediatrician. He said Johnny's gaining weight so it wasn't that serious. Anyway he set up an appointment with a nutritionist who works at his office. She told me some things to try but none of them seemed to work.

Interventionist:  Why do you think they didn't work?

Mother:  I don't know.

(P. Winton, 1991, p. 11)

As illustrated in this example, a drawback to linear questioning is that it tends to focus blame or responsibility on an individual. This may convey the attitude that somebody is doing something wrong, and if that can be figured out then the problem or need could be resolved. In this illustration, it is evident that once it was determined the father was not involved in feeding, all attention was directed toward the mother. The series of questions to the mother that follow in the illustration provide little information related to possible solutions. A likely outcome of this interview would be that another feeding assessment might be recommended.

## CIRCULAR QUESTIONING

| | |
|---|---|
| Interventionist: | How are things going at home right now with Johnny? |
| Father: | Pretty well . . . we have our ups and downs. Right now a big problem is getting him fed. |
| Interventionist: | Could you tell me a little bit about what feeding him is like? |
| Father: | Well, it's a mess. We're trying to get him to feed himself, but that's not working. And when she feeds him, she can't tell what's going in. |
| Interventionist: | Sounds difficult . . . (to the mother) Who all has been involved in feeding Johnny? |
| Mother: | Just me really. He's [Dad] given up . . . says he can't do it. |
| Interventionist: | (to Dad) What happens when you've tried? |
| Father: | She usually starts telling me what I'm doing wrong, and she's right. I can't get anywhere with him. |
| Interventionist: | How do you react to that? |
| Father: | Well, I just turn it over to her . . . |
| Mother: | You mean, you just leave . . . |
| Father: | Well, it all gets so chaotic, I do get the urge to just get out of here. |
| Interventionist: | What else is going on that makes it chaotic? |
| Mother: | The other kids are hungry, and they start asking for snacks and getting into things and that gets me upset. |

Interventionist:     Have you gotten any advice on this that has been helpful?

Mother:     Not really. I've talked to my pediatrician about it and he says it's not a real problem because Johnny is gaining weight. He sent me to a nutritionist. She had lots of advice, but none of it seemed to work (sounding discouraged).

Interventionist:     You sound pretty discouraged.

Mother:     I am.

Interventionist:     If things could be different during Johnny's feeding time, what would be the thing that would make the biggest difference?

Mother:     Um (thinking)—I guess if I had some peace and quiet.

(P. Winton, 1991, pp. 112–113)

The preceding example illustrates that circular questioning can clarify the context surrounding a family's concerns or interests. In this illustration the approach to questioning led to a more complete understanding of how family members have been and currently are involved in feeding Johnny. Of particular importance, the family's major interest related to feeding—having some peace and quiet—has been identified. Without an understanding of how families define events and what their priorities are in terms of solutions, professionals are likely to focus attention on areas that are more *their* concern than the families'. Circular questions provide a means for keeping the focus on the family. They increase the likelihood that the solutions which follow fit within the family's values and belief system. They provide a strategy for following the recommendation of Gallimore, Weisner, Kaufman, and Bernheimer (1989), that the amount or level of stimulation specified in intervention goals is less important than the extent to which the goals can be sustained within the family's ongoing routine.

Specific examples of circular questioning strategies that might be useful during this intervention phase are provided in Table 12-1. The questions reflect social systems and empowerment principles underlying current priorities in family-centered intervention.

## GENERATING EXPECTED FAMILY OUTCOMES

### What Is the Purpose of Generating Expected Family Outcomes?

Identifying family outcomes is another recent component of the intervention process that has created concern and confusion among professionals. Summers et al. (1990) stated that there "is a lack of a theoretically-grounded, empirically-based, and family-friendly framework for conceptualizing expected family outcomes of early intervention" (p.19). Johnson et al. (1989) proposed that family outcomes can focus on any area of child development or family life that a family feels is related to its ability to enhance the child's development. If we accept this definition, then the possible family outcomes are limitless and dependent on how each family defines events. This clearly negates the narrow definition that some might bring to this phase of intervention—that is, family outcomes are limited to only those goals in which the family is the target of change. An IFSP might specify only child-related outcomes, but if those outcomes have been identified by the family then they could be considered family generated and family centered.

## How Are Families Involved in Generating Family Outcomes?

Theoretically, since the passage of PL 94-142 in 1975, there has been a mechanism for ensuring that intervention outcomes are generated in collaboration with families. However, research on the IEP process indicates that collaboration has not occurred (Turnbull, et al., 1986). Brinckerhoff and Vincent (1986) reported that 75% of IEPs were developed by professionals before the IEP meeting took place. This suggests that we cannot look to past practices for direction.

Simply asking families to define their goals is not likely to evoke specific responses. Interviewing skills derived from the family therapy literature have direct application for this phase of the intervention process.

*Reflexive questioning* has been described in the family therapy literature (Tomm, 1987) as a means of encouraging families to generate their own solutions and problem-solving strategies. In order to do this, the questions serve two purposes. One is to stimulate the family to think about the future implications of current events, needs, or problems. This encourages the family to think about how they would like things to be at a future point in time and facilitates goal setting in this regard. The second purpose is to stimulate thinking about possible actions or options that would accomplish the anticipated outcomes. For example, asking families how much progress they think they can expect, or how they will know when an identified outcome has been achieved, are ways of incorporating their knowledge and beliefs into all aspects of goal setting. This approach conveys respect to the family. It is a way of recognizing their abilities to problem-solve on their own and allows them to generate solutions that fit with their values and understanding of what works for them.

The reflexive approach to questioning has been contrasted with strategic questioning (Tomm, 1987). Strategic questions are designed to influence a family and are often used when an interventionist has definite ideas about what the family ought to be doing. Through strategic questioning the interventionist attempts to get the family to agree to the needed changes. In this questioning mode the interventionist operates much like a teacher, instructor, or judge.

Findings from the field of business suggest that imposing one's goals on another person is less likely to be an effective means of getting that person to achieve the goals than if the person generates the goals themselves (Latham &

TABLE 12-1 ▆▆▆▆▆▆▆▆▆▆▆▆▆▆▆▆▆▆▆▆▆▆▆▆▆▆▆▆

## OPEN-ENDED QUESTIONS TO ELICIT INFORMATION ON FAMILY PRIORITIES AND RESOURCES

| DOMAINS OF INTEREST | QUESTIONS |
| --- | --- |
| *Opening Question:*<br>Finding out where family wants to focus (addressed to each family member in turn so each has a chance to respond) | How are things going with (child's name)? |
| Understanding family's perspective on child | What kinds of things does (child's name) enjoy doing? What makes him or her happy? |
| | What kinds of things do each of you enjoy doing with (child's name)? |
| Understanding family's definition of child's delay or handicap | What have you been told about (child's name) (hearing, vision, motor, etc.—using words of family members)? |
| | How does this fit with what you know and believe about (child's name)? |
| | What else do you know about (child's identified disability)? |
| | In what ways has this information been helpful? Or not helpful? |
| | What do you think (child's name) needs help with, if anything? |
| | What kinds of things have you tried that worked? That didn't work? |
| Understanding family's informal and formal support system | What kinds of advice have you been given? |
| | Whose advice has been helpful? Not helpful? |
| | What happens in a crisis? (if crises have been described as happening in the past). |
| Understanding family ecology surrounding events of importance to family members | If family has identified a particular event that they want to focus on, asking what a typical (mealtime, trip to the park, etc.) is like. |

TABLE 12-1
*(continued)*

## OPEN-ENDED QUESTIONS TO ELICIT INFORMATION ON FAMILY PRIORITIES AND RESOURCES

| DOMAINS OF INTEREST | QUESTIONS |
|---|---|
| Understanding family ecology surrounding events of importance to family members | Can you think of a time that (the event—mealtime, trip to the park, etc.) went well or worked the way you wanted it to? What was happening that made it work? |
| | Who or what was helpful? Who or what was not helpful? |
| Understanding critical events that aren't directly related to child | What other things are going on now that are important to you? |

From P. Winton, 1991, pp. 117–118

Locke, 1979). This provides an immediate challenge to interventionists who are used to operating and being seen as experts whose opinion is often actively sought by families. This is not to say that those opinions and expert suggestions should never be given. What should be considered is that the manner and timing of how this information is shared may be critical in terms of the family being able to incorporate this information into their ideas about what will and will not work for them.

What follows are transcripts of the outcome generation phase of a family interview, demonstrating strategic and reflexive questioning approaches to this phase. This is a continuation of the family interview illustrating circular and linear questioning.

## STRATEGIC QUESTIONING

Interventionist: Why don't you ask your husband to help?

Mother: I do, but he says he can't take the yelling.

Interventionist: (to Dad) Could you try and help out ... maybe you could help with the other kids?

Father: When I try to help, everything I do is wrong.

Mother: That's because you just let the kids eat anything they want and it spoils their dinner.

| | |
|---|---|
| Interventionist: | (to Mom) Can you fix the kids a snack earlier so they won't bug you while you're feeding Johnny? |
| Mother: | They say they're not hungry earlier and don't want anything. |
| Interventionist: | This sounds like a problem you two need to work on. I could make a referral to the psychologist on our team. |

(P. Winton, 1991, p. 114)

This example illustrates how ineffective the interventionist was when he or she tried to generate goals, based on what he or she thought ought to happen.

## REFLEXIVE QUESTIONING

| | |
|---|---|
| Interventionist: | (to Mom) Going back to what you said about wishing there could be some peace and quiet, what is different about the times when there is peace and quiet? |
| Mother: | Um hum . . . it has been so long—I guess I can't remember what was different except that Johnny wasn't born. |
| Interventionist: | What will it take to get some peace and quiet at mealtime now? |
| Mother: | A miracle, and that's not going to happen. |
| Interventionist: | If things continue like they are now when you're trying to feed Johnny, what do you think might happen? |
| Mother: | I don't know . . . I might go crazy . . . I'm not seeing any improvement in the way things are and it really is getting me down. |
| Interventionist: | (to Mom) If you were to share with him (nodding to Dad) how down you are about this situation, what do you think he might think or do? |
| Mother: | I don't know. |
| Interventionist: | (to Dad) What do you think you might think or do? |
| Father: | Well, I guess I didn't realize how upset she was . . . I guess I would try to figure out how I could help. |
| Interventionist: | (to Dad) Will that be hard to do? |

Father:          Yes, because in the past I've never done it right.

Interventionist:  (to Mom) Can you think of ways that he has helped and gotten it right?

Mother:          (pause) Um . . . well, yes . . . a couple of times on a nice day he has taken the kids outside when he gets home from work. That gives me a chance to concentrate on Johnny without them badgering me. (Pause) If he could help in that way more often, I think it would make a difference.

Interventionist:  What do you think of what she said. How do you think that will work?

Father:          I think it might work, if you kids won't bug me for snacks.

Interventionist:  (to siblings) What do you kids think?

                 (P. Winton, 1991, p. 115)

This example shows how reflexive questioning might be used to stimulate family members to come forth with alternatives. By asking the family to report a time when feeding went well, the emphasis turns to possible solutions. However, in this illustration the family appears to be stuck and unable to come forth with any solutions. By asking the family to consider possible consequences to things staying the same, the interventionist was able to help the mother and father problem-solve together about possible solutions. By asking the family what they did that worked, the emphasis is on giving them credit for success. The final comment illustrates the importance of checking out with all family members how they might react to various plans of action.

Specific examples of reflexive questioning that might be useful during this intervention phase are provided in Table 12-2. These questions are related to the specific components of the IFSP—outcomes, strategies, criteria, and time-lines—mandated by law.

## SUMMARY: PRACTICING COMMUNICATION SKILLS

The circular and strategic questions in Tables 12-1 and 12-2 are provided as examples of open-ended questioning that might be integrated into a free-flowing conversation with a family. It is not suggested that these lists of questions be read to families in a formal way. However, to incorporate questions such as these into

TABLE 12-2

## OPEN-ENDED QUESTIONS FOR GENERATING FAMILY OUTCOMES

| DOMAINS OF INTEREST | QUESTIONS |
| --- | --- |
| Understanding family priorities for outcomes | If you were to focus your energies on one thing for (child's name), what would it be? |
| | If you could change one thing about (event of importance), what would that be? |
| | Imagining six months down the road, what would you like to be different in terms of (event or area of importance)? Are there some things you would like to be the same? |
| | What would you like to accomplish in six weeks? Six months? |
| | When are some times when the event of importance went well? What was happening that seemed to contribute to its success? |
| Generating solutions or strategies for achieving outcomes that fit family values | What are some ways of getting to where you want to go? |
| | Who would need to be involved in getting done what you want to do? What would each of you need to do in order to accomplish what you want? |
| Identifying criteria for success and monitoring progress | How will you know when you've done what you want to do? |
| | How will you know when (child's name) has made progress in the ways you described? |
| Setting timelines | How long do you think it will take to get to where you want to go? |

From P. Winton, 1991, pp. 119–120

your natural communication repertoire takes practice and feedback. One strategy for practicing skills is to participate as a team in a role-play exercise. The Miller family vignette and discussion questions provide a structure for practice. Table 12–3 provides a format for self-analysis and feedback that might be used to structure discussion following a role play. As a result of this kind of activity, differences in skill levels among staff can become apparent. Encouraging those with the greater skills to act as models and consultants to those with fewer skills is a way of building on the strengths of a team or agency.

The suggestions provided in this chapter require an ongoing commitment by individuals, teams, and agencies to staff development related to family communication. Supervisors and administrators play a key role in this process. Providing staff the support, the time, and the resources to examine practices and develop and refine skills are critical components to bringing about the changes described.

# Case Study: MILLER FAMILY STORY*

*Referral and Planning to Meet*

William "Billy" Miller, a 20-month-old white male, was referred to the special early intervention program by his day-care center. He had been placed in a day-care two months ago after a woman from a local church had called protective services about possible neglect in the home. This woman had delivered a Thanksgiving basket of food to the family and had been concerned because no toys were in evidence for Billy and his 6-year-old sister, June. The house was also somewhat unkempt and the parents had appeared (to her) retarded. A protective service worker had investigated and found no concerns related to children's safety or basic care, but did find the level of stimulation in the home impoverished and, with the parents' consent, had placed Billy in day-care. June was attending full day kindergarten and special services were not provided for her. Parents were supportive of the day-care placement, saying they wanted "anything that would help" their son.

At the day-care, Billy appeared passive and fearful. He did not play with toys or other children. Often he stood alone in one corner of the room and cried. He never spoke or used gestures. He did not feed himself and did not consistently eat from a spoon when a teacher attempted to feed him. He appeared frightened and visibly shrank from any contact with staff or other children. He was not a behavior problem, but appeared so inhibited that he could not enjoy or enter

*Note: This case study first appeared in *The IFSP Training Manual* (Appdx A) by M. J. Brotherson, J. Summers, P. Winton, D. Hanna, S. Brady, P. Berdine, C. Rydall, and K. Kivi, 1989, Lexington: University of Kentucky. Interdisciplinary Human Development Institute. Contact person: Dr. Mary Jane Brotherson, 114 Porter Bldg., U. of Kentucky, Lexington, KY.

into activities. Based on these behaviors, the day-care director referred the Miller family to your agency.

1. *Discussion Questions:*

   What information would you want to gather in order to proceed with this referral?

   How would you get that information?

   What issues are likely to be of concern to this family when the first contact is made?

2. *Role Play:* The day-care director has told Louise Miller that you will be calling her about Billy. Conduct a role play of the first contact with this family by telephone. During this telephone conversation you would like to set up a family meeting.

TABLE 12-3

## SELF-ANALYSIS AND FEEDBACK ON FAMILY INTERVIEW

1. Did interviewer ask for clarification of purpose, format, and confidentiality?
2. Was opening question related to purpose, but broad and open-ended?
3. Were all family members invited to speak?
4. Did the interviewer develop an understanding of the following:
   a. family's perception of child?
   b. family's definition and understanding of disability?
   c. family's informal and formal support system?
   d. family ecology surrounding events that are the focus of intervention?
   e. other events that are of interest or importance to family members?
5. What communication strategies were particularly helpful in eliciting this information?
6. Was the interviewer able to effectively identify the following:
   a. priorities for outcomes?
   b. specific outcomes?
   c. family-generated solutions or strategies for achieving outcome?
   d. criteria for success?
   e. timelines?
7. What communication strategies were particularly helpful in generating this information?
8. As the interviewer in this role play, what would you like to do the same and what would you like to do differently, if given another chance at the role play?
9. As family members, how did you feel about the interview? What part went well? What would you have liked to have been different?

- Assign roles for telephone role play (family member, professional, observers)
- Conduct role play
  *Family: Louise Miller*—you answer the phone when the professional calls. You act hesitant and uncertain but basically agree with whatever is suggested, saying you want to do "whatever will help Billy."

3. *Feedback:* Consider the telephone conversation from the professional's and parent's perspectives. What was accomplished by the telephone contact? Were parental concerns addressed? How do you think Louise is feeling about the intervention program?

## IDENTIFYING FAMILY PRIORITIES AND RESOURCES AND GENERATING OUTCOMES

The Miller house was a small frame "shotgun" house located on an alleyway behind a garage and sitting between two small warehouses. The narrow front porch of the house sat only a few feet back from the alley and little space was available between the house and warehouse. A few broken toys were in evidence under the porch. Jonas Miller, Billy's father, greeted you at the door.

The Miller front room contained two twin beds, each shoved against adjoining walls, and two chairs. A closed fireplace with an electric heater in front of it occupied one wall and a large color television turned to the cable community bulletin board channel sat in a corner. Several battered suitcases were stacked on one bed and in another corner was a pile of dirty laundry. However, the beds were made and the room appeared generally neat. No toys were in evidence.

In the room were Jonas and Louise and Louise's father, Hoyt Jordan. Louise's sister, Edna, peered cautiously from the next room. Jonas and Louise sat on a bed at one end of the room; Hoyt occupied a chair against the opposite wall. You took a seat on the other bed near the parents.

When Jonas introduced his father-in-law, he mentioned that Hoyt had just gotten out of the hospital the previous day. In response, the elderly man began a long description of his medical problems. He was 81, "not bad shape for 81, am I?" and had "high blood pressure, kidney trouble, and sugar." His most recent hospitalization was for a bout of pneumonia, but he said he was now "feeling fine, though I can't get around like I used to." After about 10 minutes of description of various illnesses and treatments, Jonas broke in to say "She's here about Billy, Daddy," and Hoyt quieted down.

In the meantime you counted at least four mice running in and out of a hole beside the fireplace. Although distracted by the mice and the TV, you proceeded with the family interview.

1. *Discussion Questions:*

   What are your major tasks during this meeting?

   Do you have strategies for accomplishing these tasks?

2. *Role Play:*
   - Conduct a role play of this meeting
   - Assign the following roles:
     a. Jonas Miller
     b. Louise Miller
     c. Hoyt Miller
     d. Interventionist
     e. Observer
   - Family members read descriptions of their roles (this information should not be read by others)
   - Role-play volunteers sit casually with observer and others in position to see them clearly
   - In role play, emphasis is on practicing communication skills

3. *Feedback:*
   - Participants will consider the questions on the Self-Analysis and Feedback from Table 12-3.

**(THIS INFORMATION IS TO BE READ BY PARTICIPANTS WHO PLAY THE ROLE OF FAMILY MEMBERS.)**

### THE MILLER FAMILY

Jonas:  Since the protective service worker came to your house, you have been fearful of having your children removed. You have heard stories of social workers who take children away from their parents and you are not sure but what the interventionist isn't trying to do that. You feel vulnerable because you do not have a job. You have never worked outside of doing small odd jobs for your landlord and are not sure you could. You are also very worried about your father-in-law's health. With repeated hospitalizations and the many medical problems, it seems unlikely he will live much longer. Since his social security check is the major income for the family, you wonder how you'll survive after he is gone. Billy's problems appear minor to you, although you know that he is shy. He is also not much trouble, the way other children you've seen seem to be and you like him that way.

Louise:  You have always been very shy around people, but you actually kind of enjoy social opportunities if you don't have to talk much. Since last December when a local church brought some food and toys by for the kids, you have been riding the church bus to Sunday school with the children. The people at the church seem nice and although you don't know her name, one woman always speaks to you and you've begun to think of her as a friend. You were the next-to-youngest daughter and always felt responsible for taking care of your father and your sister Edna who is not quite right in the head. You know that your father can't live much longer and you have wondered about the possibility of getting a job, but think you probably would not be able to work. You know Billy can do more than he shows at the day-care, but you sympathize with his painful shyness. You never felt comfortable around people either. On the other hand, you would really like for him to have the opportunity to get a good education and a job.

Hoyt: Until 25 years ago, you worked as a farm laborer, but increasing health problems and a fall from a hay loft which left you crippled put an end to your work history. Your social security check enables you to continue to take care of your family, along with food stamps and government-subsidized housing. You are ill much of the time, and although you try to keep a bright outlook, you know that you are frequently irritable. You expect Edna, Louise, and Jonas to stay around the house to take care of you. You have taken care of them and you feel it is only what you deserve. You are worried about your impending death which you believe to be very near and can't understand why all the fuss is being made about Billy.

# REFERENCES

Andrews, J., & Andrews, M. (1990). *Family-based treatment and communicative disorders.* Sandwich, IL: Janelle.

Bailey, D. B., & Blasco, P. M. (1990). Parents' perspectives on a written survey of family needs. *Journal of Early Intervention, 14* (3), 196–203.

Bailey, D., Simeonsson, R., Isbell, P., Huntington, G., Winton, P., Comfort, M., & Helm, J. (1988). Inservice training in family assessment and goal-setting for early interventionists: Outcomes and issues. *Journal of the Division for Early Childhood, 12,* 126–136.

Benjamin, A. (1969). *The helping interview.* Boston: Houghton-Mifflin.

Brinckerhoff, J., & Vincent, L. (1986). Increasing parental decision-making at the individualized educational program meeting. *Journal of the Division for Early Childhood, 11,* 46–58.

Dunst, C., Trivette, C., & Deal, A. (Eds.). (1988). *Enabling and empowering families.* Cambridge, MA: Brookline.

Fullan, M. (1982). *The meaning of educational change.* New York: Teachers College Press.

Gallimore, R., Weisner, T., Kaufman, S., & Bernheimer, L. (1989). The social construction of ecocultural niches: Family accommodation of developmentally delayed children. *American Journal on Mental Retardation, 94*(3), 216–230.

Gorden, R. (1969). *Interviewing: Strategies, techniques and tactics.* Homewood, IL: Dorsey Press.

Havelock, R., & Havelock, M. (1973). *Training for change agents.* Ann Arbor: University of Michigan.

Ivey, A. (1971). *Microcounseling: Innovations in interview training.* Springfield, IL: Thomas.

Johnson, B., McGonigel, M., & Kaufman, K. (1989). *Guidelines and recommended practices for the individualized family service plan*. Washington, DC: Association for the Care of Children's Health.

Johnson, T., Chandler, L., Kerns, G., & Fowler, S. (1986). What are parents saying about family involvement in school transitions? A retrospective transition interview. *Journal of the Division for Early Childhood, 11*(1), 10–17.

Latham, G., & Locke, E. (1979). Goal-setting: A motivational technique that works. *Organizational Dynamics*, 45–54.

O'Hanlon, W., & Weiner-Davis, M. (1988). *In search of solutions: A new direction in psychotherapy*. New York: W. W. Norton.

Summers, J. A., Dell'Oliver, C., Turnbull, A. P., Benson, H. A., Santelli, E., Campbell, M., & Siegal-Causey, E. (1990). Examining the IFSP process: What are family and practitioner preferences? *Topics in Early Childhood Special Education, 10*(1), 78–99.

Tomm, K. (1987). Interventive interviewing: Part II. Reflexive questioning as a means to enable self-healing. *Family Process, 26*(2), 167–184.

Turnbull, A., Turnbull, R., Summers, J., Brotherson, M., & Benson, H. (1986). *Families, professionals and exceptionality*. Columbus, OH: Merrill.

Weber, T., McKeever, J., & McDaniel, S. (1985). A beginner's guide to the problem-oriented family interview. *Family Process, 24*, 357–363.

Weiner-Davis, M. (1990). In praise of solutions. *The Family Therapy Networker, 14*(2), 42–48.

Winton, P. (1988a). Effective communication between parents and professionals. In D. Bailey & R. Simeonsson (Eds.), *Family assessment in early intervention* (pp. 207–228). Columbus, OH: Merrill.

Winton, P. (1988b). The family-focused interview: An assessment measure and goal-setting mechanism. In D. Bailey and R. Simeonsson (Eds.), *Family assessment in early intervention* (pp. 185–205). Columbus, OH: Merrill.

Winton, P. (1991). *Working with families in early intervention: An interdisciplinary preservice curriculum* (2ed.), Chapel Hill, NC: Frank Porter Graham Child Development Center.

Winton, P. J., & Bailey, D. B. (1990). Early intervention training related to family interviewing. *Topics in Early Childhood Special Education, 10*(1), 50–62.

Winton, P., & Bailey, D. (1988). The family-focused interview: A collaborative mechanism for family assessment and goal-setting. *Journal of the Division for Early Childhood, 12*(3), 195–207.

Winton, P., Turnbull, A., & Blacher, J.(1984). *Selecting a preschool: A guide for parents of handicapped children*. Austin, TX: PRO-ED.

# 13

# PARENTS AND THE EDUCATIONAL SYSTEM

*Bonnie Strickland*

## INTRODUCTION

The notion that the family plays a central and vital role in determining the services their children with disabilities receive has been underscored repeatedly in the establishment of policy and best practice during the past two decades. Previous chapters have addressed early intervention and the central role of the family in the design and provision of services to infants and toddlers as a result of PL 102-119. From age 3 through 21, the educational needs of children with disabilities are addressed through special education programs in public schools. The legislation governing these programs is PL 101-476. This chapter focuses on the opportunities provided by this legislation for parent participation in the planning and implementation of special education services once a child reaches school age.

On the surface, many of the basic elements governing the provision of services to school-aged children appear to be similar to those of early intervention services to infants and toddlers. Both require the provision of services to children with identified disabilities; both require comprehensive and nondiscriminatory assessment of the child; both require the development of a written plan; both adhere to a concept of least restrictive environment; both provide a system of due process and parent participation. But beyond these broad commonalities, PL 102-119 and PL 101-476 differ significantly in regard to the roles that parents and family members assume. Understanding these differences is critical for both parents and professionals—critical for parents because their own role may change significantly when their child enters school for the first time, and critical for professionals because they must facilitate a smooth transition for parents and children from the family-focused model of early intervention to the child-focused model of the school system.

## DIFFERENCES BETWEEN EARLY INTERVENTION SERVICES AND SPECIAL EDUCATION SERVICES

Differences between the parents' role in early intervention and their role in the public school special education program can be influenced by a number of factors including (1) systemic differences; (2) differences in the role expected of parents and family; and (3) differences in the way services are designed and provided. Because these differences can often pose problems for families as they move between these systems, a brief discussion is provided here.

## Systemic Differences

Systemic differences refers to the probability that agency responsibility for the provision of services may change once the child becomes school aged. The responsibility for early intervention differs from state to state. In some states, the school system is the public agency responsible for coordinating all services for children with disabilities from birth through 21. In other states, the educational system may not begin to provide services until the child reaches age 3. At the age of 3, however, preschool special education services take the place of the early intervention services. For the family, this may mean that procedures for obtaining and negotiating services will change, service providers will change, and a new structure, that of special education, will have to be learned.

Another systemic difference is that of eligibility. Children who have received early intervention services from birth through the age of 2 may not, upon reaching age 3, qualify for services within the educational system. This may happen for two reasons. First, it is the purpose of early intervention to provide specialized services to children and families early on in order to minimize the need for special education upon entering school. If early intervention has been successful, the child may not require special education at the age of 3. Second, the child may not meet the eligibility criteria established by the public school system. Unlike the early intervention system, there is not usually a provision for "at-risk" children in public school special education programs. Although most states are attempting to create a seamless continuum of services that will enable qualifying children to move easily from one service sector to another, it is unlikely that all children who receive early intervention services will be eligible for special education at age 3. In states that do not educate typical children at the age of 3, children who continue to be "at risk" may not be eligible for any publicly provided services between the ages of 3 and 5. Parents and professionals should consider early on whether the child is likely to qualify for special education at the age of 3, what services are likely to be required, and how those services will be obtained if not through the public school.

## Differences in Parental Roles

Both PL 102-119 and PL 101-476 emphasize the critical nature of parent participation in planning and implementing of services for the child with a disability. However, the *way* in which parents participate in their child's program may change significantly once the child enters the public school system. In the early intervention system the *family* is likely to be central not only in the planning and decision-making process, but may also be recipients and participants in the early intervention services themselves. Early intervention services often include the family to the extent that family strengths and needs might be assessed to determine how best to enhance the development of the child through the family, services might be provided directly to the family, and outcomes on the IFSP often reflect family-oriented goals. Within the public school program *parents* are recognized as participants in planning and decision making regarding educational services to be provided to the child, but are not likely to receive or participate in the provision of special education. Whether by design or as a result of implementation, parents, upon entering the public school system, primarily participate in procedural and decision-making capacities. There is little, if any, provision for assessment of, or services to, the parents or family of school-aged children with disabilities. Even the use of the term *parents* in the terminology of PL 101-476 conveys a narrower interpretation than the use of the term *family* in PL 102-119.

Despite less involvement in some aspects of services, school entry may have significant advantages for many parents. Special education services are usually consolidated to ensure their provision during the school day. In addition, schools are responsible for providing transportation to and from school, and to and from any specialized services necessary for the child to benefit from the special education program. Such arrangements can create new flexibility for parents who have had primary responsibility for caregiving and transportation to and from early intervention services. In addition, school entry provides a natural opportunity for increased independence for both parents and children.

## Differences in Service Delivery

The written service document, the individualized education program (IEP) for school-aged children, differs significantly from the individualized family service plan (IFSP) developed for families and children in the early intervention system. Rather than focusing on the strengths, resources, and needs of both the family and the child, the IEP focuses on the educationally related needs of the child and the specially designed instruction to be provided. Related services, such as speech and language therapy, physical therapy, and occupational therapy, are provided only if those services are necessary to enable the child to benefit from special education. Rather than being continually reviewed and revised, the IEP is required to be reviewed and revised only annually unless a change in the child's program occurs or the parent or teacher requests a review of the program. The almost exclusive focus on the *child* within the *educational environment* and the infrequent requirement for review and revision of the IEP reflect the decreased emphasis on the integration of parents in programming once the child enters the school system.

A final difference in regard to service provision is the conceptualization of the least restrictive environment. During the period from birth to 2, the least restrictive environment is considered to be where typical children of this age are found. Because many such children remain at home, many early intervention services are provided at home. This fact alone increases the involvement of the family in the services provided to the young child with a disability. However, once the child enters school, the home might be considered a more restrictive environment for that child because typical children of the same age do not remain at home. By the time a child reaches kindergarten age, the regular classroom is recognized as the location where typical peers receive their education, thus this setting is also the preferred educational setting for children with disabilities.

If the needs of a child with a disability cannot be met in the regular classroom, even with the use of supplemental aids and materials, a range of alternative settings must be available, including (1) short periods of specially designed instruction in a resource room; (2) part-time placement in a special education classroom; or (3) full-time placement in a special education program. At this point a program provided at home might be considered most restrictive because access to children is more limited than in any other setting. It should be noted that in the public school, the location of services must be based on the identified needs of the child, which must be determined at least once a year.

Because early intervention and the public education systems differ in their focus, methods of interaction between parents and professionals also differ between the two systems. Upon entering school the focus of involvement moves from one in which parents may be both planners of and participants in the services provided to the child to one in which their primary role is planning, approving, and monitoring the educational program provided to the child. The IEP meeting is the primary way in which parents participate in the planning and decision-making process within the educational system. It should be noted that although the IEP must be reviewed and revised only annually, both the parents and the school may request a meeting to discuss, review, or revise the IEP at any time.

Another forum, the due process hearing, provides a mechanism for resolving disputes between parents and educators when differences arise regarding the provision of an appropriate education to the child. This forum allows either parents or the school to contest the actions or decisions of the other party regarding the child's program. A third forum, the mediation conference, is often selected as an intermediate step between the IEP conference and the due process hearing. Although not required by law, and not to be used to postpone a due process hearing, the mediation conference attempts to resolve differences of opinion through negotiation, and can be a beneficial alternative in resolving conflict without resorting to a costly, and adversarial, due process hearing.

Regardless of the particular forum, successful parent-professional interaction requires that all parties possess adequate knowledge and the requisite skills to participate effectively in the decision-making process. The purpose of this chapter is to translate the applicable legislative policies of PL 101-476 into procedural guidelines and competencies regarding two of the three forums for parent-professional decision making: the IEP conference and the mediation conference. The third forum, the due process hearing, is addressed in the next chapter.

# DEVELOPING THE IEP: A FORUM FOR EDUCATIONAL PLANNING ███████████

For a school-aged child with a disability, the IEP conference is the forum provided for educational planning and decision making. The IEP conference provides an opportunity for parents and professionals to formulate an educational program that is tailored to the individual needs of the child. The goal of the IEP conference is to reach consensus or general agreement between parents and professionals on the nature and content of the child's educational program, and to capitalize on the uniqueness and relevance of each participant's information and insight concerning the needs of the child. Because the IEP conference may be one of the few planned opportunities for parents and professionals from a variety of disciplines to meet together for the specific purpose of curriculum planning around the needs of the child, every effort must be made to ensure that the interaction during the process is productive and fosters future cooperation and communication. Specific legislative requirements define the minimal parameters for affording parents the opportunity to participate in the IEP process. These legal requirements include (1) provision of adequate notice that provides parents with full information about the meeting; (2) scheduling the meeting at a time and place mutually convenient to both parents and professionals; and (3) documenting efforts to include the parents when they cannot attend the meeting. However, meeting these minimal requirements of the law does not guarantee that parents will participate actively in the development of an educational program for their child. Substantive participation requires that a mutual relationship be established through which parents and professionals can communicate and plan on behalf of the child.

Although the intent of the IEP process is shared decision making between parents and professionals, the skills and attitudes necessary to achieve this outcome do not necessarily come easily. Naturalistic observations of IEP conferences in the early years of the IEP requirement (Goldstein, Strickland, Turnbull, & Curry, 1980) indicated that the IEP conference could generally be described as the presentation of an already developed IEP to the parent by the special education teacher. Even though the IEP requirement has existed for more than a decade, attendance and active participation of parents in IEP planning and decision making can still be characterized in this way (Singer & Butler, 1987; Turnbull & Hughes, 1987; Vaughn, Bos, Harrell, & Lasky, 1988).

Low levels of parent participation may indicate that some parents do not consider their own active participation to be a vital component of an appropriate education for their child ( Allen & Hudd, 1987; Witt, Miller, McIntyre, & Smith, 1984). However, it is also likely that existing professional attitudes and practices encourage and contribute to low levels of parent participation in the IEP process (White & Calhoun, 1987) . During the early years of the IEP conference, professionals indicated that parent participation was considered most appropriate in gathering and reporting information relevant to the child's program, and that activities which included judging program alternatives and finalizing decisions were less appropriate for parents (Yoshida, Fenton, Kaufman, &

Maxwell, 1978). Today, it appears that similar attitudes may still prevail. Parent participation is often viewed as helpful but not essential to the development of the IEP ( Gerber, Banbury, Miller, & Griffin, 1986). Further, professionals appear to view the IEP conference as a meeting to obtain the parents' signature on an already developed IEP (White & Calhoun, 1987).

While these findings are somewhat troubling considering the clear legal preference for meaningful parent participation in the planning and decision-making process, it should be pointed out that PL 101-476 provides the opportunity for parents to participate to the extent they wish, not a mandate to measure up to an established standard of participation. The fact that many parents do not participate in the IEP meeting may mean that, even though provided adequate opportunity, some parents may choose not to participate. It should also be noted that parents may not view their active and vocal participation in the IEP meeting as the primary indicator of their satisfaction with the conference proceedings and outcome. Witt et al. (1984) found that parent satisfaction may be more influenced by the adequacy of time allowed for the conference and by parents' perceptions of the professional's concern for their child than by whether parents perceived themselves as contributing significantly to the conference.

Balancing the individual preferences of parents regarding the nature and level of their participation, the legal requirements for encouraging participation, and the professional desire for efficiency of time and effort are all critical considerations in planning and implementing the IEP conference. Regardless of how parents ultimately choose to participate, it is incumbent on the school to ensure that opportunites for maximum participation do, in fact, exist.

Despite its many technical difficulties (Smith, 1990), professionals and parents both tend to agree that the IEP process is a valuable mechanism for enhancing the understanding of the child, and for providing an opportunity for parents and professionals to meet together in a positive way (Goldstein et al., 1980; Salisbury & Evans, 1988; Strickland & Turnbull,1990; Vaughn et al.,1988). Perhaps, then, the single most important purpose of the IEP conference is to establish positive and trusting relationships between parents and professionals that provide a basis for mutual planning and decision making on behalf of the child.

Obviously, merely extending the right to parents to participate in the development of the IEP does not ensure a meaningful interaction at the conference. The implementation of systematic strategies for eliciting active involvement of parents warrants careful consideration by professionals and parent advocates. The next section provides suggestions for enhancing meaningful parental involvement organized according to six major components of the IEP conference:

1. preconference communication
2. initial conference proceedings
3. interpretation of evaluation results
4. development of the curriculum portion of the IEP
5. decision of placement and related services
6. conclusion of the meeting

Table 13-1 contains a list of suggestions for professionals for facilitating parent participation in the IEP conference.

## Preconference Communication

The major objective of the preconference communication component of the IEP conference is to provide notice to parents regarding the conference and to encourage their participation. The notice must contain the purpose, time, location, and names of persons who will be in attendance at the meeting. Further, the notice must be provided early enough to ensure that parents will have an opportunity to attend, and the meeting must be scheduled at a mutually convenient time and place (Federal Register, 1990). The notice is of crucial importance, since it can build the foundation for collaboration and communication at the conference. Stylistic features warranting consideration include avoiding educational and legal jargon, personalizing the letter as much as possible, emphasizing the importance of the IEP, and clarifying precisely the role of the parents at the conference. In order to clarify the parental role, an agenda of the meeting; a sample IEP form; and a list of questions for parents to consider before the conference could be enclosed with the notice. Sample questions might include the following:

1. What are your goals for your child this year or for the next few years?
2. What skills do you think are most important for us to work on at school?
3. Would you object to your child leaving his or her classroom to receive special education services?
4. Are there ways you help your child at home that might be good ideas for us to use at school?
5. What do you want to tell us about your child?
6. What questions can we answer for you?

In addition, if an IEP has been drafted by professionals prior to the IEP meeting, a copy of that draft should be provided to parents prior to the IEP meeting. Providing information such as a list of questions and copies of planning documents before the IEP conference enables parents to think about the information and insights they would like to share prior to the meeting. Thus they may be more likely to anticipate the meeting with an organized plan for information sharing and a feeling of confidence in knowing what to expect.

In addition to the required written notice pertaining to the IEP meeting, additional methods for preconference communication include phone calls, home visits, individual conferences, and group parent meetings. Some teachers have held informative group parent meetings at the beginning of the year to show parents a videotape of an IEP conference, followed by an opportunity to role-play various components of the conference. This strategy goes beyond the requirement of PL 101-476 in more fully preparing parents for active decision making in the IEP conference.

TABLE 13-1

## PROFESSIONAL SUGGESTIONS FOR FACILITATING PARENTAL INVOLVEMENT IN THE IEP PROCESS

1. Provide appropriate written notices to parents regarding their involvement in IEP committees, including the requirements of stating the purpose of the IEP, arranging a mutually convenient time and location, and informing parents of the persons who will be attending the meeting.

2. Demonstrate skills in informing parents of evaluation results and IEP involvement using, in addition to the written notice, the strategies of parent-teacher conferences, phone calls, and home visits.

3. Prepare parents for meaningful IEP involvement prior to their attendance at the conference by training them in their specific roles and responsibilities.

4. Create an atmosphere in the initial portion of IEP committees that will contribute to effective parental involvement such as greeting parents, making introductions, and ensuring that parents understand their particular role and responsibilities as committee members.

5. Communicate with parents by displaying respect for the child, sensitivity to the parents' feelings, recognition of the parents' right to the confidentiality of their private life, and the willingness to listen to and respect the parents' viewpoint.

6. Initiate strategies for involving parents in active decision making, if they do not automatically assume this role, by modeling the role of asking questions and stating diverse viewpoints, reinforcing parental responses, and directing questions to parents.

7. Inform parents of their legal rights in understandable and jargon-free terminology.

8. Review evaluation results with parents in terms of specific strengths and weaknesses of their child and relating this information to the child's performance at school and home.

9. Discuss and negotiate the following aspects of IEP development with parents: (a) levels of performance; (b) annual goals; (c) short-term objectives; (d) evaluation procedures; (e) special education placement and related services; (f) extent of time in the regular class; and (g) method of reviewing the IEP on at least an annual basis.

10. Elicit special concerns from parents related to their child and to ensure that these concerns are carefully considered by the IEP committee.

11. Clarify with parents the particular follow-up responsibilities of IEP committee members and negotiate preferred strategies for parent-teacher communication throughout the school year.

12. Devise strategies for appointing, training, and involving parent surrogates for the IEP conference when the child's parents (biological, guardian, foster, or adoptive) cannot be located.

# Initial Conference Proceedings

The initial portion of the IEP conference should create an atmosphere of openness and respect, which enhances effective parent participation during the meeting. Parents should be greeted and welcomed when they arrive at the conference and appropriate introductions should be made. In one instance, a father of a child with a disability reported his discomfort when he sat through the entire IEP conference with four school representatives, knowing the name of only one of them. Sometimes even when introductions are made, it can be difficult to remember the names of all the conference participants. When the conference is attended by more than three or four persons who have not previously known each other, name tags should be used to ensure that participants can address one another by name.

In regard to the number of persons attending the IEP conference, it should be recognized that parents differ in their preferences for large and small meetings. In some instances, parents can feel intimidated and outnumbered when a large group of professionals attend the meeting. In other instances, parents may view a large number of professionals attending as indicating interest and comprehensive attention to the needs of the child (Witt et al., 1984). The required participants include (1) the child's teacher; (2) a representative of the school system other than the teacher who is responsible for providing or supervising special education; (3) the parents; (4) the child, when appropriate; and (5) an evaluator in cases in which the child's disability has been identified for the first time and other members of the committee are not knowledgeable about the evaluation procedures used with the child and the results. In determining who should attend the meeting beyond the required participants, emphasis should be directed at keeping the attendance at a level that protects and encourages the active involvement and participation of the parent.

The chairperson of the meeting should ensure that all committee members have been introduced and identified according to their particular role in the education of the child. If parents are not familiar with the role of each person, clarification should be provided. For example, merely stating that a conference participant is an occupational therapist may not be an adequate explanation of the person's particular role in relationship to the child. Rather, enumerating specific duties and potential services to the child could enhance not only the parents' understanding but that of all committee members.

The purpose of the meeting should be stated and the agenda and timeline for the meeting reviewed. Although the purpose of the meeting is included in the preconference notice, it warrants further definition at the beginning of the meeting to help all committee members focus on the task at hand. Reviewing the agenda at the outset of the meeting typically serves to remind participants of the decisions that must be made and the necessity of using time efficiently.

Finally, it is important to reiterate and adhere to the established timeline for the meeting, since both professionals and parents are likely to have other commitments that require their attention after the meeting. If the full agenda cannot be covered in the available meeting time, the goal of the meeting may be to complete a portion of the IEP and to reconvene at another time to complete the remaining portion. Both parents and professionals are likely to agree to additional meetings if they know that timelines will not exceed those established.

Research suggests that parents may participate more when specific strategies are used to encourage interaction at the IEP conference (Goldstein, et al 1980). For example, another member of the IEP committee may assume the role of parent advocate, either on a formal or an informal basis. In this role the parent advocate might encourage the active participation of the parent by directing questions to parents, reinforcing comments made by parents, and requesting clarification of information that is presented. A school or community with a strong and effective parent advocacy component might also consider providing parents experienced in the IEP process to talk with new parents before the actual conference to explain the process from the parent perspective, review questions that might arise, and even to attend the meeting, if the parent wishes.

Finally, it is important at the beginning of the conference to inform parents of their legal rights. These rights should be explained in as jargon-free language as possible, and any questions regarding rights should be discussed prior to proceeding with the conference. The parents should also be given a written copy of their rights, such as that illustrated in Table 13-2.

## Interpretation of Evaluation Results

PL 101-476 requires the school system to provide the parents with a written notice informing them of evaluation results. The content of this notice must include the following information:

1. a full explanation of all procedural safeguards;
2. actions proposed and rejected by the agency with a rationale included for each proposal and refusal;
3. a description of each test and procedure used in the evaluation process as a basis for the proposed action; and
4. a description of any other factors considered in the agency's proposal or refusal. (Federal Register, 1990)

Since the IEP is an outgrowth of the evaluation process, it is important to review the evaluation results with the parents at the IEP conference. One of the most often criticized aspects of IEP development is the lack of apparent relationship between the evaluation process and the instructional planning process (Salvia & Ysseldyke, 1988). The purpose of the evaluation review is to identify the child's specific strengths and weaknesses as a basis for planning the educational program. Evaluation information that specifically reflects instructional aspects of the child's program should always be included in this discussion. If the parents have received written notice of evaluation results prior to the IEP meeting, the meeting can serve to review the content of that notice and to build on the relevant outcomes of evaluation in the development of an instructional program. However, if written notice has not already been provided, the parents must re-

TABLE 13-2

# PARENT AND CHILD RIGHTS IN PL 101-476

As a parent of a child who has been identified as having a disability, the following rights are provided through federal legislation (PL 101-476):

1. A free appropriate public education with necessary related services to meet your child's needs (i.e., speech therapy, physical therapy, counseling, and transportation) must be provided by your local school system.

2. Your child should be educated in classes with typical children if such classes are appropriate to the needs of your child. This means, for example, that your child may not be removed from regular class placement to be put in a special class attended only by children with special needs unless you and the school personnel believe that the special class would be the best placement.

3. Your child may not receive an initial evaluation in order to be placed in a special education program unless you are previously informed and voluntarily give your consent. If you do give your consent, you may withdraw it at any time.

4. You are entitled to receive an explanation of all evaluation results and an explanation of any action proposed or rejected in regard to evaluation results.

5. You have the right to request an independent evaluation (conducted by someone outside of the school) and have the results considered in discussions regarding the school placement of your child.

6. You may inspect all educational records and request explanations of information contained in the records. You may also request that the information be amended if you do not agree with it.

7. The privacy of all school records must be maintained. You may request copies of your child's school records. Furthermore, you may obtain information from the chairperson of the special services committee concerning the particular individuals who are allowed to see your child's records.

8. You have the right to request an objective hearing (due process hearing) at any time when you disagree with the proposed procedures for evaluation and/or placement of your child. At the hearing you may have counsel, present evidence, cross-examine witnesses, and obtain written findings of the proceedings. If you normally communicate in a language other than English, the hearing must be conducted so that all communication is completely understandable to you.

From B. Strickland and A. P. Turnbull. *Developing and Implementing Individualized Education Programs.* Columbus, OH: Merrill, 1990.

ceive this information for the first time at the IEP conference, thus requiring allocation of more time to provide an in-depth explanation of evaluation results and their relationship to the development of the IEP.

Regardless of which method is used, a clear interpretation of evaluation results must be provided to the parents. Important pointers in explaining evaluation and assessment results to parents and all committee members include (1) using behavioral rather than technical terms; (2) providing a comprehensive and well-integrated interpretation of results; (3) highlighting strengths, as well as clearly specifying the child's weaknesses; and (4) systematically relating evaluation and assessment information to the areas to be addressed in IEP development. Further, if the child has been classified as having a particular disability by the school, this classification should be reviewed and discussed with the parent. Classifications established for educational purposes do not always coincide with medical diagnoses with which parents may be familiar. For example, a child with Down syndrome may be classified by the school as having mental retardation, and/or may be provided special education in a program serving children with developmental disabilities. School personnel must ensure that parents are aware of the meaning and implications of these classifications.

Parents should be encouraged to ask questions and to provide insights concerning the interpretation of evaluation data. The role of the parent advocate, as discussed in the previous section, can be particularly important in clarifying information and eliciting parental comments during the discussion of evaluation results.

## Development of the Curriculum Portion

The curriculum portion of the IEP refers to the specifications of the current level of performance, annual goals, short-term instructional objectives, and the evaluation schedules and procedures that will be used to determine if the instructional objectives have been achieved. This portion of the IEP determines what specially designed instruction will be provided to the child. The curriculum portion of the IEP can be developed in alternative ways (Strickland & Turnbull, 1990). Because parents differ in their desire for more or less participation, options should be discussed prior to the meeting to ensure that an appropriate strategy for developing the IEP is selected. For parents who prefer to review a completed draft, a two-hour meeting in which the entire IEP is developed by all committee members might diminish the likelihood that the parents will return for another meeting. Likewise, parents who wish full participation will likely resent being presented with a draft IEP that requires only a signature for completion.

A frequent practice is for one or more committee members to draft curriculum sections of the IEP before the conference. The development of a draft IEP before the meeting can provide a frame of reference for parent-professional communication. An advantage to this approach is that significant time can be saved in meetings when every objective does not have to be devised and phrased by the full committee. Further, if the parents have reviewed the recommended goals and objectives prior to the meeting, they can react in terms of amending, approving, or rejecting items they have had an opportunity to review. A distinct disadvantage of a draft IEP is that it may be presented as a final document for the parents to sign, thus minimizing parental participation ( White & Calhoun, 1987).

An alternative strategy is to develop the total IEP in the committee meeting. The advantage of this strategy is that the opportunity is provided to capitalize on the full contributions of all committee members. Through this process parents would be afforded maximum opportunity to contribute to the specification of every objective in the child's IEP. The recommendations made earlier related to sending questions to parents in advance as part of the preconference communication can help prepare the parents to contribute to the conference and enhance the relevance of their contributions. The obvious disadvantage of this approach is that meetings might be extremely lengthy and time consuming. Further, it can be an inefficient use of time for three or more committee members to focus on the specific phrasing of each objective. In choosing the appropriate strategy to follow, two important criteria that must continually be balanced against each other are (1) the enhancement of parent-professional collaboration; and (2) the efficient use of time.

## Decision of Placement and Related Services

The curriculum portion of the IEP, once developed, serves as the basis for determining how and in what setting special education and related services will be provided. In some instances special education might be provided within the context of the regular education program; in other instances the child may participate in a different program altogether, while still having an opportunity to interact with typical students. In determining the appropriate placement and related services, the child's needs serve as the criteria for decision making as opposed to what is readily available in the school system (U.S. Department of Education, 1986).

Most educators know that students cannot be removed from the regular education program unless it is clear their needs cannot be addressed in that environment even with the use of supplemental aids and services. However, parents are likely to be unfamiliar with the array of placement options that should be available in the school system. Thus the concept of least restrictive placement should be explained to parents and a written list should be provided outlining the various placement options. Based on the child's needs, alternative placements should be discussed in detail with pros and cons identified for each placement. Through the process of discussion and consensus, a placement decision should be reached considering the opinions of all committee members.

In addition to specifying placement, related services that are necessary to implement the IEP should be determined. Related services required by PL 101-476 for school-aged children are very similar to the early intervention services required by PL 102-119 for infants and toddlers with disabilities, and include

> *transportation and such developmental, corrective, and other supportive services as are required to assist a handicapped child to benefit from special education, and includes speech pathology and audiology, psychological services, physical and occupational therapy, recreation, early identification and assessment of disabilities in children, counseling services, and medical services for diagnostic or evaluation purposes. The term also includes school health services, social work services in schools, and parents' counseling and training. (Federal Register, 1977, p. 42479)*

A written list providing a description of each of these services would be a helpful point of reference for committee members in choosing services appropriate to the needs of the child. Parents may need to be reminded that related services are provided at no cost to them. In addition to services on the IEP, the projected dates for the initiation of services and the anticipated duration of services must also be documented.

It can sometimes be difficult to make decisions related to placement and related services on the basis of consensus. Parents, for example, may firmly believe that their child needs direct physical therapy on a daily basis whereas school representatives maintain that the regular education program, with consultation from the physical therapist, can address the needs of the child. Or parents may prefer that the child remain in his or her home school and receive special education services whereas the school prefers to provide services in a centrally located program. Disagreements such as these should be specifically addressed, negotiated, and preferably resolved through discussion and compromise at the IEP meeting. If resolution cannot be reached on a specific aspect of the IEP, that aspect might be tabled temporarily until an agreeable compromise can be negotiated. Every effort should be made to reach a mutually agreeable resolution at this point, rather than at later mediation or due process proceedings when adversarial postures may adversely affect the ability of both parties to compromise.

## Conclusion of the Meeting

At the end of the conference, the chairperson should summarize the discussion in terms of decisions made, future actions (e.g., annual review procedures, method of communication throughout the school year), and persons responsible for implementing the IEP and other agreed upon activities. The purpose of this review is to clarify all decisions made by the committee. If consensus has been reached among all members of the committee, the IEP can be formally approved (as indicated by the signatures of all participants) and copies distributed to all committee members. If there are unresolvable differences among parents and professionals pertaining to such issues as evaluation results, classification of the child, curriculum content of the IEP, placement, and/or related services, mediation might be considered as a next step. Although mediation can itself be adversarial and costly, it provides an alternative to the often lengthy and complicated procedure of the due process hearing. The mediation process is discussed later in this chapter.

## Suggestions for Parents

The responsibility of parents to be active and contributing advocates for their child during the IEP conference is as important as the development of the professional's skills in facilitating parent participation. This role can be difficult for parents to assume, however, since parent education and information is not always readily available to those parents who may need it most. For a large number of parents, traditional sources of advocacy information such as workshops, newsletters, and parent groups are simply not a viable mechanism for obtaining information and education. For families who do not participate in, or have access to, existing sources of training, alternative strategies for delivering information need to be considered. Information might be provided by a series of videotapes that parents can review at home, or a mentoring parent contact might be provided to visit with parents new to special education. Parents who wish to should have an opportunity to meet with one another, share information and strategies, and develop their own system of educating one another in regard to their style of preferred participation in the IEP conference. Professionals might encourage and support this type of school- or community-wide activity by simply asking parents if they would like their name and phone number made available to other parents of children with disabilities in the same school or community.

For parents who can and do access traditional sources of education, many possible alternatives exist. PL 101-476 requires school systems to provide training to parent surrogates (e.g., a representative appointed for the child when the parents cannot be identified or located) to ensure that they are able to fulfull their responsibilities associated with free appropriate public education for the child. Making this training available to parents of children with disabilities, as well as surrogate parents, might be considered as a source of education for parents of children with disabilities. Other sponsors of education could be parent organizations (e.g., Association for Retarded Citizens), the state education agency, regional training programs, and colleges and universities. Table 13-3 provides a summary of suggestions for parents, which complements the guidelines for parent and child rights outlined in Table 13-2. The suggestions are organized according to the six components of the IEP conference discussed in this section.

## ENGAGING IN MEDIATION: PARENT-PROFESSIONAL NEGOTIATION

Most disagreements between parents and schools are resolved through informal negotiation. This process has the advantage of allowing parents and professionals

TABLE 13-3

## PARENTAL SUGGESTIONS FOR THE IEP CONFERENCE

1. Preconference Communication
   a. Check to see if written notice contains required components: time of meeting, purpose, location, and participants.
   b. Ensure that time of meeting is convenient.
   c. Reschedule meeting if time suggested by the school is inconvenient.
   d. Obtain any information you believe will be helpful at the meeting, including your child's school or medial records.
   e. Inform the school of your intent to attend the meeting and state your eagerness to be involved in the decisions pertaining to your child's program.
2. Initial Conference Proceedings
   a. If you are not introduced at the meeting to any persons you do not know, introduce yourself to all committee members.
   b. Make a note of the names and positions of everyone at the meeting.
   c. Ask questions to clarify the particular role of other committee members if this is not explained initially.
   d. If you bring a friend or advocate, introduce him or her and explain his or her role.
   e. If you have a time limit for the meeting, let other committee members know.
   f. Ask the chairperson to state the purpose of the meeting and review the agenda, if this is not done.
   g. If you have any questions about your legal rights, ask for clarification.
3. Interpretation of Evaluation Results
   a. Ensure that the teacher or psychologist reports all tests that were adminstered and the specific results of each.
   b. You may make a record for yourself or ask for a written copy of the test results and evaluation of your child. This may become an important part of your records on your child.
   c. Ensure that the classroom and educational implications of the evaluation results are identified.
   d. If any professional jargon is used that you do not understand, ask for a clarification.
   e. Ask how your child was classified in regard to a particular handicapping condition (e.g., mental retardation, learning disabilities).
   f. If you disagree with evaluation findings or classification regarding your child, state your disagreement.
   g. If your disagreement cannot be resolved within the meeting, ask for an independent evaluation to be administered by a psychologist or appropriate professional outside the school.

TABLE 13-3
(*continued*)

# PARENTAL SUGGESTIONS FOR THE IEP CONFERENCE

4. Development of the Curriculum Portion of the IEP
   a. If the school's description of your child's performance is not as you perceive it, *do give* your description of his or her performance level.
   b. State the skills and content areas that you believe are most important for your child's program.
   c. If you question the goals and objectives suggested by the school, ask for justification. Your ideas are also valid.
   d. Ensure that all subjects requiring specially designed instruction are included in the IEP.
   e. If your child receives instruction from two different teachers (regular and resource teachers) clarify the manner in which the responsibility for teaching objectives will be shared.
   f. If you are willing to assume responsibility for teaching or reviewing some of the objectives with your child, make this known to the committee.
   g. Ensure that the procedures and schedules for evaluation of goals and objectives are specified.
5. Placement Decision and Related Services
   a. State the placement (regular classroom, resource program, special class) that you believe is most appropriate for your child.
   b. Be sure all necessary related services (speech therapy, physical therapy, transportation) that you believe your child needs are included. Remember that the school is not obligated to provide related services not written into the IEP.
   c. If the school does not agree with you on placement and related services and you are convinced you are right, *do not sign the IEP.* Ask for the procedural guidelines for mediating a disagreement.
   d. If you agree on a placement but are unfamiliar with the teacher, ask about the teacher's qualifications (training and experience) in regard to students with disabilities.
   e. Ensure that your child has appropriate opportunities to interact with non-disabled children (placement in the least restrictive setting).
6. Conclusion of the Meeting
   a. If the chairperson does not initiate it, ask for a summary of the meeting to review major decisions and follow-up responsibility. Make a written record of this summary.
   b. If follow-up responsibility has not been specified, ask who is going to be responsible for each task.
   c. Specify what responsibility (teaching objectives, increasing socialization opportunities during after-school hours) you will assume.

TABLE 13-3
(*continued*)  **PARENTAL SUGGESTIONS FOR THE IEP CONFERENCE**

d.  Ensure that a tentative date is set for reviewing the IEP on at least an annual basis and preferably more frequently.

e.  State in what ways and how frequently you would like to keep in touch with the teacher. Negotiate these in light of the teacher's preferences.

f.  State your desire and intent to work in close cooperation with the school.

g.  Express appreciation for the opportunity to share in decision making and for the committee's interest in your child.

to control the process of reaching agreement and the development of a solution to the disagreement. However, if negotiation fails to resolve differences, many states include mediation as the next level of settling disputes by negotiation and compromise. The purpose of mediation in the education of children with disabilities is to resolve differences between parents and educators that cannot be effectively handled through consensus or negotiation procedures, but which may not require the more formal due process hearing for settlement. The process involves a mediator, or third party, who has the responsibility of promoting an agreement between the parents and the school. Mediation provides an opportunity for directed discussion on points of disagreement between school representatives and parents. Emphasis is placed on reconciling differences of opinion by the mutual agreement and compromise of both parties, without the additional formality of attorneys and expert witnesses.

Although mediation cannot be required as a prerequisite to the due process hearing, the procedures can be initiated on any issue related to the appropriate education of a child around which parents and professionals fail to reach agreement. However, mediation is not always an appropriate substitute for the due process hearing. When the dispute between the parent and school has gone beyond the point where informal measures might potentially yield positive results, mediation is an unlikely remedy. Likewise, when the issue is one that requires legal interpretation rather than negotiation for resolution, mediation is not an appropriate procedure. How does one decide to choose mediation instead of the due process hearing? Some general guidelines include the following:

1.  Both parties must have a desire to settle the dispute through mediation, and the procedure must be voluntary.

2.  Both parties should see the potential for progress toward resolution.

3.  There should be a continuing relationship between the parents and the school that can serve as a basis for negotiation and compromise.

4.  Parents should have standing equal to that of the school system.

5.  The mediator must be independent of both parents and the school.

When these criteria are met, mediation can serve to clarify existing issues and create new options, uncover potential alternatives, and keep both the parents and school moving toward a solution (Goldberg, 1989).

The mediator plays a key role in the process of resolving disagreements. Important criteria to consider in the identification of persons to serve as mediators include the ability to see both sides of an issue, impartiality, group process skills, and well-developed interpersonal skills. A thorough knowledge of educational programming for students with disabilities is a preferable characteristic, but not absolutely necessary. One procedure for identifying a mediator is for the school administration to maintain a list of persons who have been mutually agreed upon and recommended for this role by a committee made up of both parents and professionals. From this list of recommended persons, all parties involved in the dispute should approve the individual who will serve as mediator in resolving the disagreement.

Although mediation cannot be used to postpone a due process hearing that has been requested by the parents, most states provide for mediation in their state regulations that govern the administration of special education programs. Since mediation is not specifically required by PL 101-476 as a precursor to due process, many educators and parents do not consider it a viable alternative to resolving disputes. Further, in some instances where mediation has been implemented, results have tended to be almost as adversarial, formal, and costly to participants as the due process hearing (Boscardin, 1987).

Specific procedures for mediation proceedings are often determined by the mediator or established by school regulation or policies. It is therefore important to determine whether a prexisting procedure exists and, if so, to obtain a copy prior to beginning preparation for mediation. The model we present in this section provides a six-component framework for preparing for and participating in mediation. When at all possible, preparation skills applied to one aspect of planning should be applicable to other situations in which parents and professionals meet to discuss issues. Therefore, the planning components for mediation are organized in a similar manner to those of the IEP conference. These components include the following:

1. preconference communication
2. initial conference proceedings
3. identification of points of disagreement
4. discussion of points of disagreement
5. determination of a course of action
6. summary of proceedings

Table 13-4 includes a listing of competencies for the participants (both professional and parents) in mediation sessions covering all components of the mediation model.

## Preconference Communication

The mediator approved by both the parents and school representatives should communicate with all parties prior to the conference. The purpose of this com-

TABLE 13-4

## SUGGESTED COMPETENCIES FOR PARTICIPANTS IN MEDIATION SESSIONS

1. To identify the legal rights of children with disabilities in regard to mediation.
2. To determine when the legal rights of an individual child have been abused and what specific action constituted the violation.
3. To outline the proceedings that will occur at the mediation conference.
4. To assist parents in the development and preparation of case material to be used in mediation, including the request for witnesses, presentation of testimony, and briefing of witnesses before the conference.
5. To demonstrate general knowledge regarding school programs and procedures including testing procedures, diagnosis, programming, and placement.
6. To demonstrate specific knowledge related to the program provided for a particular child.
7. To identify briefly and state clearly the issues involved in mediation.
8. To contribute to an atmosphere of willing cooperation among the participants present at the mediation conference.
9. To identify systematically each point of disagreement among the participants at the mediation conference.
10. To be knowledgeable concerning the position taken by the other party during mediation proceedings.
11. To discuss and negotiate individual issues as presented during the mediation conference.
12. To demonstrate techniques of negotiating, reviewing, and questioning evidence during mediation proceedings.
13. To demonstrate methods of synthesizing information presented during the mediation conference on each point of disagreement.
14. To identify criteria for accepting or rejecting alternatives presented during the mediation conference.
15. To clarify with the mediator and other participants at the mediation conference issues regarding suggested compromises.
16. To arrive at a future course of action based on the agreement of the participants with the negotiations during the mediation conference.
17. To initiate strategies for monitoring the implementation of decisions made during the mediation conference.

munication is to schedule a mutually convenient time and place for the meeting and to describe the procedures to be followed during mediation. Describing the procedures can serve to reduce the uncertainty, and consequently the anxiety, that both parents and professionals may experience prior to the conference. The location of the meeting is an important consideration. Although the most frequent location is in a school facility, other, more neutral, options should be considered, including community buildings such as libraries, YMCAs, and/or churches.

As with the IEP conference, the tone and style of the preconference communication can be instrumental in setting the stage for negotiation during mediation. It should be remembered that mediation is specifically designed to provide a fair resolution to disagreement while still avoiding the formality, cost, and adversarial tone usually attributed to the due process hearing. Therefore, communication prior to mediation must set the stage for such an exchange to occur. Important factors to consider include (1) assuring all parties that their opinions and positions on issues will be respected; (2) downplaying the need for attorneys on both sides, since the mediator will represent the rights and interests of both the parents and the school; and (3) accentuating the fact that the child's right to receive a free appropriate education will be the guiding criteria in reaching decisions.

Conflict between parents and schools, if left unresolved, often develops and grows over an extended period of time (Strickland, 1982). Such delays in resolving conflict can contribute to tension and mistrust long before mediation occurs. Such an adversarial relationship may be so strong that the process of mediation is defeated even before it begins. Thus timing must be recognized as an extremely important factor. As soon as it becomes clear that a disagreement cannot be resolved through consensus or negotiation, mediation should be requested, a mediator appointed, and preconference communication initiated.

## Initial Conference Proceedings

As the mediation conference begins, the mediator should introduce all participants, review the procedures to be followed, and specify the timeline for the conference. Parents, school representatives, and the mediator must ensure that during the meeting communication remains open, respectful, and focused on the commitment to providing appropriate educational opportunities for the child involved.

The unresolved issues that led to mediation should be summarized by the mediator as an introduction to the substantive portion of the conference. Both parties should then agree that the issues as stated and understood by the mediator are indeed the issues as understood by both the parents and the school. It is unlikely that mediation can proceed in a positive and productive manner unless all parties agree on what is being negotiated. Both parents and schools should also expect an opportunity to describe the issues from their respective positions. Important characteristics of these statements include clarity, conciseness, and organization. The objective is to highlight the issues being negotiated and the remedies being sought rather than to convince other participants of the correctness of that position. Both professionals and parents should avoid personally attacking each other or making unsubstantiated accusations. All parties must be committed to a nonadversarial atmosphere in order to ensure that mediation is conducted in this manner.

## Identification of Points of Agreement and Disagreement

After issues and hoped for remedies of both the parents and the school are reviewed, the specific issues around which the school and the parents *do* agree should be pinpointed. A chalkboard or flipchart is helpful for this activity, allowing all participants to see visually that there are indeed points of agreement, and providing a mechanism for all to participate in the process by adding to or modifying the points included on the list. Once identified, points of agreement represent a common framework and perspective for working toward resolution of the conflict.

Identifying points of disagreement follows. These issues can be viewed as barriers to an acceptable resolution. At this point, attention should be focused on the identification of issues that specifically pertain to or prevent the resolution of differences. Open discussion concerning these points should be avoided at this point. Further, it is critical for the parties to focus on the issues at hand, rather than, for example, on previous disagreements that may have occurred. A systematic procedure, such as ranking identified barriers from the most to the least troublesome and prioritizing the order in which issues should be addressed, will save time and provide clear definition to the discussion portion of the conference that follows.

## Discussion of Points of Agreement and Disagreement

After specific points of agreement and disagreement are listed, it is appropriate to discuss each one individually, first by one party and then the other. The discussion should encompass reasons for the position taken on the point, along with supporting documentation when appropriate. Alternatives for compromise can also be proposed. One strategy to use in working toward a compromise is for both parents and school representatives to write down separately three acceptable resolutions. These resolutions are given to the mediator and can be shared during the discussion in focusing attention on the desired goal of each party.

Communication style, again, is particularly important. Openness to alternative points of view and avoiding arguments is crucial to a successful mediation. The educators and parents involved in mediation should be aware of counterproductive postures that can constrain an open and honest discussion. Postures to *avoid* include (1) paranoid thinking, or unwillingness to consider anything the other party presents, believing that the other party is attempting to "rip me off";

(2) continuous defense of and rationalization for one's own actions or perspectives, even when they are not being attacked; (3) avoiding attempts at reasonable or partial resolution because the time allocated is perceived as not adequate to the magnitude of the problem and therefore nothing can be accomplished; and (4) obstructing the smooth proceeding of the meeting by focusing on the procedural aspects of the meeting: "I should have gone first" or "They took more time than we did."

The mediator must play a major role in assisting both parents and school representatives to avoid these potentially dangerous barriers. Before leaving each point, the mediator should ask questions and suggest means of expanding the areas of agreement and reconciling the disagreement. After the discussion on all individual points the mediator should facilitate the negotiation between both parties. Options for negotiation include agreeing to one position already presented, reaching a compromise between positions presented, or agreeing that no compromise is possible.

## Determination of Course of Action

After each point has been discussed and resolved to the extent possible through negotiation, a decision point is reached, which involves determining whether a satisfactory solution has been negotiated or whether a due process hearing is necessary. The goal of mediation is conflict resolution. Thus parties should diligently attempt to reach a mutual agreement. It is very important, however, to refrain from settling for a decision when it is unacceptable to either party. Coercion to compromise beyond the degree to which either party feels comfortable will likely lead to continued and perhaps heightened conflict between parents and the educational system, and potentially result in a due process hearing, thus negating the time and energy expended for mediation.

In some instances, participants in mediation may wish to postpone the determination of a course of action for a few days to provide an opportunity to consider carefully the implications involved in the compromise proposed. While ultimately left to the discretion of the mediator, this option increases the likelihood that a settlement will be well considered and understood by both parties prior to finalizing the agreement.

## Summary of Mediation

The purpose of the summary in mediation is to review and document future courses of action. If a satisfactory compromise has been reached, suggested strategies for monitoring the implementation of the compromise might be agreed upon by the participants and the mediator. Although the mediator may have no authority to oversee the monitoring, strategies for following up on program changes can be suggested. It may also be helpful for parents and professionals to discuss ways to keep lines of communication open with each other through periodic conferences, phone calls, program observation, home visits, and/or notes.

If a negotiated settlement has not been reached, the mediator should review with both parties the procedures to be followed in initiating a due process hearing. Resource material that would be helpful to participants in preparing for a hearing might be suggested, along with contacts for legal aid services. A major responsibility of the mediator is to minimize tension and adversarial reactions among the persons representing different points of view who have been unsuccessful in negotiating a resolution. In these cases, the mediator should urge the parties to initiate due process immediately so that the conflict is resolved as expeditiously as possible.

When disputes between parents and the school cannot be settled by mediation, either party has the right to request a due process hearing before an impartial hearing officer. The due process hearing provides a mechanism for both parents and school to present their point of view to an impartial individual who will determine the disposition of the case based on evidence and testimony presented by both parties. The essential difference between the due process hearing and mediation is that mediation attempts to reconcile or compromise differences of opinion by the mutual effort of the disagreeing parties themselves, whereas the due process hearing takes the *decision-making authority* out of the hands of the parents and the school and gives it to a third party, the hearing officer.

Although seldom the preferred first step in negotiation, the due process hearing may have clear advantages when other types of negotiation have failed by providing (1) a legally sanctioned means of settling disputes; (2) an opportunity to address issues that lack legal clarity and interpretation; (3) a forum for bringing important educational issues to the attention of the public; and (4) a method of achieving rapid change in service delivery. The next chapter addresses the due process hearing in detail.

## SUMMARY

This chapter has presented a procedural model for the IEP conference and mediation. Implicit in the suggestions made for implementing these models is the fact that merely extending legal rights to parents of children with disabilities to participate in the educational decision-making process does not assure active participation in, or meaningful access to, these decision-making forums. To achieve these assurances, both professionals and parents must make concerted and consistent efforts to communicate with one another, share in decision making, and be accountable for their actions and decisions. With the availability of a variety of forums for negotiating vital aspects of the child's educational program, a system of accountability is established to ensure that change occurs whenever necessary, assuring the provision of quality services to children with disabilties.

# REFERENCES

Allen, D. A., & Hudd, S. S. (1987). Are we professionalizing parents? Weighing the benefits and pitfalls. *Mental Retardation, 25*(3) 133–139.

Boscardin, M. L. (1987). Local level special education due process hearings: Cost issues surrounding individual student differences. *Journal of Education Finance, 12*, 391–402.

Federal Register. (1990). Washington, DC: U.S. Government Printing Office.

Gerber, P. J., Banbury, M. M., Miller, J. H., & Griffin, H. D. (1986). Special educators' perceptions of parental participation in the individual education plan process. *Psychology in the Schools, 23*, 158–163.

Goldstein, S., Strickland, B., Turnbull, A. P., & Curry, L. (1980). An observational analysis of the IEP conference. *Exceptional Children, 46*, 278–280.

Goldstein, S., & Turnbull, A. P. (1982). Strategies to increase parent participation in the IEP conference. *Exceptional Children, 48*, 278–286.

Salisbury, C., & Evans, I. M. (1988). Comparison of parental involvement in regular and special education. *Journal of the Association for Persons with Severe Handicaps.*

Salvia, J., & Ysseldyke, J. E. (1988). *Assessment in special and remedial education.* Boston: Houghton Mifflin.

Singer, J. D., & Butler, J. A. (1987). The Education of All Handicapped Children Act: Schools as agents of social reform. *Harvard Educational Review, 57*, 125–152.

Smith, S. W. (1990). Individualized education programs (IEP) in special education: From intent to acquiescence. *Exceptional Children, 57*, 6–13.

Strickland, B. (1982). *Perceptions of parents and school representatives regarding their relationship before, during, and after the due process hearing.* Unpublished doctoral dissertation, University of North Carolina at Chapel Hill.

Strickland, B. (1983). Legal issues that affect parents. In M. Seligman (Ed.), *The family with a handicapped child: Understanding and treatment.* Philadelphia: W.B. Saunders.

Turnbull, K. K., & Hughes, D. L. (1987). A pragmatic analysis of speech and language IEP conferences. *Language, Speech, and Hearing in the Schools, 18*, 275–286.

U.S. Office of Education. (1986). *Standards and guidelines for compliance with federal requirements for the education of the handicapped.* Washington, DC: U.S. Government Printing Office.

U.S. Office of Education. (1988). *Tenth annual report to Congress on the implementation of the Education of the Handicapped Act.* Washington, DC: U.S. Government Printing Office.

Vaughn, S., Bos, C. S., Harrell, J. E., & Lasky, B. A. (1988). Parent participation in the initial placement/IEP conference ten years after mandated involvement. *Journal of Learning Disabilities, 21*, 82–89.

White, R., & Calhoun, M. L. (1987). From referral to placement: Teachers' perceptions of their responsibilities. *Exceptional Children, 53*, 460–468.

Witt, J. C., Miller, C. D., McIntyre, R. M., & Smith, D. (1984). Effects of variables on parental perceptions of staffing. *Exceptional Children, 51*, 27–32.

Yoshida, R. K., Fenton, K. S., Kaufman, M. J., & Maxwell, J. P. (1978). Parental involvement in the special education pupil planning process: The school's perspective. *Exceptional Children, 44*, 531–534.

# 14

# PARENTS AND THE LAW:
# CONFLICT DEVELOPMENT AND LEGAL SAFEGUARDS

*Craig R. Fiedler*

## INTRODUCTION

Until recently, the history of U.S. public education followed a consistent course of complete parental entrustment of children's education to schools and educators. Schools were viewed as unchallengeable. Thus parents did not question any decision made by school personnel (Wolf, 1982). For parents of exceptional children, this historical course changed dramatically in 1975 with the passage of Public Law 94–142, the Education for All Handicapped Children Act (EAHCA), which places major emphasis on parent participation in educational decision making (Turnbull & Turnbull, 1990). The regulations of PL 94-142 legitimize the parent role in the educational system by granting parents of exceptional children the opportunity to share decision making with professionals in defining the parameters of an appropriate education (Turnbull & Strickland, 1981). This theme of shared educational decision making has been carried on in more recent legislative amendments to PL 94-142. In 1986, Congress amended the EAHCA to provide for special education benefits for children up to the age of 5. Title I of PL 99-457 provides that states should make available to infants and toddlers with disabilities a statewide, comprehensive, coordinated, multidisciplinary interagency program of early intervention. Most recently, PL 101-476 has reaffirmed the parental decision-making rights originally afforded in PL 94-142, and changed the title of the act from the EAHCA to The Individuals With Disabilities Education Act. Specifically, exceptional children and their parents are guaranteed the following rights:

1. an education that is appropriate and free, provided at public expense;
2. nondiscriminatory evaluation and placement procedures;
3. an individualized education program;
4. placement in the least restricted appropriate setting;
5. parental participation in all educational decisions regarding their child; and
6. procedural safeguards to ensure that parents and children's rights will not be violated. (Turnbull, 1986)

Chapter 13 examined parents' role in developing the individualized education plan (IEP) and participating in mediation processes to resolve home-school disagreement informally. Here we address more formal home-school dispute situations and provide a context for analyzing parent-educator decision-making interactions by (1) describing the role of parents in educational decision making; (2) reviewing issues and variables associated with the development of parent-educator conflict; (3) discussing the legal safeguards and procedures for resolving conflicts between parents and school personnel; and (4) delineating strategies associated with constructive conflict resolution that seeks to promote positive parent-educator relationships.

# PARENTS AND EDUCATIONAL DECISION MAKING

Shared educational decision making between schools and parents has typically resulted in an uneasy partnership at best. However, as Losen and Diament (1978) noted, the choice for educators is no longer whether to include parents or exclude them; rather, the choice is between including them grudgingly or developing new strategies for working with parents to achieve important mutual goals. Indeed, the legislative assumptions undergirding the parent participation provisions of PL 94-142 call for active parent involvement as (1) decision makers; (2) advocates for their children's educational rights; and (3) home-based teachers to carry through their children's educational objectives (Turnbull, Turnbull, & Wheat, 1982). However, as argued by Turnbull and Turnbull (1982), not all parents, perhaps not even a majority, have embraced the role of educational decision maker. In fact, research concludes that the majority of parents participate in educational decision making in a passive rather than an active way (Goldstein, Strickland, Turnbull, & Curry, 1980; Lusthaus, Lusthaus, & Gibbs, 1981; Lynch & Stein, 1982).

The implications of the research just cited on parent participation in educational decision making is significant from at least two perspectives. First, educators and parents alike must recognize and respect the role of parents as family members. As Turnbull and Turnbull (1990) stated, "This role is based on the premise that successful family life requires that the needs of all family members, including parents, be identified and addressed" (p. 15). Indicative of family systems theory, the role of parents as family members views the family as a social system with unique characteristics and needs and appreciates the fact that family members are so interrelated that any experience affecting one member will affect all (Carter & McGoldrick, 1980). In other words, parents' desire for a passive educational decision-making role may be a legitimate response to family concerns that too much involvement in any one area of family functions (e.g., education) may jeopardize the overall family balance and functionality by neglecting the needs of parents as individuals, partners, or as parents to their nondisabled children. So a clear implication of this line of research is that blanket assumptions about parent participation in educational decision making ignore the basic reality that all families are unique, and thus should not be approached from the same uniform assumptions. Instead, the same notion of individualization that is the linchpin of special education services for exceptional children also must apply to educators' assumptions and interactions with parents of exceptional children.

Second, for parents who are willing and able to fulfill the active parent participation assumptions of PL 94-142, it must be understood that normal differences of opinion among parents and educators are often inevitable, healthy, and conflict producing. Simpson (1990) recognized this reality when he stated,

> . . . normal differences of opinion among parents, family members, and professionals should be viewed as indications of open communication, interpersonal maturity, and the basis for meeting the individualized needs of exceptional children and adolescents most effectively. Consistent with this perception, the educator should not actively seek strategies for avoiding healthy conflicts but rather ways for arbitrating differences and selecting mutually satisfying solutions to problems. (p. 332)

In the next section we explore the issues and variables associated with the development of parent-educator conflict.

## VARIABLES ASSOCIATED WITH THE DEVELOPMENT OF PARENT-EDUCATOR CONFLICT

This section describes variables identified by Deutsch (1973) as affecting the development of conflict, including parental characteristics for waging conflict, the prior parent-school relationship, the nature of the issue giving rise to the conflict, the social environment within which the conflict occurs, and interested audiences to the conflict.

### Parental Characteristics for Waging Conflict

According to Deutsch's (1973) model of conflict development, characteristics of the conflicting parties refer to their respective intellectual, financial, and personal resources for entering into and waging conflict. In this section, the following personal characteristics of parents of exceptional children are briefly discussed: financial resources to hire legal representation in pursuing due process remedies; knowledge of legal rights and procedures involved in the education of exceptional children; and time and energy to initiate a legal action.

**Financial Resources.** Several studies have shown that parents who utilize the due process hearing option tend to be well educated and from the middle to upper socioeconomic levels (Budoff & Orenstein, 1982; Budoff, Orenstein, & Abramson, 1981; Lay, 1977; NASDSE, 1978, Strickland, 1983). Lay (1977) reported that parents involved in due process hearings in Massachusetts were middle class, highly educated, and at the higher end of the occupational scale. This report was confirmed by the findings of the National Association of State Directors of Special Education (NASDSE) showing that parents who initiate due process hearings were overwhelmingly of middle and upper income levels (NASDSE, 1978).

In considering the financial costs associated with pursuing a due process hearing, it can be surmised that financial ability to afford legal representation is an important determinant of whether or not a parent resorts to legal processes in an effort to resolve a conflict with the school. Indeed, parents' financial status may affect their ability to win or lose a case (Kotin, 1976).

### Knowledge of Educational Rights and Due Process.

To a large extent, parent knowledge of educational rights and due process procedures is dependent on the degree to which local and state educational agencies conscientiously abide by the notice requirements of PL 94-142. Yoshida, Fenton, Kaufman, and Maxwell (1978) found that many parents do not receive adequate notice of their procedural safeguards as accorded by PL 94-142. Perhaps part of the problem related to ensuring adequate notice to parents about their legal rights and procedures is the rather high readability level of the disseminated material. Thus a nationwide survey of state departments of education (McLoughlin, Edge, Petrosko, & Strenecky, 1981) revealed that materials disseminated to parents consistently had a 14th- to 15th-grade level readability rate. Such a high readability level restricts access to information by parents with limited educational background. Roit and Pfohl (1984) also expressed concern that parent information materials distributed by educational agencies may not be comprehensible to a large number of parents of exceptional children. In addition, these authors suggested that school personnel assume greater responsibility for evaluating the knowledge acquired by parents through the disseminated materials.

### Commitment of Time and Energy.

Finally, involvement in formal conflict situations requires not only intellectual and financial resources, but also personal commitment of time and energy. Mitchell (1976) reported that almost 100% of the parents in her study who were involved in due process hearings reported visiting their child's school frequently to see the facilities, discuss the nature of the educational program with the teacher, coordinate home activities, and discuss the child's progress. Other researchers have commented that parents who are involved in due process generally have numerous contacts with the school over a long period of time (Lay, 1977; Yoshida, 1979). Any two parties have a greater chance of experiencing conflict as their opportunities for personal interactions increase (Deutsch, 1973). In parent-school interactions, therefore, greater parent involvement means more opportunities for actively involved parents to confirm or disconfirm that their expectations for their child are being met at school.

Undoubtedly, some parents lack sufficient time and energy to be actively involved in their children's education. Therefore, compared to more actively involved parents, they do not have as many opportunities to realize differences of opinion or conflict with school personnel.

It is also anticipated that some parents who are unhappy with their exceptional child's education will consciously decide to avoid the due process hearing system because of the inordinate time and energy associated with that formalized process. Simpson (1990) suggested that the time and resources required for resolution is an important variable associated with conflict resolution. Parents and school personnel have time and energy resource limitations. Conflict resolution is possible only when the resolution mechanism is within participants' resource limitations. As a conflict-resolution mechanism becomes increasingly burdensome and time consuming, the prospects for effective and efficient conflict resolution decrease. Consequently, the conflict either continues to escalate, one of the parties concedes, or the parties' relationship is terminated.

## The Prior Parent-School Relationship

Without a history of previous interactions it is highly unlikely that conflict will materialize between parents and school personnel. Conflict develops over time and is highly dependent on the quality of interpersonal interactions and the resulting relationship between parties (Deutsch, 1973).

Losen and Diament (1978) recognized the importance of initial interactions between parents and school personnel. Thus a positive or negative initial contact may determine whether parents view school personnel as allies or adversaries. The individualized education program (IEP) conference represents a primary point of parent-school personnel interaction. Although this conference should promote mutually cooperative relationships between parents and schools, a substantial number of parents have indicated that school personnel's behavior at these conferences was discouraging and left them feeling devalued as educational planning partners (Budoff, 1975; Yoshida, Fenton, Kaufman, & Maxwell, 1978). According to Budoff (1975), until the IEP conference, all parents in his study expressed strong hopes of being able to work with the school in developing an appropriate program. Subsequently, these parents reported stress stemming from difficulty in scheduling the meeting at a convenient time, changing the meeting at the last minute on several occasions, and delay tactics in conducting the conference.

## The Nature of the Issue Giving Rise to the Conflict

The nature of the issue that sparks the conflict and its perceived importance to both parents and school is a major determinant of the course and ultimate resolution of a dispute (Simpson, 1990). Major components in assessing the nature of any issue include the scope, rigidity, and perceived importance of the issue to the parties involved. Conflict over large issues of principle is less likely to be resolved cooperatively than conflict over specific issues relating to the application of a principle, for example. Issue rigidity refers to the availability of satisfactory alternatives for outcomes initially at stake in the conflict (Deutsch, 1973). If the parties perceive no mutually satisfactory alternatives to resolve their conflict, the conflict is likely to become more rigid with neither party willing to compromise. The third component involves the perceived importance of the issue. Issues perceived as being significant are associated with more steadfastness and resolve than issues considered to be less significant. When both parent and educator perceive an issue as extremely important, conflict resolution becomes more difficult (Simpson, 1990).

Deutsch (1973) identified five basic types of conflict issues. One involves a dispute over control of resources where one party seeks exclusive possession or use of a resource. A second type centers around personal preferences. In such conflict situations, the activities or tastes of one person typically impinge upon another's preferences or sensitivities. Third, a difference in values is often at the heart of confrontations, such as conflicts over what "should be." A fourth type of conflict issue includes beliefs about what "is" or the reality of a situation as experienced by the two parties. Finally, the nature of the relationship between parties constitutes a fifth conflict category. Two people may experience conflict because of opposing views or desires in their relationship. Although Deutsch's typology of conflict issues is theoretical, its components can be found when investigating the issues involved in special education due process hearings.

Specifically, several studies have catalogued the issues involved in due process hearings. Most hearings center on appropriate placement of exceptional children with parents requesting more specialized educational services than the school considers appropriate (Bureau of Education for the Handicapped, 1980; Mitchell, 1976; Yoshida, 1979). Substantiating these findings, study by the National Association of State Directors of Special Education showed that approximately 40% of the due process hearings involved a placement dispute with the parent requesting private school placement. The remaining 60% of the cases related to the appropriateness of public school programs (NASDSE, 1978).

Kammerlohr, Henderson, and Rock (1983) analyzed 314 due process hearings held in Illinois during 1978, 1979, and the first quarter of 1980. The overwhelming majority of cases (67.5%) involved parental objection to the proposed placement of an exceptional child. Other issues included objections due to a belief that services were in an amount insufficient to meet the child's needs (11%); failure of the school to provide appropriate transportation (5.4%); and failure to provide placement consistent with the case study evaluation (5.1%).

Based on a study of 38 states and a total of 3,691 due process hearings, Smith (1981) provided strong confirmation that the majority of due process cases involve placement disputes. Thus he found that 89% of the due process hearings in his study concerned placement.

In another study, Budoff and Orenstein (1982) found that disputes between parents and schools were based on three major issues: how to define the child's special needs (the diagnosis); what types of services were required to meet these needs; and what degree of program intensity was necessary. In addition to conducting parent and school personnel interviews, Budoff and Orenstein had observers attend 60 due process hearings. Observers took notes on the testimony and documents presented at the hearing to determine how parents and schools perceived the central issues. Both parties usually agreed on the nature of their disagreement—most commonly the child's diagnosis and the content of the educational plan. Parents also tended to doubt the school's ability to deliver an acceptable program, even if they approved of the plan on paper. Furthermore, the majority of parents wanted their child to be placed in private school.

## The Social Environment Within Which the Conflict Occurs

Conflict between parent and school does not develop in isolated interpersonal interactions; instead, it is closely tied to the social environment established by the school district. The school district's social environment refers to the rules and procedures followed in handling parent-school conflict. Whether conflict can be resolved informally by the parties involved or whether it must be resolved formally through legal processes depends greatly on the school district's institutionalization of conflict rules and procedures.

Proper institutionalization and regulation of conflict decreases the likelihood of conflict taking a destructive course (Deutsch, 1973). Conflict institutionalization refers to a set of norms and patterns of action that endorse, regulate, and reward legitimate disagreements as one way of preventing formalized (and destructive) conflict (Himes, 1980). Conflict institutionalization is founded on three major goals: (1) by endorsing legitimate conflict, it aims to encourage and support people to seek legitimate ends by approved means; (2) it seeks to pattern and regulate conflict, thus making conflict both comprehensible and predictable; and (3) it gives some assurance that conflict conducted in this fashion will lead to success (Himes, 1980).

McGuire (1984) identified three types of conditions that affect conflict in school districts: (1) those that influence participants' definitions of the situation as one of conflict rather than cooperation; (2) those that generate rules allowing conflict; and (3) those that influence the choice of a competitive conflictual strategy from among the range of available strategies. A competitive view of parent-school conflict is promoted by a zero-sum view of issues, in which achieving one's own goals means defeating others or assuring that others receive less (Gray & Starke, 1980). An organization's rules can generate conflict by instilling the view that competitive strategies are legitimate and suitable means of achieving goals. Organizational rules may also foster rational discussion, consensus, and cooperation in decision making. Finally, regarding the choice of competitive or cooperative strategies, the most important considerations are the parties' beliefs about each other's cooperativeness and relative power (McGuire, 1984). For instance, if parents perceive school personnel as competitive in conflict situations, they will most likely respond in kind. Similarly, if the school district places undue emphasis on its power vis-à-vis parents, school district conflict resolution strategies will tend to be highly competitive to exploit their power advantage over parents.

## Interested Audiences to the Conflict

Whenever a conflict extends beyond the parties most directly involved (i.e., parent, exceptional child, and school personnel), escalation of the dispute can be expected, together with increased competition and use of adversarial processes (Deutsch, 1973). Several explanations may be given for this phenomenon. First, extended public debate by the parties tends to harden their views, making conflict resolution more difficult (Mack & Snyder, 1973). In parent-school conflict situations, as more persons become interested in the particular dispute, both parties feel compelled not to back down. Deutsch (1973) refers to this as the need to "maintain face." Also, if one party has been made to look foolish and weak before a significant audience, that party is more likely to retaliate than if their exploitation by the other party had not led to public loss of face.

Additionally, school districts are concerned with the precedential potential of some disputes, especially when a particular parent-school conflict could result in costly expenditure of limited school district resources. For example, as the issue in the *Board of Education v. Rowley* (1982) case became public and well known, the school district grew increasingly concerned about the potential financial drain on its fiscal resources if they lost and parents of other hearing impaired children began to request full-time sign language interpreters for their children. The cost of an interpreter for Amy Rowley could undoubtedly be borne by the school district; the cost of interpreters for 100 students like her could break the district's budget. So, as a conflict encompasses a larger interested audience, both parent and school tend to become more entrenched in their positions, making a mutually satisfactory resolution of the conflict problematic.

## LEGAL SAFEGUARDS AND PROCEDURES FOR RESOLVING PARENT-EDUCATOR CONFLICT

The legal mechanism for resolving parent-educator conflict is embodied in the principle of procedural due process. Procedural due process is based on the belief that fair procedures tend to produce acceptable, correct, and fair results (Turnbull, 1986). As applied to special education conflict situations, due process requirements have emphasized the formal adversarial procedures characteristic of courts (Kotin & Eager, 1977). Turnbull and Strickland (1981) summarized the most often cited reasons for utilizing a due process hearing model: (1) due process hearings provide an impartial, legally sanctioned means of settling disputes; (2) due process hearings provide a means of clarifying issues that lack legal interpretation; (3) due process hearings provide a means by which issues may be brought to the attention of public and state education agencies; and (4) due process hearings provide a sanctioning method in the event that the rights of any party are found to be abused.

The procedures involved in due process are best analyzed by dividing the special education decision-making process into two principal stages: (1) referral, evaluation, and placement; and (2) appeal (Kotin & Eager, 1977). Each stage involves a number of due process components.

## Referral, Evaluation, and Placement

The primary purpose of the following procedural requirements regarding notice, consent, evaluation, access to records, and surrogate parents is to accord parents and their exceptional children due process safeguards during the referral, evaluation, and placement decision-making stage.

**Notice.**  The local educational agency must give prior written notice to the parent or guardian whenever it proposes to initiate or change, or refuses to initiate or change, a child's identification, evaluation, or placement (Sec. 615 (b) (1) (C) and (D) of the Education of the Handicapped Act as amended by PL 94-142). Further, PL 94-142 requirements specify when notice must be provided, what must be contained in the notice, and that the parent must understand the content. That is, parents should be given sufficient information to ensure that they are in a position to determine whether they agree or disagree with the school's proposed decision.

**Consent.**  Parental consent must be obtained for an initial evaluation and placement of a child into a special education program (Sec. 300.504(b)). Consent means that (1) the parent has been fully informed in his or her native language of all information relevant to the activity for which consent was sought; (2) the parent agrees in writing that the activity may be carried out; (3) the consent describes the proposed activity; and (4) the parent understands that his or her consent is given voluntarily and may be revoked at any time (Turnbull, 1986). According to Kotin (1979), application of parental consent requirements to the early decision-making points (referral, evaluation, and placement) is indicative of an emphasis on early parental involvement in the special education process.

**Evaluation.**  Three general requirements were formulated by Congress in regard to evaluation (Turnbull, 1986): (1) school districts must establish procedures to ensure that evaluation methods are not racially or culturally discriminatory; (2) evaluation materials or procedures must be administered in the child's native language; and (3) no single procedure may be the sole criterion for determining an appropriate educational program for a child. In addition, parents are entitled to an independent educational evaluation of their child (Sec. 300.503); under certain circumstances, the independent evaluation must be conducted at public expense. Nondiscriminatory testing procedures reflect an attempt to prevent mis-classification and inappropriate placement of exceptional children.

**Access to Records.** A child's parents must be informed by notice of the proce-dures used by the school district to maintain the confidentiality of student records and must be permitted to inspect and review any records relating to their child that are collected, maintained, or used by the public agency (Sec. 300.561). In addition, parents may request explanations and interpretations of their child's records, request copies, have a representative inspect those records, request amendments to the records, and be afforded a hearing if a dispute arises regarding proposed amendments (Sec. 300.562).

**Surrogate Parents.** To ensure that the child's rights are protected, the law pro-vides for the appointment of a surrogate parent when the child's parents cannot be identified, or located, or when the child is a ward of the state (Sec. 300.514). The basic criteria for selecting a surrogate is that the individual have no conflict of interest and possess the skill to represent the child. Conflicts concerning who the surrogate should be may be resolved by a due process hearing.

# Appeal

The second decision-making stage where parents or schools may invoke due process protection is at the appeal stage. Whenever the public agency proposes or refuses to initiate or change the identification, evaluation, or educational placement of the child or the provision of a free appropriate public education to the child (Sec. 615 (b) (1) (E)), the parent or a public educational agency may initiate a due process hearing. Regulations governing the due process hearing establish minimal legal specifications with respect to the qualifications of the hearing officer, the rights of each party at the initial hearing and on appeal, and procedures for appeal and review of decisions rendered (Turnbull, 1986). At the initial hearing and on appeal, each party has the right to be accompanied and advised by an attorney and other experts; to present evidence and confront, examine, cross-examine, and compel the attendance of witnesses; to make writ-ten and oral arguments; to receive a written or electronic verbatim record of the hearing; and to receive a written account of findings of fact. Furthermore, no evidence may be introduced by any party unless it was disclosed at least 5 days before the hearing; and the parents have the right to have their child present and to have the hearing open to the public (Sec. 615 (d) and Sec. 300.508).

Any party who is unhappy with the hearing officer's findings may appeal to the state education agency (Turnbull, 1986). In conducting its review, the state education agency is required to examine the record of the hearing as a whole to see if due process was met and if facts were properly considered during the conduct of the hearing (Sec. 615(c)). The reviewing agency makes an independent decision and sends a copy of the decision to both parties within 30 days. When this decision is made, it becomes a final determination of a state administrative agency and may be appealed to an appropriate state or federal court.

In theory, the due process hearing model is a mechanism whereby parents and schools have an opportunity to air their concerns and have them fairly examined and weighed so that the result is an impartial decision (Essex, 1979). In many instances, the due process hearing model fulfills its stated purpose and does so in an admirable fashion. Strickland (1982b) identified the following possible positive outcomes of a due process hearing: parents are treated more as equal partners after a hearing; enforcement of parental rights embodies educational value; the due process hearing raises important issues before the public; and there is the potential of policy clarification of difficult issues.

Budoff and Orenstein (1982) also recognized some of the positive aspects of the due process appeals system. While generally viewing the due process appeals system as a potential agent of change, they specifically maintained that the due process appeals system (1) has legitimized parents' rights directly while indirectly benefiting many exceptional children; (2) lends credence to parents' right to question programs offered their exceptional children; (3) serves to pressure political and administrative organizations to become more responsive to exceptional children's needs; and (4) has led some school systems to reconsider their mode of operations and make appropriate changes where necessary.

Finally, Turnbull (1986) cited many of the positive theoretical precepts underlying the due process hearing model. First, he emphasized that the due process hearing provides schools and parents with a mechanism to test whether an exceptional child is receiving an appropriate education. Other possible benefits of the due process hearing model include its effect on advancing the notion of shared decision making between parents and schools; its use as a means of contributing to the advancement of shared interests; its use as a public sounding board for concerns and needs relating to the education of exceptional children; its use as a mechanism for increasing the potential for communication between school personnel and parents; and its function as a method of boosting public confidence in the public schools (Turnbull, 1986).

Despite the due process hearing model's advantages as a vehicle for assuring positive outcomes for exceptional children, their parents, and schools (Budoff & Orenstein, 1982; Strickland, 1982b; Turnbull, 1986), a substantial potential for deleterious consequences is associated with the widespread use of the due process hearing as the primary dispute-resolution mechanism between parents and school personnel. Mintzer (1978) captured the concerns of many legal and educational commentators when he opined the following:

> The special education hearing has shown itself to be a legal process more than an educational process . . . somewhat different from the notion of those who originally conceived of a hearing as a relaxed, informal arena where parents and educators could reason together toward the common goals of educating the child. Instead, the hearing tends to be expensive, long, formal, adversarial, and occasionally laden with subsidiary issues seemingly unrelated to the education of a child. (p. 1)

We now identify a number of possible negative consequences and limitations resulting from parent-school participation in a due process hearing, including (1) financial and emotional costs to both parents and school personnel; (2) loss of confidence in public education; (3) damaging effects on the parent-school relationship; (4) negative effects on the exceptional child; (5) overlegalization of the special education profession; (6) inaccessibility of the hearing system; and (7) consideration of the consequences of parent-school conflict.

## Financial and Emotional Costs

Both parents and school systems face significant financial burdens as a result of due process hearings. For parents, the costs of such items as attorneys' fees, payment of expert witnesses, independent evaluations, consultations with specialists, copying of records, and telephone calls have been estimated at between $300 and $4,000 (NASDSE, 1978; Yoshida, 1979). Due to the legalistic and formal nature of most due process hearings, most parents have recognized that the absence of an attorney can place them at a considerable disadvantage (Strickland, 1982b). Yet legal representation can be especially costly. According to Budoff and Orenstein (1982), parents spent from $200 to over $2,000 for advocates or attorneys alone. Financial costs to parents may also appear as time away from work or as loss of a job due to repeated absenteeism necessitated by preparation for the due process hearing.

Associated costs of the hearing include staff time, hiring of hearing officers, making transcripts, duplicating materials, and attorneys' fees (Jacobs, 1979). In one study, schools incurred attorneys' fees of up to $8,000 per hearing, with an average of $800 to $1,000 (NASDSE, 1978). In addition, schools should not underestimate the amount of both professional and clerical staff time required by a due process hearing. Kammerlohr, Henderson, and Rock (1983) estimate the amount of staff time allocated to a typical hearing at 73 person hours.

Perhaps the emotional trauma and distress experienced by parents and school personnel over the course of meetings, preparation for due process hearings, and the hearings themselves is more debilitating than the financial expenditures (Budoff & Orenstein, 1982; Michaelis, 1980; Strickland, 1982b; Yoshida, 1982). As a result of their parent interviews, Budoff and Orenstein (1982) reported that 56% of the sample found their participation in an appeals dispute "extremely upsetting" and 19% indicated they were "somewhat upset." Asked to agree or disagree with the statement that "the emotional costs of using the hearing system are high," 70% agreed. The intensity of emotional distress associated with due process hearing involvement is best conveyed through such parent responses as (Budoff & Orenstein, 1982): "I've been through seizures and everything else with her, and this has been the worst affair of my life" (p. 115). "It's been hell. Absolute hell. I very seldom speak about it, even to my husband, because I find that it gets me very upset" (p. 115). "It's horrible. It's just so horrible. It aggravates me so that I can scream" (p. 116).

School personnel also reported experiencing emotional trauma and anxiety as a result of their due process hearing participation (Budoff & Orenstein, 1982). Thus numerous due process hearings can have a damaging effect on school staff morale and confidence (Michaelis, 1980). Special educators' self-image is often hurt because they tend to see themselves as advocates within their school systems for more humane treatment of children. This self-concept is typically under attack at a due process hearing. Further, educators involved in due process hearing disputes have reported that it is extremely disturbing to have their professional judgment and/or competence questioned in a public forum (Budoff & Orenstein, 1982).

## Loss of Confidence in Public Education

The fairness and efficiency by which parent-school disputes are handled can be an important ingredient in either losing or restoring public confidence in school systems. Unfortunately, both Budoff and Orenstein (1982) and Strickland (1982) reported that, following a due process hearing, parents and school personnel were significantly less confident that the due process hearing was an effective means of settling disputes. In fact, the due process hearing system weakened support for public education among parents who had once considered themselves as advocates for the public schools (Budoff & Orenstein, 1982).

## Damaging Effects on the Parent-School Relationship

Ideally, due process safeguards, including hearings, enable parents and school personnel to develop collegial, sharing, and mutually supportive relationships on behalf of exceptional children (Budoff & Orenstein, 1982). To the extent that the due process hearing model does not foster satisfactory relationships between parents and schools, escalating conflict and more adversarial and legalistic posturing by both parties become even more likely (Winer, 1982).

Daynard (1980) concluded that the due process hearing model typically leaves school personnel with feelings of suspicion and cynicism toward parents. Similarly, Budoff and Orenstein (1982) maintained that hearings widen the gulf between parents and schools and thus make it more difficult for both parties to cooperate in future educational planning for the child. Personal attacks and impugning of the other party's motives appear to be common strategies in many due process hearing confrontations. For example, one parent in the Budoff and Orenstein (1982) study criticized school personnel because, "Instead of admitting that I had legitimate concerns about my child's progress, they tried to make it appear that I was in it for the money" (p. 109). The result of behavioral responses such as personal attacks is that they usually foreclose constructive future communication. Parents involved in due process hearings also expressed strong beliefs that school personnel had been vindictive toward them after the hearing (Budoff & Orenstein, 1982). Finally, the attitude typically prevailing at the hearing stage is to win at all costs. It becomes a we/they situation in which the ultimate goal is victory rather than problem solving to reach a solution that is best for the child (Budoff & Orenstein, 1982).

## Negative Effects on the Exceptional Child

When the due process hearing system works as well in reality as it is supposed to in theory, and when both parents and school personnel willingly comply with the hearing officer's decision, the hearing process can be expected to benefit exceptional children. However, parents' due process hearing involvement entails several possible negative effects on their exceptional children.

Budoff (1976) interviewed parents involved in due process hearings and found that 20% of them felt their children's attitude toward school deteriorated during the appeal process. Strickland (1982b) speculated that informal sanctions against the exceptional child may be an unfortunate by-product of many due process hearing disputes. For example, some school personnel's defensiveness and loss of professional pride as a result of due process hearings may lead to unusual harshness or indifference toward the child at school. Altogether, the entire educational atmosphere may be unpleasant for a child whose parents have filed for a due process hearing. At the same time, parents may impose undue pressure on their children while preparing them to testify at a hearing. Thus the child may get caught in the middle, not knowing whom to please—parent or teacher. Yet, when asked about the effects of the hearing process on their child, parents consistently reported little or no effect (Budoff & Orenstein, 1982). The emotional effects on the child undoubtedly depend on the child's age at the time of the due process conflict and the parents' effort to shield the child from anxieties associated with the educational dispute.

## Overlegalization of the Special Education Profession

Kauffman (1984) was sharply critical of the special education profession's tendency to turn over questions of ethical judgement or educational programming to attorneys and the legalistic methods of the hearing process. In fact, school personnel and parents may increasingly be allowing attorneys to shape policy and practice that rightfully should be shaped by parents and school personnel themselves (Audette, 1982). This is a true dilemma of the due process hearing model. Kauffman (1984) eloquently summed up his concern about the overlegalization of special education when he wrote;

> We live, as many observers have noted, in a litigious society. We tend today to look for a legal solution, sometimes through legislation but more often through the courts, to every problem with which we are confronted. Somehow we appear to have become convinced that legal or quasi-legal proceedings will not only crystalize the moral and ethical issues of contemporary life, including issues in

*education, but yield decisions that are ethically superior to those that could have been reached outside the courtroom or hearing. However, many of the moral and ethical issues involved in our business as special educators can probably be addressed more adequately by educators and social scientists than by lawyers and judges. (p. 67)*

## Inaccessibility of the Due Process Hearing System

The vast majority of due process hearings tend to be formal, legalistic, and adversarial in nature (Budoff & Orenstein, 1982; Strickland, 1982b; Yoshida, 1979). One undeniably necessary condition for the operation of an adversarial system is that the two opposing sides be relatively equal in strength (Riley, 1976). Undoubtedly, schools will either be represented by an attorney or have trained school personnel presenting the district's case with backup legal advice available if required. Therefore, parents in this adversarial process will most likely need legal representation. The problem is this: How many parents can afford such representation? Nader (1976) has estimated that 90% of all lawyers in this country represent only 10% of the people. Accessibility to the due process hearing system, therefore, is largely dependent on one's financial status (Kotin, 1976).

Research findings have consistently shown that the due process hearing system is accessible primarily to parents with money, namely, those parents in the middle and upper income levels (Budoff & Orenstein, 1981; Budoff, Orenstein, & Abramson, 1981; Lay, 1977; NASDSE, 1978; Strickland, 1983). As a result, the fiscal burdens associated with due process particularly abridges the due process rights of parents from lower socioeconomic backgrounds (Salend & Zirkel, 1984). This finding is especially noteworthy, since there is a strong relationship between low socioeconomic status and special education placement (Buss, Kirp, & Kuriloff, 1975). Thus the issue of hearing costs and accessibility becomes extremely important in evaluating the effectiveness of due process procedures in special education (Salend & Zirkel, 1984).

## Consequences of Parent-School Conflict

Disputants' expectations of the consequences of entering into and waging conflict can have a significant impact on the development of conflict between two parties. In particular, each party's estimations of success and the cost of conflict in relation to possible gains are important (Deutsch, 1973; Himes, 1980).

How might estimations of the cost of conflict affect a party's willingness to enter into conflict and/or continue a conflictual relationship? Himes (1980) maintained that a party who is facing almost certain defeat, or who has accomplished limited ends, is more likely to decide that withdrawal or termination of the conflict is the best option. In rational conflict situations, both parties conduct a cost-benefit analysis. If both perceive a possibility of reaching an agreement in which each party would be better off, or, at least, no worse off, than if no agreement is reached, they will be more willing to negotiate (Deutsch, 1973). This kind of thinking can change the tone of conflict from win/lose to a more productive win/win philosophy (Filley, 1975; Fisher & Ury, 1981; Simpson, 1990).

As we discussed previously, a considerable amount of research literature supports the emotional toll on parents and the damage to their long-term relationship with school personnel as two additional ingredients in a parent cost-benefit analysis of whether or not to proceed with a due process hearing (Budoff & Orenstein, 1981, 1982; Strickland, 1982b). Parents vividly recount the emotional drain and negative impact of such disputes on themselves, their marriage, work, and family (Budoff & Orenstein, 1982). A further result of the adversarial hearing process is that it seems to inflame rather than reduce the antagonism between parent and school and leads to increasing alienation of the contending parties (Budoff & Orenstein, 1982). At the very least, both parents and educators must consciously consider all possible consequences of waging conflict and, in particular, participating in a due process hearing conflict situation. To do otherwise would blindly lead into due process conflict without a clear analysis of possible consequences.

## STRATEGIES AND TACTICS EMPLOYED BY PARENTS AND SCHOOLS ENGAGED IN CONSTRUCTIVE CONFLICT

As mentioned, conflict has become a common and almost inevitable aspect of public education in the United States (McGuire, 1984). Conflict has often been viewed as a negative, disruptive, unnatural force to be avoided if at all possible. Araki (1983) suggested that a more healthy perspective would view conflict as natural and inevitable with the following potential benefits:

> When conflict is accepted, a great deal of the energy tied up in suppressing it becomes available for other uses as the conflict is brought into the open. Moreover, the differences underlying conflict often represent diversity or complementarity which has potential value to the organization. Participants may develop a wider range of responses to nonstandard behaviors. Both individuals and the system may increase in innovativeness as the diversity of viewpoints is shared and explored. Individuals may gain an increased understanding of their own positions, strengths, assumptions about people, and value structure as they are forced to articulate their views and generate supporting arguments. (p. 11)

The question, then, is how to foster the constructive rather than destructive potential in conflict situations. Deutsch (1973) considered conflict to be destructive if the involved parties are dissatisfied with the outcomes and feel they have lost as a result of the conflict. These feelings characterize the results of many adversarial due process hearings (Budoff & Orenstein, 1981, 1982; Strickland, 1982b). Constructive conflict, on the other hand, exists if the involved parties are satisfied with the outcomes and feel they have gained as a result of the conflict (Deutsch, 1973).

When parents or school personnel see the other party as being hostile or uncaring, a destructive chain reaction occurs—one or both parties becomes defensive and withdraws from the relationship. Such withdrawal reduces communication and mutual understanding of each other's goals and attitudes, while increasing mutual suspicion and further confirming the interpretations of hostility and uncaring, thereby exacerbating the initial conflict (Friedman, 1980).

Simpson (1990) emphasized the importance of expressing differences of opinion and position as a necessary and vital means of maintaining an open and effective parent-school relationship. Without an opportunity to express differences, conflict, expressed as anger, hostility, or fear, may become the sole form of expression (Simpson, 1990).

Constructive conflict resolution is characterized by open and honest communication of all relevant information between the parties; recognition of the legitimacy of each other's interests and the necessity of searching for a solution that is responsive to both parties' needs; and a trusting, friendly attitude that increases sensitivity to the parties' similarities and common interests, while minimizing differences (Deutsch, 1973). When school personnel and parents find themselves in disagreement on a child's program or educational progress, the school should reassure the parents that the school staff is aware of their concerns and considers them legitimate; persuade the parents to give the school program sufficient time; and reassure parents that school personnel will consider a new program after a sufficient trial period (Losen & Diament, 1978). To bring about constructive conflict resolution, Turnbull (1983) maintained that educators and parents need knowledge and skills in constructive communication including listening, assertiveness, use of positive reinforcement, nonverbal communication, and group decision-making techniques such as agenda setting, reaching closure, and planning.

Constructive conflict resolution is highly dependent on effective parent-educator interpersonal interactions and relationships. Much has been written about how to conduct successful parent-school conferences and establish good parent-school relationships, but little empirical research is available on the effects of parent-school relationship variables on due process conflict. Fiedler (1985) conducted a study to determine the relationship between perceived satisfaction with parent-school interpersonal interactions and involvement or noninvolvement in due process conflict. The remainder of this section briefly introduces the parent-school interpersonal interaction variables deemed important from that investigation.

## Different Assumptions/Expectations Regarding the Child's Abilities and Future Needs.
Establishing substantial agreement between parent and school concerning the child's strengths, weaknesses, and educational needs primarily determines whether the parents will be satisfied with the appropriateness of their child's education. Canady and Seyfarth (1979) saw differences between teachers and

parents as arising from their fundamentally different ways of viewing the child; that is, parents have particularistic expectations, whereas teachers hold universalistic expectations. Writing from her perspective of growing up as an exceptional child, Diamond (1981) related that her parents and teachers were often adversaries because of their different expectations about what she could and could not do.

Several barriers hinder the development of a mutually satisfying agreement between parent and school regarding the educational expectations and needs of an exceptional child. First, agreement can be barred if parents feel that the school has not committed adequate attention to their concerns and, instead, has questioned their motives for arguing that their child is not receiving an appropriate education (Budoff, 1979). To a large extent, parents consider their child's needs to be met if someone at the school listens and responds when they want to discuss the child's needs (Simpson, 1990). Second, conflict over educational expectations can develop when parents believe that their child's assessment was inaccurate or conducted by incompetent and poorly trained school personnel. Finally, some parents do not accept their child's limitations realistically and, consequently, maintain unrealistic expectations for their child's educational program. For example, some parents secretly hold on to the belief that their child's problem will somehow go away or that the child will grow out of it (Seligman, 1979). Further fuel is added to the conflict fire when school personnel attempting to help parents assess their child's abilities and needs realistically, are perceived by parents as insensitive, uncaring, or uninformed (Simpson, 1990; Turnbull & Turnbull, 1990).

**Effective and Open Communication.**  Budoff and Orenstein (1981) summed up their due process conflict findings as follows: "The predominant impression left by the study is the extreme difficulty that school system professionals have in establishing responsive and respectful communications and dialogues with parents" (p. 42). In her due process investigation, Strickland (1982b) confirmed the importance of effective and open communication between parents and school personnel in bringing about a cooperative working relationship and an appropriate education for exceptional children. The seeds of many due process disputes are found in the failure of school personnel to listen to and honor parents as partners (Budoff & Orenstein, 1982). In addition, Winer (1982) found that poor home-school communication, such as mixed messages and ambiguous statements, lack of openly expressing one's feelings/concerns, and insensitive remarks, precipitated due process conflict.

Parents involved in due process conflicts with schools have reported patterns of unresponsive, condescending, and misleading communication on the part of school personnel, as well as withholding of relevant information (Fiedler, 1985; Strickland, 1983). All the information about a child that is available to the school should be available to the parents (Turnbull & Turnbull, 1990). Further, if accurate and understandable information is to be communicated to parents, educators must avoid educational jargon and be willing to clarify any misunderstood information.

**Objectivity.** The ability to remain objective is important in preventing unnecessary parent-school conflict and a necessary skill in problem solving and refraining from personalizing a dispute when a conflict emerges (Fiedler, 1985). Both parents and school personnel have reported defensiveness and blame-casting behaviors as being characteristic of their due process conflict experiences (Budoff & Orenstein, 1982; Fiedler, 1985; Strickland, 1982b).

In discussing a child's academic characteristics and needs, school personnel must be objective and as data-based as possible to accurately reflect their findings about a child (Simpson, 1990). Decisions and recommendations that are based on objective data force educational planners to articulate the basis for such decisions. Also, quantifying a child's problem allows parents and school personnel the opportunity to ascertain the magnitude of their disagreement. In contrast, subjective data are susceptible to many interpretations and, thus, do not provide a firm foundation for resolving parent-school differences.

An additional aspect of objectivity is the ability to refrain from personalizing a dispute or becoming defensive when a disagreement arises or when a personal opinion is questioned. The destructive impact of school personnel's defensive behavior is illustrated in the following examples of common defensive reactions identified by Losen and Diament (1978): not acknowledging one's limitations or mistakes; making excuses or complaining excessively; making precipitous recommendations; forming prejudicial opinions; fitting a case into a favorite theory; overusing a favorite technique; and using language parents do not understand. School personnel must be able to handle criticism.

**Trust.** The development of a cooperative and problem-solving relationship between parents and school personnel will largely depend on the establishment of trust (Simpson, 1990; Turnbull & Turnbull, 1990). Thus Fisher (1983) noted that each party in a negotiating situation can expect greater influence over the other party if they have established a well-deserved reputation for candor, honesty, integrity, and commitment to any promise they make. That is, if the parties trust each other, they will be more committed to solving their own problems.

Simpson (1990) suggested a trusting relationship involves three basic components: an atmosphere in which a shared feeling of safety exists; reassurance and modeling of risk-taking behavior; and reinforcement of both parties for risk-taking efforts. Several other factors associated with the development of parent-school trust include a willingness to contribute to a common cause; an acknowledgment that both parties have a commitment to children; assertive advocacy on behalf of exceptional children; a positive outlook; a willingness to both reinforce and confront; a sensitivity to each other's needs; a feeling of wanting to trust one another; and honesty (Simpson, 1990).

**Different Opinions of the Child's Educational Progress.**   Home-school cooperation will be impeded if parents and school maintain different opinions about the child's educational progress. Disenchantment with a current educational program grows as parents see little or no progress in their child's academic and social skills (Losen & Diament, 1978). Parent-school disagreement also occurs when school reports of a child's performance problems do not coincide with what the parent observes about the child's performance at home (Winer, 1982).

Parents interviewed by Budoff and Orenstein's (1982) reported becoming very upset when public school programs apparently failed to help their child. Compared to school personnel, parents were more likely to consider their child's exceptionality as severe, since the exceptional condition was frustrating their expectations for the child. Thirty-one percent of the parents interviewed felt their child was falling further and further behind while the school kept assuring them that no additional special help was needed. Thus a recurrent theme in Budoff and Orenstein's (1982) study was that school personnel tended to defend the effectiveness of current programming while ignoring parental unhappiness with its results.

**Flexibility.**   The degree of parent and educator flexibility is important in establishing a good working relationship between home and school (Fiedler, 1985; Winer, 1982). A flexible educator or parent is open to alternative ideas and suggestions, is willing to compromise to meet the concerns and needs of both parties, and is amenable to trying different educational strategies or methods. Flexible approaches to a child's education are characterized by open-mindedness and the ability to suspend earlier impressions of a child as new evidence proves earlier assumptions to be wrong (Canady & Seyfarth, 1979).

When the school behaves in an overly rigid manner, parents often feel impotent in their legitimate attempts to have input in the planning process (Diamond, 1981). This situation can cause feelings of frustration and spark future conflict between parents and school. An unwillingness to consider alternatives forecloses the possibility of compromising in an attempt to find a mutually satisfactory solution for both parties (Fisher & Ury, 1981). As Fisher and Ury warned, such inflexibility is marked by either/or thinking and a tendency to bargain over positions rather than addressing the particular concerns of both parties.

# SUMMARY

This chapter has described the complex interpersonal dynamics involved in parent-educator decision-making interactions. Special education law imposes a legal context for those parent-educator interactions; and legal safeguards exist for a number of very valid reasons. However, as we pointed out, both parents and educators must fully realize the costs associated with a conflict resolution approach that invokes the formal legal mechanism of a due process hearing. The lesson to be learned is not to avoid or ignore parent-educator conflict, but to recognize that conflict, if handled properly, can be healthy and positive. Furthermore, the legal trappings of a formal due process hearing should only be contemplated as a last resort after all other conflict resolution attempts have been exhausted.

# REFERENCES

Araki, C. T. (1983). A practical approach to conflict resolution. *Educational Perspectives, 22*(1), 11–16.

Audette, D. (1982). Private school placement: A local director's perspective. *Exceptional Children, 49*(3), 214–219.

*Board of Education of the Hendrick Hudson School District v. Rowley,* 102 S. Ct. 3034 (1982).

Budoff, M. (1975). Engendering change in special education practices. *Harvard Educational Review, 45,* 507–526.

Budoff, M. (1976). *Procedural due process: Its application to special education and its implications for teacher training.* Paper presented at the meeting of the American Educational Research Association, San Francisco.

Budoff, M. (1979). Implementing due process safeguards: From the user's viewpoint. *Criteria Study 4: Developing Criteria for Evaluating the Due Process Procedural Safeguards Provisions of Public Law 94–142.* The United States Office of Education, Bureau of Education of the Handicapped.

Budoff, M., & Orenstein, A. (1981). Special education appeals hearings: Are they fair and are they helping? *Exceptional Education Quarterly, 2*(2), 37–48.

Budoff, M., & Orenstein, A. (1982). *Due process in special education: On going to a hearing.* Cambridge, MA: Ware Press.

Budoff, M., Orenstein, A., & Abramson, J. (1981). Due process hearings: Appeals for appropriate public school programs. *Exceptional Children, 48*(2), 180–182.

Bureau of Education for the Handicapped (1980). *Study of procedures for determining the least restrictive environment placement for handicapped children. Final report activity 3: Legal analysis.* Silver Spring, MD: Applied Management Sciences.

Buss, W., Kirp, D., & Kuriloff, P. (1975). Exploring procedural modes of special education. In N. Hobbs (Ed.), *The classification of children* (Vol. 11). San Francisco: Jossey-Bass.

Canady, R. L., & Seyfarth, J. T. (1979). *How parent-teacher conferences build partnerships.* Bloomington, IN: Phi Delta Kappa Educational Foundation.

Carter, E. A., & McGoldrick, M. (Eds.) (1980). *The family life cycle: A framework for family therapy.* New York: Gardner Press.

Daynard, C. (1980). *Due process: The appeals hearing under Chapter 766.* Unpublished doctoral dissertation, Boston University.

Deutsch, M. (1973). *The resolution of conflict: Constructive and destructive process.* New Haven: Yale University Press.

Diamond, S. (1981). Growing up with parents of a handicapped child: A handicapped person's perspective. In J. L. Paul (Ed.), *Understanding and working with parents of children with special needs* (pp. 23–50). New York: Holt.

Fiedler, C. R. (1985). *Conflict prevention, containment, and resolution in special education due process disputes: Parents and school personnel's perceptions of variables associated with the development and escalation of due process conflict.* Unpublished doctoral dissertation, University of Kansas, Lawrence.

Filley, A. C. (1975). *Interpersonal conflict resolution.* Glenview, IL: Scott, Foresman.

Fisher, R. (1983). Negotiating power: Getting and using influence. *American Behavioral Scientist, 27*(2), 149–166.

Fisher, R., & Ury, W. (1981). *Getting to yes: Negotiating agreement without giving in.* Boston: Houghton Mifflin.

Friedman, P. G. (1980). *Communicating in conferences: Parent- teacher-student interaction.* Urbana, IL: ERIC Clearinghouse on Reading and Communication Skills.

Goldstein, S., Strickland, B., Turnbull, A. P., & Curry, L. (1980). An observational analysis of the IEP conference. *Exceptional Children, 46*(4), 278–286.

Gray, J. F., & Starke, F. (1980). *Organizational behavior.* New York: Merrill.

Himes, J. S. (1980). *Conflict and conflict management.* Athens: University of Georgia Press.

Jacobs, L. J. (1979). Hidden dangers, hidden costs. *Amicus, 4*(2), 86–88.

Kammerlohr, B., Henderson, R. A., & Rock, S. (1983). Special education due process hearings in Illinois. *Exceptional Children, 49*(5), 417–422.

Kauffman, J. M. (1984). Saving children in the age of big brother: Moral and ethical issues in the identification of deviance. *Behavioral Disorders, 10*(1), 60–70.

Kotin, L. (1976). *Due process in special education: Legal perspectives—The state of the states, PL 94-142 and systems design.* Boston: Massachusetts Center for Public Interest Law (ERIC Document Reproduction Service No. ED 135166).

Kotin, L. (1979). Recommended criteria and assessment techniques for the evaluation by LEA's of their compliance with the notice and consent requirements of PL 94-142. In Department of Health, Education, and Welfare, Office of Education, *Due process: Developing criteria for the evaluation of due process procedural safeguards provisions.* Philadelphia: Research for Better Schools.

Kotin, L., & Eager, N. B. (1977). *Due process in special education: A legal analysis.* Cambridge, MA: Research Institute for Educational Problems.

Lay, C. A. (1977). Due process in special education (Doctoral dissertation, Boston University, 1977). *Dissertation Abstracts International, 37*, 7687A.

Losen, S. M., & Diament, B. (1978). *Parent conferences in the schools: Procedures for developing effective partnership.* Boston: Allyn & Bacon.

Lusthaus, C. S., Lusthaus, E. W., & Gibbs, H. (1981). Parents' vote in the decision process. *Exceptional Children, 48*(3), 256–257.

Lynch, E. W., & Stein, R. (1982). Perspectives on parent participation in special education. *Exceptional Education Quarterly, 3*(2), 56–63.

Mack, J., & Snyder, R. (1973). Conflict resolution. In F. E. Jandt (Ed.), *Conflict resolution through communication.* New York: Harper & Row.

McGuire, J. B. (1984). Strategies of school district conflict. *Sociology of Education, 57*, 31–42.

McLoughlin, J. A., Edge, D., Petrosko, J., & Strenecky, B. (1981). PL 94-142 and information dissemination: A step forward. *Journal of Special Education Technology, 4*(4), 50–56.

Michaelis, C. T. (1980). *Home and school partnerships in exceptional education.* Rockville, MD: Aspen.

Mintzer, B. (1978). The role of the lawyer in special education appeals hearings. In *Appeal News, 3*, Boston: Department of Education.

Mitchell, S. (1976). *Parental perceptions of their experiences with due process in special education: A preliminary report.* Paper presented at the meeting of the American Educational Research Association, San Francisco.

National Association of State Directors of Special Education (1978). *The implementation of due process in Massachusetts.* Washington, DC: Author.

Nader, R. (1976). An overview. In R. Nader & M. Green (Eds.), *Verdicts on lawyers* (pp. 7–18). New York: Crowell.

Riley, D. (1976). The mystique of lawyers. In R. Nader & M. Green (Eds.), *Verdicts on lawyers* (pp. 80–93). New York: Crowell.

Roit, M. L., & Pfohl, W. (1984). The readability of PL 94-142 parent materials: Are parents truly informed? *Exceptional Children, 50*(6), 496–505.

Salend, S. J., & Zirkel, P. A. (1984). Special education hearings: Prevailing problems and practical proposals. *Education and Training of the Mentally Retarded, 19*(1), 29–34.

Seligman, M. (1979). *Strategies for helping parents of exceptional children.* New York: Free Press.

Simpson, R. L. (1990). *Conferencing parents of exceptional children.* Austin, TX: Pro-ed.

Smith, T. E. C. (1981). Status of due process hearings. *Exceptional Children, 48*(3), 232–236.

Strickland, B. (1982a). *Perceptions of parents and school representatives regarding their relationship before, during, and after the due process hearing.* Unpublished doctoral dissertation, University of North Carolina, Chapel Hill.

Strickland, B. (1982b). Parental participation, school accountability, and due process. *Exceptional Education Quarterly, 3,* 41–49.

Strickland, B. (1983). Legal issues that affect parents. In M. Seligman (Ed.), *The family with a handicapped child: Understanding and treatment.* New York: Grune & Stratton.

Turnbull, A. P. (1983). Parental participation in the IEP process. In J. A. Mulik & S. M. Pueschel (Eds.), *Parent-professional partnerships in developmental disability services* (pp. 107–122). Cambridge, MA: Ware Press.

Turnbull, A. P., & Strickland, B. (1981). Parents and the educational system. In J. L. Paul (Ed.), *Understanding and working with parent of children with special needs* (pp. 231–263). New York: Holt.

Turnbull, A. P., & Turnbull, H. R. (1982). Parent involvement in the education of handicapped children: A critique. *Mental Retardation, 20*(3), 115–122.

Turnbull, A. P., & Turnbull, H. R. (1990). *Families, professionals, and exceptionality: A special partnership.* Columbus, OH: Merrill.

Turnbull, H. R. (1986). *Free appropriate public education: Law and implementation.* Denver: Love.

Turnbull, H. R., Turnbull, A. P., & Wheat, M. J. (1982). Assumptions concerning parent involvement: A legislative history. *Exceptional Education Quarterly, 3*(2), 1–8.

Winer, M. E. (1982). Parental involvement in special education decision-making: Access and alienation. *Dissertation Abstracts International, 43,* 1116A. (University Microfilms No. DA 8220975)

Wolf, J. S. (1982). Parents as partners in exceptional education. *Theory Into Practice, 21,* 77–81.

Yoshida, R. K. (1979). *Developing assistance linkages for parents of handicapped children.* Washington, DC: Department of Health, Education, and Welfare, Bureau of Education for the Handicapped.

Yoshida, R. K. (1982). Research agenda: Finding ways to create more options for parent involvement. *Exceptional Education Quarterly, 3,* 74–80.

Yoshida, R. K., Fenton, K., Kaufman, M. J., & Maxwell, J. P. (1978). Parental involvement in the special education pupil planning process: The school's perspective. *Exceptional Children, 44,* 531–533.

# 15

# ETHICAL ISSUES IN PROVIDING SERVICES FOR FAMILIES: POLICY AND CLINICAL CONSIDERATIONS

*James L. Paul, Lee Kern-Dunlap, & George D. Falk*

## INTRODUCTION

The development of professional services for families with members who have disabling conditions accelerated during recent years with the provisions for parent participation in PL 94-142, The Education for All Handicapped Children Act of 1975, and subsequent amendments including PL 101-476, The Individuals With Disabilities Act of 1990 (IDEA). There has been an increasing recognition of the interdisciplinary needs of families and the complexity of meeting those needs. This has presented challenges for policymakers, who must develop policies that facilitate the delivery of best practices from different disciplines, and for clinicians, who must make their services effectively available to families.

There are many significant barriers to policy development and effective clinical practice, including (1) as with most educational and professional human services, resources are limited; (2) we lack evaluated models and we have a limited research base for providing interdisciplinary services to families and children with severe disabling conditions; (3) there are deep territorial interests staked out by different agencies and disciplines that have traditionally provided services; (4) our definitions of families and our understanding of the rearing of children do not reflect the rich cultural diversity that exists in the United States; and (5) there is an inadequate supply of well-trained professionals available to work with families and children with severe disabilities.

In addition to the lack of knowledge, resources, experience, and a sufficient supply of appropriately trained professionals, there are other equally challenging issues having to do with the moral and ethical dilemmas facing those who make clinical or policy decisions. These decisions involve adequately and fairly representing relevant interests.

Each discipline has its own code of ethics to guide professionals in making moral choices about appropriate practice. These codes are necessary to protect the interests of clients and the profession. It is necessary to protect the client's interest, for example, by guaranteeing confidentiality of information, protecting the client from harm, and ensuring state of the art or science of practice. Each of these is an ethical matter involving the rights and interests of the client. On the other hand, the professional has the right to practice and to be able to provide treatment according to the current state of knowledge. The professional's right to provide state of the art or science of practice may conflict with the client's and/or the family's perception of the preferred practice. When this conflict arises, the resolution is necessarily an ethical matter.

The need for codes of ethics became apparent when the moral complexity of the client-professional relationship was recognized. Whenever one person representing a recognized and valued body of knowledge has the right to collect personal information and make decisions about the treatment of another, the rights and interests of both the one making the decisions and the one about whom the decisions are made must be understood and protected.

Difficult issues arise in providing services for infants with disabilities and their families that require thoughtful resolution and adjudication. For example, who ultimately has responsibility for the child? If the parents' religious beliefs prohibit certain medical interventions that a physician considers necessary to improve the child's quality of life significantly, who should have the final say? If a social worker believes that the parents of a medically fragile infant are not intellectually capable or morally motivated to provide appropriate care in the home, should the baby be removed from the home?

Less dramatic, how can we guarantee informed choices about treatment? An informed choice requires an adequate understanding, which often involves an educational process. When the parents have a limited educational background or have limited proficiency in English, informing the parents may involve more than telling them in English and using professional jargon. If the professional considers informed consent as nothing more than procedural compliance where the professional really knows best, then the extra effort may not be invested in helping the parent make an informed choice.

In treatment issues, under what circumstances does the person to be treated have the final say in his or her treatment? If parents and doctors are thought to know best, it is necessary to consider when and under what circumstances the child's right to speak for him or herself will be recognized and supported.

In these and many other matters where the questions of interests and rights are so complex and involve ethical decisions, it is essential that the decision makers be informed about the ethics code for their profession. These codes have been carefully considered by professionals who have sought relevant moral precepts or principles to guide the decisions. They must know what their own profession has determined that every professional in a situation similar to their own should decide.

Decisions that are easily made with obvious criteria may require little attention. The decisions that could have several different outcomes, where there are different and competing principles involved, are much more difficult and make it essential to have a clear and explicit code of ethics. An example of a difficult decision is the necessity of choosing between a family's interest or their child's interest where, in a particular instance, a poor family with several children living in a rural area wants to keep their child at home and a professional team believes it is in the best interest to place the child in a medical institution where needed services could be provided. The professional's decision is complicated by the fact that, under ordinary circumstances, the home would be the least restrictive and, therefore, the most desirable placement. In this instance, however, in the view of the professionals, the treatment needed by this child could not be reliably provided by the family.

Always involved in ethical choices are the personal values of those making the decisions. The professional codes will provide formal guidance to a point. However, it is essential that professionals be aware of their own philosophy of care and the force of their own values in the ethical positions they take. Each of us has a history with a particular ideological content. We have our view of what constitutes a family, what is responsible conduct, and so forth. The helping process that respects the culture of the client is likely to be the most successful and the most morally defensible. In order to facilitate or guide such a process, the clinician must have some awareness of his or her own values and moral beliefs and be assured that the values of the client can be respected and protected. For example, a student in a university classroom recently commented that, as a Christian, he could not work with a gay couple with an adopted child with a disability. He said he could not view this couple and child as a family. It is important to recognize the implications of this person's perspective for his potential to provide professional services to families.

In addition to the clinical issues that pose ethical dilemmas, there are equally complex policy issues that require resolution on ethical grounds. Policymakers, like clinicians, function with assumptions about children, families, disabilities, and treatment and they have a duty to be informed about current practice. They have their own values and beliefs about the way things ought to be. They have their own views about the diversity in family structures and child-rearing practices.

Those who participate in the policy process often include professionals, bureaucrats, parents, and others. Each person comes with his or her own knowledge base and beliefs. Often, one person is representing a class of individuals. A parent may be representing parents, for example, and thus represents the "consumer perspective." This raises interesting questions about the relationship between the individual representative's point of view and the sometimes less well-defined point of view of a group or class of individuals. If the parent has a child with Down syndrome, how well will he or she represent the interests of parents of children with autism, for example? Interest is an ethical matter. Whose interest? Represented by whom? These issues are sometimes difficult to sort out in the process of formulating policy. Self-interest is always at issue, and not just with parents. The self-interest may be the interest of a discipline, where a social worker (or some other discipline) may want to be sure that social workers (or some other discipline) work with families. The self-interest may be the interest of a particular agency where, for example, the mental health agency wants to be sure that the mental health needs of the child or family are addressed by mental health professionals.

Another matter of considerable ethical significance in the policy process involves the allocation of resources. Resources are always finite and more or less limited. In that context, then, who will be served? An answer to the question, Who will be served? answers a corollary question, Who will not be served? In formulating the definition of the populations to be served by Part H of PL 101-476, for example, policymakers must address who will and who will not be served. Will the most needy, that is, children with the most severe disabilities, or those who could make the most use of the resources, that is, the most treatable, be targeted for resources appropriated in Part H of PL 101-476? While informed by epidemiological and intervention data, this is an ethical decision.

Whether at a clinical or policy level, there are many decisions that are fundamentally ethical in nature. How are these decisions made when there are no data to guide the decision maker? As has been mentioned, there are some well-developed codes of ethics in each of the disciplines involved in providing professional services to children and families. However, often these codes are not adequate to provide the needed guidance. In these instances, decision makers must rely on ethical principles to provide some rational grounding and moral defense for their decisions. In an excellent chapter on professional ethics and morals, which discusses moral issues from a family systems perspective, Turnbull and Turnbull (1989) have described six traditional approaches to dealing with moral questions. They present practical examples of making moral judgments in problematic situations. These approaches to ethical questions are described briefly here.

Greek philosophers, such as Socrates, Plato, and Aristotle, and later St. Thomas Aquinas, emphasized the ability to reason as the attribute that defined a person's uniqueness from other species. We must use our intellectual faculty to approach life thoughtfully and reflectively and to attain satisfaction and fulfillment, or happiness. This requires leading a balanced life and avoiding extremes or excesses. The test for ethical decisions using this principle is that there is respect for the intellectual life of the person and that we have avoided excesses in any remedy.

The Judeo-Christian perspective emphasizes two principles, both of which focus on the relationship between persons. One is the emphasis on interpersonal reciprocity, suggesting that you should treat others as you would like to be treated. The other emphasizes unconditional love of another as yourself. The test of an ethical decision by these standards, then, would be the extent to which we are comfortable with the idea that we would want someone to make a similar decision about us, or that the decision is what we would decide for ourselves under similar circumstances.

Empathetic reciprocity is a secular doctrine that emphasizes our obligation to see in others the needs for love and respect we have in ourselves. Like the Judeo-Christian doctrine, we need to take the position of the other in making a moral judgment. Our position can be evaluated by the extent to which we enhance the ability of the other to gain love and respect.

Kant's categorical imperative argues that any reason offered as justification for a moral act be one that would apply to all people universally regardless of gender, race, creed, culture, or period of history. Therefore, no one person or group should receive any kind of "special consideration" that would privilege them differently from another is the deciding factor when considering one's duty. Kant views duty as an objective reality understood to be the same for all rational persons facing similar conditions; subsequently, any decision we make, or any action we take, in a given situation must be defended on the basis that it is what any rational person would have done under similar conditions.

Utilitarianism is a doctrine developed by English philosophers Jeremy Bentham and John Stuart Mill. This view holds that right action is that which promotes the greatest good for the greatest number. This requires attention be given to the effects of decisions and their impact on others.

Causalism is a perspective that considers the harm to society produced by a decision. If there is harm or a negative effect on the general welfare of others, then the decision is wrong.

When there is no empirical or logical answer to a problem or moral dilemma, then it is useful to consider principles such as those briefly reviewed here in making a decision. In the following section, ethical issues facing policymakers and approaches to addressing these issues are discussed.

# ETHICAL CONSIDERATIONS IN POLICY ISSUES

Gallagher (1990) presents a concise definition of policy as "the rules and standards by which societal resources are allocated" (p. 1316). He highlights five issues the policymaker must determine: (1) the client to be served; (2) the services and resources to be delivered; (3) the agencies and personnel responsible for service and resource delivery; (4) the accessibility of services and resources; and (5) the criteria for determining eligibility for services and resources. In considering these issues policymakers must assume a technical (interpretive) role and a social (stewardship) role (Paul, in press). That is, as technicians, they are faced with the task of interpreting the intent of the lawmakers, and as stewards, ensuring, through the development of policy, the best possible fit between the resources available and the interventions necessary. They must examine principles that govern who will receive benefit from the policy and how that benefit will be distributed.

Three areas of concern often faced by policymakers include child-centered issues, family-centered issues, and professional-centered issues (Paul, in press). Child-centered issues focus on matters pertaining to the child as the client. An example of a child-centered issue is defining who will and who will not be served, and service priorities. Family-centered issues focus on factors affecting the family. Interventions that violate the family's right to privacy is an example of a family-centered issue. Finally, professional-centered issues focus on the quality of professional practice and the rights as well as responsibilities of a professional to provide state of the art or science of practice.

How a policymaker responds to each of the issues presented is significantly influenced by the following: (1) her or his philosophical perspective or approach to dealing with moral issues; (2) her or his knowledge base and access to relevant research; and (3) her or his self-interests.

## Philosophical Perspectives

*Mr. Jackson and Mr. Brown serve on a state committee to establish policy for Part H of PL 101-476. Mr. Jackson believes that children with mild disabilities, or those who are considered at risk for developmental disabilities, should receive most of the limited resources. He believes that allocating limited resources for children with profound intellectual disabilities is an excessive intervention. Mr. Brown takes the perspective that most of the limited resources should be available to those children with profound disabilities because of the intense demands the disabling condition places on the daily lives of their families. Their conflicting perspectives threaten to deadlock the committee on several issues they are to consider, including determining who the client is and defining eligibility criteria for prospective clients.*

This case illustrates differing philosophical perspectives that individual policymakers bring to the decision-making process. If the resources available for implementation of policy were unlimited, the likelihood of the conflict occurring would be greatly reduced. The reality is that resources available for the implementation of policy are limited. Understanding the philosophical beliefs of committee members helps to clarify the positions they take and ultimately assists in resolution. It is helpful to the group if time can be devoted to discussion of the beliefs and values of each member as they relate to policy issues to be considered. Setting aside sufficient time for the group to hear and sympathetically consider each member's moral perspectives and his or her vision of the desired outcomes of the service system to be developed is useful in resolving difficult issues when they arise.

## Knowledge and Access to Research

*Ms. Quan and Ms. Alvarez serve on a committee to determine interdisciplinary policy for children "at risk" for developmental disabilities. Ms. Quan, a social worker, emphasizes a systems model of intervention. She proposes that assessment for children who are developmentally at risk be determined by multiple factors. In order to meet eligibility criteria, a combination of several at-risk factors should be present. Ms. Quan believes the Department of Social Services would be the logical lead agency in determining eligibility. Ms. Alvarez, an elected superintendent of a large school district, thinks Ms. Quan's plan is much too complicated and impractical to implement. Ms. Alvarez's concern is that in the long run the costs of identifying the client would disproportionately use the resources that otherwise could be used for intervention. Based on her belief that socioeconomic status is a major factor in increasing the potential of children at risk for developmental disabilities, she believes that children should be identified on the basis of whether they qualify for the free lunch program. Ms. Quan fears that primarily considering only SES in determining at risk is too limiting and would exclude many who may need help and include some who may not. Another committee member suggested that a thorough review of all available research would aid in resolving this issue. Unfortunately, the little research available did not directly address the predictive factors, and the committee was forced to rely on limited information from which to generate the best possible policy.*

This case highlights two closely related issues. First is the knowledge policymakers bring with them to the committee. Policy-making bodies usually have members who represent several disciplines, each with its own knowledge base. Ms. Quan is accustomed to working with families in her profession, whereas Ms. Alvarez is more concerned with administrative and financial efficiency. The knowledge base of committee members will impact how they view the issues at hand. Individuals who have a high degree of specialization in one discipline may find it difficult to generate alternate solutions outside of their discipline (Gallagher, 1989). Questions of territoriality, who will be the lead agency, and which agency will receive government funds for implementing the policy further complicate interdisciplinary cooperation. Increasingly, legislation reflects a shift from a child focus to a family focus in intervention necessitating interdisciplinary collaboration. This broadened focus will require increased multidisciplinary collaboration to ensure that policy meets the needs of the population to be served.

The second issue is the availability of relevant research to guide policymakers. Sincere attempts to bridge the gaps among the knowledge bases of policymakers often is frustrated by the lack of adequate research. Gallagher (1990), reviewing the development of policy, described the lack of scientific data as a major obstacle to be overcome by most policy-making committees. Frequently policymakers must make ethical decisions based on less scientific research than would normally be acceptable. This condition of having limited or relative knowledge available requires decision makers to rely on their own values and beliefs in making important decisions that affect the lives of children and families.

## Self-Interest

*Mr. Gibson and Mrs. Harding are part of a committee to establish policy for adolescents at risk of not completing high school. Mr. Gibson is a school counselor. Mrs. Harding has a teenager labeled with severe emotional disturbance who just recently was suspended from his high school. Both Mr. Gibson and Mrs. Harding have a vested interest in the success of the policy that would be established. Mr. Gibson has accepted the idea that, due to resource limitations, passage of a comprehensive policy to prevent school dropout is highly unlikely. His goal is to spread the available money among all students at risk for dropping out. Mrs. Harding's position is that, if there are only limited resources available, it would be better to offer those resources to a smaller group, like the adolescents with emotional disabilities, than to spread the resources thinly among all the adolescents who are at risk for dropping out of high school.*

This case illustrates the impact of self-interest on a policy-making group. The school counselor saw many children at risk for dropping out of school. The mother's focus was the needs of her son. She was representing her family's interests and possibly the interests of other families who have adolescents with emotional disabilities, whereas the school counselor was attempting to represent the interests of all adolescents at risk. Again, it is important for policymakers to clearly understand their own self-interests and the self-interests of others in the group. It is easier to reach consensus on ethical decisions if the biases and assumptions that individual policymakers bring with them are openly discussed.

The second issue in the case presented is that policy decisions are sometimes the result of compromise, often based on the belief that it is better to have something in place than nothing at all, with the hope that in the future a policy closer to the ideal may be established. Policy decisions are based on several criteria: (1) scientific information; (2) resources available (financial and time); and (3) political sensitivity to controversial policies (Gallagher, 1990). There is no uniform ranking of the criteria for policy decision making. Scientific information may be weighted heavier than available resources in one setting and significantly lower in another setting.

In the process of both interpreting legislative intent and disbursing limited resources, policymakers are faced with many difficult decisions. The preceding scenarios highlight some of the ethical dilemmas policymakers must work through. Several approaches to guide policy choices are discussed in the following section.

## Approaches to Ethical Issues

Three commonly used approaches are briefly presented here: cost-effectiveness analysis, cost-benefit analysis, and ethical method analysis. The first two approaches are monetary in nature and require extensive collection of data to support their hypotheses. They examine the consequences of actions to determine what is a good distribution of resources. The ethical method analysis proposed by Kendrick (in press) relies less on statistical verification and more on moral and legal reasoning. It includes the consequentialist perspective as one framework within which to examine the relationship of actions to ends; however, it allows people to include notions of duty and actions based on principles that are not justified by an appeal to consequences alone.

Cost-effectiveness and cost-benefit analyses argue that the savings derived from a treatment program will outweigh the costs of implementing the program (MacRae, 1989). The prime feature that distinguishes cost-effectiveness analysis from cost-benefit analysis is that with cost effectiveness the cost and effects are examined in distinctly different units of measurement. For example, in the health-care industry, for a given investment or cost, members of society are able to enjoy a better quality of life through improved health care. The effectiveness of the investment in health care is examined in relation to improved quality of life; however, quality of life cannot be measured by dollars. With cost benefit, the benefits can be expressed in monetary terms. Early intervention programs are often proposed from a cost-benefit position where it is argued that the expenses involved in preventative measures in early childhood programs for at-risk children will directly and significantly reduce monies that would otherwise be spent on these children later in life.

The ethical method described by Kendrick (in press) examines policy issues from a moral perspective. Monetary considerations are secondary to moral considerations. The model is designed to enable participants to recognize and process significant differences in important values effectively. Ethically informed policy would emerge from the efforts of policymakers to formulate their positions so that all important terms are clearly and unambiguously defined (e.g., family) and all values are consistently applied. It is through understanding each other's perspectives, biases, and self-interests that the group is able to explore the reasoning used by another when there is disagreement, and to evaluate the reasoning using the standards of clarity and consistency.

Paul (1992) presents a succinct summary of the ethical method's five phases. First, describe the problem sufficiently so the group achieves consensus about it. Second, generate several possible solutions for the problem. Third, identify potential value conflicts through examining possible self-interests in the group, and then work through the value conflicts using the moral analysis criteria (Kendrick, in press). Fourth, check the possible solutions against the moral analysis criteria. Finally, based on the four phases, select the solution that represents the best fit for the problem described in the first phase considering society's values and those of the individual policymakers.

# ETHICAL CONSIDERATIONS IN CLINICAL ISSUES ███████████

Embedded within recent legislation is a clear intent to strengthen the role of parents in the planning and implementation of their child's intervention (Gallagher, in press). To successfully achieve this goal, parents and professionals must work together to establish a mutual relationship of trust, respect, and communication. The trend toward increased parent involvement has many potential promises. Mesibov and La Greca (1981) described two ways a successful relationship can benefit the child and family. First, parents know their child well because of the many hours of care they invest; professionals have training in working with individuals with disabilities. By working together, a deeper understanding of the child's individual characteristics and needs can be transmitted so that effective interventions can be individually designed to meet the needs of both the child and family. In addition, professionals may impart greater objectivity than parents who may have a greater emotional investment in various intervention goals. By combining parental concern with professional objectivity, the likelihood of identifying potential areas of need to achieve both short-term objectives and long-term goals is increased.

Although there are many advantages in parent-professional partnerships, there are also potential sources of conflict. With increased parental decision-making responsibilities comes the need for consideration of a wider range of perspectives. Because of differences in cultural traditions, religious beliefs, individual experiences, and socioeconomics, parents and professionals sometimes have very different ideas concerning a child's needs and the appropriate intervention. These differing perspectives cannot always be resolved through standard professional practices or policies. When the values of professionals are in conflict with the values of parents, a resolution may involve agreement on ethical principles that requires thoughtful and informed choices.

All human service professionals are guided by the codes of ethics of their major professional associations (e.g., AMA, APA, NASW, CEC). Many authors have discussed the responsibility of clinicians to consider ethics when making clinical decisions. Allen and Allen (1979) argued that because of the extreme vulnerability of some individuals with handicaps, professionals must consider the ethics of intervention. Mesibov and La Greca (1981) pointed out that ethical considerations may contribute to the achievement of reasonable solutions allowing professionals to be more effective in their work. Turnbull (1982) stated that professionals must establish standards of professional conduct beyond the minimal standards provided by the law. According to Rosenberg, Tesolowski, and Stein (1982), professionals have a moral duty to be advocates for their clients.

The future of effective clinical practice will require clinicians not only to establish relationships of trust, respect, and communication with the parents they work with, but also to apply ethical considerations when integrating divergent perspectives in interventions. Earlier in this chapter, several approaches were described that may assist clinicians in making informed and reasoned decisions. Presented here are several areas in which clinical decisions may require ethical judgments. Individual cases are described illustrating different and potentially conflicting perspectives of parents and professionals. The purpose of these examples is to illustrate the ethical reasoning in informed and thoughtful decision making. It should become clear that ethical issues may not have a right or wrong answer, but informed and reasoned judgments should create more definitive bases for intervention decisions.

## Working With Families

*Dana, a 5-year-old boy with autism, had been receiving services at a local clinic. His therapist set up a program to encourage Dana's use of language and social interaction skills within his natural environment. The program required his parents to organize peer play groups and to respond consistently to Dana's spontaneous speech. Dana's language use and social interactions had shown significant and steady improvements over a 5-month period, but then his speech and interaction abruptly and almost entirely stopped. After a lengthy discussion with Dana's mother, the therapist found out that Dana's father had lost his job and had begun to drink heavily. This pattern of behavior was creating marital discord. Because of the stress and pressures of her husband's situation, Dana's mother felt that the family had neither the patience nor the time to implement Dana's interventions. Dana's therapist felt that Dana's mother had a responsibility to implement the strategies which had been previously successful with her child.*

As this case illustrates, it is important to establish a communicative and open parent-professional partnership so that the clinician can stay informed of changing family patterns that may affect the child. Without sufficient information, decisions may be made that work against the goals for the child and family. There are times when professionals can and should question the manner in which families care for their children. However, before this is done it is important that professionals consider all the factors that may be affecting a family's behavior. A second issue that clinicians often must address is "Who is the client?" In order to answer, it is important for the clinician to understand how changing family dynamics influence the behavior of individual family members so that the rights and needs of both the parents and the child can be considered.

The family systems perspective views the family as a whole with unique characteristics and needs. Because family members are interconnected, experiences affecting one member will also affect all members of the family. For this reason, clinical decisions must take into account the interests of all family members. In this situation, the utilitarian perspective may assist in making an appropriate decision by suggesting that it is necessary to determine what action would promote the greatest good for all parties involved. Focusing only on the implementation of Dana's intervention may increase the anxiety Dana's mother is experiencing. It may be that by temporarily focusing on Dana's parents' problems, more members of the family will ultimately benefit.

Family-professional partnerships are becoming recognized as an important element to integrate and optimize a child's opportunities. An understanding of the diverse characteristics and dynamics of families requires an ongoing open and communicative relationship. Clinicians with a thorough understanding of family values and lifestyles are in a position to provide informed ethical perspectives.

## Evaluation and Referral

*Dr. Mathieson, a diagnostic clinician, is asked by school personnel to evaluate a 2-year-old boy, Tommy. The district feels that he may be "at risk" because his four siblings all have developmental disabilities. Dr. Mathieson travels to Tommy's home, which is located in a very rural area. Following an initial assessment, Dr. Mathieson believes that Tommy shows signs of developmental delays. She feels that Tommy would benefit from services provided by a clinic in the nearest town; however, she knows that Tommy's parents do not have access to transportation for the 50-mile trip. Dr. Mathieson does not know whether to make a referral to an agency that, for practical purposes, is not accessible to the family.*

Two major issues must be considered in this example. First, the cost and benefit of the intervention must be evaluated. Families often experience significant financial burdens as a result of evaluation and interventions that may have very limited chances of success. The decision of what is an acceptable cost and how the benefits should be evaluated must be carefully considered. Second, access to services may be a critical issue. Many times major facilities are located in urban areas, such as university campuses, which may not be easily accessible to families living in rural areas. Although professionals may know that services cannot be accessed, they often feel that doing nothing is unacceptable. In the situation just described, Dr. Mathieson may attempt to place herself in Tommy's position or his mother's position and imagine how it might feel to access such services or at least be informed that the services are available. This may lead her to make the referral, which would be an example of using the principle of empathetic reciprocity. Parents have ultimate responsibility for their children and also need to make informed decisions. It may be that an option Dr. Mathieson is not aware of has yet to be explored.

The movement toward increased family involvement in clinical decision making is accompanied by the responsibility to keep family members informed in all matters concerning their child. The application of principles of reciprocity may assist professionals in understanding the responsibilities family members may be feeling.

## Intervention

*Kevin, Mr. Kent's son, was diagnosed with a developmental disability and has been receiving individual therapy at a local center since he was 2. When Kevin turned 3, Mr. Kent decided to enroll him in preschool. Mr. Kent found an integrated preschool close to his house that agreed to admit Kevin. The program uses a sensory stimulation approach with children with disabilities that involves stroking the children with soft large brushes when they show signs of discomfort or begin to tantrum. Kevin's private therapist is familiar with the strategies used by the preschool and does not believe they will be effective with Kevin. However, Kevin's father has had difficulty finding an integrated program for Kevin near his neighborhood and believes that the techniques may help Kevin.*

It is not unusual for parents and professionals to disagree sometimes on which intervention approach would be most beneficial for a particular child. Professionals have an ethical obligation to be informed of the best practices in the field. However, this is often difficult when efficacy data for a particular intervention show mixed results. When making intervention decisions several factors need to be considered. First, it is important to determine the goals of intervention. Agreeing on specific goals often facilitates the selection of strategies to achieve that goal. It is also essential that professionals understand the needs of the family. For example, are time constraints a consideration such that Mr. Kent needs to have Kevin in a preschool near his home? The family values and cultural framework should be carefully considered. For example, in some cultures interdependency is highly valued and may lead to a reluctance to embrace intervention goals that would produce independent behavior.

In the example just described, several questions need to be addressed. Treatment efficacy needs to be considered as well as family needs. Sometimes a combination of ethical principles can be applied to a single issue in trying to gain clarity. If we chose to consider the perspective of empathetic reciprocity, very different conclusions may be reached depending on whether the perspective of Kevin is taken or the perspective of his father. For example, by taking Kevin's perspective, the therapist may view the preschool's strategies as ineffective and advocate against the placement. However, by taking Mr. Kent's perspective, the convenience of the preschool's location may outweigh other factors. In this situation it may be useful to also consider the utilitarian perspective by considering what action would promote the greatest good for the greatest number of people. By considering both individual needs and cumulative benefits, the clinician may able to reach an equitable decision more easily.

Factual information concerning intervention must be used to guide ethical decision making. However, when factual information is limited, ethical considerations become increasingly important. Sometimes very different conclusions may be reached depending on the perspective taken and the principles applied. At these times it may be beneficial to consider a wide range of perspectives and apply a variety of principles to assist in decision making.

## Least Restrictive Environment

*Sally has been diagnosed with a severe language delay. The school she is attending has suggested that she be placed in a classroom for students with language impairments. The school personnel feel that this is the best placement for Sally because the classroom is staffed with a well-qualified teacher with specific training and experience in working with children such as Sally. In addition, the student-teacher ratio in the classroom is much smaller than a regular classroom. Sally's parents feel that she would not make adequate progress in a classroom with peers who also had language difficulties. They would rather have her placed in a regular classroom where she would have more opportunities to learn age-appropriate language skills from her peers. The school personnel believe that Sally's language delay would prohibit her from understanding much of what happened in the classroom and that she would not easily make friends with her classmates.*

According to the concept of least restrictive setting, individuals should be exposed to typical life experiences as much as possible, regardless of their disability. This concept is an important component of appropriate placement decisions that has important ethical implications. On the one hand, it is difficult to argue with the philosophy that individuals with disabilities should be provided with as normal an experience as possible. On the other hand, individuals have sometimes been placed in integrated environments without adequate support. This has resulted in deleterious effects on all parties involved.

When determining appropriate settings for individuals with disabilities, a variety of issues should be considered. The parents and professionals should evaluate what supports are needed for successful integration. It may be worthwhile to explore the willingness or responsibility of individuals within the system to make setting accommodations to alleviate potential problems. For example, it may be possible to make modifications in the regular classroom, such as finding a peer partner for Sally or simplifying some of the academic tasks so that Sally's educational experience can be positive and productive. The parties involved may also want to consider both present and long-term effects to achieve a balance between Sally's individual needs and the long-range goals of integrated social systems.

The widespread establishment of integrated educational settings over the last decade demonstrate a commitment to the concept of least restrictive environment. However, ineffective program strategies have resulted in conflicts affecting service delivery. As a result, families and professionals together continue to face ethical issues when determining how to best meet a child's needs in the least restrictive setting.

## Family Research

*Jose, a student labeled with severe emotional disturbance, and his family had been receiving family services from a mental health facility for several years. The director of the program received a grant to conduct a study in the area of social skills. In order to collect accurate data, it would be necessary to videotape Jose and his peers interacting. Jose's parents were very ambivalent about his participation in the research project. They felt they had received valuable services in the past and would like to assist the program director in this new endeavor. However, they had strong views about family privacy and felt that allowing Jose to be videotaped would violate those values. In addition, they were concerned about not knowing who would view the videotapes and also the possibility that Jose may someday have access to the tapes. They believed that eventually Jose would no longer exhibit problems with social interactions, and seeing the videotapes in the future may be traumatic for him.*

Although systematic research has made important contributions to the development of effective interventions, issues sometimes emerge in the process of designing and conducting research that may conflict with family values, cultural characteristics, and needs, as the example just cited illustrates. How research should be understood and evaluated requires a consideration of underlying values. Turnbull and Turnbull (1989) specified five principles resulting from the Consensus Conference on Family Research. First, research should be a means, not an end. The purpose of research should be to gain information and test strategies that will enhance the lives of people with disabilities and their families. Second, research should be a collaborative endeavor. Research should be a participatory process characterized by collaboration, mutual respect, honest communication, and trust. Third, research should be culturally sensitive. Researchers should be aware of cultural, ethnic, socioeconomic, and lifestyle pluralisms. Fourth, research should consist of many paradigms and methodologies. The complexity of family systems may best be studied through the use of a diversity of research strategies. Last, there should be sufficient funding to assure that quality research can be conducted. Funding for family research should be increased so that methodological and other considerations are not hindered.

Professionals responsible for conducting research face a diversity of ethical decisions, including formulating relevant research questions, selecting appropriate methodologies, and remaining sensitive to idiosyncratic needs and values of the families with which they work. Potential benefits to both the individual participants and the research literature must be carefully considered.

# SUMMARY

The trend toward increased family involvement in clinical and policy decisions has been accompanied by the need to redefine the roles of both parents and professionals in order to integrate a more diverse range of perspectives successfully. The issues described in this chapter illustrate the myriad of challenges that sometimes arise when individuals with differing values and interests work together. Although many professional organizations have codes of ethics, they are often limited and do not fully address the changing roles of families and professionals. In these situations, it is often helpful to apply traditional ethical principles to moral judgments. It is also important for families and professionals to understand and appreciate one another's knowledge bases, interests, philosophical orientations, and needs. An understanding of differing viewpoints facilitates the constructive resolution of disagreements. A family-professional partnership holds great potential for providing services and care that accommodate the idiosyncratic needs of the child within his or her environment. With a mutual understanding and respect of each other's values and differences, this goal can be met.

# REFERENCES

Allen, D. F., & Allen V. S. (1979). *Ethical issues in mental retardation: Tragic choices/living hope.* Nashville: Abingdon Press.

Gallagher, J. J. (1989). The implementation of social policy: A policy analysis challenge. In J. J. Gallagher, P. L. Trohanis, & R. M. Clifford (Eds.), *Policy implementation and PL 99-457: Planning for young children with special needs* (pp. 199–215). Baltimore: Brookes.

Gallagher, J. J. (1990). Emergence of policy studies and policy institutes. *American Psychologist, 45*, 1316–1318.

Kendrick, S. B., Jr. (in press). Ethical method and policy formation. In Paul et. al, *Handbook for the development of implementation policies for P.L. 99-457 (Part H)*. Chapel Hill, NC: Frank Porter Graham Center Policy Institute.

MacRae, D., Jr. (1989). The use of outcome measures in implementing policies for handicapped children. In J. J. Gallagher, P. L. Trohanis, & R. M. Clifford (Eds.), *Policy implementation and PL 99-457: Planning for young children with special needs* (pp. 183–198). Baltimore: Brookes.

MacRae, D., Jr., & Haskins, R. (1981). Models for policy analysis. In R. Haskins & J. J. Gallagher (Eds.), *Models for analysis of social policy: An introduction* (pp. 1–36). Norwood, NJ: Ablex.

Mesibov, G. B., & La Greca, A. M. (1981). Ethical issues in parent-professional service interaction. In J. L. Paul (Ed.), *Understanding and working with parents of children with special needs* (pp. 154–179). New York: Holt.

Paul, J. L. (in press) Introduction to ethics and policy development. In *Handbook for the development of implementation policies for P.L. 99-457 (Part H)*. Chapel Hill, NC: Frank Porter Graham Center Policy Institute.

Paul, J. L., Gallagher, J. J., Kendrick, S. B., Thomas, D. D., Young, J. F. (1992). *Handbook for Ethical Policy Making*. Chapel Hill, NC: North Carolina Institute for Policy Studies.

Rosenberg, H., Tesolowski, D., & Stein, R. (1983). Advocacy: Education responsibility to handicapped children. *Education and Training of the Mentally Retarded, 18*, 266–270.

Turnbull, A. P., & Turnbull, H. R. (1989). Professional Ethics and Morals. In A. P. Turnbull & H. R. Turnbull (Eds.), *Families, professionals, and exceptionality: A special partnership* (pp. 384–410). Columbus, OH: Merrill.

Turnbull, H. R. (1982). Youngberg v. Romeo: An essay. *Journal of the Association for Persons With Severe Handicaps, 8*, 3–6.

Turnbull, H. R., & Turnbull, A. P. (1989). *Report of consensus conference on principles of family research*. Lawrence, KS: Beach Center on Families and Disability.

# 16

## THE FUTURE OF PROFESSIONAL/FAMILY RELATIONS IN FAMILIES WITH CHILDREN WITH DISABILITIES

*James J. Gallagher*

## INTRODUCTION

The purpose of this final chapter is to project current trends and past history of the so-called families' movement into an uncertain future. The role of the prophet is an unenviable one. He or she must rely on the poor memory of those who have heard past predictions in order to maintain status as a seer. Predicting the future requires us to (1) correctly assess current trends; (2) decide whether these trends can be extended in a linear projection or whether they are the end of a cycle and are folding back; and (3) understand the interaction between these trends and other social forces at work in the society.

It now seems clear that interest in the family, and the role it is expected to play in programs for children with disabilities, has been steadily increasing over the last decade. One of the more obvious developments is the professionals' switch in interest from the mother-child dyad—which was really what the interest in "the family" added up to in the 1960s and 1970s—to extending that interest to the *family system*, with a much greater concern shown for father, siblings, and the interactions among all family members (Gallagher & Vietze, 1986). As we have become more interested in different family models, the *extended family* has also become a key player (see Chapter 7).

One of the strongest indications of the continuing and growing interest in the family was evidenced in the passage of Part H of PL 99-457, now referred to as IDEA (Individuals With Disabilities Education Act). This section of the law mandates a comprehensive, multidisciplinary, interagency-based service system for infants and toddlers with disabilities and their families for all states that elect to participate in the program (all of the states are participating at the time of this writing) (Gallagher, Trohanis, & Clifford, 1989).

This law continues the explicit *family empowerment* concept that was begun in PL 94-142, the Education for All Handicapped Children Act, with its stress on parent participation in the development of the individual education plan (IEP), due process, and other features. Part H proposes that families become involved in policy development as well, by mandating that at least three parents sit on the Interagency Coordinating Council, a structure designed to contribute to formulation in the law's implementation. This expectation that parents should play a significant role in policy represents a step above their merely participating in the plans for their own child.

During this era (1970–1990), parents tended to shed some of their inhibitions in dealing with the professionals who provided services for their child. A fine example of the increased assertiveness of parents toward professionals is presented by Gorham et al. (1975) in the following orientation to parents:

> You are the primary helper, monitor, coordinator, observer, record keeper, and decision maker for your child. Insist that you be treated as such. It is your right to understand your child's diagnosis and the reasons for treatment, recommendations, and for educational placement. No changes in his treatment or educational placement should take place without previous consultation with you. (pp. 184–185)

Any determination of future desirable actions rests upon a correct assessment of family needs and the role societal forces will play in the family.

## ASSUMPTIONS ABOUT FAMILY NEEDS

But legislation such as IDEA is merely based on a set of assumptions as to what the family is like and what it needs. The question as to the true *needs* of the family, or of the diversity of families faced with raising young children with disabilities, must be answered before public policy can be effectively designed. Simeonsson and Simeonsson, in Chapter 2, have detailed some of the psychological dimensions of family interactions.

MacKeith (1973) proposed four major crisis periods that are associated with the developmental model of the family of handicapped children:

1. When the parents first become aware of the fact that their child is handicapped.
2. When the child becomes eligible for educational services.
3. When the child leaves school.
4. When aging parents can no longer assume care and responsibility of their handicapped offspring.

In each of these crisis periods, the nature of the stress experienced by families and the demand for coping skills is slightly—or considerably—different. A parent can be courageous in one situation and come unstrung in another. So we should not be surprised that some parents who seem to have adapted so well to their child with disabilities in one stage are suddenly in a state of panic and disarray when the child leaves school and thus moves into a different life stage, creating a new set of problems and stresses. The ability to anticipate these transitional problems from a professional standpoint and to help parents adapt to it would be a major expected gain in the 1990s. It is obvious that vastly different support services are required at each of these crisis points. Having conceptualized them, we now have the opportunity to try to design services that might meet the special character of the crisis at each family development stage.

In addition to such significant crisis events as noted by MacKeith, there has been a growing awareness of a family life cycle, experienced by most families, which requires repeated coping to new life situations. This life cycle (see Table 16.1) is then complicated by the presence of a child with disabilities (Turnbull, Summers, & Brotherson, 1986).

The particular type of crisis that the family must deal with changes over various stages in the life cycle. For example, in Table 16.1 we find, at the pre-

TABLE 16.1

## FAMILY LIFE CYCLE WITH A CHILD WITH DISABILITIES

| STAGE | AREAS OF SPECIAL STRESS |
|---|---|
| Couple | ▪ Usual expectations about having children<br>▪ Usual adaptations to living with partner |
| Childbearing and Preschool | ▪ Fears that child is abnormal<br>▪ Diagnosis<br>▪ Finding treatment<br>▪ Telling siblings and extended family about the handicap |
| School Age | ▪ Reactions of other children and families to the exceptional child<br>▪ Schooling |
| Adolescence | ▪ Peer rejection<br>▪ Vocational preparation<br>▪ Issues around emerging sexuality |
| Launching | ▪ Living arrangements<br>▪ Financial concerns<br>▪ Socialization opportunities |
| Postparental | ▪ Long-term security for the child<br>▪ Interactions with service providers<br>▪ Dealing with the child's interest in dating, marriage, and childbearing |
| Aging | ▪ Care and supervision of handicapped child after parents' death<br>▪ Transfer of parental responsibilities to other family subsystems or service providers |

Source: Adapted from A. Turnbull, J. Summers, & M. Brotherson (1986), "Family Life Cycle," in J. Gallagher & P. Vietze (Eds.), *Families of Handicapped Persons*. Baltimore: Brookes. Used by permission of A. Turnbull and the publisher.

school level, a major source of stress—finding the right kind of treatment resources for the child. At school age, there are reactions of other children to the child with special needs, and this is a likely source of family concern. Vocational needs and emerging sexuality then become important issues around adolescence. The family that has met the problems of one particular stage must still be flexible enough to cope with the related—but different—problems coming up in the next stage.

Although all families have concerns about their offspring throughout the children's lifetime, the concerns of parents with a child with disabilities seem to be particularly sharp, and continue through the entire life span of both parent and child.

## The Father's Role

One of the foci of attention during the 1980s was the role of the father in a family with children with disabilities (see Parke, 1986; Wikler, 1986). Although some theorists would suggest that fathers of children with disabilities would play a *greater* child-care role within the family than fathers of children without disabilities—based on marriage being a sharing and balancing of stressful conditions—the evidence points to a different conclusion (Bristol, Gallagher, & Schopler, 1988; Wikler, 1986). In many families with a child with disabilities, the father can show *less* involvement with the child.

For example, in a study of 56 two-parent families, 31 of which had a child with disabilities, Gallagher, Scharfman, and Bristol (1984) found that fathers of children with disabilities were less involved with their child than were fathers of children without disabilities. Such a finding appears to be due to a variety of reasons, including the father's lack of knowledge about how to care for or interact with the child with disabilities, a denial of responsibilities by the father and a desire to flee from an unpleasant situation, or a pact with the mother on how the energies of the family can best be distributed.

## Siblings

As the focus extended beyond the mother-child dyad, there came increased attention to the siblings of exceptional children. Reviews of this literature (Powell & Ogle, 1985; Simeonsson & Bailey, 1986) delineate the various patterns of responses found in siblings—from uncomfortable feelings about how their peers will see their sibling with disabilities, to anger that the parents spend so much time with the affected child, to a sense of responsibility for caring for the child. The often deep emotional reactions, such as reported in the following passage by a girl who slapped her baby brother, will illustrate why *family-focused* programs are needed.

*In that instance, I learned something of human nature and the nature of those who would reject people like George. I had been one of them: sullen, uncaring, and unwilling to care for someone who came into the world with fewer advantages than I myself had. I am a better person for having lived through both the good and the bad times that our family has experienced as a result of my brother's autism. . . . Best of all, I have my brother—who loves me with all the goodness in his heart. (Warren, 1985)*

# Coping With Stress

A significant contribution to the understanding of the complex nature of family adaptation to the child with disabilities was made by Hill (1949), who proposed a three-factor theory of stress, later updated by McCubbin and Patterson (1983). Hill maintained that there can be three major contributors to the manifestation of stress in the individual. The first of these is the nature of the *stressor* itself (in this instance the level and severity of the handicapping condition). The second contributor to stress is the presence of *family supports* (in this instance the presence of a helpful extended family, supportive neighbors, and/or strong professional support for child and family, all of which would be indicative of a lower stress level).

The third major dimension related to stress is the individual's *perception* of the nature and meaning of the situation (a crisis situation can be interpreted as helping one grow strong, or a challenge from God, rather than an unfortunate set of events delivered upon an unlucky couple). The more positive the interpretation, the less the stress level. Using the formula "Stress $\longrightarrow$ f (A)(B)(C) . . . n," it is easy to see how a family with a child with a severe handicap might seem to be under less stress than a family with a child with a mild handicap, given a favorable set of factors in the family support area and a positive perception of the situation.

Bristol, Gallagher, and Schopler (1988) tried to determine what factors were linked to stress and marital problems with having a child with disabilities. They found that families with a child with disabilities seemed to be at greater risk for marital difficulties (fitting earlier work on increased prevalence of divorce in such families—Love, 1973), a greater sense of disruption of family life, and lower ratings on observed parenting. There were more mothers in the group at risk for depression in the children with disabilities category, and their depression seemed linked to the lack of perceived spousal support. In addition, the researchers found that many families seemed to have found effective ways to cope with this family crisis and not show any unusual stress or marital difficulties. One assumption that needs to be modified is that all families are in need of extensive personal counseling. Some have adapted quite well on their own.

# Cultural Diversity

One of the most difficult aspects of policy development is when the target population is extraordinarily diverse, as certainly occurs in Part H of IDEA. There are families from all levels of income, from many different cultural heritages, and from very different religious persuasions.

Arcia, Gallagher, and Serling (1992) found only 7% of families who did not have at least one indicator related to underutilization of services (poverty, maternal employment, ethnic minorities, teen motherhood, etc.). In families from cultural minorities, there are many opportunities to misunderstand the professional from the perspective of a family member from a different cultural background. A special effort has to be undertaken to help families from cultural minorities feel at home in service programs and to staff these service programs with representatives from such minorities.

## SOCIETAL INFLUENCES ON THE FAMILY

The family, too, is affected by larger societal factors that pressure family members to behave in certain specified ways toward each other. The role that the mother or father will play toward their children and each other is often related to cultural values held by various societal groups with which the parents are affiliated. The diversity of cultural heritages in the United States makes it more likely that there will be differences of opinion in the appropriate role to be played by a parent.

Farber (1978, 1986) identified a variety of family models that exist simultaneously in society and create substantial role differences for wives and husbands, depending on which model one or both of the parents follow. Farber found a societal movement away from the *entrepreneurial family model*, which stresses the pooling of family members' resources to a common goal, to the *companionship model*, where togetherness and common goals were stressed. That model, in turn, seems to be giving way to the *pluralistic family model*, where the family is seen as an instrument for achieving personal rights and meeting personal needs.

Such a pluralistic family model, where each member seeks to maximize his or her own personal rights and needs, can be a special problem in terms of deciding who should take the responsibility for caring for a dependent member such as an infant with disabilities. Much of the substantial family stress currently seen in American society may well be due to the differing perceptions of the appropriate roles to be played by the various family members. If, for example, the husband is playing the male role in the *companionship* model, only to find that the wife is playing the role of the female in the *pluralistic* family model, then there are likely to be major marital problems, even without the complicating factor of a child with disabilities in the family.

### Legislation

The purpose of legislating is to allocate scarce resources to clearly desirable social purposes and also to ensure that such allocation is done within the appropriate settings and conditions. In the case of Part H of IDEA for infants and toddlers, there have been deliberate attempts to upgrade the role of the family by providing for family members on the Interagency Coordinating Council, insisting on an individual family service plan with parents participating, and giving family needs prime consideration.

There is often little said about what happens when these conditions are not met. Too often in the past, this has meant a gut-wrenching effort at due process, court hearings, and acrimonious interchanges with professionals. One of the future goals is to find paths to some type of *conflict resolution* short of the devastating choice of court hearings, which often damage the relationship between parents and professionals beyond any benefits gained.

It is not surprising in this era of changing roles that there would be a multitude of clashes over whose new role will be sustained. The rights of parents are important to establish and maintain, but maintaining them often causes great family crises in its own right. The attempt of parents to invoke the due process clause in the Education for All Handicapped Children Act (PL 94-142) has often led to painful confrontations with school personnel (see Chapter 13).

# Courts

One of the other societal forces of importance over the past two decades has been the courts. The courts have been one of the allies of families seeking a more significant role with professionals and societal institutions such as the public schools. A variety of court decisions have helped to reaffirm the rights of children with disabilities and their families. Among the decisions that were supportive are the following:

- A handicapped child cannot be excluded from school without due process. No child shall be denied a free appropriate education. (*PARC v. Commonwealth of Pennsylvania*, 1972)
- Children should not be labeled "handicapped," or placed into special education, without adequate diagnosis that takes into account different cultural and linguistic backgrounds. (*Larry P. v. Riles*, 1979)
- Bilingual exceptional children need identification, evaluation, and educational procedures that reflect and respect their dual-language background. (*Jose P. v. Ambach*, 1979)

One limitation to the generally favorable court decisions was the *Board of Education v. Rowley* (1982) case, where the court ruled that a handicapped child is entitled to an *appropriate*, not an *optimum*, education—on the grounds that since no child gets an optimum education in this society, that should not be the standard for children with disabilities either. Nevertheless, the courts have generally been friendly to children with disabilities and their families, a point that has been noted by the professional community.

The organized parent advocacy groups, which have lobbied successfully at the state and federal level for increased resources for education of children with disabilities, have also funneled resources to the professional community that professionals could not have obtained solely on the basis of their own pleading. This, too, has raised the status of families in the eyes of the professional community (Kirk & Gallagher, 1989).

## PROFESSIONAL INTERVENTION IN FAMILIES

Washington and Gallagher (1986) synthesized information regarding family relationships, which have often formed the *deep structure* (Skrtic, 1990) for the various family intervention programs, as follows:

1. The perceptions and expectations of the family members, rather than objective data, will determine the family tone of unhappiness/happiness.
2. The greater the dissatisfaction with the way that responsibilities are allocated, the greater the potential for family disharmony.
3. The greater the stress placed on the family unit (such as the presence of a child with disabilities), the more important become the potential resources of the extended family and social support systems.
4. The importance of each domain to family harmony changes over different stages of family evolution.
5. The more support available in a particular domain from outside sources, the less important it is that the partner provides such support. (p. 263)

The multidisciplinary team providing professional services has a variety of tasks on which to work with these families. One of the increasing concerns of these professionals working with families who have a child with disabilities is assessing the *needs* of that family. Chapter 12 by Bailey and Winton presents the technical aspects of this problem, along with some suggestions about how to deal with the issue.

A recent study by Arcia, Gallagher, and Serling (1992) focused on the demographic portrait of families that might need services through the infants and toddlers section of IDEA. They estimate that over 20% of all young minority children live in families likely to underutilize available health and social services. Sizable changes in the established delivery systems seem called for if we are to provide services to this special group of families. Among such changes would be arranging for transportation so that services are more accessible, arranging for services to be available to mothers in the work force, recruiting service providers from ethnic and racial groups that compose much of the client population, and allowing families to choose times for meetings and services that do not interfere with their work schedules.

### Family Needs for Self-Efficacy

Rutter (1982) identified two substantial myths that seemed to be interfering with proper treatment for poor children with special needs and their families. The first of these misconceptions is that there are single causes for the problems that we see in these children; the second is that causes can be eliminated merely through direct treatment of the child. These propositions have become generally accepted as false. The focus of attention now is to how to build the strengths of the family and how to increase the effectiveness of the support networks—both within and outside the family—that impact so strongly on the family.

Rutter (1982), as well as Sameroff and Fiese (1990), believes that the family will find itself facing a crisis situation based on the number of risk factors present in its environment, rather than on what the particular risk factors are. With so many negative pressures zeroing in on the family from so many different directions, it becomes extremely difficult for the family to cope effectively with any of its responsibilities.

Dunst and Trivette (1990) emphasize helping the family to become empowered, to take control of their lives and their future. They make a distinction between enabling families and empowering families. *Enabling* families means creating opportunities for family members to become more competent, independent, and self-sustaining in their ability to mobilize social networks to reach desired goals. *Empowering* families means carrying out interventions in a manner in which the family members acquire a sense of control over their own developmental course.

This family empowerment orientation is a reaction to past professional/parent relationships that often tended to make the family *more* dependent on professional help, rather than helping the family to develop a sense of self-efficacy and a greater ability to handle their own problems without outside help—or at least to exert executive control over the situation by orchestrating needed help for their own family members.

Dunst and Trivette (1990) describe a four-step process for attaining family empowerment:

1.  Identification of family concerns, issues, and priorities using needs-based assessment procedures and strategies.
2.  Identification of family strengths and capabilities as a basis for emphasizing the things that the family already does well, and for identifying the intrafamily resources that increase the likelihood of the successful mobilization of extrafamily resources to meet needs.
3.  "Mapping" of the family's social network in terms of existing sources of support and resources and of untapped, but potential, sources of aid and assistance.
4.  Use of a number of different help-giving roles to enable and empower families, so they may become better able to mobilize resources to have their needs met and achieve desired goals. (p. 343–344)

This ecological approach to the family system is quite a contrast to the individual counseling of a mother, which was the standard procedure only a decade or so ago. It represents respect for the family and a faith that there are hidden strengths within the family system that can be tapped.

Most of the programs, past or present, have been designed around certain assumptions about individuals or about families. Gallagher (1990), in a recent review of the family as a focus for intervention, proposed five assumptions that lie at the base of most of our current family intervention efforts:

1. Changing children will change other family members.
2. Providing information and teaching parenting skills can change families.
3. Personal counseling can change families.
4. Increasing parent empowerment can change families.
5. Providing more support services can change families.

There would seem to be little evidence to support the first proposition or assumption (that changing the child will change other family members), and this lack of evidence is one reason for the trend toward family-focused interventions. On the other hand, Gallagher (1990) reported that providing information about how to parent and building parental skills seemed to show considerable gains in both parental skills and attitudes. Bailey and Simeonsson (1988), summarizing research on parent training, concluded that a variety of intervention methods seemed to help parents implement correct and consistent behavior change programs that also resulted in meaningful changes in child outcomes.

The role of personal counseling is less clear cut. There are elements of personal counseling in all of these various interventions, but it does seem to help the parents' own feelings of self-efficacy (Bandura, 1989) to become more capable at performing needed tasks. There is some additional evidence from a 10-year follow-up study (Seitz, Rosenbaum, & Apfel, 1985) that such effects are lasting in mothers and children.

Another aspect of self-efficacy involves increasing parent empowerment over public policy, a different sense of control than controlling just the program for one's own child. Hocutt and Wiegerink (1983) reported that parental satisfaction was directly related to their level of activity in the program and to their feelings that they had an influence in its administration-parental empowerment. Providing informal and formal support systems (health care, education, social services, etc.) seems to help families adapt more effectively (Parke, 1986; Tracy & Whittaker, 1987).

# FUTURE PROJECTIONS

What lies ahead for families of children with disabilities? Will they receive greater acceptance than they currently have? Will they have to fight for their rights in the courts? How will the service delivery system adapt to meet their diverse needs? Some of the current issues give clues as to how these problems will be handled. It should be pointed out, however, that while the sum total of such decisions on family participation adds up to a portrait of societal priorities, no one individual or group sat down and consciously designed or considered the desirability—or the undesirability—of such an aggregate portrait in the first place.

## Changed Service Delivery System

We are tempted to say there will be a drastically changed service system, but prudence and experience argues for a term such as *substantial.* Despite the obvious intentions of policymakers to see a multidisciplinary team approach, there are defenders of the status quo in personnel preparation and credentialing (e.g., professional associations, higher education institutions, etc.) who will slow any major changes. Still, the role of the professional is bound to change in the direction of more attention to cross-disciplinary contacts, and such transdisciplinary efforts as "arena assessment" are likely to be seen more and more often. The team approach to service coordination, a tacit recognition that the child and family need the expertise of a variety of professionals, should become closer to the norm than individual practitioners who may only occasionally refer their patients to other disciplines for special diagnostic reasons.

## Less of a Diagnostic/Prescriptive Approach

There will be a more general acceptance that the model of diagnosing the patient as a means for prescribing the treatment, while useful in various illness conditions where the treatment is directly related to the diagnosis, is not helpful for many of these families. More of an ecological approach will develop, one that tries to identify the important forces impacting on the child and the family unit in order to see what can be done to influence these forces. Since there is no true "cure" for many of these problems, but only methods of improving the developmental and social progress of the children, it becomes important to inventory the entire scene, not just focus on the affected child.

## Service Systems Respond to Family Diversity

The future demographic picture of families reveals more ethnic and racial diversity and a continuing unfortunate level of poverty for such families. These facts should slowly change the service system to help take into account the differing values, attitudes, and family practices represented by such diversity. An increasing number of minority individuals will be joining the ranks of the professionals themselves, although it has currently been difficult to interest members of such groups in the occupational virtues of social services and education.

The fact that Part H is a mandate, forcing services to all qualified children and families, guarantees that attention will be paid to the family diversity issue. Also, the two-working-parent family, or the one-parent working family, will cause service systems to change the methods of service delivery and perhaps even the times in the week that such services are delivered.

## Family Empowerment Moves Slowly Ahead

The concept of family empowerment has been, by and large, a middle-class concept, assuming that families shop for services and have a type of executive control over family decisions (if we don't like the advice we get from our pediatrician, we will fire him or her and get another). The teenage parent and the dysfunctional family (drug abuse, mental illness, AIDS, etc.) has played little part in the current policy discussions, which have largely been preoccupied by how to assure true parent empowerment for effective families.

We should begin soon to see increasing attention paid to how to provide services to the dysfunctional or inadequate family in ways to strengthen the family members to the point where they can enjoy the full privileges of family empowerment.

## Personnel Shortages That Will Force Change

Any analysis that views the needs for professionals as against the supply (see, for example, Yoder, Coleman, & Gallagher, 1990) has to conclude that there is no way such enormous shortages can be met under current models of service delivery or personnel preparation. Given this fact, it would seem that two major shifts will take place. Some members of the service delivery team will be authorized to deliver services traditionally provided by another profession (e.g., speech lessons by a special educator, physical therapy from an occupational therapist, etc.) and many of the services will be provided by paraprofessionals under some type of professional supervision. This will be done not because it is part of a bright new plan, but because it will not be possible to provide services in any other feasible manner.

## Social Reform and Social Services Support Will Continue

This is a prediction made with much less confidence, since it depends on the attitudes of the American public, a traditionally unpredictable population. The fact that we have lagged behind most of the nations of the Western world in providing comprehensive health and social services has not been a powerful motivating force to improve, to this date. Yet we seem to be edging toward some form of universal, comprehensive health care and, if we are able to pay for it, the situation for children with disabilities and their families should also improve.

# Parent Assessment

Parents are expected to participate in the planning for their own child through the individual family service plan (IFSP). However, one of the carryovers of past professional domination of the professional/parent relationship was the provision in Part H for an assessment of the families' strengths and needs. As pointed out by many parents, such an assessment process again places the professional in a dominant position in the parent/professional relationship. One of the compromises that many of the states have reached in order to meet the requirements of the law, yet keep the intent of parental equity, is to allow the parents to state their own needs, in an open-ended interview, without being interrogated by professionals through the use of interviews or tests (Place & Gallagher, 1991).

# A Replacement Extended Family

Hopefully, architects and urban planners will be more conscious of the need to design neighborhoods that can replace the standard models for the extended family, which has all but disappeared in the middle class. We can hope for a better balance between self-interests and the needs of others on the part of parents and professionals, so that the rights of the child will not be a major social issue. The parents of children with disabilities would seem, in the next decade, to have a good chance to experience a better professional and psychological environment for their child as a result of the improvements in professional knowledge and attitudes, and our increased understanding of the complex interactions between child and parent.

# Professional Coordination

Breathes there a professional with a soul so dead, who never to himself or herself hath said, we need more *coordination*? Like motherhood, the flag, and apple pie, coordination is one of those virtues that is universally applauded, if infrequently implemented. The design of the departments of human resources at the state level is an attempt to meld various social and health programs. These adventures in coordination at the federal and state level have not been universally applauded, to say the least. The establishment of the U.S. Department of Education has signaled an abandonment of the attempt to coordinate programs across health, social, and educational disciplines at the federal level as was tried with the Department of Health, Education, and Welfare.

# The Emergence of Family Service Centers

There will likely be, in the next decade, the recognition that the program coordination which really counts is that coordination which operates at the local level and comes into direct contact with the family and its multiple needs. What seems required is a one-stop service center, a supermarket of family services offering health, social, and educational services, or the easy brokering of such services. One of the future models that we will undoubtedly see is the current school being transformed into a community service model which can provide family counseling, child-care services, weekend training, and other services to meet diverse family needs. If the advocacy groups for parental rights and causes are looking for new worlds to conquer, they could do worse than to focus their attention on the establishment of local or regional family centers devoted to a full-service concept.

We have been gradually accepting the complex interrelationships that exist between child, family, neighborhood, and society, where any major effect, at any level, reverberates throughout the system. If we want an effectively adapted child and a wholesome family, then the larger society will need tending to as well—and that may be where the new emphases will be placed in the 1990s.

# REFERENCES

Arcia, E., Gallagher, J., & Serling, J. (1992). *But what about the other 93 percent?* Chapel Hill, NC: Carolina Policy Studies Program, Frank Porter Graham Child Development Center, University of North Carolina at Chapel Hill.

Arcia, E., Serling, J., & Gallagher, J. (1992). *Review of state policies to empower families and reach populations typically underserved.* Chapel Hill, NC: Carolina Policy Studies Program.

Bailey, D. & Simeonsson, R. (1988). Home-based intervention. In S. Odom & M. Karnes (Eds.), *Early Intervention for Infants and Children with Handicaps.* (pp. 209–230) Baltimore: Brookes.

Bandura, A. (1989). Human agency in social cognition theory. *American Psychologist, 44,* 9, 1175–1184.

Bristol, M., Gallagher, J., & Schopler, E. (1988). Mothers and fathers of young developmentally disabled and nondisabled boys: Adaptation and spousal support. *Developmental Psychology, 24,* 441–451.

Dunst, C., & Trivette, C. (1988). Toward experimental evaluation of the family, infant, and preschool program. In H. Weiss & F. Jacobs (Eds.), *Evaluating family programs.* New York: Aldine de Gruyer.

Dunst, C., & Trivette, C. (1990). Assessment of social support in early intervention programs. In S. Meisels & J. Shonkoff (Eds.), *Handbook of early childhood intervention* (pp. 326–349). New York: Cambridge University Press.

Farber, B. (1978). Family organization and crises: Maintenance of integration in families with a severely mentally retarded child. *Monographs of the Society for Research in Child Development, 75.*

Farber, B. (1986). Historical context of research on families with mentally retarded members. In J. Gallagher & P. Vietze (Eds.), *Families of handicapped persons* (pp. 3–24). Baltimore: Brookes.

Gallagher, J. J. (1990). The family as a focus for intervention. In S. Meisels & J. Shonkoff (Eds.), *Handbook of early childhood intervention* (pp. 540–559), New York: Cambridge University Press.

Gallagher, J. J., Scharfman, W., & Bristol, M. (1984). The division of responsibilities in families with preschool handicapped and non-handicapped children. *Journal of the Division of Early Childhood, 8,* 3–11.

Gallagher, J. J., & Vietze, P. (Eds.). (1986). *Families of handicapped persons.* Baltimore: Brookes.

Gallagher, J., Trohanis, P., & Clifford, R. (1989). *Policy Implementation & P.L. 99–457.* Baltimore: Brookes.

Gorham, K., Des Jardins, R., Page, E., & Scheiber, B. (1975). The effects on parents of the labeling of their children. In N. Hobbs (Ed.), *Issues in the classification of children: A handbook on categories, labels, and their consequences* (pp. 154–188). San Francisco: Jossey-Bass.

Hill, R. (1949). *Families under stress: Adjustment to the crises of war separation and reunion.* New York: Harper.

Hocutt, A., & Wiegerink, R. (1983). Perspectives on parent involvement in preschool programs for handicapped children. In R. Haskins & D. Adams (Eds.), *Parent education and public policy* (pp. 211–229). Norwood, NJ: Ablex.

Kirk, S., & Gallagher, J. (1989). *Educating exceptional children* (6th ed.). Boston: Houghton-Mifflin.

Love, H. (1973). *The mentally retarded child and his family.* Springfield, IL: Thomas.

MacKeith, R. (1973). The feelings and behavior of parents of handicapped children. *Developmental medicine and child neurology, 15,* 524–527.

McCubbin, H., & Patterson, J. (1983). The family stress process: The double ABCX model of adjustment and adaptation. *Marriage and Family Review, 6,* 7–37.

Parke, R. (1986). Fathers, families, and support systems: Their role in the development of at-risk and retarded infants and children. In J. Gallagher & P. Vietze (Eds.), *Families of Handicapped Persons* (pp. 101–114). Baltimore: Brookes.

Place, P., & Gallagher, J. (1991). *Part H policy development for families: A case study report.* Chapel Hill, NC: Carolina Policy Studies Program.

Powell, T., & Ogle, P. (1985). *Brothers and sisters—A special part of exceptional families.* Baltimore: Brookes.

Rutter, M. (1982). Prevention of children's psychosocial disorders: Myths and substance. *Pediatrics, 70,* 883–894.

Sameroff, A. J., & Chandler, M. J. (1975). Prenatal risk and the continuum of caretaking casualty. In F. Horowitz, M. Hetherington, S. Scarr-Salaopatek, & G. Siegel (Eds.), *Review of child development research* (Vol 4) (187–244). Chicago: University of Chicago Press.

Sameroff, A. J., & Friese, B. (1990). Transaction, regulation, and early intervention. In S. Meisels & J. Shonkoff (Eds.), *Handbook of early childhood intervention* (pp. 119–149). New York: Cambridge University Press.

Seitz, V., Rosenbaum, L., & Apfel, N. (1985). Effects of family support intervention: A ten-year follow-up. *Child Development, 56,* 376–391.

Simeonsson, R., & Bailey, D. (1986). Siblings of handicapped children. In J. Gallagher & P. Vietze (Eds.), *Families of handicapped persons* (pp. 67–80). Baltimore: Brookes.

Skrtic, T. (1990). *Behind Special Education.* Denver, CO: Love Publishing Co.

Tracy, E., & Whittaker, J. (1987). The evidence base for social support interventions in child and family practice: Emerging issues for research and practice. *Children and Youth Services Review, 9,* 249–270.

Tseng, W., & McDermott, J. (1979). Triaxial family classifications: A proposal. *Journal of the American Academy of Child Psychiatry, 18,* 1:22–24.

Turnbull, A., Summers, J., & Brotherson, M. (1986). Family life cycle: Theoretical and empirical implications and future directions for families with mentally retarded members. In J. Gallagher & P. Vietze (Eds.), *Families with handicapped children* (pp. 45–66). Baltimore: Brookes.

Warren, F. (1985). Call them liars who would say all is well. In H. Turnbull & A. Turnbull (Eds.), *Parents speak out* (2nd ed.). Columbus, OH: Merrill.

Washington, B., & Gallagher, J. (1986). Family roles, preschool handicapped children, and social policy. In J. Gallagher & P. Vietze (Eds.), *Families of handicapped persons* (pp. 261–272). Baltimore: Brookes.

Wikler, L. (1986) Family stress theory and research on families of children with mental retardation. In J. Gallagher & P. Vietze (Eds.), *Families of handicapped persons* (pp. 167–196). Baltimore: Brookes.

Yoder, D., Coleman, P., & Gallagher, J. (1990). *Personnel Needs—Allied Health Personnel Meeting the Demands of Part H, P.L. 99-457.* Chapel Hill, NC: Carolina Institute for Child and Family Policy, University of North Carolina at Chapel Hill.

# INDEX